CONDUCTORS

John Holmes was born in Sydney in 1925; after serving in
the Royal Australian Air Force in World War II, he
graduated in Economics at the University of Sydney,
joined the Australian Public Service and in 1961 went
abroad in the Australian Trade Commissioner Service.
He has lived in London, Los Angeles, Tel-Aviv, Berlin
and Vienna, as well as in countries in South-East Asia
and Africa. He experienced the great development in
musical life in Sydney after the war, influenced by
Goossens, Cardus, and others, and has been interested
in music and in recordings all his adult life, from the time
of 78 r.p.m. discs. His life overseas has brought him into
contact with many musicians, orchestras and opera
houses; in the Far East he was a newspaper critic, and
arranged concerts for visiting artists. The author of
Conductors on Record (1982), he is married, with two
children, and lives in Canberra.

CONDUCTORS

A Record Collector's Guide

including compact discs

JOHN L. HOLMES

LONDON
VICTOR GOLLANCZ LTD
1988

First published in Great Britain 1988
by Victor Gollancz Ltd
14 Henrietta Street, London WC2E 8QJ

First published in Gollancz Paperbacks 1988

British Library Cataloguing in Publication Data
Holmes, John L.
    Conductors: a record collector's guide.
    1. Conductors (Music)—Biography
    I. Title
    785′.092′2   ML402

    ISBN 0-575-04088-2

Photoset by Rowland Phototypesetting Ltd
Bury St Edmunds, Suffolk
Printed in Finland by Werner Söderström Oy

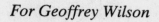

For Geoffrey Wilson

A list of compact discs available for recordings
mentioned under individual entries is given
at the back of the book.

INTRODUCTION

Standing on the podium before an orchestra of perhaps a hundred instrumentalists, the conductor is an impressive figure. In the audience and in the orchestra, all eyes follow his movements. He is performing on the supreme musical instrument, the modern symphony orchestra. Yet it is an instrument on which he cannot practise, unlike the players he is directing. When he appears before them to rehearse a work which will be performed later at a public concert he must be fully prepared: he must know the score thoroughly, he must be perfectly sure about phrasing, dynamics and balance; in short, he must have determined in his mind's ear exactly how the work should sound, how it should be shaped, and how he is to bring the notes on paper to dramatic life.

Orchestral players devote most of their lives to perfecting their instrumental skills; some conductors start their musical careers as instrumentalists themselves before they accede to their profession. Some may play a number of instruments quite well. But the conductor of the orchestra is the one who must understand the whole score so well that he is able to indicate to each and every instrumentalist, with the greatest clarity and conviction, how the work is to be performed—in detail, and in its broad architecture. We constantly hear of great conductors whose control of the orchestra is absolute: some have achieved it in the past with something like terror, others with charm and persuasiveness, and some others, the very great ones, by creating a sense of awe and utter respect in the musicians, by their concentration, conviction and profound insight into the music they are conducting.

Reading about them, one is struck by the variety of personality and method in the profession. It is not possible to say that all conductors conform to a stereotype. Some, for example Georg Szell, were ruthless men who treated their players with condescension and brutal authority. They were certainly great artists, but the status of musicians has changed so much in modern times that it would be very difficult nowadays for them to behave in this way. Some conductors are sticklers for precision, others not so concerned with small errors. Some—Leonard Bernstein is perhaps the best example—are remarkably demonstrative, and unconsciously depict the changing emotions in the music with extravagant gestures. Others, curiously including one of Bernstein's teachers, Fritz Reiner, use the smallest motions of the baton, and appear almost immobile to the audience behind them. Some always use a baton, others never. Some always conduct with the score in front of them, others from memory. Many convey their directions to the players with their eyes, yet Karajan conducts with his eyes closed.

What makes a conductor 'great'? Or putting the question another way, why are there many good conductors but few great ones? The answer can perhaps be found in the major entries in this book, for example those for Toscanini, Furtwängler, Nikisch, Beecham, Stokowski, Koussevitzky and Carlos Kleiber. First of all, these men have a burning conviction of the rightness of their interpretation of the score, sometimes to the point of regarding all others with contempt. They have studied the score exhaustively; they have, often, a profound knowledge of the composer's life, the cultural milieu in which he lived, the language he spoke, and the style in which he wrote. Their preparation of the score is meticulous and comprehensive. They have a clear aural concept of the music in their minds before they step in front of the orchestra. Arturo Toscanini had a reputation for his short temper and violent explosions at rehearsals. But we should not misjudge him. He was not fulminating against the musicians: he was angry with himself, because he could not achieve in sound the concept of the music in his mind.

The conductor's task then is to bring the concept to life through communicating it to his players. It is not just a question of good technique with the baton, or gesture; time and time again conductors who teach others say that learning the basics of beating with the baton can be taught in a very short time, but the ability to communicate the concept can scarcely be taught at all. It must be inborn, almost. Somehow there is an indefinable alchemy by which a great conductor creates his own special sound with the orchestra, and without apparent effort unfolds his magnificent interpretation of the music. So it appears over and again in this book: Nikisch's control was so complete that the players felt that he was hypnotising them. The sound he created with the orchestra could be recognised in hardly more than a bar. The same is true of so many others; those present were astonished when Eugene Ormandy once conducted the London Symphony Orchestra: the sound when he started to conduct was as if it were the Philadelphia Orchestra.

To attempt to explain how this minor miracle works is anything but easy. The balance of sound the conductor creates by controlling the tonal volume from each section of the orchestra is very important: some conductors automatically emphasise the lower instruments, such as cellos, basses and bassoons, and their tone is characteristically full of depth and 'meaning'. Some seek the greatest clarity possible, whereas others create a thick orchestral sound, rather like an organ. Tempi of course have much to do with it. Another point is the upbeat: the conductor's composure at that initial critical point sets the attack, and the mood of the music to follow. A seemingly indecisive beat leads to a diffused sound, which the conductor may be seeking deliberately; a sharp decisive beat brings its own quality to the tone. Some conductors make a point of emphasis of every climax, large or small; others pace the whole movement, sometimes the entire symphony or opera, so that there is one great point of climax. Some give the music tension by their very appearance in front of the orchestra; to others, creating tension is a conscious effort.

It is true that the more distinctive the sound and the orchestral texture obtained by the conductor, the more difficult it may be for him to capture the style of the piece he is performing. It was, and is, apparent with Stokowski and the Philadelphia Orchestra, Koussevitzky and the Boston Symphony Orchestra, and with Karajan and the Berlin Philharmonic Orchestra, all of which have been long associations, that their characteristic sound is much more suitable for the style of one musical epoch than another. Few conductors and their orchestras have embraced all styles: Szell and the Cleveland Orchestra were wonderful exponents of the classical style of Haydn, Mozart and Beethoven, but their performances of the late romantics such as Tchaikovsky and Mahler, while brilliantly executed, were certainly not spontaneously expressive. Today we have a special problem in that the preferred performance style for baroque and early classical music is for orchestras with instruments and the performing conventions of the time, rather than the essentially 19th-century approach inherited by the great orchestras and conductors. The young conductors of today have the baffling task of learning a range of styles of music they will be called on to perform, from the baroque, the classical, the romantic, the French impressionists, the national schools of, say, Czech and Russian music, to atonal and contemporary music. We should not be too critical if they cannot achieve this universality: Toscanini very rarely conducted the Mozart operas, admitting that the style was beyond him. Karajan's Bruckner is perfect, but not many would say that of his Mozart and Haydn. On the other hand, the baroque specialists of today would not be the first choice for the Bayreuth Festival.

The great conductors of the past have each had their own inimitable qualities. There seems little doubt who were 'great': Mahler, Nikisch, Strauss, Toscanini, Weingartner, Furtwängler, Mengelberg, Klemperer, Kleiber (Erich, the father of Carlos), Walter, Beecham, Koussevitzky, Szell, Reiner, Stokowski—I am sure that others can be added to this list. Sometimes one hears the plaint that there are no great ones before the public today, to take their place. This, I believe, is difficult to sustain. There are a number of fine, maybe great conductors performing today, and I am sure that careful attention to their performances in concert halls and opera houses, as well as to their gramophone records, will make this evident. If we define greatness as the performance of great music with convincing musical insight, Karajan and Mravinsky certainly rank among the immortals, but they are now at the close of their careers. Of the younger generation, Abbado, Muti, Carlos Kleiber and Haitink, and maybe others, would in my judgement qualify as great.

Judging conductors by their gramophone records is fraught with danger. Time and again conductors and other musical interpreters point out that a record captures one performance at one point in time. The variables operating at any musical performance are such that no two performances of the one work can be the same. For a conductor, the players of the orchestra, the acoustics of the auditorium, the mood of the moment, are only some of the factors which can vary, even if only to a small degree. Some conductors, too, follow Nikisch's advice that every performance should be an improvisation, and so every time a work is performed the artists are really recreating it. Often a conductor will say after a performance that he was not satisfied with the result, to a greater or lesser degree, and that he looks forward to the next time he conducts the work, to get it right. Furtwängler was probably the greatest of the improvisors, and he never felt comfortable with his performances being frozen for all time on a gramophone record. Collectors of his recorded performances can be expert in identifying the differences. Many conductors, too, dislike hearing their own records, as they know that if they recorded the work again, they would do it differently, even slightly, and that their second thoughts would be better.

The process of making records these days can also rob the performance of spontaneity, and critics who demand note-perfect recordings can take a good part of the blame for both musicians and recording engineers being anxious to sacrifice spontaneity to perfection. Conductors react differently to the recording studio: some revel in it and are tempted to believe that the process of repetition, editing, 'soling and heeling' as it is called, will produce that perfect performance that they believe the public demands. Maybe, but generally they delude themselves. The wonderful thing about those great conductors of the past is that they were individuals, and although their performances may have been impossibly idiomatic at times, they did not believe that they were attempting to record *the* definitive performance of the work in question. Their reading was special to themselves. This is amply demonstrated by comparing, say, recordings of Beethoven's *Eroica* symphony by Furtwängler, Klemperer, Toscanini, Walter and Kleiber.

Another delusion is the belief that somehow what one hears on the stereo hi-fi at home is superior to the performance in the concert hall or opera house. In extreme cases it obviously is, and some conductors, such as Karajan, have said that Mahler symphonies are best heard on records, as the clarity is so much better than in the concert hall. No doubt playing good music on gramophone records brings much pleasure to countless people, but it is inevitably a synthetic experience. In music we have the eternal triangle: the composer, the performer, and the listener, and it really can only exist when the performer is presenting the music in the presence of the listener. Moreover, listening to music performed live calls for our entire attention, a condition rarely met in our homes with gramophone records. Then, when we go to a concert or opera our anticipation of the event adds immeasurably to our experience of the music. I do not deride records; they have their place, but their limitations must be recognised. On the other hand, we are fortunate living at a time when we have readily available records of the great artists of the past. Despite the limitations we can gain at least some impression of their styles and interpretations; we can more readily appreciate that there is more than one 'right' interpretation of a great work, and we thus have the opportunity to compare different interpretations. It should be added that it would be wrong to conclude from such a comparison that one performance is the best one: there can be no best, despite the pronouncements of the record critics in their learned volumes and magazines. All are different and if we are clever we will learn from each performance what it is that makes them so. To call one 'best' is a way of declaring that we have a subjective preference for that particular style of performance. Our judgement may be true for ourselves but certainly is not true for others. The eternal comparison between Toscanini and Furtwängler, who are made to represent two opposing poles of interpretation, is interesting enough, but it becomes absurd if the conclusion is that one is right and the other wrong. My belief is that we are lucky to have both.

Most records of the older conductors might be difficult to find in the record shops now, but fortunately some are appearing in wonderful recreations on compact disc. Furtwängler, Mengelberg, Reiner, Toscanini, Walter and Klemperer are well represented on the silver discs, and let us hope that Beecham, Stokowski, Koussevitzky and the other great ones will not be slow to follow. They are important for their own sakes, but more important, they are our precious heritage, and all have had an important influence on the conductors of today. A good proportion of the entries in this book are for contemporary artists, some unquestionably great, but most of lesser stature, and their entries are somewhat short. Should someone write the same book again in 50 years' time, the perspective on each artist could be quite different. For conductors not included in the book, I can only refer the enquirer to my book, *Conductors on Record*, which is as comprehensive as I could make it, with a cut-off date at 1977.

A

ABBADO, Claudio (b. 1933). Born in Milan into a most musical family, his father a violinist and teacher at the Giuseppe Verdi Conservatory there and his mother a pianist, Abbado studied the piano and composition before entering the Verdi Conservatory. After graduation he attended Carlo Zecchi's master classes at the Accademia Chigiana in Siena, and in 1956 went to the Vienna Academy of Music to study conducting with Swarowsky; one of his fellow pupils was Zubin Mehta, and the two of them later went to the United States together. As a child Abbado had heard Toscanini, Walter, de Sabata and Kubelik, and he has said that his decision to become a conductor came when he was eight years old and heard Guarnieri conducting Debussy's *Nocturnes*. When he was at the Academy in Vienna he took the opportunity to observe the rehearsals of conductors such as Klemperer, Krips, Böhm and Karajan. He was a conductor from the beginning, and did not graduate from the position of an orchestral player. His first opportunity came in 1958 in Trieste, and in that year he also won the Koussevitzky Prize at the Berkshire Music Center in Massachusetts. His career nonetheless started slowly; he taught chamber music at the Parma Conservatory for two years, and then took part in the Dmitri Mitropoulos International Conductors' Competition in New York in 1963, and emerged as co-winner with Calderón and Kosler. One of the awards following the competition was service for a year as assistant conductor of the New York Philharmonic Orchestra, where he closely observed Bernstein and Szell, but an unexpected result of this experience was his poor opinion of the New York Philharmonic, who 'play well but don't love music'.

After hearing Abbado conduct in Berlin, Karajan invited him to conduct at the 1965 Salzburg Festival, where he led Mahler's Symphony No. 2, and for that performance he was awarded the Philips Prize. The next year he appeared at the Edinburgh Festival with the New Philharmonia Orchestra in Mahler's Symphony No. 6, and made a marked impression. He first conducted at La Scala, Milan, in 1965, and in the following year conducted Bellini's *I Capuleti ed i Montecchi* there, a performance which was taken on tour to Expo '67 at Montreal. In 1968 he was appointed permanent conductor at La Scala, graduating to artistic director in 1971. During that time the La Scala company and orchestra developed into a considerable ensemble, and with the company he gave performances at Munich at the time of the Olympic Games (1972), toured on exchange to the Bolshoi Theatre, Moscow, (1974) and to Covent Garden (1975), and went to Washington for the United States bicentennial celebrations (1976). He was awarded the Mozart Medal in Vienna (1971), was appointed principal conductor of the Vienna Philharmonic Orchestra (1971), principal guest conductor (1972) and then principal conductor (1979) of the London Symphony Orchestra, succeeding Previn, and principal guest conductor of the Chicago Symphony Orchestra (1982). In 1977 he also became musical director of the European Community Youth Orchestra, for which he receives no remuneration. He is also director of the Chamber Orchestra of Europe.

Abbado is one of the handful of distinguished young conductors who have emerged to take the place of the disappearing older generation who dominated European and American opera houses and concert halls in the decades after World War II. Many believe that he has assumed the mantle of Toscanini, and he has many characteristics similar to those of the great maestro—intense musicality, tension, concentration and vigour in his conducting, a phenomenal memory, a distaste for publicity, a scrupulous regard for the composer's intentions, and a repugnance of Fascism, which was intensified by his mother's imprisonment by the Nazis during the war for sheltering a Jewish child. He is a man of wide cultural and social interests, with a modest and reticent personality; he has a marked disdain for acclamation, and never seeks to promote himself or to lobby for appointments. He dislikes the conventional applause at the end of performances. Although he has a large repertoire, from Bach to Nono, he is not in a hurry to present major works for which he does not think himself completely prepared. His musical sympathies are the broadest, and he has worked unobtrusively to widen the repertoires at La Scala and Vienna. At La Scala he doubled the length of the season, introduced cheaper-priced performances for students and people with lower incomes, and introduced works novel to the audience. For instance, *Wozzeck* was presented, although it required 40 rehearsals.

Because he feels it brings him into closer contact with his players and singers, he usually conducts without a score. At rehearsals he is calm and precise, and avoids verbal explanations, believing his players should learn to respond to his direction through his hands and eyes. He has said that the conductor must have a complete knowledge of the score, should learn all that is possible about the composer, and should also study the composer's chamber music and vocal works so that he can acquire a better feel for the style of the music. 'He should have studied composition, be able to play an instrument, have a good sense of rhythm and good pitch, enough psychology of people, tenacity. It is important to love what he is doing, to have a passion for music, otherwise the work would become routine and that's the end, that's death. He should understand and respect other musicians and singers who may have personalities different from his own. This is especially necessary when working on an opera when so many other people are involved, or with soloists, because it's impossible for two or more people to have exactly the same conception of a work, and great soloists are great personalities. So a conductor must understand and communicate with them at a very profound level.'

Despite their immense vitality and drive, Abbado's performances on record and in the concert hall can sometimes be disconcertingly impersonal, calculated and hard-driven, and can fail to come to life. His utter fidelity to the score and his refusal to introduce subjective exaggerations of expression perhaps add to this occasional impression of coldness and over-attention to detail. On the other hand, in works such as Beethoven's Symphony No. 3 and Tchaikovsky's Symphony No. 6, his interpretations can be overpowering in the brilliance of their execution and the intensity of their dramatic expression; William Mann wrote after a performance of the Tchaikovsky work in Edinburgh that Abbado was 'conducting the symphony that Tchaikovsky composed, not a subjective revision of it'. Abbado is in addition an exceptional accompanist, seeking always to adapt his orchestral contribution to a concerto to the style of the soloist. He has been a major recording artist for Decca and DGG, and has made many brilliant records of both symphonic music and opera. His first disc was produced in 1967, an outstanding performance of Beethoven's Symphony No. 7 and *Prometheus* overture, with the Vienna Philharmonic Orchestra; since then his recorded repertoire has ranged from the *Brandenburg Concertos* (with the La Scala Orchestra for CBS) and Mozart's Symphonies Nos 40 and 41, to Berg's *Lyric Suite* and Nono's *Como una ola*. If one were to select the most impressive, it would probably be the Mahler symphonies, of which he has now recorded Nos 1, 2, 5, 6 and 7 with the Chicago Symphony Orchestra, and Nos 3 and 4 with the Vienna Philharmonic

Orchestra *et al.* His opera recordings have included *La cenerentola*, *Il barbiere di Siviglia*, *Il viaggio a Reims*, *Carmen*, *Simon Boccanegra*, *Aida* and *Macbeth*. Many of these, and his other major recordings, have been issued on compact disc.

ABRAVANEL, **Maurice de** (b. 1903). Born in Salonika, Greece, Abravanel moved with his family to Switzerland when he was 6, studied medicine at Lausanne University, and there organised a student orchestra. He abandoned medicine for music, studied with Kurt Weill in Berlin, and there made his début as a conductor. Coming to Paris in 1933 he was musical director of Balanchine's ballet company, toured Australia with the British National Opera Company, conducted at the New York Metropolitan Opera (1936–8) and at the Chicago Opera (1940–1), directed musical comedy on Broadway (1941–9), and again toured Australia (1946). In 1947 he was appointed music director of the Utah Symphony Orchestra, where his tenure was the longest of any conductor with an orchestra in the United States except for Ormandy and the Philadelphia Orchestra. He retired from the orchestra in 1979, but from 1955 was director of the Music Academy of the West at Santa Barbara. He made an extensive series of recordings with the Utah Symphony Orchestra for Westminster and later for Vanguard of over 80 discs, including the complete symphonies of Brahms, Tchaikovsky and Mahler, being the first American conductor to record the Mahler symphonies complete. Although he may have been a little detached and cool-headed in his readings, the interpretations were straightforward, cleanly executed and absolutely honest, even if they may not have been memorably distinctive.

ALMEIDA, **Antonio de** (b. 1929). Almeida was born in Paris, the son of a Portuguese father and an American mother, who migrated to Argentina when he was a boy. He studied under Ginestera at Buenos Aires, under Hindemith at Yale University and later under Szell, Koussevitzky and Bernstein. In the United States he played horn, bassoon, oboe, clarinet and cello in various student orchestras. He was conductor of the Portuguese Radio Orchestra and at the Lisbon Opera (1957–60), was principal conductor of the Stuttgart Philharmonic Orchestra (1960–4), a guest conductor with the Paris Opéra (1964–8), with the Houston Symphony Orchestra (1969–71), and with the Nice Municipal Opera (1976–80). He has been the general editor of Offenbach's collected works, including the instrumental works as well as the operas, locating the original versions of *Les Contes* *d'Hoffmann* and *La Belle Hélène*, and presenting the restored version of *La Grande Duchesse de Gérolstein* at the New York City Opera. He has been a visiting conductor with major orchestras in Europe and the United States, and has toured Australia several times. His repertoire is catholic, extending from the baroque and classical eras to Mahler and Shostakovich; he has recorded a number of the symphonies and the opera *L'infedeltà delusa* of Haydn, for the Haydn Foundation. His other discs include rarely-heard French music, of Schmitt, Duparc, Chausson, Fauré, Dukas, and Bizet, and Mahler's Symphony No. 5, and, on compact disc, accompaniments for the mezzo-soprano Von Stade.

ANSERMET, Ernest (1883–1969). Born in Vevey in the French-speaking region of Switzerland (Suisse Romande) where both his mother and grandfather were musicians, the young Ansermet was himself a musician from childhood. As it was not possible for him to follow a career as a musician, he studied mathematics at Lausanne University and the Sorbonne, and while he taught mathematics at the high school at Geneva (1903–9) he studied music with several eminent teachers, including Ernest Bloch. At first his ambition was to become a composer, but after coming into contact with Nikisch, Weingartner and Mottl he decided in 1910 to be a conductor. His first concert was at Montreux, where he substituted for someone else at a performance of Beethoven's Symphony No. 5, and this led to his appointment to direct the Kursaal concerts at Montreux. There he remained until 1913, when he directed concerts at Geneva; Stravinsky recommended him to Diaghilev and in 1915 he became conductor with the Ballets Russes. He conducted at their season in London in 1919 and was active with the company on and off until 1923, touring with them in Europe, North and South America, and leading the world premières of Ravel's *La Valse*, Falla's *The Three-cornered Hat* and some ballets of Stravinsky. In 1920 he presented a concert of Stravinsky's music in London, giving a lecture beforehand about the composer, and conducted the first performance in Germany of *Le Sacre du printemps* in 1922. Later, in 1928, he was conductor, with Fourestier, of L'Orchestre Symphonique de Paris.

Ansermet's career culminated in 1918 with the foundation of L'Orchestre de la Suisse Romande. His name was inseparable from the orchestra for 50 years, until he handed over its direction to Paul Kletzki. At the end of World War I, Suisse Romande had no professional symphony orchestra, except for a small one at the Geneva Theatre, but with the help of some influential enthusiasts, Ansermet assembled a number of musicians, mostly foreigners, to form the orchestra—French wind-players, Viennese brass, and string players from Belgium, Italy and from Switzerland itself. His aim to develop local talent finally led to four out of five of the orchestra's membership in 1946 being Swiss. In 1935, when the Swiss Radio formed its orchestra in Lausanne, the Suisse Romande Orchestra was reformed in Geneva, with the support of the city and state authorities and from private subscribers. Ansermet worked towards widening the repertoire so that it was more representative than that of the other two major Swiss orchestras, the Zurich Tonhalle and the Winterthur. Under him the Suisse Romande Orchestra presented regular concerts in Geneva, Montreux and Vevey, as well as a limited opera season, mainly of French operas. With guest appearances in England, Germany, France, Poland, Scandinavia, Belgium, Holland, the United States and South America, he acquired an international reputation during the years between the two world wars for the intelligence and brilliance of his interpretations. After 1945 he was invited to Paris, Brussels, the Hague and London, and in 1948 and 1949 successfully toured the USA, conducting the NBC Symphony Orchestra and those at Chicago, Dallas, Cleveland, Philadelphia, and in some other cities. Many first performances in the USA were included in his programmes.

Reserved in his gestures, Ansermet was nonetheless precise in his directions to the orchestra. He recognised that many orchestral players need no advice about how to play; the conductor is superior to them because of his broader outlook and his understanding of the music, historically and culturally: 'he has more fantasies, references and background.' While he believed it necessary for the conductor to know the score by heart, he always conducted with the score, as in conducting from memory he saw the danger of following the main melodic line and neglecting the secondary voices. Because of his association with the ballet and its composers, he concentrated for most of his life on performing the music of Stravinsky, Prokofiev, Ravel, Debussy and also Hindemith, Bartók and others, but in his last decades he turned more to the classical repertoire. Disagreeing with Boulez, who said that music must be interpreted in the spirit of the time, Ansermet believed that it must be interpreted in the spirit of the composer. He quoted Rimsky-Korsakov's remark that there are two kinds of music: one where you just play the notes, and you have everything, and the other where you must play the notes in a certain manner, with a certain feeling for the right sound. Ravel, Ansermet said, can be performed exactly as written, but Debussy requires an understanding of the music, and then the performer has to realise the musical idea. An orchestra's style is not simply perfection in playing, but the method in which it plays, which corresponds to a way of feeling, and it is the conductor's task to bring the musicians to participate in this feeling. The orchestra's regular conductor can form the orchestra's style, which is scarcely altered by a guest conductor: Ansermet himself had difficulty performing Debussy and Stravinsky with the Vienna Philharmonic because he found that their special style had not the equality of sound and the exact rhythm required by the music. Some conductors, such as Toscanini, impose their own personality on all the music they conduct, but Ansermet tried in his own style to illustrate as much as possible the composer's style. He emphasised that the indications in the score are relative, and that performances require much more than just observing the text: 'Making music cannot be reduced to performing what is written, because music is not an acoustic phenomenon: it is something which is inside the musical phenomenon and as truth cannot be formulated.' As each performer sees the same piece from a different point of view and has his own vision of this truth, there can be more than one satisfactory performance of the same piece.

Despite the catholicity of his musical sympathies, Ansermet was only a truly convincing interpreter in a restricted range of music, notably Stravinsky, Debussy, Ravel, Bartók and some other modern composers. He championed Stravinsky, whose technique, writing and conception he admired, but he fell out with him on aesthetics. Contemporary atonal music roused his hostility; to him it had no meaning, and could only be of interest to a coterie. To enunciate his position he published in 1916 *The Foundations of Music in the Human Consciousness*, in which he deprecated the tonal disintegration of the music of Schoenberg, arguing that structural complexity did nothing to replace traditional forms based on the intervals of the third, fourth and fifth. He also recorded a lecture, with musical illustrations, making much the same point.

Ansermet's recording career started in 1929; in the 1930s he assisted Stravinsky to prepare recordings of some of his music, but fame as a recording artist came in 1946 when he signed an exclusive contract with Decca, with whom he recorded until his death. His first records, which included sensational readings of *Petrushka* and *L'Oiseau de feu*, were with the London Philharmonic, London Symphony and Paris Conservatoire Orchestras, but all his later discs except the very last, which was a final *L'Oiseau de feu* with the New Philharmonia Orchestra, were with the Suisse Romande Orchestra. He recorded a prolific amount of music, and many of his successful discs were re-recorded for stereo, but sometimes he could not quite repeat the same magic. He knew this, and believed that the reason was that the recording technicians were tending to supplant the musicians, and that musical values were lost. Recently Decca have issued compact discs of some of his most notable recordings. His recorded repertoire first concentrated on the music congenial to him, such as Debussy, Ravel, Stravinsky, Honegger, Roussel, Chabrier, Lalo, Bartók and the Russian nationalist composers. Later his repertoire widened to include the *Paris* symphonies of Haydn, the complete symphonies of Beethoven and Brahms, and a range of other 19th-century romantic music. His characteristic style, his elegance and clear texture, were always evident, but too often his cool musical temperament and intellectual objectivity were in the way of the necessary emotional involvement to make his readings absolutely convincing, as if his wish to present the style of the composer had caused him to neglect his own feelings for the music. He should however be judged by his records of the music for which he had a special affinity, which was French and Russian rather than German, and which requires a heroic style neither he nor his orchestra possessed. Other conductors have since recorded alternative readings of the French repertoire, superb in their own right, but Ansermet's will always command admiration.

ASHKENAZY, Vladimir (b. 1937). Born in Gorky in the USSR, where his father was a popular musician, Ashkenazy showed extraordinary musical talents at a very early age, and attended the Central School attached to the Moscow Music Conservatory, his teacher being Sumbatian, and then was at the Conservatory itself, with Zemlyansky his teacher. At the age of 18, in 1955, he won second prize in the Chopin Competition in Warsaw, and two years later first prize in the Queen Elisabeth of the Belgians' Piano Competition in Brussels, after which he toured the USA (1958). In 1962 he shared first prize with John Ogden in the Tchaikovsky Competition in Moscow, after which he toured Britain, Italy, the Netherlands, Scandinavia and again the USA. Because of his growing dissatisfaction with artistic conditions in the USSR, he and his wife Dody, formerly an Icelandic pianist whom he had met in Moscow, and their first child, left the Soviet

Union to live in London, joining there the intense musical circle of young musicians of whom Barenboim, Mehta and Perlman were leading members. His recording activities with Decca were also centred in London. By 1968 the number of his annual concerts had settled to about 130 each year. In that year he and his growing family moved to Iceland, and finally in 1978 Lucerne in Switzerland became their permanent residence. He has toured many countries throughout the world as a pianist, and has a liking for performing in out-of-the-way towns; in 1979 he visited China to take part in a BBC programme about the Shanghai Conservatory.

Ashkenazy was always passionately interested in orchestral music since childhood, and attended numerous symphony concerts in Moscow. When he was 17 he heard the Boston Symphony Orchestra during its tour of the Soviet Union and this to him was an incredible event, the first time he had heard what an orchestra should sound like. He first conducted in 1969 in Iceland, where he led occasional concerts with the Iceland Symphony Orchestra. In England he conducted the Northern Sinfonia in Newcastle and the Royal Liverpool Philharmonic Orchestra (1976), and the outcome of a successful series of concerts with the Philharmonia Orchestra (1977) led to a regular association with the orchestra. He was appointed its principal guest conductor in 1981, but two years later relinquished the position. Other orchestras he conducts regularly are the Cleveland and the Amsterdam Concertgebouw, and conducting now occupies one-third of his time. As a pianist he has had a life-long devotion to Mozart, Beethoven, Chopin, Brahms, Schubert and Schumann, as well as Russian composers, although he cannot identify himself with Tchaikovsky's Piano Concerto No. 1. He has said that he is constantly surprised by the denigration of Russian composers such as Rachmaninov, Prokofiev and Shostakovich by German critics, who sometimes dismiss their music as little more than *Unterhaltungmusik* (light music). His repertoire as a conductor includes works by Mozart, Beethoven, Brahms, Bartók, Rachmaninov, Mahler, Richard Strauss, Stravinsky, Scriabin, Sibelius, Berg, Schoenberg, Shostakovich, Prokofiev, Wagner, Walton and Elgar, and his concerts with the Philharmonia Orchestra have frequently included concertos by Mozart with himself as both soloist and conductor. At the Adelaide Festival in 1984 he conducted the Philharmonia Orchestra in the nine Beethoven symphonies as well as playing the five concertos in a six-concert series, as part of a world tour. Very little contemporary music appeals to him: 'I rarely find that anything new is expressed. . . . I don't really know what to think about the long-term future of music. It may be that it is a dead end, but on the other hand there are always extraordinary people, one or two geniuses who appear in a lifetime. If there was a Beethoven or a Wagner, maybe there will be another composer of similar stature who will find the appropriate musical terms with which to convince us that the true musical expression on the most exalted and communicative level is not dead.' But a career as a conductor exclusively does not appeal to him, and he has no intention of becoming involved in the competitive jockeying for appointments and the manipulation of contracts that are virtually inescapable for full-time conductors. He has pointed out that musical life in Soviet Russia is closely connected with political life; playing skills are developed for the brilliant performances needed to win competitions, and in the end the Communist Party may decide that 'all types of cultural manifestation may have to be reduced or cut out because they provide too much scope for individuality to assert itself, which is basically anathema to communism'. He believes in the genuineness of Volkov's controversial version of Shostakovich's memoirs, which were attacked by the Soviet press as a forgery, thus agreeing with other Russian emigré musicians such as Kondrashin and Barshai. In addition to his numerous records as a pianist, he has recorded symphonies of Beethoven, Sibelius, Tchaikovsky and Rachmaninov, a number of piano concertos of Mozart which he both plays and conducts, and other orchestral works and concertos.

ATHERTON, **David** (b. 1944). Born in Blackpool, Atherton grew up in a musical family, learned the piano, recorder and clarinet as a child, and played in the National Youth Orchestra during his school holidays. He graduated with a BA in music from Cambridge, where he came under the influence of Willcocks and Leppard, and organised concerts including Berlioz's *Béatrice et Bénédict*. Lord Harewood, who heard the performance, drew him to the attention of Solti, then the musical director of the Royal Opera House, Covent Garden, who in 1967 invited Atherton to join the staff at Covent Garden. He was promoted to conductor there in the next year, and was the youngest conductor in the House's history. In 1967 he also founded the London Sinfonietta and as its musical director (until 1973) gave the first performances of many important works of contemporary British composers. At Covent Garden he led a number of repertory operas, as well as Tippett's *King Priam*, conducted with the Welsh National Opera and the San Francisco Opera, and became in 1968 the youngest conductor in the history of the Henry Wood Promenade Concerts. He was principal conductor of the Royal Liverpool Philharmonic Orchestra (1980–3), musical director of the San Diego Symphony Orchestra in California (from 1980), and principal guest conductor with the Royal Liverpool Philharmonic Orchestra (from 1983). He has conducted the major orchestras in Britain and has appeared in Europe, the Middle East, North America, the USSR, Japan and the Far East, Australia and New Zealand. His awards include the Edison Award, the Grand Prix du Disque, Conductor of the Year in 1971, and the Koussevitzky Award. Most of his records have been of music by British composers: Walters, Mathias, Williams, Milner, Hoddinott, Bennett, Birtwistle, Tippett, Hamilton, Dick and Taverner. But his most important achievement on disc has been a five-record set of the entire music for chamber ensembles of Schoenberg, which was issued by Decca in 1974, the year of the composer's centenary.

B

BARBIROLLI, Sir John (1899–1970). Born in London of Italian and
French parentage, Barbirolli studied at the Trinity College of
Music and the Royal Academy of Music, and joined the Queen's
Hall Orchestra as a cellist at the age of 16. After two years in the
army he resumed his career as an orchestral player in London,
played in several string quartets, and in 1925 made his début as a
conductor with the John Barbirolli String Orchestra. He joined
the British National Opera Company as a conductor in 1926,
conducted the Covent Garden Opera Company (1929–33), and
also conducted orchestras in London and at the Leeds Festival.
In 1933 he was appointed conductor of the BBC Scottish
Orchestra in Glasgow, and in 1936 he was a guest conductor with
the New York Philharmonic-Symphony Orchestra, which led to
his appointment as its principal conductor in succession to
Toscanini. His contract was initially for 1937–40, then renewed
for a further term, 1940–3. His time in New York was controversial: those who disapproved of his appointment, including
some other conductors and newspaper critics, constantly deni-
grated him and intrigued against him, and his task was made no
easier by Toscanini's return to New York in 1937 as the conductor of the NBC Symphony Orchestra. Barbirolli was of course a
sharp contrast to Toscanini: 'there was no baton-breaking,
score-hurling or bullying since he became head of the
Philharmonic-Symphony, yet he had no trouble whatever in
maintaining discipline,' wrote John Erskine in his history of the
orchestra. Barbirolli was remiss, perhaps, in failing to cultivate
the orchestra's wealthy patrons, and in addition his programmes
often ventured beyond the conventional, which no doubt
counted against him. But there is no question that his tenure
with the orchestra was not the musical disaster his critics
claimed: audiences increased during his time, his performances
of Brahms, Schubert, Ravel and Debussy in particular were
highly regarded, and when he was invited back to New York in
the 1950s his reception was enthusiastic. The main reason for his
departure was his British citizenship, which prevented him from
becoming a member of the Musicians' Union, necessary then
for both conductors and players in the USA. He enjoyed the
deep respect of many of his great contemporaries: one was
Fritz Kreisler, with whom he had recorded the Beethoven and

Brahms violin concertos in London in 1936, but his reputation as an excellent accompanist was used to disparage him, and caused him to be adamant later in refusing to accompany on record.

Barbirolli was in New York in his late 30s, and was not then quite the great conductor he later became. The next memorable phase of his career came with his return to England in 1943 at the height of the war, answering a call from the Hallé Orchestra in Manchester. He was permanent conductor of the orchestra – the first since 1933 – until 1958, when he stepped down to become conductor-in-chief, finally becoming conductor laureate for life in 1968. His leadership transformed the orchestra from the original 33 members in 1943 to an ensemble that could rival the major orchestras in London, at least until the arrival of the Philharmonia and Royal Philharmonic Orchestras in 1946 and 1947, when Barbirolli had to suffer the poaching of his best players by these and the other London orchestras. He conducted again at Covent Garden in 1951, was principal conductor of the Houston Symphony Orchestra, Texas (1961–7), from 1961 was guest conductor with the Berlin Philharmonic Orchestra, toured overseas with the Hallé, Philharmonia and BBC Symphony Orchestras, appeared at festivals in Europe, and led many successful concerts with orchestras in other countries. He married the oboist Evelyn Rothwell in 1939.

Barbirolli was an outstanding interpreter of the later classics and romantics, particularly Brahms, Sibelius, Bruckner and Mahler. British composers enjoyed his warmest advocacy, and he was one of the finest performers of Delius, Vaughan Williams and Elgar. He performed the two Elgar symphonies and *The Dream of Gerontius* with the greatest personal conviction, and recorded both symphonies twice; his tempi were markedly slower than those of Boult or of Elgar himself. His scores were meticulously prepared and he would never consider undertaking a performance or recording unless he was completely ready. In his early years his performances were clean and with marked rhythms, although some critics noted a certain restlessness. In Beethoven, Brahms, Strauss and Mahler he became, as he grew older, expansive and grand, with an inclination to linger over melody and detail; his recordings of Beethoven's Symphony No. 3 (with the BBC Symphony Orchestra), the Brahms symphonies (with the Vienna Philharmonic Orchestra) and Strauss's *Ein Heldenleben* (with the London Symphony Orchestra) are superb examples of his late style. He was 54 before he first conducted a complete Mahler symphony, and it was the critic Neville Cardus who drew his attention to the composer. He found in these works an inspiration and a challenge that he could not discover in contemporary music, and his performances of the Symphony No. 9 in particular drew extravagant praise from his fellow conductors. His recording of this symphony with the Berlin Philharmonic Orchestra was one of the finest ever made of a Mahler symphony when it was released in 1964; it was the orchestra themselves who had requested that they should record the work with Barbirolli after an overwhelming concert. The recordings he also made of the Symphonies Nos 5 and 6 of Mahler, with the New Philharmonia Orchestra, are similarly part of recording history. He was short in stature, and despite his continental parentage and temperament, remained very British, even to the point of being a lover of cricket. He was amicable towards orchestral players, although he retained their respect and could enforce discipline. While he wore spectacles to read scores, he would not conduct with them, as they hindered his communication with his musicians.

In a recording career that started in 1911 and finished in the year of his death in 1970, Barbirolli recorded an enormous range of music, from Purcell to Schoenberg. His very earliest records were as a cellist and as a member of string quartets; he then directed on record the John Barbirolli Chamber Orchestra, and in the years 1928 to 1938 made numerous discs for HMV, including accompaniments for many of the leading singers and instrumentalists. In his years with the New York Philharmonic-Symphony Orchestra his recordings included the first two Sibelius symphonies, Brahms' Symphony No. 2 and a number of other works, but when he returned to England in 1943 he recorded a vast number of works with the Hallé Orchestra, first for HMV and then for Pye. He returned to EMI (the successor to HMV) in 1962, and the discs he made included the ones mentioned earlier of symphonies of Beethoven, Brahms and Mahler and *Ein Heldenleben*, as well as Verdi's *Requiem* and *Otello* (with the New Philharmonia Orchestra *et al.*) and *Madama Butterfly* (with the Rome Opera Orchestra *et al.*); in the last-named, the *Penguin Stereo Record Guide* wrote, 'the conductor emerges as the central hero, not through ruthlessness but sheer love. Players and singers perform consistently with a dedication and intensity rare in opera recordings made in Italy, and the whole score glows more freshly than ever.'

BARENBOIM, Daniel (b. 1942). Born in Buenos Aires, son of a professor of music and a music teacher, both of Russian descent, Barenboim learnt the piano from his father and gave his first recital in

Buenos Aires at the age of 7. Two years later the family moved to Europe and he gave concerts at Salzburg and played Bach's *Concerto in D Minor* at the Salzburg Festival in 1952, at the age of 10. There he studied chamber music with Mainardi and joined Markevitch's conducting class, applying the knowledge he had gained previously from his father. He also met Furtwängler. The family moved to Vienna and then to Israel in 1952, which was to become their home. He was awarded a scholarship by the American-Jewish Cultural Foundation, which took him to Paris to study composition with Nadia Boulanger, and in 1956 became the youngest person to receive the diploma of the Accademia di Santa Cecilia in Rome. Even at this point his repertoire as a pianist included fifteen piano concertos and all the Beethoven sonatas. He was also then speaking five languages.

Although Barenboim wished to conduct from an early age, he became known first as a young but greatly gifted pianist. In 1956 he played a Mozart concerto in London under Krips, and the next year appeared in New York with Stokowski and the Symphony of the Air. While he was receiving a normal schooling in Israel he was a regular soloist with the Israel Philharmonic Orchestra, and toured the United States, South America and Australia. In 1961 he made his first professional appearance as a conductor with the Haifa Symphony Orchestra, and conducted with the Sydney and Melbourne Symphony Orchestras the next year; in 1964 he was a soloist with the English Chamber Orchestra in London and a year later conducted them from the keyboard in a Mozart concerto. He became a regular conductor of this orchestra and for many years has spent two months of each year with them, as well as touring abroad and recording with them. At this time Barenboim was appearing with the Berlin Philharmonic and New York Philharmonic Orchestras as a pianist, and in 1965 toured the USSR. He also performed in that year at the Edinburgh Festival and in 1967 played the entire Beethoven sonatas in a series of recitals in London, Tel-Aviv and Vienna. Later, in 1975, he was to perform and direct the complete Mozart piano concertos in London, New York and Paris with the English Chamber Orchestra, and in Tel-Aviv with the Israel Philharmonic Orchestra.

Barenboim's career as a conductor became firmly established in 1968 with his début in New York with the London Symphony Orchestra, substituting for its regular conductor, Kertész; he had been an apprentice conductor with the Copenhagen Radio and the Hallé Orchestras. The orchestras he has regularly conducted include the Israel Philharmonic, Chicago Symphony, New York Philharmonic, Cleveland, Berlin Philharmonic and the London Philharmonic. He has also appeared at La Scala, Milan, has directed Mozart operas at the Edinburgh Festival, and led *Tristan und Isolde* at the Bayreuth Festival, where he has been engaged to conduct the *Ring* cycle. Since 1975 he has been musical director of the Orchestre de Paris; his activities are now centred in Paris and in recent years he has restricted his appearances as a guest conductor. Simultaneously he has pursued his career as an outstanding piano recitalist and concerto performer, chamber player and accompanist to singers who have included Fischer-Dieskau and Janet Baker; in 1985 he performed the cycle of Beethoven sonatas, again, in Paris and Munich. In 1967 he married the British cellist Jacqueline du Pré.

Through playing duets and playing the scores with his father, Barenboim became familiar with the symphonic repertoire as a child. Both Edwin Fischer and Furtwängler have had a deep influence on him as an interpretive artist: 'Furtwängler astonished me by his all-round vision. He really understood the inner logic of music, and through inter-relating themes and subtle changes of tempo he was able to make a movement seem like a single organic growth. I can truly say that there is not a day passes when I don't think "I wonder what Furtwängler would think about this".' He is quick to add that a superficial imitation of Furtwängler's interpretations is pointless, and in any case impossible. He played Furtwängler's piano concerto in Berlin in 1964 on the tenth anniversary of the great conductor's death; his performance with Mehta and the Los Angeles Philharmonic Orchestra has been available on a private label. Fischer gave him the idea of conducting from the keyboard; he told him however that to direct Mozart concertos from the keyboard effectively it was first necessary to become a conductor and learn to understand the orchestra thoroughly.

Other musicians who have influenced him are Nadia Boulanger, Barbirolli, Rubinstein and Arrau. Boulanger gave him an understanding of the dual approach to every musical challenge: the structure, and the intangible elements inside the piece. Barbirolli revealed to him the art of accompanying with an orchestra. Rubinstein's contribution was his wonderful sense of well-being, and Arrau impressed him with his scrupulousness in his attention to the text, to its smallest detail. Barenboim's symphonic repertoire is catholic, ranging from Bach, Haydn, Mozart, Beethoven, Schubert, Schumann, Brahms, Bruckner, Tchaikovsky and Elgar to the Second Viennese School. He performed the nine Bruckner symphonies in Paris, for the first time, to give the orchestra a style appropriate for the Austro-German repertoire. He is an enthusiastic advocate of Elgar and has conducted the symphonies in the USA and Europe with orchestras who had never performed the music before.

Philips recorded Barenboim as a pianist when he was aged 13, then later, between 1967 and 1970, EMI recorded the complete Beethoven sonatas, as well as the Mozart piano concertos, of which the final disc appeared in 1975. For the latter series he conducted the English Chamber Orchestra from the keyboard, and with this orchestra he also recorded the mature Mozart symphonies, from No. 29 to No. 41. These performances confirmed him to be an outstanding Mozart interpreter, but some critics expressed reservations about some of the symphonies, particularly the last three. In his other orchestral and choral recordings, which include Schumann's four symphonies, Bruckner's nine, and the two symphonies and other orchestral pieces of Elgar, and numerous other major works by many composers, his unusually subjective temperament leads to intensely romantic readings, immediately reminiscent of Furtwängler; his emphasis on the dramatic aspects of the work, and the choice sometimes of unconventional tempi are also evident. Despite the large number of records he has made, he regards them as purely coincidental in his musical career, and that they have little real musical value. Any one performance, on record or in concert, can never possibly realise the full musical content or potential of any piece, so that, in his own words, 'recordings are bound to be barren aural aids – at best'. To him the major objection to records is that the listener is not required to make a conscious act of submission and concentration as he would at a live performance. The most enjoyable and important thing about music, to Barenboim, is that it takes one away from one's objective surroundings, which is possible in the concert hall but much less likely when one places a record on the turntable at home in everyday life.

BARSHAI, Rudolf (b.1924). Born in Labinskaya, in the Krasnador district of the USSR, Barshai studied with Zeitlin at the Moscow Conservatory and Academy of Music, and with Musin at the Leningrad Conservatory. He performed as a violist and in chamber groups with Shostakovich, Richter, Oistrakh and Rostropovich. In 1955 he formed the Moscow Chamber Orchestra, which was the first in the USSR, and led its first concert after six months' training. The orchestra soon became internationally famous for its superb tone, ensemble and style. Barshai orchestrated and arranged baroque and contemporary music for it, including Shostakovich's String Quartet No. 8. With the orchestra he performed and recorded the symphonies of Beethoven (except No. 9), believing that the chamber orchestra of today is indistinguishable from that of a full symphony orchestra of the classic and early romantic periods. In fact, he and his orchestra were most at home with the music of Bach, Haydn, Mozart, Beethoven and Schubert. He conducted other major symphony orchestras in the Soviet Union. A Soviet Jew, but claiming no interest in political dissent, Barshai left the USSR in 1977 and emigrated first to Israel, where he became the conductor of the Israel Chamber Orchestra, and in 1982 he was appointed conductor of the Bournemouth Symphony Orchestra. Western orchestras have found him an exhausting and meticulous rehearser.

BÁTIZ, Enrique (b. 1944). Born in Mexico City, Bátiz studied as a pianist at the Juilliard School and as a conductor in Poland. In 1971 he was appointed general music director of the Mexico State Symphony Orchestra which was created by Carlos González, the governor of the State of Mexico, and has its home at Toluco, a small town west of Mexico City. Most of the players, who come from Europe, the United States and Mexico, were under the age of 35. With the orchestra Bátiz toured Guatemala and Venezuela (1974) and the USA (1975), and he has been a guest conductor in North America, West and East Europe. In the last year or two Bátiz has been very active in recording studios in Britain, and a number of discs have been issued in which he has directed the London Philharmonic, London Symphony, Royal Philharmonic and Royal Liverpool Philharmonic Orchestras. He has also recorded with his Mexico State Symphony Orchestra music of Spanish and Mexican composers, of which he is a specially idiomatic interpreter. In music such as Dvořák's Symphony No. 8, Tchaikovsky's Symphony No. 5, and *Petrushka*, he is revealed as a most dramatic and expressive musical personality, extrovert in his interpretations, with every attention to detail. He certainly has no inhibitions in bringing music alive in the presence of the microphone instead of the live audience, but one could add the reservation that his very forthrightness sometimes leaves little room for charm.

BAUDO, Serge (b. 1927). Baudo was born in Marseille; his father was professor of oboe at the Paris Conservatoire and his uncle the cellist Paul Tortelier. He studied at the Paris Conservatoire under Fourestier and won prizes for percussion, chamber music and conducting, played the timpani with the Lamoureux, Paris Opéra and Paris Conservatoire Orchestras under Walter, Munch, Knappertsbusch *et al.* (1946–57), and in 1950 first conducted in Paris. His initial appointment came with the Radio Orchestra at Nice (1959–62); he conducted regularly at the Aix-en-Provence Festivals (from 1959); at Karajan's invitation he took over from him the conducting of Debussy's *Pelléas et Mélisande* at La Scala, Milan, and was appointed by Munch permanent conductor of the Orchestre de Paris (1967). He had been permanent conductor of the Paris Opéra (1962–5). He then became artistic conductor of the Rhône-Alpes regional orchestra. Like his compatriot Fournet, he believes in the importance of regional orchestras in French musical life and the need to support the musicians and musical public involved in them. He has appeared in the Paris Opéra-Comique, the Berlin Deutsche Oper, La Scala, the Vienna State Opera and the New York Metropolitan Opera and with major orchestras and festivals in Europe, in addition to visiting Israel, Canada, Japan and other European countries. He has a reputation as an interpreter of French music—his recording of the five symphonies of Honegger for Supraphon are excellent examples— and has given many first performances of contemporary works, including Messiaen's *Et exspecto resurrectionem mortuorum*, which he premièred at Chartres in 1965.

BEECHAM, Sir Thomas (1879–1961). Beecham was born at St Helens in Lancashire, into a wealthy family which derived its fortune from manufacturing patent medicines, more especially the famous Beecham's Pills. He showed early precocity in music, and after attending his first concert at the age of 6, started piano lessons. Although he received no formal training in music, he studied composition thoroughly and mastered several instruments; later in life he was scathing about the value of musical academies and conservatories, and had to suffer the jibes of some of his great contemporaries that he was an amateur. After 18 months at Wadham College, Oxford, he returned to St Helens to join the family business; he formed the St Helens Orchestral Society, and gave his first public concert with them in 1899. In that year, his father, Joseph Beecham, became mayor of St Helens, and engaged the Hallé Orchestra under Hans Richter for an inaugural concert at the town hall. Richter was unavailable at the last moment, the young Thomas Beecham substituted for him, and conducted without score or rehearsal Beethoven's Symphony No. 5, Tchaikovsky's Symphony No. 6, the overture to *Tannhäuser* and the prelude to *Die Meistersinger*.

In 1900 Beecham travelled in Europe, came to London in 1902 to take a post conducting a touring opera company, collaborated with Charles Kennedy Scott in founding the Oriana Madrigal Choir, and in 1905 conducted his first London concert with an ensemble drawn from the members of the Queen's Hall Orchestra. He established and conducted the New Symphony Orchestra (1906), formed another, the Beecham Symphony Orchestra (1908), and in 1910 gave the first of his Covent Garden opera seasons with the financial backing of his father who was a noted patron of music and who eventually became the landlord of the Royal Opera House at Covent Garden. He brought Diaghilev's Ballets Russes to London (1911), took his orchestra to Berlin, and during the next years conducted concerts and directed the Beecham Opera Company at Covent Garden and in other London theatres, where he introduced many new and unfamiliar operas. At the end of his life he estimated that he had conducted nearly 90 different operas, covering the Italian, French, German and Russian repertoires, and English operas when he could find them. During World War I he was indefatigable in keeping music alive in Britain, touring with his opera company, and conducting the Hallé and London Symphony Orchestras. Financial difficulties brought a hiatus in 1920; his opera company became the British National Opera Company, and when he conducted again it was in 1923 with the London Symphony Orchestra. He performed in Britain, Europe and the United States, became director of the Leeds Triennial Festival and the Norwich Festival, and in 1929 led the great Delius Festival in London, where he conducted all the programmes from memory.

Anxious to establish and lead a full-time orchestra in London which would be comparable to the best in Europe and the US, Beecham first negotiated unsuccessfully with the British Broadcasting Corporation and the London Symphony Orchestra; the BBC founded its own BBC Symphony Orchestra in 1930 which, under Boult, became itself a most distinguished ensemble. Beecham recruited many of the best available British instrumentalists and founded the London Philharmonic Orchestra, and the first concert was in the Queen's Hall in October 1932. The programme was a typical Beecham choice: the overture *Le Carnaval romain*, Mozart's Symphony No. 38, Delius's

Brigg Fair and *Ein Heldenleben*. From then until he left it in 1940 it took its place amongst the finest in Europe; Beecham thought it reached its peak in performance during its German tour in 1937. During those years he also conducted memorable seasons at Covent Garden, invited Reiner, Kleiber, Walter and Furtwängler to share the direction, organised and conducted a Sibelius Festival of six concerts in London (1938), and conducted in Brussels and Paris. He left England at the beginning of World War II, toured Australia, Canada and the USA, and finally ended up with the Seattle Symphony Orchestra, which he conducted from 1941 to 1943. When he returned to Britain in 1945, the connection with the London Philharmonic could not be re-established, and so in 1947 he founded his last great orchestra, the Royal Philharmonic, which he directed until his death in 1961. In 1960 he invited Rudolf Kempe to be the orchestra's associate conductor. He led his second Delius Festival in 1946, appeared at the Glyndebourne and Edinburgh Festivals, organised a festival of the music of Richard Strauss (1947), toured extensively, particularly in the USA (1951), returned to Covent Garden for memorable performances of *Die Meistersinger*, was made a Companion of Honour (1957), and published an autobiography, *A Mingled Chime* (1944), and a biography of Delius (1959).

Wood and Boult would also have to be considered if one were to name the greatest British conductor, but for the international public, Beecham has pride of place. He is indisputably of the first rank of conductors, and with both the London Philharmonic in the 1930s and the Royal Philharmonic later he led orchestras of the greatest eminence. His impact on British musical life was enormous: he founded five orchestras, kept opera alive in England for almost a decade, although he lost a fortune doing it, and was a major influence in the revival of the music of Mozart, of whom he was one of the finest interpreters. He did as much as anyone to establish Sibelius in the repertoire, and through his complete dedication to the task he almost convinced his countrymen that Delius was a great composer. He said that he was first attracted to Delius's music because he was a composer he had never seen or heard before, whose music was not like any other, and nobody seemed to know what to make of it: 'I found it as alluring as a wayward woman and determined to tame it . . . and it wasn't done in a day.' At the same time he avoided giving first performances of Delius's music: 'I always let somebody else make a damned fool of himself with the music, and then I came along later and showed how it's got to be done.' His Delius performances are legendary; Eric Fenby, Delius's amanuensis and also at one time Beecham's secretary-assistant, regards Beecham's recordings of 1929 as his best, especially *In a Summer Garden*, *On Hearing the First Cuckoo in Spring* and *The Walk to the Paradise Garden*. With Delius, Beecham exaggerated the composer's own nuances for greater expression, and took care that the melodic strands passed from one voice to another.

Although Beecham's musicianship was fundamentally intuitive, it was based on careful scholarship and preparation, an extraordinary memory, and a unique ability to inspire his players. When he first conducted *Der Rosenkavalier* in London he led the rehearsals from memory; he usually conducted without a score, but he experienced several disastrous lapses in the concert hall and opera house. During his career he created miracles with many orchestras of the second, or even the third rank, inspiring them to play much better than they imagined they could, and so demonstrated Mahler's adage that there are no bad orchestras, only bad conductors. For his own orchestras he recruited the best players, trusted them to play as well as they could, and allowed them freedom in phrasing the solo passages. He fervently believed that music must be enjoyed, and that the most important thing is the lyrical line: 'The grand tune is the only thing in music that the great public really understands, and flexibility is what makes it alive.' He also said: 'If I cannot sing a work, I cannot conduct it.' Musicological scholarship concerned him not at all: he performed Haydn from corrupt editions, and the researches of Robbins Landon passed him by. In his recording of Handel's *Solomon* he used his own edition, which omitted some numbers, and re-orchestrated and re-arranged the order of the rest. For his third recording of *Messiah* in 1960, he commissioned Eugene Goossens to re-arrange the work for modern symphony orchestra, and then made his own embellishments to Goossens' score, justifying the result by saying that Handel would have scored the work this way if he were alive today. The recording remains one of the most extraordinary aberrations in the history of the gramophone record. He arranged ballet scores from Handel's works—*The Faithful Shepherd* and *The Great Elopement* were the two most famous —and even assembled a piano concerto from his music.

As a conductor, Beecham had little interest in the scores of Elgar and Mahler, which have explicit directions throughout; these appeared to restrain his scope in interpreting the music. He called Elgar's Symphony No. 1 'the musical equivalent of St Pancras Station', and after conducting the Vaughan Williams

Pastoral Symphony was heard to say 'A city life for me!'. He gave exemplary performances of Strauss and Wagner, but generally had little sympathy for the great German composers; he once remarked: 'I would give the whole of Bach's *Branden-burg Concertos* for Massenet's *Manon* and would think I had vastly profited by the exchange.' Bruckner was beyond his horizon, and although he is reputed to have been ill-at-ease with Beethoven and only interested in Brahms' Symphony No. 2, the composers he most often performed during his years with the London Philharmonic were Beethoven and Brahms, as well as Mozart, whom he revered most of all. He had no time for most of the music of the 20th century: 'No composer has written as much as 100 bars of worthwhile music since 1925. *Wozzeck* is ingenious, but uncivilised and uncharming.' Also: 'For me much of Schoenberg is unintelligible, and remains unintelligible, much as I study his scores,' and of Stravinsky: 'There is behind his façade of ingenious notes and patterns no continuous personality.'

At rehearsals Beecham talked little, despite all the quips and banter heard in the LP rehearsal record that was issued in the 1950s. Details did not concern him, except maybe in Mozart and Delius, and he was always relaxed, with the score in front of him, as if refreshing his memory. His usual procedure was to run through a complete movement of a work, comment at the end about points of interpretation, then play the piece again. He said to the orchestra: 'Forget about bars. Look at the phrase, please. Remember that bars are only the boxes in which the music is packed.' Sometimes he showed remarkable patience in achiev-ing his objective, and once took a full three hours' rehearsal session perfecting the first four minutes of the overture to *William Tell*. But like Nikisch and Furtwängler, his concert performances were true improvisations, and what occurred at rehearsal was no guide to the final performance. His scores of Handel, Mozart, Schubert, Rossini, Berlioz, Bizet and Delius were marked with the greatest detail, and aspiring conductors could well study his recording of *Scheherazade* to learn how carefully he phrased and balanced the music. Between the final rehearsal and the concert he would sometimes re-mark the orchestral parts, and the players would have to be quite sure they followed his instructions. Occasionally he would arrive at the concert hall and would assemble the principals and give them final directions about certain points in the score for them to pass on to their sections. So every concert was a new performance and a separate act of interpretation; running through in his mind the scores to be performed at the concert would reveal to him an improved phrasing, or a better balance. He was rarely satisfied with any one performance, and set out to make each better than the last one of the work. During the performance itself he always looked directly at the players in solo passages; all the members of his orchestras spontaneously gave of their best. Noticeably at the beginning of a concert, he bowed first to the orchestra, and then to the audience. During a speech at a luncheon to celebrate his 80th birthday he said: 'I just get the best players and let them play. . . . At rehearsal they play the piece through; any mistakes they know about as well as I do, so we play it through again; *they don't know what I am going to do* . . . so that at the performance everyone is on his toes, and we get a fine performance.'

From the earliest days of the gramophone record until the era of stereophonic sound, Beecham was one of the most active and successful contributors to the record catalogues. His first recording was made in 1910, and his last was *Ein Heldenleben*, made in 1959. With his two great orchestras, the London Philharmonic and the Royal Philharmonic, he was as much concerned with producing recorded performances as concerts. His recordings up to 1932 were as varied as his later ones, and probably the most successful were *Messiah* (1928) and the Delius performances mentioned earlier. The London Philharmonic discs were legendary; at the centre were the Mozart and Haydn symphonies he recorded, but others such as Franck's *Symphony in D Minor*, Beethoven's Symphony No. 2, Brahms's Symphony No. 2, Tchaikovsky's *Francesca da Rimini* and Sibelius's Symphony No. 4 were the most notable of the major works, and there were of course numerous overtures and other pieces where his care and musicianship often transformed minor or neglected works into ones of great charm and character. The Handel arrangement, *The Faithful Shepherd*, was one of the most evocative and beautiful recordings he ever made. The Royal Philharmonic records generally repeated his basic repertoire, but some wonderful items were added: Goldmark's *Rustic Wedding* symphony, *Scheherazade*, Berlioz's *Harold in Italy* and *Symphonie fantastique*, Strauss's *Don Quixote* and *Ein Heldenleben*, to name but a few. Three of his opera recordings were also exceptional: *Die Zauberflöte*, *La Bohème* and *Carmen*, but all of these were made with orchestras other than the London Philharmonic and the Royal Philharmonic.

To the man in the street, Beecham was more widely known for his wit than as a musician: Neville Cardus said that he was the best English wit since Oscar Wilde, and some of his sallies frequently aroused attention if not indignation. Maybe his public image was a cloak to hide his true self, which, as several close to him have pointed out, was of a rather uncertain and timid personality, with possibly a sense of inferiority stemming from his provincial upbringing. Sometimes his witticisms had a touch of malice which offended some; there were enough to be brought together by Harold Takins and Archie Newman in their *Beecham Stories* (London, 1978). As an example, he once engaged for a performance of *Messiah* a soprano who was unfamiliar with the work. When he met her later he asked her how she was progressing in learning her part. 'I've been working hard on it,' she replied. 'The score goes with me everywhere—to work, to meals, up to bed at night. . . .' 'Then,' he replied, 'I trust we may look forward to an immaculate conception?'

BEINUM, Eduard van (1901–59). The successor to Mengelberg as musical director of the Amsterdam Concertgebouw Orchestra, van Beinum was born in Arnhem and at the age of 16 became a violinist in the orchestra there. He studied at the Amsterdam Conservatory, was first a choral conductor, then was conductor of the Haarlem Symphony Orchestra (1927–31), assistant conductor (1931–8) and then principal conductor with Mengelberg (1938) of the Concertgebouw Orchestra. After Mengelberg was banished from musical life in the Netherlands in 1945, van Beinum was chief conductor of the orchestra until his death in 1959. He was also principal conductor of the London Philharmonic Orchestra for the 1948–9 season, and from 1956 spent two months of each year with the Los Angeles Philharmonic Orchestra.

Both as a musician and as a personality van Beinum was at the opposite pole to the flamboyant and autocratic Mengelberg. Van Beinum's style was modest, reserved and undemonstrative; his creed was to let the music speak for itself. He believed that the emotional content of the music manifested itself more effectively this way, rather than seeking to exaggerate every nuance. This was true, but only up to a point; his Beethoven and Brahms were found to be somewhat sober and understated, and performances of the romantics sometimes unexciting. In all his performances the most striking aspects were the discipline, balance and precision of the orchestra, a sustained tension and an acute alertness to the pulse of the music. He saw himself as on the same level as the players in the orchestra and his relations with them were based on mutual respect. Even when the work was a Beethoven symphony, he always had the score in front of him. His repertoire was firmly based on the Viennese classics, Haydn, Mozart, Beethoven and Schubert; he also gave memorable performances of Bach, and he frequently performed Debussy, Ravel and Bruckner. His Berlioz was exceptionally successful; Mahler entered his repertoire only after 1945, as Mahler's music was proscribed in Nazi-occupied Europe. The modern composers he conducted were Bartók, Kodály, Stravinsky, Janáček, Roussel, Szymanowski, Shostakovich and Britten, Russians such as Tchaikovsky and Rimsky-Korsakov, and also Strauss and Wagner.

His early death limited van Beinum's recording career to a dozen years, but he made many significant records, mostly for Decca and Philips. Recordings with the Concertgebouw Orchestra and the London Philharmonic Orchestra ranged from Bach's orchestral suites to the four sea interludes from Britten's *Peter Grimes*; the most noteworthy were Bartók's *Concerto for Orchestra*, Berlioz's *Symphonie fantastique*, Brahms' Symphony No. 1, *Le Sacre du printemps*, Mahler's Symphony No. 4 and Bruckner's Symphonies Nos 7, 8 and 9.

BERGLUND, Paavo (b. 1929). Born in Helsinki, Berglund learned the violin as a boy with an instrument made by his grandfather, and studied at the Sibelius Academy in Helsinki and in Vienna and Salzburg. His first professional appointment was as a violinist with the Finnish Radio Symphony Orchestra (1949); he helped form the Helsinki Chamber Orchestra and became its conductor (1952), was appointed assistant conductor of the Finnish Radio Symphony Orchestra (1956), became its principal conductor (1962–72), was conductor of the Finnish Radio Chamber Orchestra (1965), and musical director of the Finnish Philharmonic Orchestra (1975–81). He toured Europe, Japan and Australia, and directed the Finnish Radio Symphony Orchestra's first English tour in 1967. In 1972 he was appointed musical director of the Bournemouth Symphony Orchestra, in succession to Silvestri, who had developed it into one that could be compared without loss to the major London orchestras, and under Berglund the orchestra maintained, perhaps enhanced, this standard. His connection with the Bournemouth Symphony terminated in 1979, but he continues to conduct the London orchestras and has toured with several of them. He appears as a guest in many of the major US orchestras, in 1981 was appointed principal guest conductor of the Scottish National Orchestra in Glasgow, and in 1985 toured Spain with the Chamber Orchestra of Europe.

As a Finn, Berglund has an intense interest in presenting the music of Sibelius, and his idiomatic and convincing recordings of Sibelius's music have done much to fire the recent revival of interest in the composer. He has recorded the seven symphonies, in addition to the early *Kullervo* symphony, with the Bournemouth Symphony Orchestra for EMI in vivid, energetic performances that capture the composer's unique qualities and which set forth the grandeur of the music as well as its instrumental colour. He was also concerned to ensure that the editions of the scores were correct. Sibelius did not publish the *Kullervo* symphony, and Berglund edited certain passages in it which he thought needed amendment. The entire series is now being recorded again by EMI with the Helsinki Philharmonic Orchestra, including the *Kullervo* symphony. He has also made records of other orchestral works by Sibelius. Shostakovich is another composer whom he has recorded extensively, with discs of a number of the symphonies, one of which is the neglected Symphony No. 7, the *Leningrad*.

BERNSTEIN, Leonard (b. 1918). Born in Lawrence, Massachusetts, of a family of Jewish migrants who had come from Rovno, Russia, Bernstein had shown exceptional musical talent as a child, composed a piano concerto at the age of 13, and a year later took piano lessons from Helen Coates, who was later to be his personal secretary. He attended his first concert at the age of 16, hearing the Boston Symphony Orchestra under Koussevitzky, and as a schoolboy produced and directed comedies, operettas and operas with the Boston Public School Orchestra. At Harvard (1935–9) he studied with Merritt, Piston and Edward Burlingame Hill, and met Copland and Mitropoulos who were to become lasting influences. From 1939 to 1941 he was at the Curtis Institute in Philadelphia, studying conducting with Reiner, piano with Vengerova and orchestration with Randall Thompson; he was a conducting pupil of Koussevitzky at the Berkshire Music Center at Tanglewood (1940–1). Rejected for military service, he worked as an arranger and transcriber in New York, then was engaged by Rodzinski as assistant conductor with the New York Philharmonic-Symphony Orchestra (1943–4). When Bruno Walter fell ill before a concert in November 1943 Bernstein substituted and made a sensational début with a programme that included *Don Quixote*, Schumann's *Manfred* overture, and the prelude to *Die Meistersinger*.

Engagements as a guest conductor followed, but at that time

he began making his mark as a composer, with his Symphony No. 1 (*Jeremiah*), the ballet *Fancy Free* and the musical *On the Town*. Now financially independent, he was able to accept an honorary appointment as conductor of the New York City Symphony Orchestra (1945–8) which was an important period in his development. At this time he conducted many orchestras throughout the United States and Europe, and as far afield as Prague and Tel-Aviv. He was music adviser to the Israel Philharmonic Orchestra (1948–9), head of the orchestra and conducting department at the Berkshire Music Center (1951–5) and professor of music at Brandeis University (1951–6). He launched a series of television lectures on music (1955) with an estimated audience of eleven million, achieved success with his musical *Wonderful Town* (1953), wrote scores for *Candide* (1956), *West Side Story* (1957) and the film *On the Waterfront*, made his operatic début with *Medea* at La Scala, Milan (1953) and conducted the opening concert at the Frederick H. Mann Auditorium in Tel-Aviv (1957). After appearing frequently as a guest conductor with the New York Philharmonic Orchestra, he was appointed co-principal conductor of the orchestra with Dmitri Mitropoulos (1957–8), then sole musical director (1959–69). This gave him the distinction of being the first native-born American to lead a major US orchestra, and on his resignation in 1969 he was honoured with the title 'laureate conductor'.

Bernstein's retirement after twelve years with the New York Philharmonic was partly the result of his desire to give more time to composition, but afterwards he increasingly turned his attention to opera and has appeared with great success in Vienna, New York and London. He sees that the symphony orchestra is now undergoing a crisis because it is not being fed a living stream of music as it was in the periods of its evolution, from Mozart to Mahler. He believes that as a composer he can do something to contribute to the orchestra's repertoire of contemporary music. At the same time he feels that the lifestream of music in the present day is not to be found in the concert hall, and that the orchestra is basically now a vehicle for performing the great works of the classical and romantic eras and has little contact with modern composition. He is not, of course, alone in this assumption; for instance, his successor with the New York Philharmonic, Boulez, took active steps to remedy the situation.

Bernstein's array of talents have made him one of the most widely known, publicised and popular musicians of the day. As well as being a conductor he is an accomplished pianist and has recorded piano concertos by Mozart, Ravel and Shostakovich; his television talks, for which he has prepared over 100 scripts ranging from a discussion of the *St Matthew Passion* to explanations of jazz, were published in part in two books, *The Joy of Music* and *The Infinite Variety of Music*, and his Charles Eliot Norton lectures at Harvard (1973) entitled *The Unanswered Question* have received wide circulation. He has in these ways attempted to bridge the gap between the world of pop and the musically naïve, and the world of the symphony orchestra and its great repertoire. In 1974 he led the New York Philharmonic in a concert at Central Park, New York, which was attended by 130,000 people. He by nature needs to communicate, to explain, to educate and to share his own private joy with all.

Some of Bernstein's musical comedy and ballet scores were immediately successful; *West Side Story* is a significant work in that it brought the Broadway musical into the concert hall. His serious music has been less durable. Some of the compositions have religious implications, and while he is a man of wide religious sympathies the emotional outlook of these pieces is essentially Jewish, and deliberately so. He premièred his Symphony No. 1 (*Jeremiah*) with the Pittsburgh Symphony Orchestra in 1944; his Symphony No. 2 (1949, entitled *The Age of Anxiety*) has an important piano part, and in the scherzo, harp, celeste and percussion join the piano in a jazz passage. The Symphony No. 3, the *Kaddish* (1963), has a spoken part which is a somewhat familiar colloquy with God, and although Bernstein has pointed out with justification that the questioning of God is a time-honoured Jewish tradition, to many the composition's overstatement is an embarrassment. His *Mass* was written for the opening of the Kennedy Center for the Performing Arts in Washington DC (1971). It goes further than the *Kaddish* symphony; some hold it to be blasphemous. Bernstein himself gives this 'theatre piece for singers, players and dancers' great personal significance, saying that it is a composition that he has been writing all his life. Critical assessment of the work has been contradictory, from the verdict that it is a 'sincere expression of a crisis of faith', to Martin Bernheimer's judgement that it is a 'pretentious exercise in well-crafted banality', which is not far removed from Olin Downes' comments written after *The Age of Anxiety* in 1950: 'wholly exterior in style, ingeniously constructed, effectively orchestrated, and a triumph of superficiality'. Probably the *Mass* should be seen live on the stage if it is to find any justification as music, drama or religious experience, for its combination of incongruous musical styles in the form of a

Broadway spectacle can be completely unconvincing, if not repellent, on record. Bernstein, however, has written one piece with religious inspiration which does not descend to bathos: the *Chichester Psalms*. His one orchestral work which is a popular concert piece, at least in the USA, is the overture to his less-than-successful musical comedy, *Candide*. Composition appears to be no problem to him, and he says that musical ideas come freely, but that he throws away at least ten times as much as he saves.

As a conductor, Bernstein's repertoire extends from the baroque of Bach and Vivaldi to modern European composers such as Bartók, Vaughan Williams, Stravinsky, Prokofiev, Shostakovich and Britten, and includes the Americans Ives, Copland, Harris, Thompson and Schuman. He has had little time for twelve-tone music, and in his hundreds of records there is no Berg or Schoenberg. He is essentially a romantic interpreter, attracted by the emotional surge and dramatic impact of the music. The self-discipline of the classical style is possible, but difficult for him, despite his superb recordings of Haydn symphonies. The lack of reserve in his interpretations is matched by his extravagant gestures on the podium, evident from his very first years as a conductor, and more than one critic has found it intolerable to watch his choreographic feats and facial expressions. Bernstein himself is not conscious of these movements, and orchestral players report that he is exactly the same at rehearsals when there is no audience. No music in his hands is allowed to speak for itself; it is projected with such intensity and expressiveness that the composer's intention can sometimes be lost, and it is only too evident that Bernstein must, above all, arrest and rivet the attention of the listener. He is in no sense a stylist, but of much of the repertoire he gives passionately committed performances.

Prior to his association with the New York Philharmonic, Bernstein made a number of records with various orchestras. His years with the New York Philharmonic and his contract with Columbia at that time made him one of the most recorded conductors ever, and of all conductors his art is one of the most exhaustively represented on disc. He has also recorded with other orchestras, and more recently he has been contracted by DGG for recordings with the Vienna Philharmonic Orchestra. From Bach's *St Matthew Passion* to Bloch's *Sacred Service*, his discography with the New York Philharmonic encompasses the complete symphonies of Beethoven, Schumann, Brahms, Sibelius and Mahler, as well as innumerable records of the music of Haydn, Mozart, Bartók, Berlioz, Copland, Debussy, Ravel, Dvořák, Ives, Mendelssohn, Nielsen, Prokofiev, Strauss, Shostakovich, Stravinsky, Tchaikovsky, Vaughan Williams, Wagner, Messiaen, Roussel and of course himself. Probably the most outstanding have been the six *Paris* symphonies of Haydn and the nine Mahler symphonies. The Haydn symphonies won the most enthusiastic praise from the eminent Haydn scholar, H. C. Robbins Landon, who called Bernstein 'one of the greatest, if not the greatest, interpreter of Haydn's music we have either [in the USA] or in Europe'. The Mahler symphonies have a searing intensity: the music finds a ready mirror in Bernstein's own temperament. In Mozart, Beethoven, Schumann, Schubert and Brahms, Bernstein encounters problems of style which his innately romantic musical nature does not help him to solve. Nonetheless, his Beethoven Symphony No. 3 with the New York Philharmonic must be listed among his best records. The others? Probably *Harold in Italy* and *Symphonie fantastique* (with the New York Philharmonic and, more recently, with the French National Orchestra), Bach's *Magnificat*, Bartók's *Concerto for Orchestra*, Brahms' Piano Concerto No. 2 (with Watts), the discs of pieces of Copland and Gershwin, the Franck symphony, Mendelssohn's Symphony No. 3, Mussorgsky's *Pictures at an Exhibition*, Shostakovich's Symphony No. 5, Sibelius's Symphony No. 5, Strauss's *Till Eulenspiegel* and *Don Juan*, and *Le Sacre du printemps*; to these must now be added the nine Beethoven symphonies and the four Brahms symphonies with the Vienna Philharmonic.

Bernstein in addition has made a major mark as a conductor of opera. He directed the US première of *Peter Grimes* at Tanglewood in 1946, and in 1953 was the first American-born musician to conduct at La Scala, Milan, where his *Medea* aroused some controversy. He returned to La Scala many times, but his first real triumph was with *Falstaff* at the New York Metropolitan in 1964. His performance of *Der Rosenkavalier* in Vienna in 1967 was also sensational, and this production was eventually recorded and released in 1972. In 1973 his *Carmen* in New York, and in 1983 his *Tristan und Isolde* with the Bavarian Radio Symphony Orchestra were issued by DGG, for whom he also recorded his own three symphonies and other orchestral music with the Israel Philharmonic Orchestra. He is the most significant and accomplished American conductor to have appeared so far. His vast talent and musicianship must be given high praise, but even so his final place among the great conductors is a problem. He represents, to the rest of the world, so many familiar aspects of American cultural life: charisma, brilliance given to overstatement, and a certain lack of emotional restraint that makes it difficult for him to distinguish between sentiment and sentimentality. But he is still in his sixties, not old for a conductor, and when one considers Walter, Toscanini, Beecham, Monteux and Klemperer beyond that age, there may be wonders yet to be revealed.

BLOMSTEDT, **Herbert** (b. 1927). Born in Springfield, Massachusetts, the Swedish conductor Blomstedt studied at the Royal School of Music at Stockholm, at the University of Uppsala, then with Tor Mann in Stockholm, with Markevitch at Salzburg, and with Bernstein at the Berkshire Music Center in Massachusetts. He also took part in a course in contemporary music in Darmstadt, and in the performance of old music at the Schola Cantorum in Basel. After making his début as a conductor with the Stockholm Philharmonic Orchestra in 1954, he became conductor of the Norrköping Radio Orchestra (1954), won first prize in the International Conductors' Competition at Salzburg (1957), was chief conductor of the Danish Radio Symphony Orchestra (1967–77) and of the Stockholm Radio Symphony Orchestra (since 1977). He has conducted the Dresden Staatskapelle since 1969, in 1972 became the orchestra's permanent guest conductor, and in 1975 its chief conductor, and in 1978 took up the position of general music director, leading it in tours of Japan, the USA and Europe. He is now musical director of the San Francisco Symphony Orchestra. Since 1961 he has taught conducting at the Stockholm Conservatory, and became a professor there in 1965. He has also taught conducting at summer courses in Monte Carlo, and at Aspen and Loma Linda in the USA. In Sweden he has been awarded the Knighthood of the Northern Star and is a member of the Royal Music Academy, and in Denmark he received the Knighthood of the Dannebrogen Order. Blomstedt has recorded in two separate spheres, in Scandinavia and in Dresden in DR Germany. Chief among his records at the first are the six Nielsen symphonies, with the Danish Radio Symphony, which were welcomed as a fine achievement. With the Dresden Staatskapelle he has recorded, inter alia, the nine Beethoven symphonies and *Leonore* (the first version of *Fidelio*), and symphonies of Mozart, Schubert and Bruckner. Admittedly, the Beethoven and Schubert symphonies tend to weightiness and a certain stolidity, but the Bruckner Symphony No. 7, issued on a compact disc, has shown him in a much more favourable light.

BÖHM, **Karl** (1894–1981). Born in Graz, Austria, Böhm studied law at
the University of Graz, at the same time taking lessons in piano
and theory at the Graz Conservatory. His father, an amateur
musician and a lawyer, and friend of Hans Richter, believed that
he should have a profession to fall back on if he was unsuccessful
as a musician. Böhm continued his musical studies at the Vienna
Conservatory under Mandyczewski, and after being injured
while serving in the Austrian army in World War I he returned to
civilian life, received the degree of Doctor of Laws at Graz
(1919) and became a prompter at the Graz Opera. He never
studied conducting formally, but accepted Richter's advice that
he would know immediately if he would make a conductor by
standing in front of an orchestra. He finally abandoned law for
music and was appointed first conductor at Graz (1920). While
he was conducting a performance of *Lohengrin*, Karl Muck was
present in the audience, was impressed and offered to assist him
in the study of Wagner's operas. Muck also recommended him
to Walter, then to the Munich Opera, who engaged him (1921).
Böhm was deeply influenced by Walter's great performances of
the Mozart operas at Munich, although he came to believe that
Walter's readings of Mozart were too sentimental: 'You will find
every emotion in Mozart's music,' he said, 'but he is never
sentimental.' On the other hand, he thought Strauss's tempi too
fast for Mozart. After Walter's departure from Munich, Böhm
worked with Knappertsbusch, and then left for Darmstadt
where he became first conductor (1927–31), was for the next two
years in Hamburg, then succeeded Busch as music director in
Dresden (1934–43), finally moving to the Vienna State Opera.
In Dresden he enjoyed ideal conditions, worked continuously
with the same singers and orchestral players, and was not
disturbed by travel and other conducting engagements. His
recordings with the Saxon State Orchestra for HMV when he
was in Dresden were some of the most remarkable in the
pre-war 78 r.p.m. catalogue, the major works including
Beethoven's Symphony No. 9, Violin Concerto (with Strub) and
Piano Concertos No. 3 (with Kolessa), No. 4 (with Gieseking)
and No. 5 (with Fischer), Brahms's Violin Concerto (with
Schneiderhan) and Piano Concerto No. 2 (with Backhaus),
Bruckner's Symphonies Nos 4 and 5, *Till Eulenspiegel* and *Don
Juan*, and the complete Act III of *Die Meistersinger*.

In Darmstadt Böhm conducted one of the first performances
of Berg's *Wozzeck* (1928); Berg himself was present for the last
days of the rehearsals. From then on Böhm was a leading
interpreter of the two Berg operas, *Wozzeck* and *Lulu*, and

recorded both for DGG. He also enjoyed a close association with Richard Strauss, which began in 1933 when Strauss visited him in Hamburg during his preparation of *Arabella*. Later, in Dresden, Böhm gave the first performances of *Die schweigsame Frau* and *Daphne*, which Strauss had dedicated to him. Böhm conducted most of Strauss's major orchestral works and operas in the presence of the composer, and said that Strauss always insisted that, above all, the words of the libretto be clearly audible. When *Die schweigsame Frau* was being rehearsed for its première, Böhm complained that the thickness of the woodwind passages made it impossible to hear the words, and Strauss rewrote and lightened the wind parts. In addition, Böhm heard Strauss conduct many of his symphonic poems and operas, and these experiences gave him such a profound insight into their interpretation that his own performances had an unmistakable authority. In 1936, after Böhm brought the Dresden State Opera to Covent Garden to present *Der Rosenkavalier* and *Tristan und Isolde*, he was invited back to conduct *Elektra* and *Salome* on the same programme, but refused on artistic grounds.

After World War II Böhm was permitted to appear again as a conductor in 1947, and was director of the Vienna State Opera (1950–3). His first appearance in Vienna had been much earlier in 1933, with *Tristan und Isolde*. He was engaged for a five-year contract in 1954 and conducted *Fidelio* at the first performance of the reconstructed opera house on the Ringstrasse the next year, but drew strong local criticism through his absences from Vienna, particularly in South America where he was the director of the German repertoire at the Teatro Colón in Buenos Aires (1950–4). He resigned after his contract had run only fifteen months, and was succeeded by von Karajan, although he was to continue to conduct in Vienna. He was not the first, nor the last, great conductor to break with the Vienna State Opera before completing his contract; von Karajan, and Maazel more recently, were to do the same. Böhm first appeared in the United States in 1956 when he was a guest conductor with the Chicago Symphony Orchestra; Rudolf Bing, who had known Böhm previously when he was on the staff at Darmstadt, engaged him for the New York Metropolitan Opera, where he made his triumphant first appearance with *Don Giovanni* (1957). Later he was to lead notable performances at the Met. of *Die Meistersinger* (1959), *Wozzeck* (1959), *Parsifal* (1961), *Fidelio* (1963), *Daphne* (1964), *Der fliegende Holländer* (1965), *Salome* (1965), *Die Frau ohne Schatten* (1966) and *Lohengrin* (1966). Despite his concentration on the German repertoire at the Met. and at the Teatro Colón, Böhm conducted much Italian opera, both in Italy and Germany; once he prepared *Falstaff* at Dresden and had 25 ensemble rehearsals and 15 stage rehearsals. Altogether, he conducted 150 different operas in his career. In 1962 he led an exceptionally intense *Tristan und Isolde* at Bayreuth, which fortunately has been preserved on disc; he toured with the Berlin Philharmonic Orchestra in Japan, and first conducted *The Ring* at Bayreuth in 1963, which was also recorded, and in 1967 conducted the Vienna Philharmonic Orchestra when they toured the USA and Canada. In 1970 he received the Great Gold Medal for distinguished service to Viennese music, and was also named General Music Director of Austria. In 1973 he conducted the London Symphony Orchestra at Salzburg, and in 1977 was named the orchestra's president, in succession to Sir Arthur Bliss.

Böhm came to occupy a position of eminence among European conductors, and more particularly he was one of the very finest interpreters of Austro-German music. As a personality he was authoritarian and sometimes unfairly critical of some players in his orchestras; he talked quietly, but quickly gained the respect of the orchestra. His gestures were economical and he commanded an immense dynamic range with little effect. Like so many other great conductors, it was his eyes that communicated most to his players. His interpretations were poised, unaffected by mannerisms and quite devoid of eccentricity. He made no special effort to point up details or to exaggerate a dramatic point or to heighten a climax, but he was perfectly precise in matters of tempi, dynamics and phrasing. In Mozart, Beethoven, Schubert, Brahms and Bruckner, all of whose symphonies he recorded, his performances were unfailingly spacious and beautiful, as exemplified by the recordings of Beethoven's Symphony No. 6 and Bruckner's Symphony No. 4 with the Vienna Philharmonic Orchestra. But in music that calls for a touch of demon or virtuosity, such as Beethoven's Symphony No. 7, the smoothness of his conducting lacked tension and the final incandescence was missing. His Mozart was urbane, supremely well-judged and balanced; the sound was big, perhaps too big to be truly authentic in style, and sometimes there was a hint that while the music was left to speak for itself, craftsmanship may have imperceptibly replaced inspiration. He was in another world from the pointed elegance of Beecham, the intense lyricism of Walter and the crisp accuracy of Szell. Böhm's art is extremely well-documented on gramophone records and he was, for almost five decades, one of the major recording artists, in his last phase recording with the Berlin and Vienna Philharmonic Orchestras. His discography rarely departs from the central repertoire of the German and Viennese classics, with the exception of the inclusion of the two Berg operas and Tchaikovsky's last three symphonies, but Haydn was almost completely neglected. With the astonishing number of records he made both of opera and symphonic music, it is inevitable that in some he may not have scaled the heights as he undoubtedly did in others. But his unfailing taste and the integrity of his profound musicianship could never be called into question.

BONYNGE, Richard (b. 1930). Bonynge was playing the piano at the age of 4, then studied the bassoon and piano at the New South Wales State Conservatory of Music at his birthplace, Sydney; there he came under the influence of its director, Sir Eugene Goossens. After appearances in Australia as a concert pianist he travelled to England and attended the Royal College of Music, where his attention turned to opera and ballet. He had met his fellow Australian, the soprano Joan Sutherland, whom he coached in the *bel canto* style of singing; the two were married in 1954 and since then their two careers have been inseparable. He started as a conductor in 1962 when he took over at short notice at an orchestral concert at which Joan Sutherland was appearing in Rome. He first conducted in the United States at the Hollywood Bowl in 1962; his first opera was *Faust*, in Vancouver in 1963, he first conducted at the New York Metropolitan Opera in 1966, and his first appearance at Covent Garden, London, was two years later. He was artistic director of the Vancouver Opera Association (1974–8), and from 1975 has been musical director of the Australian Opera in Sydney. Bonynge has made an intense study of the operas of Bellini and his period, and has introduced into Sutherland's performances of this repertoire embellishments and ornaments from many sources. In more recent years he has made a similar study of French operas of the middle and late 19th century. His sympathy for the singers makes him an effective and distinguished opera conductor, although his musical interests range beyond the opera house. As he customarily conducts for all of Sutherland's operatic and concert appearances around the world he has exceptional opportunities to excel in this medium. He gives little attention to modern operas, saying that present-day composers do not write for singers: 'This is why I think if we are to enjoy singing we have to go back and do the composers who wrote for singers, who knew what singing was all about.' He made his first records in 1962, and virtually all his subsequent recordings have been made for Decca, and he has conducted almost every recording in which Sutherland has appeared.

BOSKOVSKY, Willi (b. 1909). A Viennese, Boskovsky enrolled at the Vienna Academy at the age of 9, studied the violin with Mayrecker and Moravec, and graduated at 17 having won the Fritz Kreisler Prize. He soon made a name as a solo violinist and continued making solo appearances until 1939. He joined the Vienna Philharmonic Orchestra in 1932, and in 1939 Knappertsbusch made him one of the orchestra's four leaders. In 1937 he founded the Boskovsky Trio, and in 1947 the Boskovsky Quartet and the Vienna Octet, of which he remained the leader until 1958. His career as a conductor started in 1954 when he was asked to direct for the first time the Vienna Philharmonic's New Year Concert, and he continued to do so until 1979. Boskovsky is renowned for his superb recordings for Decca of the music of Johann Strauss and others of the Strauss family, and of the dance music of Mozart. In the entire Strauss discography his records lead the field, and the complete dances, marches and minuets of Mozart were issued by Decca between 1964 and 1967, with him leading the Vienna Mozart Ensemble. Later the group recorded all the Mozart cassations, serenades and divertimentos, except those for woodwind, and its unerring sense of style and impeccable playing defy analysis.

BOULEZ, Pierre (b. 1925). Born in Montbrison, France, Boulez learned the piano as a boy; he was encouraged by the soprano Ninon Vallin to take formal teaching, but after several unsuccessful attempts to enter the conservatoires at Lyon and Paris as a piano student, he eventually came to Paris and studied composition with Messiaen, Leibowitz and with Honegger's wife, Andrée Vaurabourg, at the Paris Conservatoire. From there he graduated with honours in 1945, and immediately became known as an *enfant terrible* and as an outspoken opponent of the conservative elements in music by leading a demonstration at a concert of some of Stravinsky's neo-classical pieces in Paris. In 1945 he also heard for the first time Schoenberg's Quintet for Wind Op. 26, which struck him as the most radical revolution in music since Monteverdi, and as the only possible musical language for our time. His first appointment was in 1946 as musical director of the Compagnie Renaud-Barrault, and in his first appearance at the theatre he played the Ondes Martenot, an electronic instrument, in some incidental music to *Hamlet* by Honegger. With Barrault's company he toured Europe, North and South America and the Far East. At this time and with the help of Barrault and his actress wife, Madelaine Renaud, he founded and organised the Domaine Musical concerts in Paris, which were devoted to performances of contemporary music and to rarely heard masterpieces of the past. The Domaine Musical concerts scored a triumph in 1957 when Stravinsky directed the first performance of *Agon*. Boulez conducted in public for the first time in 1965 when he substituted for Rosbaud at the première of his *Le Marteau sans maître*, and in 1957 Scherchen entrusted him with conducting his own *Visage nuptial* in Cologne, and so started his distinguished international career.

In 1960 Boulez left Paris and joined the South-West German Radio at Baden-Baden, where he made his home; the Radio had offered him a small income for the right to the first performances of his works. Under the influence of Rosbaud, then the musical director of the Radio Orchestra, he developed as a conductor, at first of his own music. In 1963 he returned to Paris to lead a remarkable first performance there of *Wozzeck*, and after making his London début in 1964 with the BBC Symphony Orchestra he progressed rapidly as an international celebrity. He made his début in the USA with the Cleveland Orchestra (1965), appeared at the Edinburgh Festival (1965), conducted *Parsifal* at Bayreuth (1966), conducted *Tristan und Isolde* with the Bayreuth Company on tour to Japan, led performances of *Pelléas et Mélisande* at Covent Garden (1969) and finally was appointed chief conductor of the BBC Symphony Orchestra (1971–5), musical director of the New York Philharmonic Orchestra (1971–7) and principal guest conductor of the Cleveland Orchestra. In 1975 he became director of the Institut de Recherche et de Co-ordination Acoustique/Musique at Beaubourg in Paris, which was the result of an initiative by the late President Pompidou, financed by the French Government, with the aim of bringing together performers, composers and scientists to find new approaches to composing and performing modern music. The Institut provides the best possible environment and equipment for composers, and aims to bring new works into the repertoire. In 1976 Boulez returned to Bayreuth to conduct the controversial *Ring* production by Chéreau, which became known to a vast audience through its distribution in video form. He is now president of the Ensemble Intercontemporain in Paris.

Although his commitments as a conductor have in the past

brought a diminution to his output as a composer, Boulez remains one of the foremost composers to emerge since World War II. He attempts to apply serial techniques to all the elements of music, in addition to melody, as it originated with Schoenberg. His early piano sonatas created an immediate impression, which was later confirmed by *Le Soleil des eaux* (1948), *Structures* (1952), *Le Marteau sans maître* (1955), *Pli selon pli* (1960), *Doubles* (1958), *Domaines* (1968) and a work in memory of Stravinsky, *Explosante-fixe* (1973). However, his leadership of the avant-garde in Paris was uncompromising and abrasive; differences about aleatoric music (that is, where elements in a composition are left in an indeterminate state) have divided him from most of his contemporaries, and despite his high regard for Stockhausen he has given little attention to electronic music. He once contemplated collaborating in a stage work but he has no ambition to write an opera. He regards his former teacher Messiaen as the only great French composer to appear between the two world wars; to him Debussy is the only French composer of the last two centuries who is universal, and among British composers he is interested in Goehr, Davies, Bennett and more particularly Birtwistle. As a conductor he is not concerned with much of the music of the 19th-century classics, such as Brahms, Tchaikovsky and Strauss, since they were not innovators compared to Beethoven, Berlioz, Debussy and Wagner, who have accordingly earned his admiration. He prefers to perform rarely heard classical and modern pieces and to develop new ways of including them in his programmes.

Conducting started for Boulez as a hobby, to give him the chance to hear his own music and to learn what was practical when writing for the orchestra. When he accepted the appointments in London and New York he attempted to bring about a vast and radical change in orchestral programmes and in the organisation of concert life. For him musical life must be revitalised so that it is part of a genuine living culture and part of the musical creative activity of our time, not a 'kind of second-rate enjoyment'. At present, he says, 'audiences try to rediscover at concerts the first emotions they felt on hearing classical music', but he feels no obligation to provide them with that opportunity. Audiences have to be brought into contact, readily and willingly, with music written today, but this implies being familiar with the music from which it springs, that is the Second Viennese School of Schoenberg, Berg and Webern, who provide that indispensable link between Strauss, Mahler, Debussy and the other late romantic and impressionist composers, and the composers of today. His mission then has been to have the music of Schoenberg, Berg and Webern accepted as part of the regular orchestral repertoire, and in London and New York he had ample opportunity to work towards these ends. He re-arranged concert programmes, found new ways and places to have concerts to bridge the gap between audiences and performers. His influence was certainly marked, if not profound; in New York the result was that the audience for the New York Philharmonic concerts became decidedly younger as the more elderly and conservative members drifted away (perhaps to return with the advent of Zubin Mehta); in London the BBC Symphony Orchestra was only one of a number of orchestras giving regular concerts but, under Boulez, it became highly proficient at performing contemporary music.

Despite the self-imposed limitations of his repertoire, Boulez is undoubtedly one of the finest conductors of the day. Klemperer called him 'the only man of his generation who is an outstanding conductor and musician'. Technically he is exemplary: he uses no baton, and his left hand is employed merely to measure a crescendo. His ear is extremely acute and his ability to single out one player in the orchestra for correction has brought many players to despair. His sound is unique; no matter how much he insists that his orchestra is simply playing the notes accurately, the lean, clear, Boulez sound emerges. When he conducted the Philadelphia Orchestra their characteristic tonal bloom vanished and the cool sound of the Boulez orchestra took its place. His profound understanding of musical structure gives continuity and coherence to the music, and it never becomes a series of brilliant episodes. He reacts strongly against the traditional readings of the great musical masterpieces and casts an iconoclastic eye at the interpretations of the great conductors of the past. His generation, he feels, has no use for the traditions of the past; 'for me, the right tradition is to give a new face to each generation. Generally, the danger of maintaining a style or tradition is that, on the contrary, you maintain mannerisms.' He believes his generation sees the music of the past through a different perspective from earlier performers: 'my generation wants to combine a high degree of precision with a great deal of interpretative freedom'. Scores, he says, 'must be interpreted in the spirit of the time. How Bach was played in 1920 is not how we like to hear him today. The superficial elegance that people appreciated in Mozart is not what we admire in him now.' His conducting of *Pelléas et Mélisande* illustrated this point; to him it is cruel and mysterious, not sweet and gentle, as it is in the usual

French tradition. His recording of *Parsifal* was too much for those who had been affected by Knappertsbusch's devoted reading. Desmond Shaw-Taylor wrote of its 'chilly effect, as though of a deconsecrated cathedral through which we are shepherded in pretty smart time'. Even so, it has been noted that the cold precision of his earlier recordings has given way more recently to something much warmer and more humane. In *Gurrelieder*, which was issued in 1975, Boulez appeared to relax his former severity in managing this huge, sensuous score, as if he were coming closer to the aesthetic of the late romantics, which he had earlier despised.

Rehearsals with Boulez are calm and even-tempered. He gives more time to the music that interests him, sometimes to the detriment of other music in the programme. Usually he goes through a piece completely, then bit by bit, repeating passages and sometimes separate groups of instruments until he is satisfied. His manner at concerts is completely without any trace of flamboyance and his facial expression rarely betrays emotion. 'I do get excited,' he explains, 'but I am not obliged to look excited.' In the words of Winthrop Sargent: 'His attitude seems to be that of a strict physician who is going to see that you take your medicine whether you like it or not.'

Boulez's recordings have inevitably been of the composers he applauds: Berlioz, Bartók, Stravinsky, Debussy, Ravel, Wagner, Mahler, and of course Schoenberg, Berg and Webern, as well as his own music. His recordings of opera have been *Pelléas et Mélisande*, *Wozzeck*, *Lulu*, *Parsifal* and the four operas of the *Ring*. All are completely characteristic of his style and outlook. The *Symphonie fantastique* was an outstanding example of his musicianship, but a Beethoven Symphony No. 5, which he recorded with the New Philharmonia Orchestra, was almost a curiosity with its slow tempi and uncommitted air.

BOULT, **Sir Adrian** (1889–1983). The son of a Liverpool merchant, Boult was born in Chester, Lancashire, and studied at Christ Church, Oxford, where he was awarded a D. Phil. in Music (1914). At Oxford he came into contact with Sir Hugh Allen, who was then professor of music. Afterwards he went to the Leipzig Conservatory, where he observed Nikisch and studied with Reger (1912–13). He returned to England, gave some orchestral concerts in Liverpool, conducted opera at Covent Garden where he assisted with the Bodanzky performance of *Parsifal* (1914), and came into prominence in 1918 when he directed several concerts of the Royal Philharmonic Society. In that year he also conducted the première of Holst's *The Planets*. He was with the War Office and the Commission Internationale de Ravitaillement in World War I, and has told the story that at one point he helped to organise the supply of footwear to the British Army; in his office, surrounded by boots, Vaughan Williams made the first revision of his *London Symphony*. From 1919 to 1930 he was a member of the teaching staff of the Royal College of Music; among his students were Leslie Heward and Constant Lambert. His subject was conducting; in 1921 he published *A Handbook on Conducting* and 42 years later produced another volume, *Thoughts on Conducting*. In the early 1920s he conducted the British Symphony Orchestra, which had been formed by ex-servicemen musicians, the London Symphony Orchestra, Diaghilev's Ballets Russes and the British National Opera Company, conducting *Die Wälkure*, *Parsifal* and *Otello*.

Boult's first major appointment was with the City of Birmingham Orchestra (1924–30); at about this time he was also musical director of the Bach Choir (1928–31). In 1930 he was named director of music at the BBC and permanent chief conductor of the newly-formed BBC Symphony Orchestra. His work with the orchestra in its formative years was possibly his greatest contribution to British music. When it was assembled most of the best players in Britain were recruited for the front desks, and as it was a permanent radio orchestra there was ample rehearsal time and its standards were higher than those then prevailing in the country. He said later that he did not go abroad very much then; 'If I went away, I had to make do with two or three rehearsals when I was a guest conductor. I had unlimited rehearsals at home, and I didn't really want to go about much.' In the BBC Symphony Orchestra's first concert in October 1930 was included Brahms's Symphony No. 4, for which Boult had 12 to 15 rehearsals. The orchestra became one of the leading ensembles in Europe until World War II; the London Philharmonic, formed by Sir Thomas Beecham in 1932 because he had been precluded from conducting the BBC Symphony, was a rival. Toscanini had the highest regard for the BBC Symphony and conducted it on visits to England in 1935, 1937, 1938 and 1939, the greatest occasion being the seven-concert Beethoven cycle in 1939. The exceptional results which Toscanini achieved with the orchestra in his recordings in England were not accidental.

Boult remained with the BBC until 1950 when he was obliged to resign, having reached the retiring age for a civil servant. In his 20 years with the orchestra he led 1,536 concerts, an average of 77 a year. He toured in Vienna (1933), Boston and Salzburg (1935), New York (1938 and 1939), and led the BBC Symphony on tour in Europe in 1936 and to Brussels in 1937. In the USA he was one of the very few guest conductors with the Boston Symphony Orchestra. All his life he was a consistent champion of British music both on record and in concert, especially Elgar, Vaughan Williams and Holst; Bliss, Moeran, Ireland and others also received his patronage, and he believed that Parry, Stanford and Rubbra are the most underrated British composers in this century. Curiously, Boult never recorded Delius and gave him virtually no attention. He was knighted for his services to music in 1937 and was awarded the Gold Medal of the Royal Philharmonic Society in 1944. After retiring from the BBC he became principal conductor of the London Philharmonic Orchestra (1950), but resigned from the position after leading them on a tour to the USSR in 1956. He nonetheless retained a close connection with the London Philharmonic, and in 1959–60 spent the season with the City of Birmingham Symphony Orchestra. Also, from 1962 to 1966 he returned to the staff of the Royal College of Music.

Boult was a modest, patient and undemonstrative musician, and kept his personal life completely private. He had catholic tastes, although Beethoven, Schubert and Brahms were at the centre of his affections. Despite his success with *Wozzeck*, which he presented after intensive preparation with the BBC Symphony and soloists in the 1933–34 season, he professed to have little comprehension of twelve-tone music; in 1931 he performed, with apparent distinction, Schoenberg's *Variations for Orchestra*, but said that when he came to do the piece again three years later in Vienna, performing it, incredibly, for the first time there, he found nothing in the score to remind him of the previous performance. He then remarked to himself that if someone had said to him that it was an entirely new set of variations on a different theme he would have believed him. He disliked showmanship of any kind, once saying that a conductor should appeal to the eyes of the orchestra and to the ears of the audience. On the podium his stance was exceptionally still; he never used his feet and his left hand came into play only sparingly. In rehearsal he was economical, and in a symphony he played to the end of the exposition before replaying unsatisfactory passages. He endeavoured to have the composer present when playing a new work, although he once found one British composer so exasperating at a rehearsal that he greeted her: 'Good morning, Dame Ethyl, and what are your tempi for today?' From his public performances it would have been difficult to detect his personal preferences, but he once remarked that he considered it his duty to make the best of whatever score he was given: 'As an executant I am not, and have no right to be, a critic of any kind, even to the extent of having preferences or favourites.'

Boult said that the greatest influences on him as a young man were Hans Richter, because of the solidity and architectural power of his conducting, and Henry Wood, whose performances had affection and beauty. In later years he much admired Weingartner, Furtwängler and Walter. Casals, too, was a profound teacher; Boult once spent a month at Barcelona observing him rehearsing his orchestra. From Nikisch Boult learned to talk with the point of his baton and not with his voice at rehearsals. In his autobiography, *My Own Trumpet* (1973), he named those who were the greatest conductors in his experience: for Bach —Steinbach and Hugh Allen; for Beethoven—Richter, Safanoff, Furtwängler and Weingartner; for Brahms—Steinbach; for Wagner—Richter, Walter (for *The Ring* and *Die Meistersinger*) and Nikisch (for *Tristan und Isolde*); for Tchaikovsky— Wood and Safanoff. Boult's own strength as a conductor was best revealed in music in large forms and breadth of structure; his emotional reserve made him less impressive, some might have said dull, in highly coloured but less significant music. His acute ear gave him an unusual capacity for achieving a fine balance among the instrumental groups, and he appealed to the musicians to listen to one another. He rarely edited a score, but in Beethoven followed Weingartner's alterations. Normally he obeyed scrupulously the composer's instructions, particularly with Elgar. He conducted familiar repertoire from memory, otherwise he used a score. Boult recorded from 1920 to 1978, from the primitive acoustic 78 r.p.m. discs to the first experiments in digital recording. After early records, which included Schubert's Symphony No. 8 in the 1920s, his series with the BBC Symphony Orchestra was one of the major contributions to the catalogues at that time. The more remarkable of these were Schubert's Symphony No. 9, Beethoven's Piano Concerto No. 3 (with Solomon—an example to all for evermore in style and the art of the accompanist), *The Planets* (the first of his five recordings of the work) and Elgar's Symphony No. 2. Later, with the London Philharmonic and other orchestras he recorded much Elgar; it is noticeable that his tempi in the Symphony No. 1 are slower than Elgar's in the latter's own recording of the work. Boult explained that Elgar 'was always in a hurry in the recording studio, because he was still imbued with that awful four-minutes-per-side business. I'm not going to say that he hurried things in live performance . . . there he always had space and time.' With the advent of the LP, Boult recorded much music for many companies, mostly with the London Philharmonic Orchestra; included were *Messiah* (twice), the Schumann and Brahms symphonies, four of the Beethoven symphonies, and the Vaughan Williams symphonies (twice, except the No. 9). He recorded the two Elgar symphonies three times each, and for Lyrita directed a number of discs of the music of Ireland, Moeran, Rubbra and Parry. A unique technical feat was achieved in the recording studio with the disc of Bach and Handel arias with the great British contralto, Kathleen Ferrier. Boult had recorded the recital originally with her and the London Philharmonic on a mono LP for Decca in 1953; in 1960, after her tragic death, he and the same orchestra assembled again and recorded exactly the same programme on stereo, accompanying Ferrier's voice which was dubbed from the other disc. The 1960 recording is now available on compact disc. In 1974 he recorded the *Brandenburg Concertos*, played with full orchestra; he felt that the current spate of recordings with smaller ensembles was insufficiently full-blooded. While history has cast him as the supremely authoritative interpreter of British music, this can obscure the wide cast of his musical sympathies, as the early LPs of Rachmaninov's Symphonies Nos 2 and 3, Mahler's Symphony No. 1 and Shostakovich's Symphony No. 6 demonstrate.

BRITTEN, Benjamin (1913–76). The eminent British composer Britten was born at Lowestoft in East Anglia, studied the piano with Harold Samuel and composition with Frank Bridge while still at school, and then the piano with Arthur Benjamin and composition with John Ireland at the Royal College of Music in London. After spending the early years of World War II in the USA he settled in Aldeburgh, Suffolk, and in 1948 Britten, Peter Pears and Eric Crozier organised the first Aldeburgh Festival of Music and the Arts. It opened with his cantata *Saint Nicholas*; the festivals were continued in June and July of each year, and many of Britten's compositions received their first performances there, although other modern British music is also performed. Celebrated local and international artists, such as Richter, Rostropovich, Shostakovich, Fischer-Dieskau, and the British musicians Kathleen Ferrier, Dennis Brain and Julian Bream, have taken part. Britten was highly honoured, received the

Companion of Honour (1953) and Order of Merit (1965), and was made a Life Peer in the last year of his life.

Like Elgar before him and more latterly Stravinsky, Britten had the good fortune to have a major record company (Decca) interested in recording his music under his own direction. Not only did this help to familiarise the musical public with his work almost as it appeared, but there now exist superbly performed and recorded documents of how Britten believed the music should sound. Luckily Britten was a competent conductor; in his younger years he was obliged to conduct the first performances of his own works, and from the time of *Albert Herring* until *Death in Venice*, when he was too ill, he led the premières of his works himself. His success as a conductor led to many more requests to conduct than he was ready to accept, as he refused to surrender more time than he had to from composition. He was an exacting musician and demanded the utmost in technique and concentration from the musicians he directed. He recorded all his major compositions for Decca, including all his published operas except *Gloriana* and *Death in Venice*, and in the records justice must be given to the immense contribution of Peter Pears. Britten also recorded some music other than his own: Bach's *St John Passion* and *Brandenburg Concertos*, Purcell's *The Fairy Queen*, *The Dream of Gerontius*, Schumann's *Scenes from Goethe's Faust*, and some symphonies and other pieces by Mozart and Schubert. He was also a fine pianist, and many consider him to have been one of the greatest accompanists of his time; his recordings of Schubert's song cycles *Die schöne Müllerin* and *Winterreise* with Pears are transfigured by the artistry and insight of both artists. Decca are now re-issuing in compact disc some of Britten's recordings, and *Peter Grimes*, the *Serenade for Tenor, Horn and Strings* (with Pears and Tuckwell), *Les Illuminations* and *Nocturne* (with Pears), have appeared. Presumably others will follow.

C

CANTELLI, Guido (1920–56). Born in Novara, Italy, Cantelli played as a boy in his father's military band, was organist at the local church at the age of 10, conducted the town's choral society and gave piano recitals at the age of 14. After studies at the Milan Conservatory, he returned to Novara in 1941 to become conductor and artistic director of the Teatro Coccia, which had been founded by Toscanini in 1899. In 1943 he was forced to join the Italian Army, but refused to support Fascism, and was sent to a Nazi labour camp in Stettin for two years; his health deteriorated but after transfer to Bolzano he escaped to Milan. He was caught by the Fascists, but was saved from a death sentence by the liberation of Italy. With the end of the war he resumed his musical career, conducted the La Scala Orchestra in a programme that included Tchaikovsky's Symphony No. 6, and appeared with orchestras in Italy, Belgium, Austria and Hungary. Toscanini heard him rehearsing the La Scala Orchestra in Milan in May 1948 and immediately invited him to be a guest conductor with the NBC Symphony Orchestra; Cantelli's first radio concert in New York was in January 1949 and he visited the United States each year to conduct the NBC Symphony, the New York Philharmonic, the Boston Symphony and other major orchestras. In 1950, together with de Sabata, he led the La Scala Orchestra at the Edinburgh Festival and in the following years conducted at the Lucerne, Salzburg and Venice Festivals. His life was tragically cut short by an air crash in Paris; he had just been appointed principal conductor at the La Scala Opera but had yet to conduct his first opera there.

From the first time he heard him conduct, Toscanini held the highest regard and affection for Cantelli, believing that he himself conducted the same way at Cantelli's age, and he attended many of Cantelli's rehearsals and concerts in New York. No doubt his musical influence on Cantelli was profound, but it would be wrong to conclude that Cantelli tried to copy Toscanini. He was in his own right an extraordinarily gifted musician, whatever his relationship with the older man. He differed from the elderly Toscanini in his musical interpretations, but Toscanini probably saw in him the lyricism and fluency of his early style. Cantelli possessed a remarkable memory and conducted without scores at both rehearsals and concerts. His passionate demands for perfection and his complete involvement in every note produced a high degree of tension at rehearsals and recording sessions, when he would repeat a passage almost endlessly to achieve what he wanted. Frequently he surprised himself at the very high standard of the performance that resulted, although on occasion he would be reduced to tears when he could not produce the desired effect. He was well characterised by C. J. Luten: 'The precision and refinement of the orchestral playing, and clearly fastidious care for attack, chording and sonority, these technical achievements were guided by exquisite musical taste. All expression occurred within the framework of the composer's instructions regarding tempo, dynamics, rhythm and phrasing and . . . Cantelli had the power to achieve rubato inside the bar, so that the barlines themselves were always equidistant.'

Cantelli recorded for RCA and EMI with the La Scala, NBC Symphony and Philharmonia Orchestras. When he visited Britain in 1950 with the La Scala Orchestra he recorded Tchaikovsky's Symphony No. 5 in London in just one day, and this disc became one of EMI's best-selling LPs. Among his other recordings were Beethoven's Symphony No. 7, Brahms' Symphonies Nos 1 and 3, Schubert's Symphony No. 8, Mendelssohn's Symphony No. 4, Schumann's Symphony No. 4, Tchaikovsky's Symphony No. 6 and *Romeo and Juliet* fantasie-overture, *La Mer*, *Daphnis et Chloé* Suite No. 2 and *Siegfried Idyll*. The advent of stereo spelt the virtual elimination of all his recordings, although some have been reissued for their historical interest. These are an invaluable document of a superb conductor, and, in the case of the Philharmonia Orchestra, of a great orchestra at the zenith of its prime.

CELIBIDACHE, Sergui (b. 1912). Born in Roman, Romania, Celibidache spent his early life in Jassy (modern Iasi), the capital of Moldavia, where his father was prefect. He studied in Paris and in wartime Berlin at the Hochschule für Musik and at the University, taking up philosophy to avoid military conscription, and wrote a thesis on the music of Josquin des Prés. He won a conducting competition with the Berlin Radio, and in 1945 became permanent conductor of the Berlin Philharmonic Orchestra, which at the end of the war had been led by Leo Borchard. He toured the United States with the orchestra, sharing the podium with Furtwängler; he left the orchestra in 1952, appeared as a guest conductor in Europe, Israel, Japan and Latin America, and has been permanent conductor of the

Stockholm Radio Symphony Orchestra, the French National Orchestra, the South-West German Radio Orchestra at Stuttgart, the Bamberg Symphony Orchestra and the Munich Philharmonic Orchestra. His compositions include four symphonies, a piano concerto and the orchestral suite *Der Taschengarten*, which he recorded for UNICEF with the Stuttgart Radio Symphony Orchestra.

Celibidache is a legend in his own time, as much for his elusiveness as for his commanding musicianship. In his years with the Berlin Philharmonic he immediately showed himself to be an indefatigable worker and painstakingly thorough, and the orchestra's repertoire soon came to include music by Berg, Hindemith, Honegger, Poulenc, Ravel, Stravinsky, Shostakovich, Britten, Copland, Barber, Piston and others, all of whom had not been played previously by them. What was, and is, remarkable about him is the extraordinary lengths to which he goes to prepare a performance. With the Berlin Philharmonic he expected ten or twelve rehearsals for each concert, and today he refuses engagements if he cannot be guaranteed five or six rehearsals. He has said that the number of rehearsals he requires for a concert depends on the quality of the orchestra and that the better the orchestra the more he rehearses it, because the possibilities are greater. He rehearses the orchestra almost to the point of exhaustion, allows absolutely nothing to pass and expects the maximum concentration and effort from the players. He appeals to the musicians' intelligence and musical sensitivity before seeking technical perfection in the performance. He prefers to work with radio orchestras, where the time for rehearsals is more generous, but nonetheless dislikes radio concerts as such. He sets a limit to the concerts he will conduct, demands very high fees, and avoids confronting new orchestras too often, as well as touring with his own orchestra. His memory is phenomenal and he rehearses without a score without making a mistake, although he says that his memory is purely functional and he has no memory for numbers in the score. His sound is unique and is partly achieved by having the bass instruments play extremely quietly. Of other conductors he admires Ferrara, Weingartner and Furtwängler, but dismisses Toscanini with: 'If music were just notes he would have been superb.' 'There is no miracle in music,' he has remarked, 'only work. Music is neither beautiful nor ugly; it either exists or it does not exist. To realise its existence in sound one has to work over it for a long period with profound concentration. I would prefer to do nothing than be content with an approximation or with mediocrity.' The final result of his approach to performance and interpretation is an amazing degree of finesse and accuracy in scores by composers such as Ravel, but in, say, a Brahms symphony his passion for the highest degree of execution counts against the lyrical spontaneity that is required to make the music convincing. Many orchestral players regard him as a genius, some as a misguided talent.

Although Celibidache recorded symphonies by Mozart, Mendelssohn, Tchaikovsky, Shostakovich and Prokofiev, and concertos by Mendelssohn and Brahms early in his career, recording is now anathema to him, and the entire concept is unacceptable: 'Like peas, music cannot be canned. It loses its flavour, its scent, its life. The tape which makes the recordings possible consists of lots of little bits stuck together from different versions. This means the end of the continuous and basic pulse necessary to bring the work to life in sound. Also the acoustic conditions of a recording are never the same as those of a live performance, and so a recording is a treason to music because the listener never hears what the artist wants him to hear.' On another occasion he compared a record to going to bed with a picture of Brigitte Bardot. However there are records available on various labels of his performances, apparently taken from radio transmissions, and if one is to take him at his word, these may interest the curious but cannot give a satisfactory impression of him as an interpretative artist. It is the concert hall or nothing.

CHAILLY, Riccardo (b. 1953). The son of the composer Luciano Chailly, Riccardo Chailly was trained at the Giuseppe Verdi Conservatory in Milan, and studied conducting with Guarino at the Perugia Conservatory and then with Caracciola and Ferrara. He made his début in the United States at the Chicago Lyric Opera in 1974, founded with Hans Werner Henze the Cantiere Internazionale d'Arte in Montepulciano in 1976, made his début at La Scala, Milan, in 1978, first conducted at Covent Garden in 1980, and at the Vienna State Opera and the New York Metropolitan Opera in 1982. He was appointed principal conductor of the Berlin Radio Symphony Orchestra in 1982, was principal guest conductor of the London Philharmonic Orchestra (1982–5), and in 1988 will become principal conductor of the Amsterdam Concertgebouw Orchestra. He has conducted many of the major orchestras in the USA, led the Berlin Radio Symphony Orchestra on its tour of the USA in the 1984–5 season, and has also toured with the Royal Philharmonic Orchestra in Japan.

One of the new generation of Italian conductors, Chailly's career has quickly taken him to several of the major positions in the field in Europe; he has established himself as a dynamic and effective artist with a wide range of sympathies, in addition to the conventional repertoire. His performances in the symphonic literature, as exemplified by his recordings of Tchaikovsky's Symphony No. 5 and Bruckner's Symphonies Nos 3 and 7, could be described as idiosyncratic, but some writers have been critical of oversights in many aspects of the interpretations. He has also recorded the operas *Andrea Chénier* and *The Rake's Progress*, as well as *Carmina Burana* and *Alexander Nevsky*.

CONLON, James (b. 1950). Born in New York, Conlon learned the piano and violin as a boy, studied conducting with Morel at the Juilliard School, and was assistant conductor when the Juilliard Orchestra visited Spoleto in Italy. While still a student he substituted for Schippers at a performance of *La Bohème*; when he made his début with the New York Philharmonic Orchestra he was the youngest conductor ever to conduct in a subscription series with the orchestra. His first appearance at the New York Metropolitan Opera was in 1976, and at the Royal Opera, Covent Garden, in 1979; he has conducted the major orchestras in the United States, Britain and Europe, and in 1983 was appointed musical director of the Rotterdam Philharmonic Orchestra. He has an exclusive recording contract with Erato, and records with the Rotterdam Philharmonic, the London Philharmonic and the Scottish Chamber Orchestras; his records display his self-assurance and high degree of musicianship, and include Liszt's *Dante Symphony*, Janáček's *Idyll* and *Lachian Dances*, Dvořák's Symphony No. 9 and a number of the late Mozart symphonies, the latter with the Scottish Chamber Orchestra.

CORBOZ, Michel (b. 1934). Born in Fribourg, Corboz was a member of the local church choir, and first heard Monteverdi through Nadia Boulanger's 78 r.p.m. records. He studied at the Fribourg Conservatory and in 1953 became the choirmaster at Notre-Dame in Lausanne, where he also led the French choral group A Coeur Joie. He teaches at the Conservatoire at La Chaux-de-Fonds, and in 1968 founded and conducted the Lausanne Vocal Ensemble, which is made up of fifteen professional singers, and which soon became famous for the standard of its performances. Other choral groups he conducts are the choir at Lausanne University and the Gulbenkian Foundation Choir at Lisbon. His recordings for Erato of music of Monteverdi (*Vespro della beata Vergine*, *La favola d'Orfeo* and *Selva morale e spirituale et al.*), Bach (*Mass in B Minor*, the *St Matthew Passion* and the *St John Passion*) and the sacred music of Vivaldi, demonstrate Corboz's profound understanding of these composers' music, as well as the high standard of the Lausanne Vocal Ensemble.

D

DAVIS, Andrew (b. 1944). Born in Ashridge, Hertfordshire, Davis
received his early musical education at the Royal Academy of
Music, London, studied the organ with Hurford and Kee, was an
organ scholar at King's College, Cambridge (1963–7) where
he was Willcock's assistant conductor with the Cambridge
University Musical Society, and studied with Ferrara at the
Accademia di Santa Cecilia in Rome (1968). Returning to
England he played the harpsichord and organ as a continuo
instrument, and in this role took part in Marriner's recording of
Die Kunst der Fuge with the Academy of St Martin-in-the-
Fields. He was chosen by Groves with three others to take part
in the Royal Liverpool Philharmonic Orchestra Society seminar
for young British conductors (1969), which led to his being
appointed the orchestra's principal guest conductor. He was
associate conductor of the BBC Scottish Orchestra (1970–1),
and came into prominence dramatically in London in 1970 when
he first substituted for Inbal and later for Rozhdestvensky in
concerts with the BBC Symphony Orchestra. He made his début
at Glyndebourne with Richard Strauss's *Capriccio*, toured the
Far East with the English Chamber Orchestra, visited Israel to
conduct the Israel Philharmonic Orchestra (1973), became a
regular conductor at the Proms concerts in London, made his
North American début with the Detroit Symphony Orchestra
(1974) and then conducted concerts with the New York Philharmonic, Los Angeles Philharmonic and Boston Symphony
Orchestras, and became associate conductor of the New
Philharmonia Orchestra (1973–6), touring Europe with the
orchestra three times. After conducting the Toronto Symphony
Orchestra in a concert which included Janáček's *Glagolitic Mass*
and Strauss's *Don Quixote*, he was appointed the orchestra's
music director (1975), leading them on a tour to China (1978).
His years with the Toronto Symphony have been remarkably
successful; he has widened the repertoire considerably, brought
the orchestra to a high level of competence and artistry, and in
1982 led the orchestra in the inauguration of the new Roy
Thomson Hall in Toronto. He has continued to conduct at
Glyndebourne, has appeared at the New York Metropolitan
and Covent Garden Opera houses, and is a regular guest
conductor with major US orchestras.

In a short time Davis has come to the fore as a major British conducting talent, and he has won the widest respect for his keen rhythmic sense, his understanding of style, the clean execution he achieves and the strong dramatic tension of his interpretations. His musical sympathies are wide, and his repertoire ranges from Bach to Shostakovich; he professes a special preference for Elgar, Schumann, Berg, Stravinsky, Mahler and Beethoven. In 1979 he led the Philharmonia Orchestra in a four-concert series of the orchestral music of Elgar, and he includes in his concert programmes in Britain and abroad music by British composers such as Elgar, Vaughan Williams and Tippett. His early youthful appearance has matured somewhat in recent years, and he retains a thoroughly British manner and personality. Before the orchestra he is self-confident, and commands the respect of the players because of his knowledge of the score and his courtesy to them. His baton technique is exemplary, and in rehearsal he talks little but sings frequently. He has an accurate ear, and prefers to play long stretches before returning for corrections, although sometimes he works on a passage phrase by phrase to achieve his aim. Barbirolli is the conductor for whom he has the greatest affection: 'He had a very distinct personality of his own. The kind of sound that Barbirolli went for is very much on my list of aims. He was fond of the string sound, always. Terrific warmth and richness and love.' He sees the kinship between Barbirolli and Furtwängler, but his preference in Beethoven is still Klemperer.

Davis has recorded with the Toronto Symphony Orchestra, with whom he has been contracted for four recordings a year for CBS. In this series there have been Sibelius's Symphony No. 2, Borodin's three symphonies, and pieces by Janáček. He has also recorded with the London orchestras; characteristic of his work have been Shostakovich's Symphony No. 10 (with the London Philharmonic Orchestra for Classics for Pleasure), Franck's *Symphony in D Minor* and Duruflé's *Requiem* (with the New Philharmonia Orchestra *et al.* for CBS) and Strauss's *Four Last Songs* (with Te Kanawa and the London Symphony Orchestra for CBS).

DAVIS, **Sir Colin** (b. 1927). Born in Weybridge, Surrey, Davis studied the clarinet, first at Christ's Hospital and then at the Royal College of Music with Thurston, and was for two years a musician in the Household Cavalry. Self-taught as a conductor, he gained his initial experience with the Kalmar orchestra (1949) and with the Chelsea Opera Group (1950), where his first appearance as a conductor was with *Don Giovanni*. In 1952 he was one of the conductors of the Festival Ballet at the Royal Festival Hall, London, and in 1957 was appointed assistant conductor of the BBC Scottish Orchestra. In 1958 he made a brilliant début at Sadler's Wells Opera with *Die Entführung aus dem Serail*, attracting attention as a fine conductor of Mozart, which was confirmed the next year when he substituted for Klemperer in concert performances in London of *Don Giovanni* with the Philharmonia Orchestra and a cast that included Sutherland and Schwarzkopf. He made his first appearances in the USA and Canada in 1959, and in the following year conducted at Glyndebourne where he substituted for Beecham in *Die Zauberflöte*, and also conducted ballet at Covent Garden. In 1962–3 he toured Japan with the London Symphony Orchestra, whom he also conducted on a world-wide tour in 1964. He was musical director at Sadler's Wells (1965–70) and of the English Chamber Orchestra, conducted first at Covent Garden in opera with *Le nozze di Figaro*, was chief conductor of the BBC Symphony Orchestra (1967–71), and was then appointed chief conductor and artistic adviser at Covent Garden (1971–86). At the same time he remained with the BBC Symphony Orchestra as joint-principal guest conductor and was appointed guest conductor of the London Symphony, the Boston Symphony and the Amsterdam Concertgebouw Orchestras. He had previously declined the appointment of musical director of the Boston Symphony. In 1983 he became chief conductor of the Bavarian Radio Symphony Orchestra. He also appears as guest conductor with the New York Philharmonic Orchestra and the New York Metropolitan Opera, and conducted *Tannhäuser* at the Bayreuth Festivals in 1977 and 1978, being the first British conductor to appear at the festivals. In 1979 he took the Royal Opera (Covent Garden) on tour to Japan and South Korea, and in 1980 he received a knighthood.

Davis is probably the major British conductor to emerge since Beecham, and the musicians who perform with him are frequently impressed with his great love of music and his sense of conviction in the works he conducts. Like Beecham, a good part of his reputation is as an interpreter of Mozart and Berlioz, and he is often claimed to be the finest living exponent of Berlioz. A modest and unassuming personality, although perfectly sure of himself, his relations with orchestral players are unlike the autocratic manner of many of his Continental colleagues. British orchestras react rather uncertainly to him, and his first years at Covent Garden were somewhat difficult, but his touch with

American orchestras is more sure. His skill in responding to the latter's susceptibilities has been expressed in the words of a musician of the Boston Symphony: 'He has a way of telling us what we need to know without insulting our intelligence.' His rehearsal methods are unauthoritarian; the work is run through first and then detailed attention is given to unsatisfactory passages. It has been suggested that he is apt to give too much attention to detail to the detriment of the music's broad line, but for composers with whom he is most sympathetic this is scarcely evident. He once expressed his attitude to conducting as 'taking care of something that has a life of its own. It's like holding the bird of life in your hand. Hold it too tight and it dies. Hold it too lightly and it flies away.'

Beyond Mozart and Berlioz, he has a name as an interpreter of Handel, Stravinsky and Tippett, and also has been acclaimed in composers such as Berg, Britten, Sibelius and Debussy. At Covent Garden his repertoire has expanded to include Wagner, and his leadership of *The Ring* (1974–6) was praised for its penetration and persuasiveness, and is quite distinctly his own. At the New York Met. he has led brilliant performances of *Wozzeck*, *Peter Grimes* and *Pelléas et Mélisande*, although in the last-named his interpretation was a little too far from the traditional for many tastes. His *Idomeneo* at Covent Garden impressed, and this opera he regards as Mozart's greatest: 'In no other opera, I think, does he so closely identify with his characters. . . . Mozart was an even greater master of this kind of *opera seria* than he was of *drama giocosa* or *opera buffa*. I don't believe that Mozart ever equalled the passion that he poured into music that expresses all the predicaments, nor did he ever again use the chorus as one of the principal characters.'

Davis eschews the literalness, intensity and fast tempi of Toscanini, feeling that his style is 'unspacious'. He does not acknowledge the particular influence of any other great conductor, and in this sense he is an original. The idea of complete faithfulness to the score he scorns: 'The score is like a two-dimensional map of Everest, not like Everest itself. We must make the score into a real experience. Music is the events that take place between key relationships, the weight, size and feel of a chord as compared with what has gone on before.' Naturally this view is antipathetic to much modern music, in which Davis cannot find any emotional meaning, although his admiration extends to Taverner, Birtwistle, Maxwell Davies and Henze, but certainly not to Stockhausen. Until the recent past the late romantics, with the notable exception of Elgar, have not had immediate attraction to him. Yet he did not hesitate to conduct Wagner at Covent Garden, and lately has expressed interest in Bruckner and Mahler. Sibelius too has become associated with him, particularly after his spectacular recordings of the symphonies with the Boston Symphony Orchestra.

As in the opera house, Davis first made his mark as a recording artist as an interpreter of Mozart, and his very first records were of the Symphonies Nos 29, 34 and 39 and the Oboe Concerto with the Sinfonia of London, and with Leon Goossens, for World Record Club in 1958. The next year he started recording for EMI, and later for L'Oiseau Lyre and Philips. In addition to Mozart symphonies and concertos he has recorded the major Mozart operas, of which *Le nozze di Figaro* (with the BBC Symphony Orchestra *et al.* in 1971) approached the standards of the great set of Erich Kleiber of 1959 in its authority and sensitivity. His Berlioz recordings include *Les Troyens*, which is an immense achievement, and the Davis/Berlioz/Philips enterprise is one of the complete and unblemished successes in the recent history of the gramophone. Tippett and Stravinsky have also had special significance among his recordings, which have included the two Tippett operas *The Midsummer Marriage* and *The Knot Garden*. In the mainstream repertoire he has recorded (*inter alia*) all the Beethoven symphonies but two, and the piano concertos (with Bishop-Kovacevich); more recently his recordings with the Concertgebouw Orchestra of the ballet suites of Stravinsky and symphonies of Haydn and Dvořák are eloquent examples of his musicianship, having a convincing precision and urgency. All of his recordings have not attracted universal admiration; in the Beethoven and Sibelius symphonies unusual tempi have occasionally drawn the critics' fire, and a certain straightforwardness has given some readings a perfunctory air. Davis's performances are quite distinct from Karajan's grand smooth line, Bernstein's dramatic intensity and Maazel's preoccupation with expressive detail. Now in his early sixties, he is still, by conductors' standards, a relatively young man and will no doubt go on to contribute much more to the catalogue of recorded music. After the acclaim that greeted his recording of *Tosca*, his Wagner productions at Bayreuth and Covent Garden, and his expressed interest in Mahler and Bruckner, it will be very interesting to see what insights he will bring to future endeavours in the studios.

DAVISON, Arthur (b. 1923). Born in Montreal, Davison is the grandson of one of Canada's most distinguished playwrights. He began playing the violin at the age of three and when he was twelve he was giving regular broadcast recitals. After studies at the Conservatoire de Musique at Montreal, with the conductor Wilfred Pelletier, and at McGill University, he came to England in 1948 with a scholarship to the Royal Academy of Music, studied there with Sammons and Beard, and played in the Philharmonia Orchestra. In 1956 he founded the London Little Symphony Orchestra and became artistic director of the Virtuosi of England, a group of superb instrumentalists. His other activities have included conducting the Royal Amateur Orchestral Society, the Croydon Symphony Orchestra and the National Youth Orchestra of Wales. During frequent tours of Canada and the United States he has conducted the New York City Ballet and for CBS Radio and Television, and has been active with the Danish Royal Orchestra and the Royal Danish Ballet. In 1974 he was awarded the CBE. Under contract to Classics for Pleasure in Britain, he has enjoyed an immense success as a recording artist; in 1974 he received an award to mark the sale of 500,000 records, and in 1977 EMI/CFP presented him with a Gold Disc for the sale of over a million records and cassettes conducted by him. His records for CFP include excerpts from *Messiah*, the *Brandenburg Concertos*, *Water Music* and *Music for the Royal Fireworks*, *The Four Seasons*, and the violin concertos of Bach (with Bean and Sillito), with the Virtuosi of England.

DEL MAR, Norman (b. 1919). Born in Hampstead, Del Mar studied with Vaughan Williams and Lambert at the Royal College of Music, and during World War II served with the Royal Air Force as a horn player in its Central Band. After the war he founded and conducted the Chelsea Symphony Orchestra in a series of concerts noted for their adventurous programmes. In 1946 he joined the Royal Philharmonic Orchestra as a horn player and in the following year Beecham engaged him as musical assistant and associate conductor for the orchestra. He then conducted part of the Strauss Festival presented by Beecham at Drury Lane. Del Mar later said: 'I owe everything to Beecham.' In 1947 he also led the Croydon Symphony Orchestra, became assistant conductor at Sadler's Wells Opera (1948), principal conductor of The English Opera Group (1949), assisted Malko with the Yorkshire Symphony Orchestra (1954–6), was conductor of the BBC Scottish Symphony Orchestra (1960–5), the Göteborg Symphony Orchestra (1969–73) and the chamber orchestra of the Royal Academy of Music (1973–7), taught conducting at the Royal College of Music (1972), was principal guest conductor with the Bournemouth Sinfonietta (1982), principal conductor of the Academy of the BBC (1974–7), and artistic director of the Norfolk and Norwich Triennial Festival (1979 and 1982), and is now principal conductor of the Arhus Symphony Orchestra in Denmark. He developed a reputation as an interpreter of Mahler and Bruckner, 20th-century music, and in particular British composers. In recent years he has been a freelance conductor of opera and in the concert hall, and was awarded the CBE in 1975. He has written an important three-volume study of the life and music of Richard Strauss (1962 and 1968), as well as other books about conductors and the orchestra. Del Mar has many recordings to his credit, almost entirely of 20th-century British music, of Elgar, Vaughan Williams, Warlock, Britten, Bax, Delius, Goehr, Tippett, Hoddinott, Maw, Crosse, *et al*.

DOHNÁNYI, **Christoph von** (b. 1929). Grandson of the composer Ernst von Dohnányi, and on his mother's side related to the psychiatrist Karl Bonhoeffer and the Protestant theologian killed by the Nazis, Dietrich Bonhoeffer, Dohnányi was born in Berlin, first studied law at the University of Munich, and then attended the Hochschule für Musik in Munich, where he won the Richard Strauss Prize for composition and conducting in 1951. He then went to the United States, where he studied piano and composition under his grandfather at Florida State College, and was a fellow at Tanglewood under Bernstein. He was first a pianist, but in 1952 Solti brought him to the Frankfurt Opera as chorus coach and third conductor (1952–7). From there he moved on to conduct the opera companies at Lübeck (1957–63) and Kassel (1963–6), was chief conductor of the West German Radio Symphony Orchestra at Cologne (1964–9), chief conductor of the Frankfurt Opera (1968–77), and artistic director and principal conductor at the Hamburg State Opera (1977–82), and then was appointed conductor of the Cleveland Orchestra (1984). He has appeared in both opera houses and concert halls in London, Vienna, Milan, Rome and many other cities, and was chosen by Henze in 1956 to lead the first performances of his operas *Der junge Lord* in Berlin (1965) and *Die Bassariden* in Salzburg (1966). In 1967 he led *Tannhäuser* at Bayreuth and later made his début in the USA with *Der fliegende Holländer* in Chicago (1969), conducted *Falstaff* at the New York Metropolitan Opera (1972) and *Salome* at Covent Garden (1974). Dohnányi is a serious personality but shows wit and charm readily; although meticulous and demanding before the orchestra, he is not an autocratic conductor and believes that the intense work of the opera house is the best training for his profession. In Berlin as a child he had attended rehearsals and concerts of the Berlin Philharmonic Orchestra under Furtwängler, and at the Hochschule für Musik in Munich one of his teachers was Rosbaud. Other great conductors he has taken as models are Busch, Beecham, Walter and de Sabata, all of whom he greatly admires. His modesty is shown in his conviction that he should thoroughly understand and perform the symphonies of Haydn and Mozart before proceeding to those of Beethoven and Brahms, and in his disapproval of display. He does not wish to become known as a specialist in any composer or era and has a strong commitment towards performing modern operas; he holds that it is more difficult to conduct an opera of Mozart than one of Berg, since Berg's wishes are more evident. However he regrets that few contemporary composers have the inclination or the ability to write a continuous piece of an hour's length. When his appointment at Cleveland was announced there were some who believed that he was not of sufficient stature as a conductor to lead this great orchestra; however it appears that he has not only preserved the orchestra's marvellous balance and clarity, but has added a certain warmth and mellowness.

Dohnányi has many distinguished recordings to his credit. Among his earliest were Henze's *Der junge Lord* (from the Berlin première performance, for DGG); with the Vienna Philharmonic Orchestra for Decca he recorded *Wozzeck*, Mendelssohn's Symphonies Nos 1, 3 and 5, *L'Oiseau de feu*, Bartók's *The Miraculous Mandarin* and *Two Portraits*, five Lieder and *Ewartung* of Schoenberg, and a suite from Berg's *Lulu* and the finale from *Salome*. In *Wozzeck*, the Schoenberg disc and the *Lulu* and *Salome* coupling, his wife Anja Silja joined him. More recently he has recorded with the Cleveland Orchestra *et al.* Dvořák's Symphony No. 8 and *Scherzo Capriccioso*, Schubert's Symphony No. 9 (for Decca) and Beethoven's Symphony No. 9 (for Telarc).

DORATI, Antal (b. 1906). Born in Budapest where his father was a violinist at the Budapest Opera and the Budapest Philharmonic Orchestra and his mother a music teacher, Dorati studied at the Franz Liszt Academy under Weiner, Bartók and Kodály, who were frequent visitors to the Dorati household. At 18 he was then the youngest person to graduate from the Academy. Immediately afterwards, in 1924, he joined the Budapest Opera as a répétiteur and made his professional début there as a conductor, and at the same time studied philosophy at the University of Vienna. In 1928 Fritz Busch engaged him as his assistant at the Dresden Opera, but in the next year he became musical director and principal conductor at the Münster Opera (1930–32). In his years at Münster he also appeared with other orchestras and opera houses in Germany, Hungary and Czechoslovakia; he moved to Paris in 1932, conducted orchestras in Great Britain and France, and after an engagement with the French National Radio he was appointed principal conductor of the Ballet Russe de Monte Carlo (1933–40), with which he toured Europe, the United States and Australia. He first conducted in the USA in 1937, appearing with the National Symphony Orchestra in Washington DC; in 1941 he took up residence in the USA and eventually became a US citizen in 1947. His first appointment was as musical director of the American Ballet Theatre (1941–45), and he was also director of the New Opera Company in New York (1941–42). When the Dallas Symphony Orchestra was reorganised in 1945 Dorati was engaged as its musical director; with Menuhin and the orchestra he was the first to record Bartók's Violin Concerto (now known as the No. 2). In 1949 he moved to Minnesota to succeed Mitropoulos as conductor of the Minneapolis Symphony Orchestra (the predecessor of today's Minnesota Orchestra), and was named its director in 1954. He left Minneapolis in 1960, believing he had achieved as much as he could with the budget allowed for the orchestra; in fact, he said much later that the problem with other American orchestras he conducted was one of finance: 'People didn't take my suggestions; it was not understood what was needed.' Returning to Europe he received a Ford Foundation grant to enable him to study Italian baroque and pre-baroque music, and conducted both concerts and opera in London, Vienna, Rome, Hamburg and other centres. His association with the London Symphony Orchestra at this time, in recording a wide repertoire for Mercury, was crucial in the orchestra's development to its later superb standards.

In 1963 Dorati was appointed chief conductor of the BBC Symphony Orchestra; when his term was completed in 1966 he toured with the Israel Philharmonic Orchestra, was principal conductor of the Stockholm Philharmonic Orchestra (1967–74), musical director of the National Symphony Orchestra at Washington DC (1970–75), senior conductor of the Royal Philharmonic Orchestra (1975–79) and musical director of the Detroit Symphony Orchestra (1979–84). He toured the USA with the Stockholm Philharmonic in 1968 and 1970, appeared as a guest conductor with almost all the major symphony orchestras and opera houses in the world, and was instrumental in maintaining the Philharmonia Hungarica, first in Vienna and later in FR Germany, and is honorary president of the orchestra, which is made up of musicians who left Hungary in 1956.

With the Philharmonia Hungarica he recorded all of Haydn's symphonies for Decca, one of the largest enterprises in the history of recording, along with the similar series by Ernst Märzendorfer, with the Vienna Chamber Orchestra for Musical Heritage Society, USA. He has finally made his home in Switzerland, and now regularly returns to Budapest, coming back, he reflects, to his roots.

Dorati has been a composer since the age of 12, but after a very prolific youth his compositional activities suffered a lapse of 20 years. Since then he has composed at least one major work a year; in his own words: 'If my creative work is not in conformity with today's trends, it is so according to the natural way of my own musical and personal development, and above all, to my artistic conscience.' His compositions include a symphony, piano and cello concertos, three serenades for orchestra, a *Missa Brevis* for mixed choir and percussion, a ballet *Magdelena*, a cantata *The Way of the Cross* and some chamber music. He has recorded the piano concerto with his wife, Ilse von Alpenheim, and the National Symphony Orchestra, for Turnabout, together with his *Variations on a Theme by Béla Bartók*, for solo piano. Of his ballet arrangements there is the familiar *Graduation Ball*, from the music of Johann Strauss.

Because he could claim to be the leading ballet conductor of his generation, Dorati has tended to be typed, unfairly, as a ballet conductor, despite his wide experience in conducting the symphonic and operatic repertoire. But his years as a ballet conductor taught him that conductors cannot remain long doing this, since, in his view, the dancer's discipline is fundamentally non-musical, as opposed to that of a singer. He has a formidable reputation as an effective trainer of orchestras and can point to the Dallas Symphony, the London Symphony, the BBC Symphony, the National Symphony and the Detroit Symphony Orchestras, where his work was eminently successful. Orchestral players once found him somewhat irascible, but now he claims to be more easy-going. Even the most difficult scores he conducts from memory. He enjoys making records, and believes that the value of recordings is that they set down the way in which music has been performed in each epoch. The danger of the record, he has said, is that 'it catches a moment's expression and eternalises it in a way which shouldn't be. No two perform-ances are alike, and what is interesting in music is that it is performed in several ways, and to know only one interpretation is not to know the music itself.'

Dorati made his first recordings in the mid-thirties, of ballet music he was then conducting in performance with the London Philharmonic Orchestra in London. Mercury Records later contracted him to make 100 recordings with the Minneapolis Symphony Orchestra and a further 50 with the London Sym-phony Orchestra. In 1971–74 he made 48 discs for Decca in the series of all 104 Haydn symphonies (hailed as 'one of the finest monuments in the history of the gramophone'), and the Haydn operas. And he has made numerous other discs for other companies, including the nine Beethoven symphonies with the Royal Philharmonic Orchestra for DGG. He counts as one of the most prolific conductors on record, his total output of records exceeding 500. Despite the excellence of many of these recorded performances he has never really stood among the greatest interpreters of the central repertoire of the German and Austrian classics. His style is too intense, clipped and hard-driven to result in performances that are stamped with the apparent intellectual profundity of the German school of con-ductors. Dorati is at the opposite pole to, say, Klemperer and Böhm, but his orchestral texture is characteristically lighter than that of Szell or Toscanini. It is not unreasonable to make these comparisons; Dorati is capable of thrilling readings both on record and in the concert hall, as his Beethoven and Brahms symphonies are dramatic and exciting. He defends himself, saying that he sees no necessity to establish a standard inter-pretation of a work: 'To me, a criterion of a great piece is its endurance to be played in many different ways. If it can be played in only one way, it's not a great work.'

Dorati detests flamboyance in a conductor. 'The flamboyance should be spiritual and not visible. What we do should only be recognised by the orchestra, not by the audience. We don't conduct the audience. Unfortunately today there are too many conductors who mime. These mime what is being heard, where-as the conductor conducts what is not being heard but will be in the flash of a second. The mime is with the beat, but that is already too late for the players!' He has remarked, too, perhaps too modestly, that he makes 'not bad music with a strong conviction and 100 per cent honesty'.

DOWNES, Edward (b. 1924). Downes graduated from the University in his native Birmingham (1944), then studied at the Royal College of Music (1944–6) and became a lecturer at Aberdeen University. In 1948 he was awarded a Carnegie Scholarship enabling him to study conducting for two years with Hermann Scherchen, after which he was engaged as a conductor with the Carl Rosa Opera Company (1950–1), and in 1952 he became a staff conductor at the Royal Opera House, Covent Garden. Until he left in 1969 he had conducted almost every opera in the repertoire, including a complete *Ring*; in 1963 he led the Western première of Shostakovich's *Katerina Ismailova* at Covent Garden. Afterwards he has devoted himself more to symphonic music, although he was musical director of the Australian Opera for five years (1972–6), leading the first performance of an opera (Prokofiev's *War and Peace*) at the Sydney Opera House after its opening in 1973. In 1980 he became chief conductor of the Netherlands Radio Orchestra at Hilversum, where he also taught at conductors' courses; he is principal conductor of the BBC Philharmonic Orchestra, and ran a course in conducting at the European Music Year Conductors' Seminar at the Royal Northern College of Music at Manchester in 1985. 'Any idiot can learn the actual beating,' he said, discussing the teaching of conducting. 'It's the musicality that counts.' He has never forgotten a piece of advice given to him by Scherchen: 'If you can hear the music in your head sufficiently clearly you can turn your back on the orchestra and waggle your bottom and they will play for you.' Among his records are Bax's Symphony No. 3 and Maxwell Davies's Symphony No. 3.

DUTOIT, Charles (b. 1936). Born in Lausanne, Dutoit studied the violin, viola, piano, percussion, composition and conducting at Lausanne Conservatory, Geneva Music Academy and then in Italy and in the USA. He was a member of the Lausanne Chamber Orchestra, and made his début as a conductor in 1959, played as an orchestral viola player and as a member of a string quartet, and in 1964 conducted the Berne Symphony Orchestra in *Le Sacre du printemps*, which led to his appointment as permanent conductor of the orchestra (1967–77) and to von Karajan inviting him to conduct at the Vienna Festival the following year. He conducted the Zürich Radio Symphony Orchestra (1964–7), the Zürich Tonhalle Orchestra (1966–71), has been music director of the National Orchestra of Mexico for two years, principal conductor of the Göteborg Symphony Orchestra in Sweden (since 1975), music director of the

Montreal Symphony Orchestra (since 1977), and principal guest conductor of the Minnesota Orchestra (1983). He regularly conducts the major European orchestras, as well as the Boston Symphony, Pittsburgh Symphony, Philadelphia, Cleveland and New York Philharmonic Orchestras, has toured South America, South Africa and Japan, and in the Far East with the Royal Philharmonic Orchestra. He made his début in London in 1966 and in the USA in Los Angeles, and with the Montreal Symphony Orchestra has toured Canada, the USA and Europe. In the 1982–3 season he made his Covent Garden début with *Faust*, and in 1982 he was made Artist of the Year in recognition of his services to music in Canada.

Dutoit's repertoire extends from Monteverdi to Messiaen, and includes opera, ballet, chamber music, oratorio and symphonic music. He has specialised in the music of Stravinsky and his first recording for Erato, *L'Histoire du soldat*, received a Grand Prix du Disque of the Académie Charles Cros. He has also recorded *Petrushka*, *Pulcinella*, *Apollon musagète*, *Les Noces*, *Renard*, and *Rag Time* (with various orchestras for Erato), and his other discs include Honegger's *Le Roi David* and Chabrier's *Le Roi malgré lui* (also for Erato), and a series with the Montreal Symphony Orchestra for Decca which established both him and the orchestra as artists of international stature. The works recorded included Falla's *El amor brujo* and *Three-Cornered Hat*; *Daphnis et Chloé*, *Scheherazade*, *Le Sacre du printemps*; Ravel's *Alborada del gracioso*, *Rapsodie espagnole* and *La Valse*; Respighi's *Feste romane*, *Pini di Roma* and *Fontane di Roma* and Saint-Saëns's Symphony No. 3.

E

ELDER, Mark (b. 1947). Born in Hexham, Northumberland, Elder was educated at Cambridge University (1966–9), and was first a répétiteur, chorus master and assistant conductor at Glyndebourne (1970–2). He made his début as a conductor with the Royal Liverpool Philharmonic Orchestra (1971), conducted opera in Australia (1972–3), joined the English National Opera (1974) and in 1979 was appointed its musical director. In the meantime he conducted for the first time at the Royal Opera, Covent Garden, in *Rigoletto*, in 1976. He became principal guest conductor of the London Mozart Players (1980), and in 1981 conducted at the Bayreuth Festival. Elder has been a strikingly successful conductor of opera at the ENO, particularly with the operas of Verdi. His one record has been of John Buller's *The Theatre of Memory* and *Proença*, with the BBC Symphony Orchestra *et al*.

ERMLER, Mark (b. 1932). The son of an eminent Soviet film director, Ermler was born in Leningrad and was educated at the Leningrad Conservatory where he studied conducting under Khaikin and Rabinovitch. He graduated in 1956, and straightaway joined the conducting staff of the Bolshoi Theatre in Moscow. His first production on his own was the première of Prokofiev's *The Story of a Real Man*; his repertoire of more than 50 operas includes works by Mozart, Beethoven, Berlioz, Verdi, Bizet and Puccini, in addition to Mussorgsky, Glinka, Borodin, Rimsky-Korsakov, Tchaikovsky and Prokofiev. He also directs ballet and symphony concerts, has conducted orchestras in the USSR and abroad, and has toured in Europe, North America and Japan. Reputed to have an extraordinary memory, he has an immaculate technique, and his records are examples of the fine sense of style and subtlety of his conducting. They include *Tosca*, *Madama Butterfly*, *Prince Igor*, Tchaikovsky's *Yolanta*, *Eugene Onegin* and *The Queen of Spades*, Glinka's *A Life for the Tsar*, Rachmaninov's *Francesca da Rimini* and Prokofiev's *The Story of a Real Man*.

F

FEDOSEYEV, Vladimir (b. 1932). Born in Leningrad, Fedoseyev studied at the Mussorgsky Music School there, at the Moscow Music Institute and at the Moscow Conservatory, where Ginzburg was his teacher for conducting. He was appointed conductor and artistic director of the USSR Radio-Television Orchestra of Russian Folk Instruments (1959–74), and also conducted concerts and opera in Moscow and Leningrad. He became principal conductor and artistic director of the USSR Radio-Television Symphony Orchestra in 1975, and has toured as a guest conductor in Eastern and Western Europe, the USA and Japan. His recordings include the operas *Tcherevichky* of Tchaikovsky, *May Night* and *The Snow Maiden* of Rimsky-Korsakov, and the eight symphonies of Glazunov. His disc of Rachmaninov's *Symphonic Dances*, which was issued in 1982, was the first digital record released in the USSR.

FERENCSIK, János (1907–84). Ferencsik was educated at the conservatory in his native Budapest, was engaged as coach at the Budapest State Opera in 1927, and became a conductor there in 1930. He was a musical assistant at the Bayreuth Festivals (1930–1) and conducted at the Vienna State Opera (1948–50 and 1964). From 1952 until his death he was musical director of the Hungarian State Symphony Orchestra, and with this ensemble toured the United States (1972) and Japan and Australia (1974); he first conducted in Britain, with the London Philharmonic Orchestra, in 1957, and in 1963 visited the Edinburgh Festival with the Hungarian State Opera and Ballet. From 1957 to 1974 he was musical director and chief conductor of the Budapest State Opera, and from 1966 to 1968 musical director of the Danish Radio Symphony Orchestra. He has also conducted major orchestras and in opera houses in many European countries, the USA, USSR and South America, and has appeared at the Vienna, Salzburg and Munich Festivals. One of the most distinguished of Hungarian musicians, his honours include the Kossuth Prize (1951 and 1961), the highest state decoration in Hungary. He has recorded much Hungarian music, particularly that of Liszt, Bartók and Kodály, one of his last recordings being an outstanding performance of Bartók's *Bluebeard's Castle*. He also recorded, *inter alia*, the nine symphonies of Beethoven, where his sober musicianship is always evident.

FISCHER, Iván (b. 1951). Born in Budapest, Fischer studied at the Béla Bartók Conservatory in Budapest (1965–70), then was a conducting student with Swarowsky in Vienna (1974). He conducted in Milan, Florence, Vienna and Budapest (1975–6), won a competition for conductors sponsored by the BBC (1976), which led to many engagements in Britain, and then became co-principal conductor of the Northern Sinfonia Orchestra in Newcastle (1979–82). He has conducted opera in Budapest, Zürich, Amsterdam, Frankfurt-am-Main, Vienna *et al.*, toured the Far East with the London Symphony Orchestra (1983), and was appointed musical director of the Kent Opera (1983). A remarkable talent, Fischer has made some fine records, including Mozart's Symphony No. 40 and Schubert's Symphony No. 9 (with the Budapest Festival Orchestra), Mendelssohn's Symphonies Nos 3, 4 and 5 and Mahler's Symphony No. 1 (with the Hungarian State Symphony Orchestra), Brahms' Violin Concerto (with Belkin and the London Symphony Orchestra) and Donizetti's *Don Pasquale* and Paisiello's *Il barbiere di Siviglia*.

Iván Fischer should not be confused with his brother, Ádám, born two years earlier, who also studied at the Béla Bartók Conservatory and with Swarowsky. Ádám was a prize winner at the Guido Cantelli Conductors' Competition in Milan (1973), was principal conductor at the Helsinki National Opera (1974–7) and assistant conductor of the Helsinki Philharmonic Orchestra (from 1975) and first conductor at the Karlsruhe Opera (1977–8), made his début at the Salzburg Festival in 1980, and has also conducted at the Bavarian State Opera, the Hamburg State Opera and the Vienna State Opera. His records include some Haydn symphonies, Schubert's *Rosamunde* music, some Rossini overtures and Goldmark's opera *The Queen of Sheba*.

FRICSAY, Ferenc (1914–63). Born in Budapest, Fricsay studied at the Budapest Academy of Music under Kodály and Bartók, and conducted his first concert, with the Hungarian Radio Orchestra, at the age of 15. His father had been a conductor before him, and he was able to play every instrument in the orchestra except the harp. In 1935 he was appointed conductor of the orchestra at Szeged, where he remained during World War II. In 1945 he conducted the first symphony concert in liberated Budapest, and also appeared for the first time at the Budapest Opera. He became general music director of the Berlin State Opera (1949) and chief conductor of the Radio-in-American-Sector (RIAS) Orchestra in Berlin, which was the first of the six radio orchestras to be established in FR Germany and West Berlin after World War II, and was unique in that it was made up entirely of new players, many of whom had migrated from DR Germany. Fricsay remained with the orchestra until 1954, and a year later it changed its status and name to Berlin Radio Symphony Orchestra. He was also music director of the Bavarian State Opera in Munich (1949–52) but resigned following disagreements with the management. Previously, in 1947, he had achieved a measure of international fame when he took over from Klemperer the preparation and direction of von Einem's opera *Dantons Tod* at the Salzburg Festival. He also conducted in Vienna, London, Holland, Israel and South America, and made his début in the USA with the Boston Symphony Orchestra in 1953. After leaving Berlin in 1954, he was engaged as conductor of the Houston Symphony Orchestra in Texas, in succession to Efrem Kurtz, but a dispute with the orchestra's management caused him to resign after conducting only a few concerts. He returned to the Bavarian State Opera for three years (1956–8), then to Berlin (1959) to conduct the Berlin Radio Symphony Orchestra, and became musical adviser to the new Deutsche Oper in West Berlin. He died in Basel at the age of 48.

Undoubtedly Fricsay's great achievement was in developing the RIAS Symphony Orchestra to be one of the finest in FR Germany, and the many records he made with it are eloquent evidence of the standard it attained. Part of this was due to the exceptionally good players he recruited, part to his strict discipline with the string players, and the meticulous preparation that preceded every performance. His manner of unfolding each work to the players at rehearsal commanded their absolute attention. He signed his first recording contract with DGG in 1948, and in the first decade of the LP record became one of DGG's most important artists. His most outstanding recordings were Mozart's *Requiem, Die Entführung aus dem Serail, Le nozze di Figaro, Don Giovanni, Die Zauberflöte, Fidelio*, Verdi's *Requiem, Der fliegende Holländer*, Dvořák's Symphony No. 9, Tchaikovsky's Symphonies Nos 4, 5 and 6, and *Le Sacre du printemps*. Many of these, such as Verdi's *Requiem* and the Tchaikovsky symphonies, were sensational in their day. He also recorded a number of the symphonies of Haydn, Mozart and Beethoven, but he was much more convincing in the later romantics, in addition to modern composers such as Bartók and Stravinsky.

FRÜHBECK DE BURGOS, Rafael (b. 1933). Son of a Spanish mother and a German father, who settled in Burgos, Frühbeck added the 'Burgos' to his name to identify himself as a Spaniard. He first took violin lessons at the age of 7, performed in public at 12, as a youth played in a local orchestra and conducted zarzuelas at small Madrid theatres. He was in the Spanish army for three years when he was a bandmaster at Santander (1953–6). From 1956 to 1958 he was at the Hochschule für Musik at Munich studying with Lessing and Eichhorn, and on his return to Spain became conductor of the Bilbao Municipal Symphony Orchestra (1959–62). In 1962 he succeeded Argenta as conductor of the Spanish National Orchestra at Madrid and became widely known in Europe and later in North and South America as a guest conductor. His other appointments, in addition to the Spanish National Orchestra (1962–77), have been general music director of the Düsseldorf Symphony Orchestra (1966–71), music director of the Montreal Symphony Orchestra (1975–6) and principal guest conductor of the National Symphony Orchestra in Washington DC (1980), and of the Yomiuri Nippon Symphony Orchestra, Japan.

After Argenta's death in 1958 Frühbeck de Burgos emerged as the leading Spanish conductor, and he has won a worldwide reputation not only as an interpreter of Spanish music but for his performances of the repertoire from Bach to Stravinsky. He was the first to perform the complete *St Matthew Passion* in Spain, and in his regular concerts in Madrid he included avant-garde music of Spanish and other composers. The one conductor who has impressed him most was Knappertsbusch, whom he heard often in Munich; Knappertsbusch, he says, conducted concerts without rehearsals, and the result could be either disastrous or a sublime experience. Frühbeck de Burgos himself conducts mostly from memory, but does not memorise contemporary pieces which he expects to perform only once. He has found that recording is the surest way to become familiar with a work, although his successful recording of *Elijah* and the many performances of the oratorio which he was later called on to give, somewhat jaded his enthusiasm for it, but this did not prevent him from later recording Mendelssohn's *St Paul*. He feels at home with orchestras on both sides of the Atlantic, and of all orchestras he considers the Berlin Philharmonic and the Philadelphia the most exciting to conduct. The problem of attracting young people to concerts of classical music he finds to be only true in the USA, and says that this probably is due to the way in which orchestras are organised and financed there. With the orchestra in Madrid a third of each series is open to the public and not the subscribers, and the average age of the audience would be in the early twenties. This is, he says, a common experience in Europe.

Counting the 40 or so zarzuelas he recorded for Spanish Columbia, Frühbeck de Burgos has made over 80 records, for EMI, Decca, DGG and Alhambra. Foremost are his many discs of Spanish music, and of the others his outstanding ones have been Mozart's *Requiem* (with the New Philharmonia Orchestra *et al.* for Decca), Schumann's Symphony No. 3 (with the London Symphony Orchestra for Decca) and *Der Rose Pilgerfahrt* (with the Düsseldorf Symphony Orchestra *et al.* for EMI), *Elijah* (with the New Philharmonia Orchestra *et al.* for EMI) and *St Paul* (with the Düsseldorf Symphony Orchestra *et al.* for EMI) and *Carmina Burana* (with the New Philharmonia Orchestra *et al.* for EMI). His approach to each piece is entirely fresh and where he feels so he does not hesitate to discard tradition. Before his recording of *Elijah* he studied the score carefully with Wilhelm Pitz, the then chorusmaster of the New Philharmonia Chorus, and established a reading in which tempi were faster than usually accepted in England. In his recording of *El amor brujo* he insisted on a true flamenco singer, certain that the music was written for that particular voice; in *Carmen* he went back to the original spoken dialogue, and in *Carmina Burana* he sought to avoid a romantic approach to the music, emphasising more the poetry of the words. A rarity which he has recorded is Falla's *Atlantida*, in the realisation by Ernesto Halffter (with the Spanish National Orchestra *et al.* for EMI).

FURTWÄNGLER, Wilhelm (1886–1954). The son of Adolf Furtwängler, a distinguished professor of archaeology, Furtwängler was born in Berlin, spent his childhood in Munich, and was given a private education. He studied music under Rheinberger, von Schillings and Beer-Walbrunn, and conducting with Mottl; at his very first concert with the Kaim Orchestra in Munich, at the age of 20, he conducted his *Adagio in B Minor* and Bruckner's Symphony No. 9, which was not then well-known. He continued to compose throughout his life, but realised that conducting would be his destiny when he found out that people did not understand or appreciate his music. Some of his compositions have appeared on gramophone records: his Symphony No. 2, written in 1944–5 and first performed in 1952, appeared on mono DGG LPs in which he conducted the Berlin Philharmonic Orchestra. It is a curious work of great length and is almost a summation of romantic music, with overtones of Brahms, Bruckner and Tchaikovsky. His piano concerto was revived by Daniel Barenboim who said that 'you must listen to it with your hat on, so that you can doff it as you meet César Franck, Bruckner, Tchaikovsky, Wagner and Strauss in it, but you suddenly realise that most of these composers didn't write a piano concerto, and this work fills some kind of gap.' It is sombre, doom-laden music, and the second movement is almost a paraphrase of Bruckner. There has also been available on record Furtwängler's *Violin Sonata in G Major*, a work lasting over three-quarters of an hour and in just two movements.

Furtwängler's rise to the most significant appointments for a conductor in Germany was swift. He succeeded Abendroth at Lübeck (1911–15), Bodanzky at Mannheim (1915–20), where he directed both opera and symphony concerts, Loewe at the Vienna Tonkünstler Orchestra (1919–24), and Mengelberg at Frankfurt Museum Concerts (1920–22), first appeared in Berlin in 1917, and succeeded Richard Strauss as music director of the Berlin State Opera Orchestra (1920). Then in 1922, at the age of 36, at the death of Nikisch he took his place as music director of the Berlin Philharmonic and Leipzig Gewandhaus Orchestras, remaining with the latter until 1928. He appeared in London in 1924 and in the USA in 1925, conducted the New York Philharmonic Orchestra (1925–7), became chief conductor of the Vienna Philharmonic Orchestra in succession to Weingartner (1927–30), first toured England with the Berlin Philharmonic in 1927, was appointed general music director of Berlin (1928), toured England with the Vienna Philharmonic Orchestra (1930), led *Tristan and Isolde* at Bayreuth (1931) where he was overall music director, was awarded the Goethe Gold Medal (1932), first appeared at the Paris Opera in 1932, conducted *The Ring* at Covent Garden (1937 and 38), first appeared at the Salzburg Festival in 1937, and resumed musical directorship of the Vienna Philharmonic Orchestra in 1939.

When the Nazis came to power in Germany in 1933 and began to implement their racial and artistic theories, Furtwängler immediately found himself in conflict with them. Performances of Paul Hindemith's operas had been banned because of his Jewish connections and because he had recorded music with two Jewish refugees, Simon Goldberg and Emanuel Feuermann. Furtwängler performed at a concert the symphony which Hindemith had arranged from part of his opera *Mathis der Maler*, which was acclaimed by the public but disapproved by the Nazi authorities. Furtwängler then wrote his famous open letter to Goebbels on the freedom of the arts, concluding with 'What would happen if vague political denunciations were constantly to be applied to the artist?', and declaring that in view of the great scarcity of great musicians throughout the world, Germany could ill afford to dispense with Hindemith. The letter received the widest publicity in the press, and at his performances with the Berlin Philharmonic and at the State Opera the day of its publication he received prolonged applause. The Nazi press attacked him crudely in the next few days, and he became isolated to the point where he resigned his posts. Later the Nazi condemnation of Max Reinhardt, Arthur Schnabel, Otto Klemperer and Bruno Walter aroused his opposition, and he succeeded in protecting many musicians or their wives who were being persecuted by the Nazis.

During the entire period of the Nazi régime Furtwängler would not leave Germany, except for tours; during the war he stayed in Germany, as the Nazis would not have allowed him to return. He was opposed to the régime, but proud of being a German. In 1936 Richard Wagner's grand-daughter Friedelind Wagner witnessed a meeting between Hitler and Furtwängler at Bayreuth and described Hitler turning to Furtwängler and telling him that he would have to allow himself to be used by the party for propaganda purposes. Furtwängler refused; Hitler got angry and told Furtwängler that in that case there would be a concentration camp ready for him. Furtwängler was silent for a moment and then said: 'In that case, Herr Reichschancellor, I will be in very good company.' It is undoubtedly true that Furtwängler believed that music should always be separate from and remain above politics, however naïve that belief might be. At the very end of the war, Speer, the Nazi minister for armaments and war production, who frequently attended Furtwängler's concerts in Berlin, advised him to go to Switzerland when he was leaving for an engagement in Vienna, as Speer had reason to fear for his safety. After the war, Furtwängler was absolved by the Allied Kommandatur of any Nazi sympathies, and in 1947 he resumed his directorship of the Berlin Philharmonic. In the last decade of his life he conducted both the Berlin Philharmonic and the Vienna Philharmonic Orchestras, was a guest conductor in London, Copenhagen, Paris and Buenos Aires, conducted at the Lucerne, Salzburg and Edinburgh Festivals, and led Beethoven's Symphony No. 9 at the re-opening of the Bayreuth Festivals in 1951. But he never returned to the United States; he had previously, in 1934, refused an offer to succeed Toscanini as permanent conductor of the New York

Philharmonic-Symphony Orchestra because of the indignation of the Jewish citizens there, and after the war an attempt to have him appointed conductor of the Chicago Symphony Orchestra came to nothing. Switzerland was his final home. His widow said that he died a tortured man, ashamed of what Germany had done, and depressed because of a worsening impairment of his hearing.

Even during his lifetime, Furtwängler was a legend. He saw himself as the embodiment of the German romantic tradition, particularly as it is expressed in Beethoven, Brahms and Bruckner. He possessed an almost mystical belief that music is the revelation of the human soul. Early in his career he became famous for his performances of Beethoven; he perceived in the sonata-form structure of Beethoven and Brahms the tragic element of all great music which results from the clash of the heroic and lyrical elements from which it is constructed. He once remarked that Bruckner was not primarily a musician at all, but a descendant of the great German mystics, and in the words of Walter Abendroth, 'he performed the Bruckner symphonies as if they were the ritual of a non-denominational religion which had found its expression in the music of the 19th century'. In his concert programmes between 1911 and 1940 he conducted Beethoven 1,045 times, of which the Symphony No. 5 appeared most frequently. Brahms was included in his programmes 519 times, and far behind came Haydn (200) and Mozart (173).

Furtwängler's interpretations were essentially improvisatory, and every performance of the same work could be different. He was at the opposite pole to Toscanini, with whom he is traditionally contrasted. Furtwängler thought about the works he performed more than most musicians and his knowledge of the scores he conducted was exhaustive. Two idiosyncrasies marked him off: his indecisive beat, and his varying tempi within movements. His baton technique has been described as insecure and uncertain, perhaps reflecting his indecision in personal, artistic and political affairs. But this lack of clarity was, in some measure, deliberate, for it produced the diffused and full string sound and the expressive intensity on the part of the players which he was seeking. Also, the character of the upbeat determined the attack of the players; a vigorous upbeat set the character for, say, Beethoven's Symphony No. 5, but something quite different was necessary for the prelude to *Tristan und Isolde*. There is a story of a concertmaster who watched his wavering baton preparing for the upbeat, and said 'Courage, maestro!' Furtwängler did not determine his tempo modifications before a programme: Daniel Barenboim, who was greatly influenced by Furtwängler, has said that 'he was one of the few musicians who managed an equilibrium between intellectual understanding and a spontaneous feeling at the actual performance. He managed to rehearse in such a way that gave him the freedom to do things in the evening that were quite different to the preparations; but the basic principles of his interpretation were always well-established. He was able to perceive structure without limiting his emotional response.'

Nevertheless, as convincing as these tempi modifications may have been in performance, they are inevitably disconcerting on a record or a broadcast, where the essential element of communication between the interpreter and his audience is missing. Furtwängler realised this, and believed that the mechanical processes involved in recording were unsympathetic to inspired musical performance. He had little interest in recording techniques. He knew that his performances were inseparable from the mood of the occasion, and more often than not they would sound eccentric or even perverse on a permanent record; many of the broadcast performances issued on record since his death could be regarded as too idiosyncratic to survive in this form. It was not until he recorded *Tristan und Isolde* with Flagstad and Suthaus and the Philharmonia Orchestra, a year before his death, that he acknowledged the value of the gramophone. He also had a reputation for slow tempi, but this was not always justified, for although he slowed down for moments of great poignancy, he hurried through passages he found less interesting, particularly in opera. His *Ring*, altogether, is faster than Solti's, and his *Parsifal* was the fastest ever. Even so, his readings did become slower as he grew older. For him orchestral tone was based on the lower instruments, especially the bassoon.

As will be evident, the contrast between Toscanini and Furtwängler was extreme, in almost every respect. Their origins, first of all, were so different, as were their cultural backgrounds. For Toscanini it was the world of Verdi and Italian opera, for Furtwängler, the symphonies of Beethoven, Brahms and Bruckner. Their conception of the music itself, too, was a complete contrast: to Toscanini, music, or at least symphonic music, had no extra-musical emotional content. He was once asked how he conceived the heroic statement of Beethoven's Symphony No. 3, to which he replied, rather curtly, that to him it was simply '*Allegro con brio*'. Furtwängler on the other hand was always searching for the meaning behind the notes, and his command of the *adagio* style, so evident, say, in Bruckner, was foreign to Toscanini; it has been suggested by one commentator (Peter Pirie) that Toscanini could not master the *adagio* style of the German symphonists because there is no *adagio* in Verdi. Both conductors, Furtwängler and Toscanini, found themselves time and again performing before the same audience, particularly in New York, and at the Salzburg and Bayreuth Festivals, and therefore were cast as the supreme rivals. But the final point of departure was their separate political stances: Toscanini, while he had a high regard for Furtwängler as a musician, was the implacable foe of Fascism and Nazism, and outrightly refused to have any truck at all with either régime or their musical manifestations; Furtwängler was the naïve artist who compromised himself by imagining that he could accommodate himself with the Nazi régime by remaining in Germany in the belief that music was superior and unrelated to the political régime about him, with all its brutalities and ugliness. Certainly, Toscanini was on the side of the angels, and Furtwängler was rejected by at least part of the musical world for failing to take a stand, and was haunted by the hideous atrocities perpetrated by the German people whose great culture he strove to preserve. Both were at opposite poles in musical interpretation—the objective, as opposed to the subjective—and both had their successors who have followed their tradition. Perhaps their greatest successors have been those who have successfully moulded both approaches in the one style, and of these Karajan is the supreme example.

Furtwängler made comparatively few recordings before World War II, but some were exceptional. These were Beethoven's Symphony No. 5 and Tchaikovsky's Symphony No. 6, both sets being with the Berlin Philharmonic Orchestra when it visited London in 1938. He made a number of studio recordings with the Vienna Philharmonic, the Berlin Philharmonic, the Philharmonia and the Lucerne Festival Orchestras after the war, and including the live concert performances that have also been released, it is possible to compile a complete set of Beethoven symphonies, the four Brahms symphonies and a wide range of the rest of his repertoire. Many of these are becoming available on compact disc, and it is interesting for the collector to note that the date of the performance is usually given, as Furtwängler's performances were so variable. Among the operas he recorded, next to *Tristan und Isolde* (one of the finest operatic performances ever recorded), the other important issue was *The Ring*, which was originally recorded in the RAI studios in Rome in late 1953 for radio transmission. For this the finest musicians were culled from all the Italian orchestras and the best German singers were assembled; each act, and *Das Rheingold* complete, were broadcast without interruption after it had been rehearsed and performed. After protracted and difficult negotiations these performances were released by EMI in 1972, and while the quality of the recording itself and the orchestral playing in no way compete with the stereo recordings by Solti, Böhm and Karajan, Furtwängler conducts with the greatest insight and understanding of this vast score.

G

GARDINER, John Eliot (b. 1943). Great-nephew of the composer Balfour Gardiner, Gardiner first heard Monteverdi in a performance by Nadia Boulanger at a Dartington Summer Music School when he was 6. He studied at Cambridge and at King's College, London, with Dart and then with Boulanger in Paris, was a conducting pupil with Dorati and Hurst, and was an apprentice conductor with the BBC Northern Symphony Orchestra. At Cambridge when he was an undergraduate he formed the Monteverdi Choir, came to prominence with a performance of his own edition of Monteverdi's *Vespro della Beata Vergine* at a Promenade Concert in London (1968), then specialised with the Monteverdi Choir and Orchestra in performances of pre-baroque and 18th-century French music, as well as 20th-century music, and in 1971 discovered Rameau's last opera *Les Boréades*. His association with Nadia Boulanger was profound, and in her will she left him her scores of Monteverdi, Carissimi, Rameau and Charpentier, among others.

Gardiner became convinced that it is necessary to use old instruments in performing music up to 1750, but believes that one must choose the type and size of the ensemble to suit the hall and acoustic conditions when presenting baroque music. He is one of the group of British musicians who have made a vast contribution to the performance of baroque and pre-baroque music with old instruments, others including Hogwood, Preston and Pinnock. He has made extraordinary recordings with the Monteverdi Chorus and the English Baroque Soloists, for DGG Archiv, of Bach's *Mass in B Minor* and orchestral suites, Purcell's *King Arthur* and Handel's *Messiah*. At the same time he has also recorded with the English Baroque Soloists and the forte-pianist Malcolm Bilson a number of the Mozart piano concertos, as well as the Symphonies Nos 29 and 33 of Mozart. However, this repertoire is one side of Gardiner's interests; as a conductor he also performs the 19th- and 20th-century symphonic repertoire, and has recorded Chabrier's *Etoile* (with the Lyon Opera), orchestral suites of Massenet, and choral music of Berlioz.

GIBSON, Sir Alexander (b. 1926). Born in Motherwell, Scotland, Gibson studied the piano at the Academy of Music in Glasgow, and attended Glasgow University, served for four years in the Royal Corps of Signals (1944–8), then studied at the Royal College of Music in London under Austin, and in 1951 was awarded the Queen's Prize. He was a conducting pupil of Markevitch at the Salzburg Mozarteum, and of van Kempen at the Accademia Chigiana at Siena, and at the Besançon Festival in 1952 he was awarded the special Enesco Prize in the competition for young conductors. He became a répétiteur at the Sadler's Wells Opera Company (1951–2), was associate conductor of the BBC Scottish Orchestra (1952–4), was a staff conductor at Sadler's Wells (1954–7), made his début at Covent Garden with *Tosca*, and was appointed music director of Sadler's Wells (1957–9) where he conducted 26 different operas. In 1959 he was engaged as music director of the Scottish National Orchestra, the first long-term resident conductor this orchestra had enjoyed in all its 60 years and he was the longest serving director of any orchestra in Britain. With financial aid from the Arts Council, Scottish Television and friends, he founded the Scottish Opera in 1962, and its scope and reputation grew to culminate in productions of *Les Troyens* (1969) and the first complete *Ring* to be staged in Scotland, under Gibson (1971). He has been a guest conductor with many of the major symphony orchestras in Britain, Europe, South America, Israel and the United States, where he made his début in 1970 with the Detroit Symphony Orchestra. In 1981 he was appointed principal guest conductor of the Houston Symphony Orchestra, performing *The Dream of Gerontius* there. In 1967 he was awarded the CBE and in 1971 he was knighted.

Gibson's contribution to the cause of opera and symphonic music in Scotland has been inestimable, and his fine and exacting musicianship has been amply demonstrated in his many records with the Scottish National Orchestra, which have included Mozart's violin concertos (with Szeryng and the New Philharmonia Orchestra), *The Dream of Gerontius* and symphonic works of Elgar, Mahler's Symphony No. 4, Rachmaninov's Symphony No. 2, the symphonies and other pieces of Sibelius, and the three symphonies of Stravinsky. In these recordings Gibson has shown himself to be an extremely sound but somewhat cautious musical personality, inclined to be reserved in music calling for the expansive romantic gesture. But this may be, to some listeners, erring on the right side. Very little has been recorded of the Scottish Opera except for a disc of excerpts from *Der Rosenkavalier*, under Gibson's direction and issued in 1975. Nonetheless his work with the company has won high praise; writing in *The Musical Times* (February, 1972), Andrew Porter commented on Gibson's reading of the complete *Ring* as 'colourful, constructed on a large scale, and urgent. By *Götterdämmerung* it had achieved greatness: the house was afire with that kind of collective ecstasy, rapture in the Wagnerian experience, associated with conductors like Furtwängler, Knappertsbusch and Goodall.'

GIELEN, Michael (b. 1927). Gielen was born in Dresden where his father was a distinguished opera producer, and emigrated to Argentina with his family. He studied the piano with Leuchtner in Buenos Aires (1942–9), in 1947 he became a répétiteur at the Teatro Colón, and in 1949 gave a recital of the complete piano music of Schoenberg. In 1950 he returned to Europe, studied in Vienna with Polnauer (1950–3), became a coach and conductor at the Vienna State Opera (1952–60) and began to win a reputation as a conductor of both the Viennese classics and of contemporary music. He was first conductor at the Royal Opera, Stockholm (1960–5), conductor at Cologne (1965–8), where he led the première of Zimmermann's *Die Soldaten*, was musical director of the Belgian National Orchestra at Brussels (1969–73), chief conductor at the Netherlands Opera (1973–5), general music director and chief conductor at the Opera at Frankfurt-am-Main (1977 onwards), replaced Boulez as chief guest conductor of the BBC Symphony Orchestra (1978), is a conductor of the South German Radio, and has been until recently the music director of the Cincinatti Symphony Orchestra. In addition to his reputation as an acute interpreter of music of the 20th century, Gielen is a composer of some distinction, and sets aside time from his conducting commitments for a period each summer for composition. One of his early LPs was a coupling of the violin and piano concertos of Schoenberg, performed by Marschner and Brendel respectively, with the South West German Radio Symphony Orchestra, and issued in 1958 by Turnabout; this recording was immensely important in introducing the music of Schoenberg's later period to a great number of people. Gielen further established himself as one of the major living interpreters of Schoenberg, with a recording for Philips of *Moses und Aron*. He has recorded many other contemporary compositions, including *Die Soldaten*.

GIULINI, Carlo Maria (b. 1914). Born in Barletta in southern Italy, Giulini learned the violin as a boy, studied in Rome, first privately, at the Conservatorio di Musica di Santa Cecilia and then at the Accademia di Santa Cecilia under Molinari. As a student he played the viola in a string quartet, and for five years in the Augusteo Orchestra under many of the great conductors of the 1930s, including Strauss, Furtwängler and Walter. During the early part of World War II he was an officer in the Italian army, but with the arrival of the Nazis in Italy he went into hiding because of his anti-Fascist sympathies. He emerged in 1944 to conduct at the Augusteo the first concert to celebrate the liberation of Rome; the programme included Brahms's Symphony No. 4. In the same year he was appointed deputy to Previtali with the Radio Italiana Orchestra in Rome, and became the musical director of the orchestra in 1946. He conducted radio performances of opera, the first being *Hänsel und Gretel*. In 1949 he conducted at festivals at Strasbourg, Prague and Venice, and in 1950 was conductor of the Milan Radio Orchestra; in Milan he became a close friend of Toscanini, after the latter had heard him conduct a radio performance of the Haydn opera, *Il mondo della luna*.

Giulini's operatic début was at Bergamo in 1951; the next year he conducted at La Scala for the first time, with Falla's *La vida breve*, and was appointed assistant to de Sabata, whom he succeeded as principal conductor in 1954. At La Scala he worked closely with Maria Callas. In 1955 he made his first appearance in Britain, conducting *Falstaff* at the Edinburgh Festival, and in the United States with the Chicago Symphony Orchestra. In 1958 came his famous collaboration with Visconti in *Don Carlos* at Covent Garden, and in these years he became widely celebrated as a conductor of opera, symphonic and choral music. He first conducted the Verdi *Requiem* in London in 1962 and recorded it several years later; his interpretation of this work was described by Alec Robertson as 'the most musical and the most spiritual one ever remembers hearing'. In 1969 he became permanent guest conductor of the Chicago Symphony Orchestra, was principal conductor of the Vienna Symphony Orchestra (1973–6), in 1978 conductor of the Los Angeles Philharmonic Orchestra, and in 1983 toured Japan with the orchestra.

In 1969 Giulini decided that he would cease to conduct opera and would devote his attention to symphonic music. He had become dissatisfied with the restricted time given to preparing roles, the inadequacy of the casts he had to work with, and with the frequent need to compromise and make do with conditions as they were. He now rigidly limits the number of engagements he accepts and avoids social occasions; his contract with the Los Angeles Philharmonic expressly excluded social activities. He has, also, no interest in orchestral administration. Routine is absolute anathema to him: he conducts for three weeks, then devotes the next four weeks to meditation and study: 'We have to deal with genius, and we are small men. We must understand what is behind the notes. We must not forget that Beethoven, Mozart and Bach wrote these things, and we must try all our lives to understand what they say. Reading the score is not enough – how many changes did the great composers make in their scores?' For him every rehearsal and performance takes the proportions of an important event. Although he is now the leading living Italian conductor, even taking into account Abbado and Muti, he is quite different in temperament from other Italians such as Toscanini and de Sabata. He is known to musicians as a gentle, gracious man, of impressive suavity and elegance, who beguiles and inspires his players rather than terrifying or bullying them. He keeps to a limited repertoire, developing it slowly, and he feels no necessity to be a missionary for new composers, as his interest is in music that has entered the bloodstream of the people. His sense of perfection and his inability to compromise with conditions less than his own demands, which caused him to give up conducting opera, also bring him to seek the highest standards in his work with symphony orchestras. Before he led the Israel Philharmonic Orchestra on a world tour in 1960 he gave them 20 purely technical rehearsals, as well as the programme rehearsals for the tour. In Los Angeles in 1975 he asked for and was given fifteen hours of rehearsals for Mahler's Symphony No. 9. He said: 'One cannot play Mahler the way one plays Brahms. One cannot even play the Ninth as one plays the First. It is a matter of getting the notes and fingers in the right place first, and then trying to understand the conception. Mahler demands a special sound, a special reception of mood and structure. The orchestra must understand this so it becomes second nature by performance time, so it becomes part of the body. Mahler demands special attention.' In fact, all music to him demands special attention.

Giulini takes recording very seriously; to him a record is a document in the development of interpretation, and brings the best performances to people who never have the chance of hearing a great orchestra. But, to its disadvantage, a recording fixes just one moment of performance, and it is impossible to do twice the same performance. There can be no perfect performance; he learned, as a player in the Augusteo Orchestra, that great conductors interpret the same piece very differently, but all were right, in their own ways. All great music has new life with changes in interpretation. The problem in recording is to bring life to the performances; to him, life is more important than perfection. His first recording for EMI was Cherubini's *Requiem Mass*; he and his musicians worked very hard, but when he heard the first complete recording he saw that it was good, but 'a most beautiful cadaver'. He said to the players: 'Take the next day off, then the next day we will do a live performance.' When the time came, he said: 'Do forget that there is a microphone. We play this piece and we try to make music.' Life then flowed into the music. He is also concerned to produce the same sound on record as one hears in the hall, and to try as much as possible to play long takes. He prefers to rehearse the piece, perform it at concerts four times, then to record it; he believes it wrong to rehearse in the recording studios because the approach to the music is false. However, his characteristic orchestral sound is not easy to record, as it has a special emphasis on the middle and lower string instruments.

Giulini's first records were for Cetra, but in 1953 EMI took him under contract and with the Philharmonia and New Philharmonia, Chicago Symphony and London Symphony Orchestras he made many brilliant recordings. Much later he recorded for DGG with the Vienna Symphony, Los Angeles Philharmonic, Vienna Philharmonic and Chicago Symphony Orchestras; he has also recorded with other orchestras. His great operatic recordings include *Don Giovanni*, *Le nozze di Figaro*, *Don Carlos*, *Falstaff* and *Rigoletto*; his recorded performances in the symphonic and choral repertoire range from symphonies of Haydn and Mozart to the Sea Interludes from *Peter Grimes*; if one were to choose his finest, Bruckner's Symphony No. 8 (with the Vienna Philharmonic Orchestra) and Mahler's Symphony No. 9 (with the Chicago Symphony Orchestra) would have to be included. In the symphonies and concertos of Beethoven and Brahms critics have found Giulini's interpretations somewhat uneven, as sometimes his depth of expression, lyrical intensity and refinement of nuance could result in slow and unsteady tempi, which give an impression of waywardness and a lack of dramatic urgency. To this degree he has been likened to Furtwängler, although he himself is not conscious of being Furtwängler's heir. These performances of Giulini contrast with the rhythmically steady and utterly straightforward readings of northern European conductors such as Karajan, Böhm, Kleiber, Klemperer and Schmidt-Isserstedt, and even more so with the crispness and tension of Toscanini. It is evident in the concert hall that he conceives the music with greater intensity than most other conductors; for instance, the *Scherzo* of Beethoven's Symphony No. 9 takes a more *musical* shape than heard with almost any other conductor. Some critics mistakenly remarked that his recording of Mahler's Symphony No. 1 was an Italianate view of the music, and *ipso facto* unidiomatic, a view which surprised Giulini. His interpretation, he said, was quite intentional; moreover, he pointed out, he grew up in the southern Tyrol, not far from the places that gave Mahler so much inspiration. 'I heard the same sounds, saw the same beauties.'

GOODALL, **Sir Reginald** (b. 1905). Born in Lincoln where he was a chorister at the cathedral, Goodall learned the piano from his father, studied the violin and piano at the Royal College of Music under Sargent, Benjamin and Reid, and then went to Munich and Vienna for further studies. He was assistant to Coates at Covent Garden (1936–9) and to Sargent with the Royal Choral Society, and during the war he conducted a symphony orchestra at Bournemouth. His true career as a conductor started at Sadler's Wells (1944) where he conducted the première of *Peter Grimes* (1945) and shared the first performances of Britten's *The Rape of Lucretia* at Glyndebourne (1946). He was then invited by Rankl to join the music staff at Covent Garden; he visited Germany and was assistant to Furtwängler, Krauss, Klemperer and Knappertsbusch, and studied Berg's *Wozzeck* with Erich Kleiber in Berlin, and later conducted the opera at Covent Garden. There he led numerous performances of Italian and German operas and conducted several Wagner operas on tour, but during Solti's directorship of Covent Garden (1961–71) he was not called on to conduct at all, his activities being confined to coaching singers in the Wagnerian operatic roles for performances by other conductors. In 1968 the Sadler's Wells Opera staged *Die Meistersinger* with Goodall the conductor; when the company moved to the Coliseum in London to become the English National Opera the four operas of *The Ring* were produced under Goodall, in the English language. Since then he has led performances of *Tristan und Isolde*, *Parsifal* and *Die Walküre*, with the Welsh National Opera. He was knighted in 1986.

In the past twenty years Goodall, even in this late stage of his life, has emerged as one of the greatest living Wagnerian conductors, and he has frequently been compared to Furtwängler and Knappertsbusch for the style and brilliance of his performances. Working with them he learned the art of keeping the pace but slowing down for the significant passages; yet his interpretations have a broad, unhurried majesty and conviction that go far beyond imitation. He insists on allowing the music to unfold naturally: 'Wagner was the last great German classical composer and every note must sound.' He stubbornly demands meticulous preparation before performance, coaches the singers and instrumentalists individually and has countless group rehearsals; both singers and players respect his knowledge and are inspired by his love of the music. He feels no bitterness about his neglect at Covent Garden before Solti's departure, and thinks that he may have matured in that time. In fact he is untypically modest for a great conductor, his soft-spoken nature bordering on shyness. He is a firm believer in presenting Wagner in English translation, as the text is as important as the music. He accepts concert engagements rarely, since he only conducts music he knows: 'Otherwise it is just traffic directions.' As a result of a collaboration between EMI and Peter Moores, he has recorded with the English National Opera Company in Andrew Porter's translation of *Das Rheingold* (1975), *Die Walküre* (1976), *Siegfried* (1974) and *Götterdämmerung* (1978). With the Welsh Opera, this time in German, he also recorded *Tristan und Isolde* (1981).

GROVES, Sir Charles (b. 1915). A Londoner, Groves was enrolled at the Choir School of St Paul's Cathedral at the age of 8, and later studied at the Royal College of Music in London. He began his career as a free-lance accompanist then joined the British Broadcasting Corporation in 1938 as a chorus master, became conductor of the BBC Theatre Orchestra (1942), the BBC Revue Orchestra (1943) and the BBC Northern Symphony Orchestra (1944–51). From 1951 to 1961 he was conductor of the Bournemouth Symphony Orchestra; it was, in 1951, the Bournemouth Municipal Orchestra, and was about to cease its existence, but Groves fought for its survival and it was reformed as the Bournemouth Symphony Orchestra, under the aegis of the Western Orchestra Society Ltd, and Groves was its first musical director. In 1950 he toured in Australia and in 1957–8 in South Africa, also conducting at other times in Europe and South America. From 1961 to 1963 he was the first full-time director of the Welsh National Opera, and from 1963 to 1977 music director and conductor of the Royal Liverpool Philharmonic Orchestra. At Liverpool he instituted the post of associate conductor, and in 1967 he himself was appointed associate conductor of the Royal Philharmonic Orchestra, although he continued to spend most of the year in Liverpool. In 1973 he was knighted, and in 1978 was appointed musical director of the English National Opera, in succession to Mackerras, but retired from the position in the following year. With the Royal Philharmonic Orchestra he visited FR Germany, Switzerland, Poland and the USA; he conducts the Munich Philharmonic Orchestra regularly and has led the annual New Year's Eve performance of Beethoven's Symphony No. 9.

Early in his career Groves was greatly influenced by Toscanini, Beecham, Furtwängler and Wood. At the BBC he prepared the choir for Toscanini's London performances of Brahms's *Ein deutsches Requiem*, Verdi's *Requiem* and Beethoven's *Missa Solemnis*. In Liverpool he became the first British conductor to perform the complete cycle of Mahler symphonies with his own orchestra. He has a special fondness for large-scale choral works such as Mahler's Symphony No. 8 and Berlioz's *Grande Messe des Morts*, but also encourages and performs new music. Anxious to avoid being labelled as a specialist, he has nonetheless become known as a fine interpreter of British music in particular, as his records demonstrate. In fact he believes that the insistence in conducting from memory on the part of many conductors is one of the causes of specialisation. He enjoys recording, and has said that he would record anything, although he clearly sees the artistic problems involved: 'The medium itself has created all sorts of problems, wonderful as it is – the idea of putting a bar in here, a bar there. I like to try and get a thing through with as few takes as possible, not to "sole and heel" so much. One wonders whether the slavish accuracy that the recording masters have imposed on us is an end in itself—I doubt it. You can have a thing accurate in itself but as dull as ditchwater.' On another occasion, when he was appointed successor to Lord Britain as president of the National Youth Orchestra, he said that the perfect recording techniques of modern gramophone records had spread the misapprehension that there was one true and only authentic version of each musical work. 'On the contrary, each experience of a piece of music should be a fresh one, to which one brings an independent judgement without preconceptions.'

Groves has made records for Saga and EMI; for the latter, most have been of British composers, including Elgar, Delius, Sullivan, Coates, Bridge, Jones, Mathias, Brian, Arnold, Bliss, Walton and Grace Williams. His Delius recordings have included *A Mass of Life*, *Koanga* and many of the orchestral pieces, and they inevitably invite comparison with the famous original recordings of Beecham of much the same music, but it is scarcely a valid criticism of Groves to suggest that, fine though they are, they do not efface the finesse and utter conviction of Beecham's own performances. Groves himself is a devout admirer of Beecham and especially of his Delius recordings, and his association with him goes back to his days at the Royal College of Music when he played in the orchestra conducted by Beecham in *A Village Romeo and Juliet*. Groves has pointed out that Beecham invariably gave intense preparation to all his scores, above all to Delius, whom he edited considerably, not only in questions of balance but in inserting expression marks. Beecham's interpretations cannot be imitated by others; they are essentially his own conception of Delius's intention. Groves is sure that he must try to find for himself what lay behind the composer's mind and to make his own estimate. 'It's bad enough to try and satisfy the memory of the composer, let alone the memory of another conductor's idea. Which still does not detract from my worshipping of Beecham's conducting.'

GUEST, George (b. 1924). Born in Bangor, North Wales, Guest was, as a boy, a chorister in Bangor Cathedral (1933–5) and at Chester Cathedral (1935–9). His father was an organist, and as a school-boy he studied the organ with Boyle at Chester Cathedral. After service with the Royal Air Force in India and Europe (1942–6) he was awarded an organ scholarship at St John's College, Cambridge (1947–51), where he succeeded Orr as organist and choirmaster (1951). He became a lecturer in music (1953–82) then professor of harmony and counterpoint at the Royal College of Music (1960–1), is a member of the council of the Royal College of Organists of which he was president (1978–80), was president of the Cathedral Organists Association (1980–2), and has been director of studies in music at St John's, Downing and Queen's Colleges in Cambridge. He was also director of the Berkshire Boys Choir in the United States (1967–70), a group assembled from boys and men from the leading American choirs. The choir of St John's College, Cambridge, with whom Guest has made over 50 LP records, has an experience and tradition going back over 450 years. Its membership is composed of choristers on scholarships who board at the college school, and the tenor and bass parts are taken by university students who enter the college as choral scholars. The choir's typical sound is somewhat more astringent than is usual with British cathedral choirs; Guest has cultivated this tone as he believes it more suited to the music of composers like Monteverdi and

Palestrina. Guest has recorded extensively for Argo; included are five of the great Masses of Haydn: the Nos 7, 8, 10, 11 and 12, and even taking into account previous recordings of some of the masses, this series has fully revealed the glory of some of Haydn's most magnificent music. The orchestra employed is the Academy of St Martin-in-the-Fields. The other records are of music by Victoria, Praetorius, Monteverdi, Palestrina, Gesualdo, Gabrieli, Byrd, Purcell, Michael Haydn, Mozart, Tallis, Weelkes, Liszt, Beethoven, Bruckner, Schubert, Duruflé, Fauré, Messiaen, Howells, Stainer, *et al.* However, the only compact disc directed by Guest is a coupling of two *Glorias* of Vivaldi, with the St John's Choir and the Wren Orchestra.

H

HAITINK, Bernard (b. 1929). Although born in Amsterdam into an unmusical background, Haitink's first interest in music was awakened when he was taken to a concert where Mengelberg conducted the Concertgebouw Orchestra, and he started to learn the violin at the age of 9. After studying at the Amsterdam Academy of Music under Hupka, he joined the Netherlands Radio Philharmonic Orchestra as a violinist; then he attended the Netherlands Radio course for conductors at Hilversum where he was a pupil of Leitner (1954–5), became assistant conductor of the Radio orchestra (1955), and then principal conductor in 1957. In the meantime in 1956 he was asked to substitute for Giulini in a performance of Cherubini's *Requiem Mass* with the Concertgebouw Orchestra, and was invited to conduct them occasionally, toured Britain with them in 1959 and was, in 1961, appointed joint permanent conductor of the orchestra together with Jochum, and in 1964 became sole permanent conductor and artistic director. His début in Britain occurred in Liverpool in 1961; in 1967 the London Philharmonic Orchestra appointed him their principal conductor and artistic adviser, and two years later he became the orchestra's artistic director, remaining with them until 1978. In 1972 he led his first performance at the Glyndebourne Festival Opera, and in 1978 he became its musical director; he will become director of the Royal Opera House, Covent Garden, in 1988. His début in the United States occurred in Los Angeles in 1957, and in 1971 he made his first appearance as guest conductor with the Boston Symphony Orchestra. He has toured overseas with the Concertgebouw Orchestra, and in 1957 visited the USSR with the London Philharmonic Orchestra. In 1971 he was awarded the Gold Medal of the Vienna Mahler Society.

Compared to so many of the charismatic conductors of his and earlier generations, Haitink is a startling contrast. He is unassuming but completely self-confident, shy but approachable; his manner on the podium is sober, incisive and such that he communicates immediately and directly with his players. He dislikes histrionics directed towards the audience, certain that this creates the wrong atmosphere. 'There is no mystique about conducting,' he said, 'but it is a job, a profession of its own. The technique is not so difficult, but you must have the gift to communicate, to *listen* to the orchestra, a certain gift to inspire the players. There are moments when you feel unhappy, when you can't get what you want, but you must work it out inside yourself. Conducting should not be made to look difficult: when I go to the theatre I don't want to be confronted with the problems of the actors. . . . I think conducting is a down-to-earth profession. The things that are not down-to-earth I keep to myself.' He settles on an interpretation after reading and re-reading the score, but he does not attempt to mark the score: 'Interpretation is something that cannot be written down. It must be in one's blood, or nowhere.' Rehearsals are neither exhaustive nor exhausting; he talks as little as possible, does not wish to impose his will on the orchestra at any cost, or rarely uses the full three hours allotted to him, believing that the standard of performance can easily be impaired, and that the extra finish must come at the concert itself. In fact, after the final rehearsal, his players wonder what the standard of the concert will be. When he is a guest conductor he never attempts to change the orchestra to fit his own ideals: 'I want to get the best out of an ensemble, but to keep its own character.' His apparent calm has its limits; more than once he has left the concert hall, taking his orchestra with him, annoyed by inattentive audiences.

Growing up in Holland in the shadow of Mengelberg and van Beinum, Haitink shares their eclecticism and their devotion to Mahler and Bruckner. After van Beinum's death he was asked to conduct a Mahler symphony for the Concertgebouw Orchestra's 75th anniversary; he had had no experience with Mahler, conducted the Symphony No. 1, became fascinated by the composer, and then learned a new symphony each year. His performances of the Mahler and Bruckner symphonies have become famous, both on record and in the concert hall; they are at another pole of expression, but not of intensity, compared with the more subjective and overtly dramatic conductors such as Bernstein and Solti. Haitink dislikes performing the Mahler symphonies too often, feeling that while Mahler's world may be absorbing, it is not healthy. Under his baton the romantic composers receive powerful, finely judged, unmannered and unexaggerated readings. Some may regard his interpretations as unremarkable and too literal to have definite character, but like his great predecessor with the Concertgebouw Orchestra, van Beinum, he is temperamentally averse to highly personal inter-pretations. His awe for the great composers he conducts obliges him to perform their music as faithfully and as clearly as he can. Beethoven was introduced rather late into his concerts, for

despite his great love for the composer, he was at first frightened
to perform his works, and even now has refused to record the
Missa Solemnis, saying that he is not ready for it. He studied the
Beethoven scores closely, read many books about him, and went
to Vienna to see the first edition of the *Eroica*, where the careful
dynamic markings of Beethoven convinced him that performances must be absolutely faithful to the scores, even to not
doubling the woodwind. He once named as his favourite music
Beethoven's late piano sonatas and string quartets, and the
Bartók quartets. He knows his limitations; he is wary of Bach,
because of the stylistic problems involved, and is content to
leave the latest modern music to others. Another composer,
Sibelius, he finds difficult to present effectively in the concert
hall. The upshot of it all is that the Concertgebouw Orchestra
has remained in the very top flight of European orchestras under
his leadership, and the London Philharmonic advanced after he
took charge to a pre-eminent position among the British orchestras. He has been reluctant to accept opportunities to take over
American orchestras, for despite his admiration for them, the
status of the conductor and the inflexibility of rehearsal times, in
particular, are not to his taste.

Haitink's many recordings are headed by the nine symphonies
of Mahler and Bruckner (with the Concertgebouw Orchestra),
the nine symphonies of Beethoven (with the London Philharmonic Orchestra), the four symphonies of Brahms and Schumann (with the Concertgebouw Orchestra), the tone poems of
Liszt, the two symphonies of Elgar, *Don Giovanni* and *Die
Zauberflöte* (with the London Philharmonic Orchestra); he is
nearing completion of the fifteen symphonies of Shostakovich
(with the London Philharmonic Orchestra). In all these performances clarity, thoughtfulness and moderation distinguish the
interpretation. In many great conductors one is aware that the
music is the vehicle for the demonstration of magnificent orchestral tone; with Haitink it is the opposite, although one is struck
nonetheless by the brilliance of the orchestral execution. He
does not aim to overwhelm with volume or expressive gestures.
In Bruckner, for instance, he keeps the pianissimi very low and
does not exaggerate the fortissimo climaxes, and with this the
music gains breadth. About the Bruckner series, Deryck Cooke
wrote: 'I can pay Haitink no greater tribute than to say that,
whatever reservations I may have about his performance of this
or that movement, the overall effect of each symphony is such
that I can think of none better, and few as good.' The recordings
of the Mahler symphonies attracted scarcely less praise from

Cooke; for example of the Symphony No. 9 he wrote: 'This great Mahler record, which in spite of the illustrious competition (from Walter, Klemperer, Solti and Bernstein), I can only hail as the ideal Ninth, beyond any criticism.' The Beethoven symphonies are usually accepted as the final test of a great conductor, and again the unmannered and straightforward nobility of Haitink's performances confirm his stature.

HANDLEY, Vernon (b. 1930). Born at Enfield, North London, and educated at Balliol College, Oxford, and the Guildhall School of Music and Drama, Handley won a conducting competition promoted by the Tunbridge Philharmonic Society, and was appointed musical director and conductor of the Guildford Philharmonic Orchestra and Choir (1962), which shortly after became a fully professional orchestra. He conducted the first orchestra and was a teacher at the Royal College of Music (1966–72), was appointed associate conductor of the London Philharmonic Orchestra (1982), and principal guest conductor of the BBC Scottish Orchestra in Glasgow (1983); he is now artistic director and principal conductor of the Ulster Orchestra. He has appeared as a guest conductor with many of the major British and European orchestras, broadcasts frequently, and his repertoire includes a high proportion of British and unfamiliar music of the 20th century. At the same time, he does not wish to be typecast solely as a conductor of British music. His conducting style has been largely influenced by Boult, whose economical gestures and placement of the orchestra he has adopted. He says: 'I cannot conduct instruments; I can only conduct people,' and tries to memorise all his players' names; he takes the view that all musicians are eager to play, but feel most of the time that they are prevented from doing so. Handley has made over 50 records, the first being with the Guildford Philharmonic Orchestra, but his most successful have been with the London Philharmonic Orchestra for Classics for Pleasure: Dvořák's Symphony No. 8, orchestral pieces of Delius, Elgar's two symphonies, *Enigma Variations*, *Introduction and Allegro*, *Serenade* and Violin Concerto (with Nigel Kennedy), Vaughan Williams's Symphony No. 2 and *Fantasia on a Theme of Tallis*, and Tippett's *Concerto for Double String Orchestra*. The Elgar Violin Concerto, also on compact disc, has been especially praised.

HARNONCOURT, Nikolaus (b. 1929). Born in Berlin, Harnoncourt studied the cello with Grümmer, attended the Vienna Academy of Music (1948–51), and from 1952 to 1969 was a cellist in the Vienna Symphony Orchestra. When still a student he became interested in early music and old instruments, and gave many concerts playing the viola da gamba. In 1953 he founded the Concentus Musicus Wien to perform music written between 1200 and 1800, and closely studied problems of performance and the technique of playing old instruments. His wife, Alice, is the leader of the ensemble. Through tours in Europe, the USA and Australia and its series of recordings, the Concentus Musicus Wien has become one of the foremost groups presenting early and baroque music played in the authentic manner. Harnoncourt has edited new editions of Bach's *Mass in B Minor*, *St Matthew Passion* and *St John Passion*, and has prepared new scores of the Monteverdi operas, *Il ritorno d'Ulisse in patria*, *L'Incoronazione di Poppea* and *La favola d'Orfeo*, which he has led in public performances and recordings. Later in Zürich in collaboration with the producer Ponnelle he directed new productions of the three Monteverdi operas, which were repeated in Vienna, Edinburgh, Milan, Hamburg, Wiesbaden and Berlin. He was appointed a professor at the Mozarteum and Institute of Musicology at Salzburg in 1972, and has given lectures and seminars in many countries, directing courses in the music of Monteverdi and Bach in Bremen and Ossiach, and in 1980 was awarded the Erasmus prize jointly with Gustav Leonhardt for their interpretations of baroque music. His work took another turn in 1981 when he became associated with the Amsterdam Concertgebouw Orchestra in recording the symphonies, operas and choral works of Mozart in new interpretations, free of 'dust and tradition'. Records have been issued of many of the symphonies, in addition to the *Requiem*, the incidental music to *Thamos*, and *Idomeneo*, the latter following a stage production in collaboration with Ponnelle.

Harnoncourt has explained that in his young years he could not believe that the 18th-century sonatas for stringed instruments were as dull as they then sounded when performed. But he found that playing them on the instruments of the time was not the full answer; 'Our first step was to discover an adequate performance and this included a lot of things which are far more important than the instruments. I think one can effect a very good performance of baroque music with modern instruments up to a threshold beyond which it is impossible to proceed. After this point certain conditions occur which the modern instruments cannot fulfill.' In his study of the old instruments in Vienna he found that they could adequately bring to life once more the timbres of the baroque era. Generally the instruments can be played well, since Bach would not have allowed his musicians to play the music badly. 'If they had been unable to play his scores then he would have written simpler music for them and I think, therefore, that Bach's works are in a sense portraits of his performers.' In the Concentus Musicus Wien each musician is a very good player on the equivalent modern instrument. Harnoncourt cannot conceive of an alternative modern method of performing baroque music; to him the modern method is 'an unsorted blend of geniality, 19th-century tradition, and ignorance'. A genuine modern interpretation he has yet to hear.

Since the *Brandenburg Concertos* were issued by Telefunken in 1966 the Concentus Musicus Wien under Harnoncourt has made a number of recordings of baroque and pre-baroque masterpieces which have brought many international awards. Then followed *inter alia* the Bach orchestral suites, *St Matthew Passion* and *Mass in B Minor*, Monteverdi's *La favola d'Orfeo*, Rameau's *Castor et Pollux*, Handel's *Belshazzar*, Bach's *Christmas Oratorio* and numerous other works of the period. Most significantly, he has undertaken together with Gustav Leonhardt the recording of all Bach's cantatas, which must rank as one of the most ambitious projects in the history of the gramophone record. By mid-1986 Cantata No. 156 had been released.

Critical reception of Bach's *Mass in B Minor* and the cantatas has, however, not always been sympathetic, and the view of some critics has been that the attempt to produce authentic performances has disposed of the baby with the bath water. In the cantatas, for instance, the players tend to eschew all the colour, sentiment and feeling for atmosphere, indeed the expressiveness that Bach intended. The Monteverdi operas have brought similar reservations; writing in *The Gramophone* Denis Arnold remarked on the participation of oboes, violins, trumpets etc. in the vocal music, and on the use of constant ornamentation by these instruments in *L'Incoronazione di Poppea*, which must be regarded as anachronistic. Yet it must be admitted that a preparation of a performing score from the original manuscripts, which differ among themselves in many respects, presents problems whose solutions will never satisfy everyone, certainly scholars with their own very definite ideas. Again, Harnoncourt's new scoring of *Il ritorno d'Ulisse in patria*, in which there are many anachronistic intrusions, could scarcely be claimed to be a re-construction of mid-17th century performing practice. Perhaps these matters may only concern experts and not the general musical public, who might recall the controversy regarding Raymond Leppard's production of *L'Incoronazione di Poppea* at Glyndebourne some years earlier. However, the recording of *Castor et Pollux*, issued in 1972, roused none of these reservations and received wide praise, and *Il ritorno d'Ulisse in patria* was listed as the record of the year in 1972 by *Stereo Review*, and the Bach Mass and Passions, *Belshazzar*, *Jeptha*, Mozart's *Requiem*, *Thamos* and *Idomeneo* attracted similar awards.

HERBIG, Günther (b. 1931). Born at Ustí nad Labem in Czechoslovakia, Herbig studied with Abendroth at the Franz Liszt Hochschule at Weimar and made his début as a conductor at the Weimar Opera in 1957. He remained at Weimar until 1962, at the same time teaching conducting at the Hochschule, and studied further with Scherchen, Jansons and Karajan, with whom he was for two years. He became music director at Potsdam (1962–6), assistant conductor of the Berlin Symphony Orchestra in East Berlin, where Sanderling was chief conductor (1966–72), was chief conductor and artistic director of the Dresden Philharmonic Orchestra (from 1972), in succession to Masur, and then returned to the Berlin Symphony Orchestra as chief conductor. Between 1979 and 1983 he was principal guest conductor with the Dallas Symphony Orchestra, and later with the BBC Philharmonic Orchestra in Manchester, and in 1983 was appointed music director of the Detroit Symphony Orchestra, following Dorati. Prior to his departure from East Germany he was a guest conductor in many East European countries, and toured with the Berlin Symphony, Leipzig Gewandhaus and Dresden Philharmonic Orchestras, touring West Germany, Britain, Poland, Spain, Czechslovakia, Italy, Austria, Japan and the USSR with the Dresden Philharmonic in 1974–6. In the USA he has also appeared as a guest conductor with the Chicago Symphony, Philadelphia, Boston Symphony, New York Philharmonic and Los Angeles Philharmonic Orchestras, and has a reputation for his performances of the major symphonic works such as those by Beethoven, Bruckner and Shostakovich. For Eterna in East Germany he has made a number of successful recordings, including Haydn's Symphonies Nos 93 to 104 (with the Dresden Philharmonic Orchestra), and the four Brahms symphonies and Mahler's Symphony No. 5 (with the Berlin Symphony Orchestra).

HOGWOOD, Christopher (b. 1941). Born in Nottingham, Hogwood studied under Leppard and Dart at Cambridge University where he organised an orchestra to perform contemporary music. He studied with the harpsichordist Puyana in Spain, and with David Munrow at Cambridge began to play baroque music on modern instruments; after his graduation in 1964 he spent a year at the Charles University in Prague, and in 1967 he and Munrow founded the Early Music Consort of London, which was devoted to introducing the performance of medieval music to the concert hall and to gramophone records. That year the quartet consisting of Hogwood, Munrow, the counter-tenor Bowman and the violist Brooks first performed at Louvain, Belgium, a year before their first appearance in London. Prior to this in 1966 Hogwood became the harpsichordist in the Academy of St Martin-in-the-Fields. His experience with the Early Music Consort, with which he had made many records and performed in concerts, finally brought him to the point when he was unable to judge whether the performances were authentic, as they were based on guesswork and assumptions. His editing of scores of baroque music for the Academy of St Martin-in-the-Fields led him to appreciate that the music of the 17th and 18th centuries offered reliable sources not possible with music of earlier periods, and also that the use of modern instruments, including the harpsichord, imposed limitations. He then gave recitals on historical instruments, joining with others interested in historical performances, and finally in 1973, in collaboration with Peter Woodland, a producer for Decca Records, he formed the Academy of Ancient Music, to record first of all the orchestral music of Thomas Arne. The success of this recording, which was issued on the L'Oiseau Lyre label, led to more recordings of the music of Vivaldi, Bach and his sons, Stamitz and Haydn, and between 1979 and 1982 Mozart's symphonic works were recorded in performances by the Academy, under the guidance of Hogwood, the concertmaster Jaap Schroder and the musicologist Neal Zaslaw creating the exact musical forces that performed the works originally. These recordings established Hogwood's reputation internationally, as a British complement to the work of Harnoncourt in Vienna. In addition to the complete Mozart symphonies, the Academy under Hogwood went on to record Handel's oratorio *La resurrezione*, *Messiah*, *Water Music* and *Royal Fireworks Music*, and Mozart's *Requiem*, the latter in an edition by Richard Maunder which omits all the posthumous additions to the score made by Sussmayr, substituting passages based on material left by Mozart. The Haydn Symphonies Nos 100 and 104 have also been recorded, and a project to place on compact discs all the symphonies of Beethoven has started with the issue of the first two.

Hogwood does not confine his conducting activities to baroque and classical music, being anxious to avoid being earmarked as a specialist, and on a tour of Australia in 1983 he conducted works by Mendelssohn, Shostakovich and Verdi. In the United States he has conducted the Boston Symphony, Chicago Symphony, St Louis Symphony and the Detroit Symphony Orchestras, and he led the Academy during its first US tour in 1985. His approach to conducting was a novelty for these American orchestras, used to the dominance of the great conductor, whoever it might be on the day: 'I'm for democracy to the point of anarchy. Your oboe d'amore player is fully aware of the art regarding his instrument, its technology and its history. You accept what he feels is best in the circumstances. Other players will make their own suggestions. You are the umpire. No one wants to get back to the maestro situation of a bunch of mice playing baroque instruments and a great conductor telling them to do it his way.' He has also followed Mozart's custom of dividing the first three and final movements of his symphonies between the beginning and end of the programmes, and encourages audiences to applaud at the end of the movements, as this was the practice on festive occasions in the 18th century.

The impact of the Harnoncourt-Hogwood revolution in the performance of pre-baroque, baroque and classical music has come about mainly through their gramophone records, which have made their performances immediately available to a worldwide audience. This in itself emphasises the value of the record – or the present-day compact disc – as a document of the performance practice of the time, as so many conductors recognise. Every interpreter inevitably is convinced that his conception of the work is the correct one, and it must be conceded that the performances of Hogwood and Harnoncourt are carefully researched and prepared. Nonetheless it would be false to conclude that with them we have reached the ultimate stage in the performance of this music. Those with long memories will recall the performances of the Bach suites and the *Brandenburg Concertos* by the Adolf Busch Chamber Players in the 1930s, then those of the Stuttgart Chamber Orchestra under Munchinger in the post-war decade, followed by the Academy of St Martin-in-the-Fields in more recent times, plus a host of others in between. Each had its special case to argue, and was greeted at the time as the state of the art. So we need to keep a sense of perspective about all these performances and to remember that new insights in performance and interpretation will always appear so long as music is performed. Even today there are alternative approaches to the performance of baroque music: in Leipzig there is another school of Bach performance, examples of which are the recent recordings of the suites and *Brandenburg Concertos* by the New Bach Collegium Musicum of Leipzig under the direction of Max Pommer. Here the use of old instruments is considered of far less importance than the style of the actual performance, which is derived from the closest study of the documents of the time. This does not for a moment dispute the freshness and originality of these performances of the Academy of Ancient Music and the Concentus Musicus Wien, which find an ideal medium in the compact disc with its clarity and dynamic range.

HORENSTEIN, Jascha (1898–1973). The son of a Russian industrialist and an Austrian mother, Horenstein was born in Kiev, and at the age of 6 was taken with his family first to Königsberg and then to Vienna. His mother taught him the piano, and in Vienna he learned the violin with Adolf Busch, studied Indian philosophy at the university and was a pupil of Marx and Schreker at the Academy of Music. In Vienna he conducted a student group, and by the time he was 20 he had determined to be a conductor. When Schreker went to Berlin to the Hochschule für Musik there, Horenstein followed him, and in Berlin he conducted the Schubert Choir. He became Furtwängler's assistant, rehearsed Bach's *Mass in B Minor* for him at Frankfurt-am-Main in 1923, and the next year made his début with the Vienna Symphony Orchestra with a programme that included the then little-known Symphony No. 1 of Mahler. In Berlin he conducted the Blüthner Concerts in 1924, the Berlin Symphony Orchestra (1925–8), and was a guest conductor for concerts with the Berlin Philharmonic Orchestra in 1926. He gave the première of Berg's *Lyric Suite* in Berlin in 1929 and made records for Polydor with the Berlin Philharmonic. As a young man he came into contact and worked with Schoenberg, Berg, Webern, Stravinsky, Rachmaninov, Strauss, Nielsen, Busoni and Janáček, and performed their music all his life.

In 1929 Horenstein was appointed director of the Düsseldorf Opera on Furtwängler's recommendation. He remained there until the Nazis forced him to leave Germany as he was a Jew, and Düsseldorf was the only permanent appointment he held throughout his life. A second-rate position was never acceptable to him, and he later said that he had never been offered a first-rate one on satisfactory conditions. He went to Paris, and in the 1930s travelled extensively, conducting in Brussels, Vienna, Warsaw and in the USSR, toured Australia and New Zealand, and was one of the four conductors, including Toscanini, to conduct the new Palestine Symphony Orchestra, and visited Scandinavia with the Ballet Russe de Monte Carlo. Settling in the USA in 1941, his début in 1942 was with an orchestra called the Works Project Administration Symphony. He became a US citizen and went on to conduct many of the major orchestras in the USA and South America. After World War II he returned to Europe, took up residence in Lausanne, and was in constant demand. In 1950 he introduced *Wozzeck* to Paris, in 1958 he conducted a memorable Beethoven *Missa Solemnis* at the Leeds Festival when he substituted for Klemperer, and in 1959 he conducted Mahler's Symphony No. 8 for the BBC, setting off the revival and enthusiasm for Mahler in Britain; in 1961 he led *Fidelio* at Covent Garden, where he last appeared with *Parsifal* just before his death, and in 1964 he presented *Doktor Faust* of Busoni in New York. In London he gave many concerts and was particularly associated with the London Symphony Orchestra, as well as the BBC Northern Symphony Orchestra in Manchester.

Although Russian by birth, Horenstein was a conductor completely nurtured in the German tradition at a critical epoch. In Vienna he was just too late to witness Mahler conducting, but as a youngster he was at concerts conducted by Nikisch, Walter and Weingartner, whose influence remained with him throughout his life. Later he remarked that he could not conduct Brahms' Symphony No. 4, Mahler's Symphony No. 9 or the *Leonore No. 3* overture without recalling the Nikisch performances he heard as a boy. His mentor, Furtwängler, was also a decisive influence; from him he said he learnt 'to search for the meaning of the music rather than being concerned with the music itself, to emphasise the metaphysical side of the work rather than its empirical one'. A lifelong interest in Indian philosophy, with its stress on the spiritual life and how it should dominate our actions, brought him to the same conclusion. Another conductor he admired was Stokowski, for the width of his repertoire, the sense of occasion he brought to every performance, the number of important works he premièred, and for his profound impact on a vast audience. Even though he was a short and seemingly frail man, he was very energetic and meticulous in preparing works for performance; routine performances would not be tolerated, even from the greatest orchestras, and with less distinguished ensembles he was quick to assess their capabilities and expected nothing less. The result was that he was always able to elicit the highest standard with every orchestra he conducted.

In rehearsal Horenstein played long stretches of the work, to establish continuity, and then proceeded to the details. In the words of Joel Lazar, his assistant in the last three years of his life: 'The exceptional unity and continuity that characterised his performances arose from the way he controlled rhythm, harmony, dynamics and tempo so that each individual moment might receive the most vivid characterisation, but the overall line and cumulative effect would not be lost.' Horenstein disregarded minor ensemble mistakes to maintain the overall flow of the music. The technique of conducting, and indeed of recording, was not important to him; it was the result that was significant. Seeking ever for the meaning behind the notes he would first start with the literal performance of them, then give careful attention to the particular style of the music and the period and influences at the time when it was written. The imposition of his own self on the music was scarcely possible. His first loves were Mahler and Bruckner and his conception of them was derived from the Vienna of Nikisch, Walter and Furtwängler; in his recording of the *Brandenburg Concertos* he used authentic instruments, including a viola da gamba played by Nikolaus Harnoncourt. In Mozart he was elegant, precise and subdued; with, for example, the trio of the Symphony No. 40 of Mozart he produced an exquisite and profound effect. In his valedictory *Parsifal* at Covent Garden, the orchestra played with a flexibility and delicacy that resembled chamber music. Some of his last words were said to be: 'One of the greatest regrets in dying is that I shall never again be able to hear *Das Lied von der Erde*.'

Before he was 30 Horenstein had recorded Bruckner's Symphony No. 7 and Mahler's *Kindertotenlieder*, and he fought against the risk of being categorised as a Bruckner and Mahler specialist. Despite the number of other records he made throughout his life, it is his recorded performances of these two composers that are his memorial. In the early days of LP he recorded Bruckner's Symphonies Nos 8 and 9, and in 1969–71 Unicorn in Britain issued a superb series with him conducting the London Symphony Orchestra and the New Philharmonia Orchestra in Mahler's Symphonies Nos 1, 3 and 4, as well as Nielsen's Symphony No. 5 and other music by Hindemith, Strauss, Panufnik and Robert Simpson. One of his most remarkable records was Beethoven's Symphony No. 9, an early LP which was the first time the entire symphony was accommodated on one disc. Perhaps his most representative recording is Mahler's Symphony No. 4, recorded by Classics for Pleasure with Margaret Price and the London Symphony Orchestra.

I

INBAL, **Eliahu** (b. 1936). A graduate of the Conservatory and the Academy of Music at his birthplace, Jerusalem, Inbal made his first appearance as a conductor with the Youth Symphony Orchestra of Israel in 1956. During his military service he was leader of the Army Symphony Orchestra, and conducted a combined Army and Youth Orchestra which won first prize at the Kerkrade Festival, Holland, in 1958. In that year he was recommended by Leonard Bernstein for a scholarship from the Israel-America Foundation to study abroad; he studied with Ferrara in Holland, Fourestier at the Paris Conservatoire (1960–63), and with Celibidache in Siena. Following the award of first prize in the Guido Cantelli International Competition for Conductors in Novara in 1963, he received many international engagements, and took part in festivals, tours and concerts in Europe, Israel, Japan, the USA, Scandinavia and Australia. He first conducted opera in 1969, with *Elektra* at Bologna, and *Don Carlos* at the Verona Festival, also conducted opera at Munich, Stuttgart and Cologne, and in 1974 was appointed chief conductor of the Frankfurt Radio Symphony Orchestra, leading the orchestra during a tour of the USA in 1980. His major recordings, for Philips, have been Schumann's four symphonies, *Symphony in G Minor* (the *Zwickau* symphony) and *Overture, Scherzo and Finale* (with the New Philharmonia Orchestra), the complete works for pianoforte and orchestra of Chopin (with Arrau and the London Philharmonic Orchestra), Debussy's *Nocturnes* and *La Mer* (with the Amsterdam Concertgebouw Orchestra) and Scriabin's Symphonies Nos 1, 2 and 3, *Poème de l'extase* and *Prometheus* (with the Frankfurt Radio Symphony Orchestra). His first recordings, of the Schumann symphonies and the Debussy coupling, invited comparison with performances of the great conductors, and although he created an impression of tending to drive the music too hard, his exceptional talent was generally recognised. He also recorded Bruckner's Symphonies Nos 3, 4 and 8, in the composer's first versions (with the Frankfurt Radio Symphony Orchestra, for Telefunken); these performances are of exceptional importance to all interested in Bruckner, as it is the later revisions of the symphonies that have generally been recorded previously.

J

JANOWSKI, **Marek** (b. 1941). Janowski was born in Warsaw and was raised in Wuppertal in Germany. He studied mathematics and later music at Cologne University, for a short time studied in Vienna, and then attended the Accademia Chigiana in Siena. He conducted concerts in Italy, at the age of 20 was a répétiteur at Aachen, and a year later was a conductor at the Cologne Opera. His first appointment was as first conductor at the Deutsche Oper am Rhein in Düsseldorf (1964–9); he then was a conductor at the Hamburg State Opera, becoming first conductor there (1969–74), was general music director at Dortmund (1975–9) and permanent guest conductor at the Deutsche Oper in West Berlin, the Bavarian State Opera, and at the opera houses at Paris, Buenos Aires, East Berlin, Dresden and Prague. He also conducts with leading symphony orchestras in Europe, is a permanent guest conductor of the Dresden Staatskapelle, and was appointed artistic adviser of the Royal Liverpool Philharmonic Orchestra (1983), and is also now conductor of the Gürzenich Orchestra in Cologne. His operatic repertoire ranges from Mozart to Strauss, but he believes that young conductors should conduct modern music, himself visiting London with the Cologne Opera to lead the British première of Henze's *Der junge Lord*. By far his most important contribution to the record catalogue has been a complete recording of *The Ring*, with the Dresden Staatskapelle *et al.*, which has been issued on compact disc; his direction was characterised by Alan Blyth as a 'thoroughly dramatic, positive interpretation', with an intimacy contrasting especially with Solti's forthright reading of the operas. Janowski's other recordings include Penderecki's *The Devils of Loudun*, Weber's *Euryanthe*, Strauss's *Die schweigsame Frau*, and Brahms's four symphonies, the latter with the Royal Liverpool Philharmonic Orchestra.

JANSONS, **Mariss** (b. 1943). Born in Riga, Jansons studied with his father, Arvid Jansons the conductor, at the Leningrad Conservatory, and then with Swarowsky in Vienna, Karajan in Salzburg and Mravinsky in Leningrad. He was awarded second prize at Karajan's International Conductors' Competition in Berlin (1971), conducted in the Soviet Union, Eastern and Western Europe, and the United States. He was appointed chief conductor of the Oslo Philharmonic Orchestra (1979), with whom he has recorded effective performances of the Tchaikovsky symphonies, released on compact disc.

JÄRVI, Neeme (b. 1937). The Estonian conductor Järvi's first teacher was his brother Vallo; he then studied at the Tallinn School of Music and at the Leningrad Conservatory, where his teachers in conducting were Rabinovich and Mravinsky. At the same time he played as a percussionist in the Estonian Radio and Television Orchestra, of which he became music director (1963–80), as well as director of the Tallinn Opera. He conducted many of the leading orchestras in the USSR, was awarded first prize in 1971 at the international competition for conductors at the Accademia di Santa Cecilia in Rome, and in that year was awarded the title of People's Artist of the Estonian SSR. He toured in many European countries, North and Central America and Japan, but left the Soviet Union in 1980 and became a resident in the USA where he made guest appearances with orchestras including the New York Philharmonic, Philadelphia, Boston Symphony, San Francisco Symphony and the National Symphony, Washington DC, and conducted at the New York Metropolitan Opera. In Europe he appeared with the Amsterdam Concertgebouw Orchestra and with radio orchestras in West Germany. His present appointments are principal conductor of the Gothenburg Symphony Orchestra in Sweden, principal conductor and musical director of the Scottish National Symphony Orchestra (from 1984), in succession to Sir Alexander Gibson, and principal guest conductor of the City of Birmingham Symphony Orchestra.

One of the prominent musicians from the USSR who have emigrated to and re-established their careers in the West, Järvi is an exciting and spontaneous artist who has quickly become much sought after and acclaimed. He has a high regard for the Scottish National Symphony Orchestra, with whom he has made a number of outstanding compact discs for Chandos, including Prokofiev's seven symphonies and excerpts from *Romeo and Juliet* and Shostakovich's Symphonies Nos 1 and 6. Of the orchestra he says: 'The string tone is special, different from any other orchestra—warm and beautiful, but also flexible. I trust the orchestra and it trusts me.' A propos recording the Prokofiev symphonies he adds: 'With orchestral musicians I try to *create* all the time and show the listener, through them, how much I like the music. I don't think now that we have to play exactly the interpretive markings Prokofiev made; instead, through our performance, we try to show how good the music is. In a recording we're freer than in a concert, when everybody is uncomfortable in evening dress, but the quality is the same. It depends on how I'm feeling at this time, and my mood; I can never repeat myself exactly—that's boring, not interesting.' With the Swedish company BIS he is also recording, with the Gothenburg Symphony Orchestra, the complete symphonies and orchestral music of Sibelius, and has recorded Stenhammer's Symphony No. 2 and *Excelsior!*, and with the Swedish Radio Symphony Orchestra he is also recording the complete orchestral works of his fellow-Estonian Eduard Tubin. Previously in the USSR he had recorded several symphonies of Haydn with the Estonian Chamber Orchestra, and works of Richard Strauss and Stravinsky, with two Moscow orchestras, for Melodiya.

JOCHUM, Eugen (1902–87). Born at Babenhausen in southern Germany into a musical family and the brother of Otto (composer) and Georg Ludwig (conductor), Jochum was playing the piano at the age of 4 and the organ at 7. After attending the Augsburg Conservatory he studied at the Munich Academy of Music (1922–4), and his first appointment was as a répétiteur at Mönchen-Gladbach. His début as a conductor was with the Munich Philharmonic Orchestra in 1926 with a programme including the *Leonore No. 3* overture and Bruckner's Symphony No. 7. Its success led to an appointment with the Kiel Opera (1926–9) where he conducted 17 operas in his first season, as well as leading the Lübeck symphony concerts at the same time. Furtwängler's recommendation was responsible for his engagement by the Mannheim Opera (1929); he was principal conductor at Duisburg (1930) and with the Berlin Radio Symphony Orchestra (1931–3), also giving concerts each season with the Berlin Philharmonic Orchestra and conducting at the Berlin State Opera. With the advent of the Nazis he left Berlin to become music director of the Hamburg Opera and the Hamburg Philharmonic Orchestra, succeeding Muck and Böhm. He remained there until 1949 and was also active in other German cities; during the Hitler era he avoided joining the Nazi Party.

In 1949 Jochum founded and was principal conductor of the Bavarian Radio Symphony Orchestra, and was with the orchestra for 25 years, raising it to become one of the most distinguished in Germany. In 1953 he conducted for the first time at Bayreuth, leading *Tristan und Isolde*, and returned in 1971, 1972 and 1973. He led the Bavarian Radio Symphony Orchestra at the Edinburgh Festival in 1957, first visited the United States in 1958, and since 1962 regularly conducted at the Berlin German Opera and in other German opera houses. On the death of van Beinum in 1961 he was appointed, with Haitink, co-conductor of the Amsterdam Concertgebouw Orchestra; Haitink became principal conductor in 1964, but Jochum remained a frequent guest conductor with the orchestra. He toured the USA and Japan with the orchestra in 1961, and was again in Japan in 1968. In 1975 the London Symphony Orchestra appointed him 'conductor laureate'. His many honours included election as president of the German section of the International Bruckner Society in 1950, the Würzburg Kulturpreis in 1967, and the Brahms and Bruckner Medals.

A tall, erect and unfailingly courteous man, Jochum, since childhood, found his musical background in the great Austro-German classics. His preferences were always for Bach, Haydn, Mozart, Beethoven, Schubert, Brahms, Bruckner, Wagner and Strauss, of whom he was recognised as one of the greatest living interpreters. As a conductor he could be identified with the romantic tradition represented most of all by Furtwängler, as opposed to the objective tradition whose greatest exponent was Toscanini. Jochum felt no compulsion to maintain exactly steady tempi, particularly in Brahms and Bruckner; in fact it was against his musical nature to do so. The search for the inner character, drama and spirituality of the music took precedence over a concern for literal accuracy in matters of tempo or historical authenticity. His own deep religious convictions were reflected in his interpretations of Bach and Bruckner in particular, which had a powerful intensity and emotional elevation equalled by very few other musicians. Bach and Wagner were his first decisive influences when he was a young man. Although he recorded no Bach until comparatively late in his life, he made sets for Philips of the *Mass in B Minor* and the *Christmas Oratorio* (with the Bavarian Radio Symphony Orchestra *et al.*) and the *St Matthew Passion* and the *St John Passion* (with the Concertgebouw Orchestra *et al.*). In performing Bach he gave virtually no attention to historical accuracy with regard to ornamentation in either the vocal or the instrumental writing, so that his interpretations never appealed to purists. But, for example, in the *St John Passion*, the Netherlands Radio Chorus under Jochum sang with such great feeling, conviction and drama that the performance has a very powerful impact, fully consistent with the text; it is an interesting contrast to Gillesberger's (on Telefunken), which seeks to reproduce the performing practices of Bach's time, but is completely without sentiment.

Jochum's performances and recordings of the Mozart symphonies revealed him as one of the very finest interpreters of this composer; the Symphonies Nos 35, 36, 38 and 39 with the Amsterdam Concertgebouw Orchestra, and the Symphony No. 41 with the Bavarian Radio Symphony Orchestra are superbly refined, and in the case of the Symphony No. 40, is an intensely moving reading with orchestral playing of great beauty. Jochum himself has confessed that Haydn came to him much later in life than Mozart; he recorded some of the symphonies with the Bavarian Radio Symphony and the Berlin Philharmonic Orchestras, and the Symphonies Nos 95 to 104 with the London Philharmonic Orchestra, but it is the discs of the Symphonies Nos 93, 94, 95 and 98 with the Dresden Staatskapelle, issued unfortunately only in East Germany, that take him to the heights in these works. He recorded the Beethoven symphonies three times over, with the Berlin Philharmonic, the Amsterdam Concertgebouw and the London Symphony Orchestras; at best his Beethoven is deeply felt and magnificently poised, but at less than best his idiosyncrasies have been described as mannered wilfulness. Again, he recorded the Brahms symphonies three times, the last two series being with the Berlin Philharmonic and the London Philharmonic Orchestras, and these performances always encountered criticism for the variations of tempi within movements. Similar reservations have been made about his Bruckner; while it is readily conceded that his performances profoundly penetrate the music's unique spiritual world, it does this at the expense of its architectural structure. Jochum said that from his earliest years he saw no problems with performing Bruckner, compared to Mozart and Beethoven, and the music came to him naturally. His changes in tempo within movements, which to others are so destructive of the music's continuity, were an integral part of his conception of the music and contributed to the intensity of the performances. He always conducted from the Novak editions, and believed that, as it is very difficult to discover Bruckner's final wishes in the various revisions of the symphonies, every conductor has to make his own decisions. He refused to conduct the Symphony No. 0, respecting Bruckner's wish that it not be heard. He first recorded Bruckner's Symphonies Nos 4 and 5 with the Hamburg Philharmonic Orchestra on 78s; later DGG recorded the nine symphonies with him conducting the Berlin Philharmonic and the Bavarian Radio Symphony Orchestras, and more recently EMI have issued the nine with the Dresden Staatskapelle. In addition to recordings of *Così fan tutte*, *Die Entführung aus dem Serail*, *Der Freischütz* and *Die Meistersinger*, and works by Schubert, Schumann, Weber, Sibelius, Mahler, Strauss *et al.*, Jochum was attracted to and performed recent composers such as Orff, Egk and Hartmann, and his recordings of *Carmina Burana*, *Catulli Carmina* and *Trionfi d'Aphrodite* were among the first of these works.

Joó, Árpád (b. 1948). The Hungarian conductor Joó started his musical studies at the Academy of Music in Budapest, went abroad to study further with Zecchi and Magaloff, at the Juilliard School in New York, and at the University of Indiana at Bloomington. He was conductor of the Knoxville Symphony Orchestra in Tennessee (from 1972), and since 1977 has been musical director of the Calgary Philharmonic Orchestra. He is also artistic director of Sefel Records, and with this company he has made a number of successful recordings, including Mahler's Symphony No. 1 (with the Amsterdam Philharmonic Orchestra) and Symphony No. 8 (with the Budapest Symphony Orchestra *et al.*), and Liszt's *The Legend of St Elisabeth* (with the Hungarian State Symphony Orchestra *et al.*).

K

KARAJAN, Herbert von (b. 1908). Karajan's family came to Austria from Macedonia; his great-grandfather was the director of the court library in Vienna, his grandfather a physician, and his father a doctor who was a clarinettist in the Mozarteum Orchestra in Salzburg, where Herbert was born. The 'von' in his name is inherited from his Viennese forebears. When he was 3 he started playing the piano, gave his first recital at 4, and toured as a pianist when he was 14. He studied at the Mozarteum under Paumgartner, who encouraged him to become a conductor; the final decision was taken when he heard Toscanini conduct in Vienna, where he was studying musicology at the University under Schalk. To give him the opportunity to conduct, his father hired the Salzburg Symphony Orchestra; afterwards Karajan substituted for another conductor at a concert in Ulm in 1927, and he was engaged as conductor there in 1928. He remained at Ulm for seven years, where his experience was comprehensive —coach and chorusmaster, as well as conductor. He held summer courses for conductors at Salzburg (1930–34), and in 1935 succeeded Busch as first conductor at Aachen, where he was later appointed music director, the youngest in Germany. In 1937, on Walter's invitation, he went to the Vienna State Opera to conduct *Tristan und Isolde*, but refused a permanent appointment there because of the unsatisfactory rehearsal conditions. In the following year he conducted the Berlin Philharmonic Orchestra in a concert, and astounded the orchestra by demanding string rehearsals for a programme made up of Mozart's Symphony No. 35, *Daphnis et Chloé* Suite No. 2 and Brahms's Symphony No. 4. After leading *Fidelio* at the Berlin State Opera in 1938, he was engaged as conductor (1938–44), and also reorganised the symphony concerts of the opera orchestra, the Berlin Staatskapelle. Before World War II he made guest appearances in Belgium, the Netherlands, Sweden, Denmark and Italy; he left Aachen finally to become music director of the Berlin State Opera, where he conducted until it was destroyed in an air raid, in 1944.

Karajan was a member of the Austrian Nazi Party from 1935; he later said that he was obliged to join the party to win the appointment at Aachen. He was the holder of an 'SD' card, which gave him many privileges, but he fell into disfavour with the party because of his second marriage to a woman of Jewish extraction. In Berlin, the Nazi leaders played him off against Furtwängler, an ironic situation for, along with Toscanini, Furtwängler was the conductor he admired most. At the end of World War II he was forbidden to conduct, and retired to Italy; in 1947 he was denazified and conducted at the Salzburg Festival in 1948. He conducted the Vienna Philharmonic Orchestra, but Furtwängler's position in Vienna prevented him from taking a permanent position with the orchestra. So he became conductor of the Vienna Symphony Orchestra, and elevated it to a standard rivalling the Vienna Philharmonic; he was also conductor of the Singverein of the Gesellschaft der Musikfreunde, and was appointed their artistic director for life in 1948; he presented an annual series of concerts and toured with the Society in Europe. His Nazi associations have lived on with him; in 1954 when he toured the United States with the Berlin Philharmonic Orchestra there were protests, but these were answered by declarations about his apolitical and exclusively musical outlook. Even now he is not welcome in Israel, and some major Jewish musicians refuse to play with him.

Karajan's emergence after the war was largely the responsibility of Walter Legge of EMI, who had heard him conduct at Aachen, and engaged him for a series of recordings with the Vienna Philharmonic Orchestra. In 1950 Legge appointed him the principal conductor of the Philharmonia Orchestra, which he had established primarily for recording purposes; Karajan remained with the orchestra until 1962, and with them made numerous recordings and toured the USA in 1956. In 1948–9 he conducted a season of German opera at La Scala, Milan, and in 1950 became the first German to be appointed a conductor and director there. He was artistic director of the Salzburg Festival from 1956 to 1960, in 1951 led *The Ring* and *Die Meistersinger* at Bayreuth, and in 1952 *Die Meistersinger* again; in 1954 he replaced Furtwängler, who had just died, as conductor of the Berlin Philharmonic Orchestra for its tour of the USA, and returned to the USA with the Vienna Philharmonic the next year. In 1954 he also toured Japan. His career reached its zenith when the Berlin Philharmonic named him its principal conductor in 1955; he accepted the position on condition that it would be a lifetime appointment. He has declined all other invitations to be principal conductor or music director of other orchestras, but from 1956 to 1964 he was the artistic director of the Vienna State Opera, and was for a season artistic adviser of l'Orchestre de Paris (1969–70). He toured the USSR with the Vienna

Philharmonic (1964) and with the Berlin Philharmonic (1969). In 1967 he established his own Salzburg Easter Festival, and in 1968 set up the Herbert von Karajan Musical Foundation. This organisation has amongst its projects examining ways of aiding sick people with music, a music school in Berlin where the section leaders of the orchestra are the professors, a biennial conductors' contest alternating with a youth orchestras' contest and research in conjunction with the University of Salzburg into the physical and psychological stress attendant on the profession of music. In 1977 he returned to conduct the Vienna State Opera for a festival of nine performances, and became artistic director of the Vienna Festival. He has been awarded the Grand Cross with Star and Epaulette of the Federal Republic of Germany.

Public attention in Europe has been attracted to Karajan almost as much for his glamorous life as for his conducting. His enthusiasm for skiing, sports cars, aeroplanes and yachts has brought him as much notice as is normally associated with film stars, and disputes and controversies have marked his career. The latest was a contretemps in 1984 with the Berlin Philharmonic when he insisted on engaging a female clarinettist, which led him to replace the orchestra with the Vienna Philharmonic at a performance at the Salzburg Easter Festival; all was eventually resolved, the clarinettist resigned, and both Karajan and the orchestra were brought to realise that they were mutually dependent. He has become the most commanding and highest paid conductor in Europe. His egomania has eclipsed that of all other conductors; Walter Legge said (in 1976): 'Previously he seemed anxious to absorb information from the people around him. Now he seems only to want praise.' Roger Vaughan, in his biography of Karajan, wrote: 'By the age of 73 [in 1981] his ego had become blinding, colossal. He doesn't argue, he doesn't discuss. He dictates. He has a particular approach to music making that he is certain is right. He would eat musical pretenders for breakfast.' However one reacts to him as a personality, there can be no doubt at all that he is a completely dedicated, utterly professional and exhaustively painstaking musician. Some would qualify this by adding that his progress to pre-eminence has been the result of a deliberate and ruthless opportunism, as much as of his own musical genius. While Beecham and Stokowski may have understood the value of gramophone records to promote themselves and their orchestras, Karajan's exploitation of recordings is so sophisticated that their attempts now appear infantile. At present he has contracts with the three major recording companies—DGG, EMI and Decca—and he decides himself what works he will record, and selects the dates, the soloists, the tapes and even the designs on the record covers. He is so successful that a third of the DGG discs sold in Britain are those of Karajan; altogether he had made some 800 recordings, whose total sales would be more than 100 million. With the Berlin Philharmonic itself the total is more than 300 records, and in 1971 alone he made 31 recordings.

Early in his career Karajan's entry into the auditorium was awe-inspiring. He would walk to the podium with an expression of acute, trancelike concentration; before the orchestra he would pause, motionless, almost interminably, before the first downbeat, and when conducting his eyes would close and his body would sway. These mannerisms have been much modified in later years. He has always conducted from memory, with some exceptions, such as Berg's *Lyric Suite*. When the tenor Jon Vickers asked him how he beat a particularly difficult passage in Act III of *Tristan und Isolde*, he immediately demonstrated his method, although he had not a score at hand nor had conducted the opera for eleven years. When he conducts he does not cue entries, and his beat does not indicate bar lines; while this presents no problem for the Berlin Philharmonic, players in other orchestras have narrowly avoided disaster. At rehearsals he uses few words (despite the constant chatter in the rehearsal record issued by DGG of the last movement of Beethoven's Symphony No. 9), he is never rude, works quickly, is completely prepared and gives scrupulous attention to all details. His patience is endless; when he first took over the Singverein of the Gesellschaft der Musikfreunde, he took the greatest pains to train the choir to sing with the tone required. For the preparation of Beethoven's Symphony No. 9 for a tour of the Berlin Philharmonic in 1970 he called for over 100 hours of rehearsals; preparation for the presentation of an opera at the Salzburg Easter Festivals begins three years before; a recording is made in 20 sessions before the opera is staged so that the cast has the opportunity to listen to themselves on tape for a whole year, and then there are another 50 rehearsals before the performance.

At first, Karajan's reputation was made with performances of Bach, Mozart, Beethoven, Brahms, Wagner, Tchaikovsky and Bruckner, but after World War II he added Verdi, Puccini, Bartók, Sibelius and others. More recently the second Viennese school and Mahler have been included in his repertoire. In 1975 a set of records in which he conducted music by Schoenberg, Berg and Webern was issued by DGG, whose advertisements for it included a statement by him that he had delayed recording the music until his orchestra was completely at one with the idiom. Even so, it would be difficult for anyone to claim that Karajan is a champion of unfamiliar composers or new music, and Henze is the only contemporary composer he performs. His repertoire is conservative and was for a long period forced to be so by the artistic strictures of the Nazi period. Generally he has followed musical taste rather than attempted to create or influence it, and has shown nothing of the enterprise of say Stokowski, Beecham or Koussevitzky. This is probably a reflection of the musical culture of which he is such a prominent ornament, and it is perhaps unreasonable to expect a conductor of his age to pioneer new music. His discovery of Mahler, on record and in the concert hall, was an event although he has pointed out that he was brought up on Mahler's music when he was studying in Vienna.

Much has been written about the Karajan 'sound', and his smooth, tensionless orchestral style. There can be no doubt that the Berlin Philharmonic had elements of this sound before he became its principal conductor. The magnificent and supple strings, the superb woodwinds, singly or blended as a group, the marvellous horns and brass, and the sumptuous basses—all these inspired just the same praise under Furtwängler as they do now under Karajan. He inherited a tradition, and enhanced it, but within five years of his coming to Berlin the orchestra was largely renewed because of retirements. His production of this sound is an inexplicable alchemy, like every other great conductor's special sound, but we can derive some clues from his own statements about his approach to music. He has discovered, he says, the importance of his pulse in relation to tempo: 'Different conductors have different pulse rates and their tempi are often mathematical proportions of this. Bach's music is nearly always the pulse of the heartbeat. Again, I know this from my long experience of yoga. I know what my heartbeat is: I feel it in every part of me. And if I fall into the pulse at the start of a piece of music it is a physical joy. In this way your whole body makes music.' Also, he explained that every musical masterpiece has one climax, and 'the end must feel as though it is the end'. Experience has taught him where to apply his concentration in the piece, at the decisive moment, in the climax; and it has also brought him to understand how to maintain one pulse through an entire work. With the heroic and tragic composers his performances are marvellous, but with others the style does not suit. Performances can appear calculated, pre-ordained and devoid of spontaneity. The very perfection of his orchestral sound brings about its interpretative weakness, for his special concern for the architecture of the piece, building it up towards the climax, gives the music its smooth surface, but mutes the sforzandos and minimises the dramatic effect of unexpected modulations or sharp changes in dynamics. Stravinsky objected to this style of performance being applied by Karajan to his *Le Sacre du printemps*; in his comments about Karajan's recording of the work he declared: 'I doubt if *The Rite* can be performed satisfactorily in terms of Herr von Karajan's traditions. . . . There are simply no regions for soul-searching in *The Rite of Spring*.' At the other end of the musical spectrum Karajan has equal difficulty in performing Haydn and Mozart, despite the excellence of some of the Mozart opera recordings; we hear superb orchestral performances but readings that are fundamentally superficial. Haydn's wit and muscle, Mozart's elegance and poignancy are often absent. It is not surprising that he has said that the most difficult movement for him in all Beethoven is the first of the Symphony No. 1; it is the closest to Haydn. Even so, it is absurd for some critics to refuse to review Karajan's records because his performances are contrived, apparently beyond tolerance. Karajan himself has taken this up, saying: 'So much nonsense is talked, particularly by some critics about "manipulating" the music. The verb is used detrimentally, and why should it be? The composer manipulates from the moment he picks up his pen. The concert hall manipulates because each seat is different. . . . And my manipulation as a conductor is that I try to bring out the sound that I want. That is my handwriting.'

Karajan has an operatic repertoire of more than 50 works. He has made many magnificent recordings of opera, yet they do not give an adequate impression of his great impact on opera performance, particularly at La Scala and Vienna. He first conducted Wagner at La Scala, but soon developed into a superb conductor of Italian opera, and in Vienna he produced as well as conducted Verdi and Puccini. Some contend that, for him, production is mainly a matter of lighting or darkening. He takes immense care in preparing operas; for *Die Walküre* in Vienna in 1957 there were 25 lighting rehearsals alone. When he was working with Vienna and La Scala simultaneously he developed a close liaison between the two houses, bringing the leading singers from La Scala to join his productions in Vienna, but this made him unpopular in Vienna, since the ensemble principle was always important there. He has, however, said that he left the Vienna Opera because of the lack of rehearsal time, and the deteriorating conditions there. More recently, he has declared that unless the great opera houses combine their resources and bring together the best available casts for particular shared productions, opera could be eclipsed, but his warning, and his offer, were not taken up. In 1965 he founded a company Cosmotel to produce opera films for television, starting with *La Bohème*, directed by Zeffirelli, and later including *Carmen* and *Otello*, which he directed himself. By assembling the finest casts for these films and conducting the Berlin Philharmonic, he believed that the public would not tolerate ensemble opera with its inevitably lower standards. But the enormous costs in producing filmed opera, particularly the last, *Otello*, brought the project to an end. Karajan also believes in the superiority of records over concert performances, as the sound is so much clearer, although, ironically, some commentators consider that his concert performances are much more exciting than his recordings of the same works.

Karajan's first record was the overture to *Die Zauberflöte*, made in 1938 with the Berlin State Opera Orchestra for Polydor. From 1939 to 1943 he made a number of recordings of symphonic works by Mozart, Beethoven, Dvořák, Brahms and Tchaikovsky, as well as other music, with the Berlin Philharmonic, the Amsterdam Concertgebouw and the EIAR Symphony Orchestras. While he was debarred from conducting in public before denazification, Walter Legge recorded him with the Vienna Philharmonic Orchestra, from 1946 to 1950, and these records were issued by Columbia on 78s, and some of the later ones on LP. They were the first discs to introduce him to the British and American public and included many distinguished performances such as Beethoven's Symphonies Nos 5, 8 and 9, Schubert's Symphony No. 9, Tchaikovsky's Symphony No. 6 and Brahms's *Ein deutsches Requiem*. The Beethoven symphonies in particular marked him as the successor to Weingartner. After he joined the Philharmonia Orchestra his association with EMI continued until the mid-1950s and resulted in a magnificent series of orchestral, choral and operatic discs, with a repertoire spanning from Bach to Bartók. Paramount were the Beethoven and Brahms symphonies, the operas *Ariadne auf Naxos*, *Così fan tutte*, *Die Fledermaus*, *Falstaff*, *Hänsel und Gretel*, *Il trovatore* and *Der Rosenkavalier*. To these should be added the recording of the 1951 Bayreuth *Die Meistersinger*. In 1959 and later he recorded for Decca with the Vienna Philharmonic Orchestra, and in 1959 he embarked on the great series with the Berlin Philharmonic Orchestra for DGG with Strauss's *Ein*

Heldenleben. A number of works were repeated a second (and some later a third) time, and he is now recording again his central repertoire for compact disc. EMI recorded him again from 1970, and he even recorded works he had already done with DGG. The scope of the music covered by these DGG and EMI discs is breathtaking in its comprehensiveness: among them are the *Brandenburg Concertos*, *Mass in B Minor*, *St Matthew Passion* and *Magnificat* of Bach, Haydn's Symphonies Nos 82 to 87 and 93 to 104 and *The Creation*, Mozart's Symphonies Nos 32, 35, 36 and 38 to 41, the complete symphonies of Beethoven, Schubert, Schumann, Mendelssohn, Brahms, Bruckner and Tchaikovsky, Mahler's Symphonies Nos 4, 5, 6 and 9, and *Das Lied von der Erde*, most of the tone poems of Richard Strauss, a survey of the works of Schoenberg, Berg and Webern, representative works of Ravel, Debussy, Shostakovich, Prokofiev, Stravinsky and many others, and a number of complete operas including *The Ring* and *Pelléas et Mélisande*. He also recorded with some other orchestras: *Die Meistersinger* with the Dresden Staatskapelle, some French music with l'Orchestre de Paris, and operas with the La Scala company. No conductor in the history of the gramophone record can approach him in the immensity and general standard of his recorded output, although there are certain parts of the repertoire where his style results in performances that are less than his best. But many discs are incomparable, particularly the Bruckner symphonies, and the Mahler and Tchaikovsky symphonies, to pick some other examples, are not far behind. As for the Beethoven symphonies, he has recorded them now four times, the first with the Philharmonia Orchestra and the last with the Berlin Philharmonic on compact disc; in the latter versions the performances have perhaps become too finely honed. Many of his early discs are being re-issued on cheap labels and his repertoire is quickly expanding on compact disc. Most music-lovers will never be able to hear Karajan in the concert hall or opera house, and these records do give a grand panorama of his art and achievement.

KEGEL, Herbert (b. 1920). Born in Dresden, Kegel studied at the school of the Saxon State Orchestra at Dresden (1935–40); he saw military service in World War II, when an injury to his hand forced him to abandon thoughts of a career as a concert pianist. He was a theatre conductor in Pirna and Rostock (1946–9), conductor (1953–8) and general music director (1958–60) of the Leipzig Radio Choir and conductor (1953–60) and chief conductor (1960–7) of the Leipzig Radio Symphony Orchestra. In

1977 he became chief conductor of the Dresden Philharmonic Orchestra, and from 1975 he has also been a professor at the Hochschule für Musik at Dresden. Now one of the major conductors in DR Germany, his repertoire includes the major composers of the 19th century, as well as music by Martinů, Hartmann, Dallapiccola, Nono, Lutosawski, Stravinsky, Bartók, Hindemith, Schoenberg, Webern, Janáček, Kodály, Orff, Shostakovich, Dessau, Penderecki, Henze and Britten, whose *War Requiem* he led at the International Bach Festival in Leipzig in 1966, and subsequently recorded. His other recordings include the sacred music of Mozart, which was widely circulated in the West on the Philips label, *Messiah*, *Carmen*, *Parsifal*, *Wozzeck*, Orff's *Der Mond*, Mahler's Symphony No. 4, and music by Britten, Hindemith, Hartmann, Penderecki *et al*. His performances of the nine Beethoven symphonies with the Dresden Philharmonic Orchestra have been issued on compact disc, and have been enthusiastically acclaimed for their balance and penetration.

KEMPE, Rudolf (1910–76). Born at Niederpoyritz, near Dresden, Kempe studied the piano as a child and later took lessons on the violin and oboe. He was educated at the Orchestra School of the Saxon State Orchestra at Dresden, and in 1929 joined the Dortmund Opera orchestra as first oboist, and very soon after was appointed first oboist with the Leipzig Gewandhaus Orchestra. A fellow member of the orchestra was Charles Munch, and in the orchestra he played under Furtwängler, Strauss, Beecham, Walter, Klemperer and Kleiber. In 1933 he became a répétiteur with the Leipzig Opera, and made his début as a conductor there with *Der Wildschütz* of Lortzing in 1935. He joined the German army in 1942, but within a year had returned to conducting, enjoying an unofficial permanent leave. From then until 1948 he was first conductor and then music director at the opera at Chemnitz (now Karl-Marx-Stadt), and also conducted at the Berlin State Opera and at orchestral concerts in Berlin, Leipzig and Dresden. After a year at the Weimar National Theatre (1948–9), he was engaged as the general music director at the Saxon State Theatre at Dresden, where he also conducted the Staatskapelle concerts (1949–52), and then was music director at the Bavarian State Opera at Munich (1952–4), also appearing as a guest conductor at other major opera houses in Europe and South America. At the Vienna State Opera he conducted Mozart, Verdi and Strauss in 1951–2, and came to London in 1953 to conduct Strauss operas with the Bavarian

State Opera Company. He was invited to Covent Garden to lead
Salome, conducted *The Ring* there in 1954 and 1956, and from
then on appeared in London frequently, but declined an offer to
become the music director at Covent Garden in 1956. His début
in the USA occurred in 1955 when he conducted *Arabella*,
Tannhäuser and *Tristan und Isolde* at the New York Metropolitan, and in that year directed Pfitzner's *Palestrina* at the Salzburg
Festival. Serious illness curtailed his activities in 1956 and later
in 1963–4. Beecham invited him to become the associate conductor of the Royal Philharmonic Orchestra in 1960, and after
Beecham's death in 1961 Kempe was first appointed chief
conductor of the orchestra, then artistic director in 1964, and
finally 'conductor for life' in 1970. Nonetheless he departed from
the orchestra in 1975 when he was engaged as chief conductor of
the BBC Symphony Orchestra, in succession to Boulez. Previously, in 1965, he had become chief conductor of the Zürich
Tonhalle Orchestra, and in 1966 general music director of the
Munich Philharmonic Orchestra. His first appearance at the
Bayreuth Festivals was in 1960, when he led *The Ring*; he also
conducted there in 1962, 1963, 1964 and 1967. He was married to
the operatic soprano Elisabeth Lindermeier.

Many orchestral musicians who played under Kempe regard
him as one of the greatest conductors of his generation, and to
them his premature death was an irreparable loss. In the earlier
stages of his career opera occupied most of his attention, but in
the last phase of his life his appearances in the concert hall were
more numerous. His experience as a conductor of opera was
vast; ironically the musical public tended to regard him as a
Wagner and Strauss specialist, but in Vienna he conducted the
Italian repertoire almost exclusively, and the opera he conducted the most times in his life was *Carmen*. He first conducted
The Ring in Barcelona in 1954, prior to his great success with the
tetralogy in London; he went to Barcelona to learn the score by
rehearsing a less-than-perfect orchestra. In opera his sympathies
extended from Mozart to Strauss, and included unfamiliar
German composers as well as Verdi, Puccini, Bizet, Offenbach
and Orff. In the concert hall he excelled in Mozart, Haydn,
Beethoven, Brahms, Bruckner, Tchaikovsky, Mahler and
Strauss; he conducted Schoenberg, Webern and Berg but had
little interest in avant-garde music. After he had performed a
very modern score he was asked what school it was, and he
replied with a chuckle, 'No school at all'. He had a remarkable
understanding of the music of Delius, which he conducted with
great insight at the Delius Festival at Bradford in 1962.

Kempe conducted most of his repertoire from memory; his technique was exemplary and his gestures and beat were models of clarity, with which he could convey to the orchestra how he wished to portray the music. At rehearsals he was relaxed, and his verbal comments were few and quietly spoken, although musicians found that he created a unique atmosphere which made them quite nervous. In performance, he was fiery and impassioned, but only for the music, and his players were then inspired to perform better than their best. He placed the second violins on the right. The music of Beethoven, Brahms, Bruckner, Strauss and Wagner was given a warm sonority, the interpretations were unmannered, unhurried, and the climaxes were paced carefully so that tension was built gradually. The music was articulated beautifully, and the drama revealed cumulatively. In the Wagner operas the music was in a continuous lyrical flow, far removed from the feverish excitement generated by fast, accurate playing. Critics were sometimes tempted to complain that he smoothed out the dramatic peaks; Harold Rosenthal, for instance, wrote about his 'chamber music' approach to *The Ring*. His warmth and sense of balance made his Brahms memorable, but just before he died he led an impetuous and fiery performance of the Symphony No. 4 with the BBC Symphony Orchestra in London. The scrupulous attention he gave to each instrumental line, as well as to the dramatic structure of the piece, made him one of the finest conductors of Richard Strauss, but in the highly charged music of Berlioz, Tchaikovsky and Rimsky-Korsakov, for instance, his restraint took away the last ounce of bravura.

For someone who was not keen on recording, Kempe has an exceptional list of records to his credit, of music ranging from Bach to Britten. His first recordings included opera sets made for Urania—*Der Rosenkavalier*, *Die Meistersinger*, *Der Freischütz* (with the Dresden Staatskapelle) and *Lohengrin* (with the Bavarian State Opera Orchestra). Then for EMI he made a number of extremely fine LPs in London, Vienna, Berlin, Dresden and Munich, the major works being the nine Beethoven symphonies (with the Munich Philharmonic Orchestra), the complete Strauss tone poems (with the Dresden Staatskapelle), Tchaikovsky's Symphony No. 6 (with the Philharmonia Orchestra), *Die Meistersinger*, the four Brahms symphonies and *Ein deutsches Requiem* (with the Berlin Philharmonic Orchestra) and *Lohengrin* (with the Vienna Philharmonic Orchestra). He also recorded with these and other orchestras numerous other works for other companies—symphonies, concertos, tone poems and overtures, the more noteworthy being Strauss's *Eine Alpensymphonie* (with the Royal Philharmonic Orchestra for RCA), Korngold's *Symphony in F Sharp* (with the Munich Philharmonic Orchestra for RCA), Janáček's *Glagolitic Mass* (with the Royal Philharmonic Orchestra for Decca), Bruckner's Symphonies Nos 4 and 5 and the four Brahms symphonies (with the Munich Philharmonic Orchestra for BASF/Acanta) and Bruckner's Symphony No. 8 (with the Zürich Tonhalle Orchestra for Tudor). His death at the age of 66, just after he had been appointed chief conductor of the BBC Symphony Orchestra, robbed the world of a great musician who was reaching the most productive period of his career. He was the natural successor to the great German conductors of a generation before him, and with whom he had come into contact early in his life. Fortunately he has left as his legacy many exceptionally fine records, through which his musicianship can be evaluated and appreciated: the Beethoven and Brahms symphonies, the Strauss tone poems, and the later opera sets, will be prized for many years to come.

KERTÉSZ, István (1929–73). Born in Budapest, Kertész studied the violin, composition and conducting at the Franz Liszt Academy, and graduated as a conductor. He was principal conductor of the Györ Philharmonic Orchestra (1953–5) and conductor at the Budapest Opera (1955–6), left Hungary after the uprising in 1956, studied conducting with Previtali at the Accademia di Santa Cecilia in Rome, and made appearances at the opera houses in Hamburg, Frankfurt-am-Main and West Berlin. He became general music director at Augsburg Opera (1958–63), conductor at the Salzburg Festival (1961–64), music director at the Cologne Opera (1964–73), principal conductor of the London Symphony Orchestra (1965–8) and conductor of the Gürzenich Orchestra of Cologne (1971–3). He was a frequent guest conductor with major symphony orchestras and in opera houses in Europe, North and South America, particularly with the Cleveland, Vienna Philharmonic and Israel Philharmonic Orchestras. His United States début had taken place with the Detroit Symphony Orchestra in 1961; he took part in many festivals in Europe, and led the London Symphony Orchestra on several international tours.

When Kertész was drowned while swimming in the Mediterranean at Tel-Aviv, at the age of 44, the world lost a most distinguished musician who was already reputed to be one of the finest conductors of his generation. His naturally warm personality was reflected in his music-making, which seemed spontaneously lyrical and heartfelt. His readings of Mozart, Schubert, Dvořák and Bruckner had this special distinction. His association with the London Symphony Orchestra was, at the end, marred by a conflict concerning the extent of his control over the orchestra's artistic policy, which is inevitably an uneasy matter for a conductor contracted to a self-governing orchestra. Nonetheless his London concerts, his tours with the orchestra and his records with the Vienna Philharmonic as well as the London Symphony, in addition to his guest appearances elsewhere, won him wide recognition. At rehearsals he was subdued and even offhand, but at concerts before the public he was transformed and the orchestra responded readily to his own delight in performing the music. He was not typically Hungarian, if one accepts that precision and dramatic tension are the qualities most characteristic of Hungarian conductors perhaps better known than Kertész; his performances were usually relaxed, sensitive and direct, and he drew beautiful playing from his orchestras. In the last decade of his life he recorded for Decca and made a number of discs, the most notable being the complete Dvořák symphonies with the London Symphony Orchestra, and the Brahms and Schubert symphonies with the Vienna Philharmonic Orchestra.

KITAENKO, Dmitri (b. 1940). Born in Leningrad, Kitaenko studied at the Leningrad and Moscow Conservatories and later with Swarowsky and Oesterreicher at the Vienna Academy of Music. He won second prize at Karajan's First International Conductors Competition in Berlin (1969), became chief conductor at the Stanislavsky and Nemirovich-Danchenko Musical Theatre in Moscow (1970), and artistic director and chief conductor of the Moscow Philharmonic Orchestra (1976). He collaborated with Felsenstein in a production of *Carmen* at the Berlin Komische Oper, and among the operas and ballets with which he has been associated in Moscow was a new production of Shostakovich's *Katerina Ismailova*. He has toured in Eastern and Western Europe and the USA; he has a broad range of musical sympathies, and his records for Melodiya include music by Mozart, Strauss, Wagner and Puccini, as well as Russian composers.

KLEIBER, Carlos (b. 1930). The son of Erich Kleiber, Carlos Kleiber was born in Berlin and left Germany with his parents in 1935 to live in South America. He began his musical studies in Buenos Aires in 1950 and first performed in public as a pianist at La Plata two years later. He returned to Europe with his family after World War II and studied chemistry at Zürich, which he soon abandoned for a musical career. His first experience was at the Gärtnerplatz Theatre in Munich (1953), and in the next year he made his début conducting an operetta at Potsdam. He became conductor at the Deutsche Oper am Rhein in Düsseldorf and Duisburg (1956–64), then was at the Zürich Opera (1964–6) and the Stuttgart State Opera (from 1966). He first appeared at the Bavarian State Opera in 1968 and at the Vienna State Opera in 1973, conducted *Tristan und Isolde* at Bayreuth and first conducted at Covent Garden with *Der Rosenkavalier* in 1974, and made his début in the USA with *Otello* at the San Francisco Opera in 1977. One of his earliest successes at Stuttgart was *Wozzeck*, of which his father conducted the première in Berlin in 1925. He centres his activities in Munich, but has no wish to accept a permanent appointment; in recent years he has rarely conducted outside Germany, he stipulates a high fee and an exceptional number of rehearsals, he abhors publicity, and gives the impression that he is reluctant to conduct at all. Despite all of this, he is one of the most sought-after conductors in Europe.

Like his father, Kleiber is a most scrupulous and fastidious musician, with an extraordinary intensity and dramatic sense which places his performances at the highest level. His repertoire is quite small, and in the opera house he rarely conducts anything other than *Otello*, *La traviata*, *La Bohème*, *Der Freischütz*, *Tristan und Isolde*, *Die Fledermaus*, *Carmen*, *Elektra*, *Der Rosenkavalier* and *Wozzeck*. But his knowledge and insight into these scores and their literary and cultural background is profound; in the words of Placido Domingo, who appeared under Kleiber at Covent Garden in *Otello*, 'he has assimilated the score to such a degree that he can read through the notes to uncover all the drama and the feeling of the music, everything the composer imagined. It seems so natural and simple: yet even with all the preparation it sounds spontaneous. We never repeat a performance. Every night is a different experience.' Like Furtwängler was, he is wary of recording, and for the same reason, knowing that every performance stands on its own and cannot be definitive, for himself or for the music. Also like many other great conductors, it is his eyes that keep the complete attention of his players. A Covent Garden instrumentalist summed him up: 'Beecham had the flair and charisma but not Kleiber's intellect; Kempe had the stick technique but not Kleiber's sensitivity. There are a lot of conductors who share some of Kleiber's qualities, but he himself has them all.' Similar remarks were made of Toscanini. However, Kleiber is unpredictable in temperament, and occasionally exhibits an almost childlike petulance which confounds the musicians working with him. When the Stuttgart State Opera took *Wozzeck* to the Edinburgh Festival, he cancelled the performance at the last moment, and at another time in Vienna he left without any explanation after a rehearsal before a scheduled concert of Beethoven symphonies.

Apart from those fortunate enough to be present at his operatic and concert performances, Kleiber is known to the worldwide musical public for his small number of superlative recordings. The first was *Der Freischütz* (with the Dresden Staatskapelle *et al.*) in 1973, and the second which was released in 1976, was of Beethoven's Symphony No. 5 (with the Vienna Philharmonic Orchestra). The latter was immediately acclaimed as a most remarkably intense and dramatic performance, even when compared to his father's outstanding recording of the work with the Amsterdam Concertgebouw Orchestra in 1957. His subsequent recordings, each extraordinary in its own way, have been Beethoven's Symphony No. 4 (with the Bavarian State Orchestra) and Symphony No. 7, Schubert's Symphonies Nos 3 and 8, and Brahms's Symphony No. 4 (with the Vienna Philharmonic Orchestra), Dvořák's Piano Concerto (with Richter and the Bavarian Radio Symphony Orchestra), *La traviata*, *Die Fledermaus* and *Tristan und Isolde*. Most of these have been issued by DGG on compact disc.

KLEIBER, **Erich** (1890–1956). Born in Vienna, Kleiber studied at the Prague Conservatory, and decided to be a conductor when he heard Mahler conducting his Symphony No. 6. He became a chorusmaster at the German Theatre at Prague, and made his début as a conductor in 1911 directing the stage music for a comedy. He was also then known as a fine accompanist, and started composing in his student years; his compositions later included violin and piano concertos, orchestral and chamber works. He was appointed third conductor at Darmstadt (1912–19), where the first opera he conducted was Offenbach's *La Belle Hélène*. His following appointments were first conductor at Barmen-Elberfeld (1919–21), at Düsseldorf (1921–2) and Mannheim (1922–3), and then in 1923 he became general music director at the Berlin State Opera. At Düsseldorf he had established a reputation with performances of *Pierrot Lunaire*, *Das Lied von der Erde* and the Verdi *Requiem*, at Mannheim with his première of Bittner's *Das Rosengärtlein*, and then in

Berlin, prior to his appointment, with a remarkable *Fidelio*. His years in Berlin (1923–34) constituted one of the most memorable epochs in German musical performance. He led great productions of Janáček's *Jenůfa* (1924), *Wozzeck* (1925) and Milhaud's *Christophe Colomb*, and also performed much modern music with the Berlin Philharmonic Orchestra—Busoni, Schoenberg, Strauss, Berg and Bartók—as well as Berlioz, Liszt and Reger, and a cycle of concerts of the unfamiliar music of Mozart. In 1925 he toured with the Vienna Philharmonic Orchestra, leading Mahler's Symphony No. 3 in Budapest, in 1926 visited Buenos Aires for the first time, and in 1927 conducted in the USSR. A close friend of Berg, he was determined to perform the Five Symphonic Pieces from *Lulu* in 1934, although he knew the Nazi régime's hostility to atonal music; like Fritz Busch, Kleiber was not a Jew, but would never tolerate interference by the Nazis with his selection of programmes. He resigned from his Berlin post in December 1934 and left Germany the next year.

Kleiber then conducted concerts and some opera in London, Prague, Brussels, Buenos Aires, Amsterdam, Salzburg and in Switzerland, and in 1939 took up residence in Buenos Aires and became an Argentinian citizen. He conducted opera at the Teatro Colón, and trained and led the symphony orchestra in Buenos Aires, also touring other countries in South America and conducting all manner of orchestras. From 1943 to 1948 he was with the Havana Philharmonic Orchestra, and in 1948 returned to Europe. In 1951 he accepted the position of conductor at the Berlin State Opera in East Berlin, but his dissatisfaction with conditions imposed on him brought his resignation in 1955. In his last years he was a guest conductor in London, Vienna and in other European musical centres, and was particularly active in Cologne and Stuttgart.

Kleiber was unquestionably a great conductor, especially with Mozart and Beethoven. He apparently had little interest in Bach or Brahms, and his enthusiasm for Mahler and Bruckner waned as he grew older. He was a warm exponent of the music of many modern composers, and loved the dances and waltzes of Mozart and Johann Strauss. An unremitting perfectionist, he sought to recreate music exactly as written by the composer; even the most familiar score was re-studied before rehearsal, and he demanded that his performers play or sing the notes exactly as they appeared. In his words: 'There are two enemies to good performance: one is routine and the other is improvisation.' His musicianship was however not simply a technical perfection of

execution; this was only the beginning. He said: 'When I conduct, I leave it to my heart, and my feelings, and my respect for
what the composer wrote, to tell me what to do. Everything else
comes second to me—if it comes at all!' He brought to his
interpretations a humanity, a vigour and a passion that made
them all unique.

In rehearsal Kleiber was careful to ensure that his musicians
understood the meaning of what they were playing, and his
explanations were short, witty and to the point. Once when
rehearsing the choir for Beethoven's Symphony No. 9, he asked
the singers to avoid sentimentality, saying it 'is like eating honey
with your fingers'. When preparing an opera, he saw to it that
each of the orchestral players had a libretto. After intense rehearsal for a concert, when he was satisfied that his musicians had
mastered the score, his direction of the orchestra changed, and
at the concert itself his movements were small and his demeanour
quiet. He never rehearsed more than necessary, but when he
was in Berlin he enjoyed five rehearsals for every concert.
Finally, on the day of the concert, no music was played; instead
he would read a long catalogue of errors committed at the
general rehearsal the previous day, adding that the composer
had drawn his attention to them. Before every rehearsal he
memorised the score as well as the numbered indications, and he
even took the trouble to learn the names and seating of the
orchestral players. At the concert itself he avoided signalling the
points of excitement or climax beforehand to the audience, and
impressed on his players not to do this in preparing their
instruments.

Kleiber's finest work for the gramophone came in the last
decade of his life when he was under contract to Decca. Then his
major undertakings were Mozart's Symphony No. 40 (with the
London Philharmonic Orchestra), Beethoven's Symphonies
Nos 3, 5, 6 and 7 (with the Amsterdam Concertgebouw Orchestra) and the No. 9 (with the Vienna Philharmonic Orchestra),
Tchaikovsky's Symphonies Nos 4 and 6 (with the Paris Conservatoire Orchestra), and *Der Rosenkavalier* and *Le nozze di
Figaro* (with the Vienna Philharmonic Orchestra and soloists of
the Vienna State Opera). These recordings of the Beethoven symphonies were one of the features of Decca's early LP catalogue;
with the possible exception of the *Pastoral* and the *Choral*,
the performances reached great heights, and demonstrated
his direct link with Weingartner in Beethoven interpretation.
Many have argued that his Symphony No. 5 was the greatest
recording ever made of that much-recorded work, maybe until

that of his son, Carlos Kleiber, was issued in 1975. Kleiber did the *Eroica* for the second time for Decca with the Vienna Philharmonic, but would not allow its release; the reason is not clear, but it has been suggested that an imperfect balance of the horns was responsible, although John Russell in his biography of Kleiber pointed out that he was never satisfied with his performances of the work, and that the music, particularly the *marcia funebre*, affected him profoundly. On one occasion he was found weeping in his room after conducting it. This Vienna Philharmonic performance is a marvellous one, and has now been released on compact disc; if comparisons have to be made, it stands with the Weingartner/Vienna Philharmonic, Klemperer/Philharmonia and the 1953 Toscanini/NBC Symphony performances as the greatest recordings of the symphony. Kleiber's meticulousness is illustrated in his recording of Beethoven's Symphony No. 7; in the last bar of the *allegretto* the strings continue to play pizzicato, whereas it is customarily played arco (i.e. with the bow, abandoning the previous marking pizzicato). When queried, Kleiber argued that from his examination of the score, it was his conviction that Beethoven meant this to be. Strauss and Klemperer also adopted the pizzicato ending. The *Rosenkavalier*, recorded in 1954, is a profoundly perceptive reading; in it Kleiber was concerned to maintain a balance between the singers and the orchestra, so that the conversational sections of the work would not be lost. *Le nozze di Figaro*—one of Kleiber's precious 'three Fs': *Fidelio*, *Figaro* and *Freischütz*—is a miracle of style and ensemble, and with Beecham's *Die Zauberflöte* and Karajan's *Così fan tutte* is one of the indispensable classics of recorded Mozart opera.

KLEMPERER, Otto (1885–1973). Born in Breslau which was then in Germany, with a father who was a businessman and a mother a professional piano teacher, Klemperer was taken with his family at the age of 4 to Hamburg, and after attending the Realgymnasium des Johanneum there, he studied at the Hoch Conservatory at Frankfurt-am-Main. In 1902 he became a student of piano and violin at the Klindworth-Scharwenka and Stern Conservatories in Berlin. When he was studying composition and conducting with Pftizner he decided he would be a conductor, and made his début in 1905 in Berlin with Max Reinhardt's production of *Orphée aux enfers*, which at that time he conducted at 50 performances. He nonetheless admired Offenbach for the rest of his life. Later that year he conducted the off-stage choir in Mahler's Symphony No. 2 at a performance under Fried and attended by Mahler. When he was on tour in Vienna accompanying a cellist, he visited Mahler and played the scherzo from the symphony from memory, having previously made a piano reduction of the entire score. Mahler gave him his visiting card with his recommendation written on it, which enabled him to obtain an appointment as choirmaster and conductor at the German Opera in Prague in 1907. During his three years in Prague he visited Munich and Vienna from time to time to assist at the rehearsals of Mahler's later symphonies.

Again with Mahler's help, Klemperer became a conductor at the Hamburg Opera (1910); there then followed a succession of appointments, at Barmen (1913), in Strasbourg (1914–16), Cologne (1916–24) and Wiesbaden (1924–7), and in those years he was a guest conductor in Barcelona (1920), Rome (1923), Moscow (1924), Leningrad (1925) and New York (1926). He continued to visit the USSR until 1936. In 1927 he was engaged as the director of the Kroll Opera in Berlin, which had just been established to present new operas and experimental productions of traditional operas. The Kroll was the third opera house in Berlin, where Kleiber was at the State Opera, Walter at the Charlottenburg Opera and Furtwängler with the Berlin Philharmonic Orchestra. Klemperer was at the Kroll until 1931 when political pressures and financial difficulties forced its closure. At the end of his life he said that this was the most satisfying period of his career, as conditions were ideal and the limitations of repertory opera were avoided. In the four years he staged *Oedipus Rex*, Schoenberg's *Die glückliche Hand* and *Erwartung*, Hindemith's *Cardillac* and *Neues von Tag*, and Janáček's *From the House of the Dead*, some for the first time, as well as the operas of Mozart, Beethoven, Wagner, Puccini, *et al.* in some experimental productions. He also conducted concerts with the Kroll orchestra, performing all Stravinsky's music. In fact Klemperer was then famous for his interest in performing contemporary music, and it was only in the last two decades of his life that he restricted himself to the repertoire from Bach to Bruckner, and became recognised as one of the foremost interpreters of Beethoven, Brahms and Bruckner.

In 1928 he visited London, returning the next year, to conduct at the Courtauld-Sargent concerts, where he gave what is thought to be the first performance in Britain of Bruckner's Symphony No. 8. After 1931 he conducted at the Berlin State Opera, but as he was a Jew, the Nazis dismissed him in 1933. (Actually, he had converted from Judaism to the Roman Catholic faith in 1919, but left the Church in 1967.) Ironically Hitler attended one of his last performances in Berlin, and Hindenburg had just presented him with the Goethe Medal for his 'outstanding contribution to German culture', when, soon after, a Berlin newspaper declared that 'his whole outlook ran counter to German thought and feeling'. He fled with his family to Austria and then to Switzerland, where he was offered the conductorship of the Los Angeles Philharmonic Orchestra. He remained in California from 1935 to 1939, conducted the New York Philharmonic-Symphony and Philadelphia Orchestras, and in 1937 organised the Pittsburgh Symphony Orchestra, although he refused to be its permanent conductor. At Los Angeles he knew Schoenberg, and performed the latter's transcription of Brahms's *Piano Quartet in G Minor* with the orchestra there. The manager of the orchestra said to him: 'I don't know why people say that Schoenberg has no melodies. That was very melodic.'

Grave physical and financial troubles followed. In 1939 he had an operation for a brain tumour which left him partly paralysed, and from then on he could not conduct with the baton. Engagements became scarcer. In 1940 he led the chamber orchestra of the New York School of Social Research in some Bach concerts, and for a short time he was conductor of the New York City Symphony Orchestra. He suffered from cyclothymia, and experienced an uncontrollable succession of euphoric and depressive states of mind; after an incident in a New York sanatorium the publicity it was given prejudiced his career further. To prove his complete sanity and competence, he hired an orchestra for a concert in Carnegie Hall, with a programme of his own transcription of a Bach trio sonata, *Eine kleine Nachtmusik*, Hindemith's *Nobilissima Visione* and Beethoven's Symphony No. 3. He made the violinists and violists stand throughout to maintain a proper tension. The concert was a success and engagements with orchestras throughout the USA resulted. He had become a US citizen in 1940, but altogether he was not satisfied with his experience in the USA, and later a controversy about his passport with the immigration authorities because of his prolonged periods overseas made him more unhappy. While he acknowledged the superb skill of the great American orchestras, he missed the warmth of the playing of those in Europe, and thought none could compare with the Vienna Philharmonic, for one.

Klemperer returned to Europe after World War II, conducted in Italy, Sweden, Switzerland and France, and made his first appearance in London in 1947. This was with the Philharmonia Orchestra, who were puzzled by his beat. The Budapest Opera engaged him as music director (1947–54), but when he was prevented from performing a work of Schoenberg there, he did not return to Budapest after a successful tour of Australia, during which he conducted Mahler's Symphony No. 2 four times in Sydney, to full houses. An accident at Montreal airport in 1951 forced him to conduct from a chair for several years. In 1954 he settled in Zürich, but most of his activities from then on were in London. Another accident, in 1958, when his hotel bedroom caught fire, stopped him from conducting *Tristan und Isolde* at the New York Met. His career came to a triumphant conclusion when he was appointed principal conductor of the Philharmonia Orchestra in 1959; in 1964 the orchestra's founder, Walter Legge, attempted to disband it, but the members re-constituted themselves as the New Philharmonia Orchestra. Klemperer was appointed president, and led them in their inaugural concert with Beethoven's Symphony No. 9 at the Royal Albert Hall. At Covent Garden he conducted *Fidelio* in 1961, *Die Zauberflöte* in 1962, and *Lohengrin* in 1963, and his Beethoven cycles in London were major events. He composed several symphonies, a violin concerto, five operas, choral and chamber music, and wrote several books of recollections; as a pianist he performed in chamber music ensembles in Berlin.

In contrast to the tribulations he experienced after his expulsion from Germany, Klemperer's final years saw him acclaimed as one of the greatest conductors of the century. In his own ironical words, 'I am the last of the classical school – when Bruno Walter died, I put my fees up.' Despite the immense success of his concerts in London and elsewhere, it was through the gramophone record that he became universally known, and Legge, who contracted him for EMI and who supervised his records with the Philharmonia Orchestra, must take the credit for ensuring Klemperer's full recognition as a great artist. Klemperer's extraordinary misfortunes gave him a heroic aura; in his early life he was a tall, overpowering figure, but to watch him in his last years being assisted to the chair at the podium, to lead a powerful performance of a Beethoven symphony with the most meagre gestures, was a moving sight. Wieland Wagner summed him up this way: 'Classical Greece, Jewish tradition, medieval Christendom, German romanticism and the realism of our time make Klemperer the conductor a unique artistic phenomenon.' As an interpreter of Beethoven, Brahms and Bruckner his performances had a rock-like inevitability that placed him in the same class as Toscanini, although their musical styles were poles apart. In one respect they were similar: both saw the score as their only authority, and the intense study of the score was the essential preparation for the performance of any music, no matter how familiar. But in contrast to Toscanini, whose tempi grew faster in later life, Klemperer's grew perceptibly slower. Exactly how and when this happened is an interesting point; recordings of performances he conducted in Budapest between 1947 and 1954 which have been recently released by Hungaroton show that his tempi were then brisk and his vitality unimpaired, but within just a few years he had assumed the slower tempi and the majestic pace of his final style with the Philharmonia recordings. Perhaps it was the accident in Montreal that was the cause. Some who watched him carefully have suggested that his tempi became slower simply because he could not beat faster, and that it was his crippling impairments that restricted his repertoire to music that he could direct with the simplest gestures.

Traditional approaches and extra-musical meanings meant nothing to him. Complete faithfulness was the beginning of any revelation about the meaning of the music. He came to every rehearsal with his mind completely made up about his interpretation, and how to resolve the music's problems, and with his commanding presence he never needed to raise his voice to the players. His gestures were severely economical from the beginning, but he conveyed his intentions very adequately with his eyes. With some orchestras unaccustomed to him, his sparse gestures were confusing, which led the players to follow the section leaders closely; some claim that this was the main reason for the high standard of playing achieved. His natural irascibility was sometimes exacerbated by his fluctuating psychological condition, and he was quite intolerant of musicians not prepared to accept unreservedly his direction or to devote themselves entirely to the cause of art.

Klemperer's performances of the repertoire from Bach to Strauss were characterised by deliberate tempi and a particular orchestral sound. He was at a loss to explain how he created this sound; like so many conductors it was so much a part of his musical personality that he probably could not recognise it himself. He could only say that he considered the upbeat very important, and that the conductor's hand should give the musicians the opportunity to play as though they were quite free. Klemperer was most concerned with clarity and balance. He sought a big sound, and gave special prominence to the woodwinds. Beauty of tone, for its own sake, never interested him. Tempi were steady, each note and pause given its exact value, and every phrase its precise measure. Second violins were placed on the right, as they are seldom in unison with the first violins, and so must be heard independently. Clear articulation of the strings was assisted by careful bowing and dynamic markings. Frequently his readings impressed with their enormous power and profundity, but this was certainly not always the case, as his slow tempi, at least in his final years, could render the music ponderous and devitalised. His performance of Beethoven's Symphony No. 9, for instance, impressed some as incredibly powerful, but to others it was simply laboured. His tempi in the Mozart operas certainly gave him the opportunity to reveal much detail, but the music was often devoid of charm or drama. His Haydn and Brahms were grave, but without sentiment; in Mahler he excused his disregard for lyrical beauty and feeling on the grounds that he was not a moralist. When he conducted in Vienna in the early 1930s, the members of the Vienna Philharmonic believed that he, not Furtwängler or Walter, was the greatest and most impressive conductor of Bruckner's symphonies. The greatness of his style is well illustrated in the recorded performance of Beethoven's Symphony No. 6 with the Philharmonia Orchestra: in the first movement, the tempo is absolutely firm and its unhurried steadiness gives the music breadth and calm. In the crescendi the clarity of the woodwinds and his careful dynamic control create an overwhelming impression. Yet, later, the scherzo is taken so slowly that the notes are separated and all vitality is lost. When he was questioned about his slow tempi, his answer was: 'You will get used to it!'

Klemperer's association with Mahler and Strauss in his early years did not make him an automatic advocate of all their music. He would not conduct Mahler's Symphonies Nos 1 and 6, but considered Symphonies Nos 8 and 9 the composer's greatest. He disliked all of Strauss after *Salome*, except *Metamorphosen*, even describing *Die Frau ohne Schatten* as an ugly and incomprehensible opera. He felt it necessary to make slight alterations to the scoring of the Beethoven and Schumann symphonies, but believed that these retouchings were only right for himself and should not be imitated by others. Of present-day conductors he especially admired Boulez, whose rehearsals and concerts he attended, approving of his Haydn and Mozart as much as his Debussy and modern repertoire. He had a sardonic sense of humour. In 1954, after Krauss and Furtwängler had died, he commented 'Ah, it has been a good year for conductors.' Once he refused to conduct the *Enigma Variations* in the Royal Festival hall, declaring that the acoustics of the building did not suit that kind of music. When he was recording *Der fliegende Holländer*, one of the singers was dissatisfied with his perform- ance and asked: 'Please may I sing again?' Klemperer growled: 'Why? It might get worse.' The singer answered: 'Ah, but it might go better,' to be crushed with 'We can't wait that long'.

Klemperer's first recordings were made for Polydor in 1924–5 by the acoustic process, and were of Beethoven's Symphonies Nos 1 and 8 and the adagio of Bruckner's Symphony No. 8. These were with the Berlin State Opera Orchestra, with whom he also recorded other major works of Mozart, Schubert, Brahms, Debussy, Strauss *et al.* before his departure from Germany in 1933. It was not until 1947 that he recorded again, this time in Vienna with the Vienna Symphony and Pro Musica Orchestras for Vox. These early LP discs included Beethoven's Symphonies Nos 5 and 6 and *Missa Solemnis*, Mendelssohn's Symphonies Nos 3 and 4, Bruckner's Symphony No. 4 and *Das Lied von der Erde*, which all drew dramatic attention to his status as an interpreter of these composers. The performances were arresting for their commitment and utter sense of com- mand. He signed a contract with EMI in 1952 but was forced to cancel it because his American citizenship and membership of the American Musicians' Union prevented him from recording in Europe. He therefore gave up his American passport, signed the contract again, took up residence in Zürich, and commenced a vast recording programme which only concluded with his death. He is one conductor who is adequately, if not exhaus- tively, represented by his records, and this series for EMI with the Philharmonia (and New Philharmonia) Orchestra is largely responsible for his pre-eminent reputation. The discography encompasses the complete symphonies of Beethoven, Brahms and Schumann, Bruckner's Symphonies Nos 4, 5, 6, 7, 8 and 9, Mahler's Symphonies Nos 2, 4, 7 and 9 and *Das Lied von der Erde*, the Beethoven Piano Concertos (with Barenboim) and Violin Concerto (with Menuhin), Brahms's *Ein deutsches Requiem* and Violin Concerto (with Oistrakh), *Messiah*, *Missa Solemnis*, the Bach suites and *Brandenburg Concertos*, *St Matthew Passion* and *Mass in B Minor*, many symphonies of Haydn, Mozart, Schubert, Mendelssohn, Tchaikovsky *et al.*, numerous overtures and other orchestral works and operatic excerpts, and the operas *Die Zauberflöte*, *Don Giovanni*, *Le nozze di Figaro*, *Così fan tutte*, *Fidelio*, *Der fliegende Holländer*

and Act I of *Die Walküre*, and his own Symphony No. 2 and
Merry Waltz. The only relatively modern music he recorded for
EMI was Stravinsky's *Pulcinella* and *Symphony in Three Movements*, Hindemith's *Nobilissima Visone* and Weill's *Die kleine
Dreigroschenmusik*. To name the greatest of all his recordings
would be virtually impossible, as his interpretations, like Furtwängler's and Toscanini's, do not command universal admiration. Today, with the reissue of some of the Philharmonia
performances on compact disc, his style and interpretative
outlook are being reappraised. For instance, many have claimed
that his Beethoven *Eroica* (the first on mono, with the old
Philharmonia Orchestra, rather than the stereo re-make) may
be his greatest record, but others deprecate it. His *Fidelio* was
described by Harold Rosenthal as 'one of the greatest operatic
recordings of the post-war period'; probably there are few
dissenters from that judgement. His other recordings with
claims to greatness are the *St Matthew Passion* and Mahler's
Symphony No. 2, but it is not going too far to say that in almost
all his performances there are elements of greatness which
transcend the confines of his style.

KNAPPERTSBUSCH, Hans (1888–1965). Born in Elberfeld, Germany,
Knappertsbusch conducted school orchestras as a boy, proceeded to Bonn University to study philosophy, then to the
Cologne Conservatory to study under Steinbach and Lohse
(1909–12). His début as a conductor was at Mühlheim in 1911,
and in 1912 he conducted at a Wagner festival in Holland. His
first appointment was at Bochum, from where he went to
Elberfeld (1913–18), Leipzig (1918), Dessau (1919–22), and
finally was engaged with a life-long contract at the Bavarian
State Opera at Munich in 1922, succeeding Walter. Here he became renowned for his performances of the operas of Wagner,
Strauss and Mozart. His unhesitating hostility to the Nazis, and
his refusal to join the Nazi party, finally led to his enforced
retirement in 1936, on Hitler's personal direction. He moved to
Vienna where he conducted at the Vienna State Opera and at
concerts of the Vienna Philharmonic Orchestra, but was obliged
to abandon these activities when the Nazis annexed Austria. He
gave guest appearances in some non-Fascist countries in
Europe; previously in 1936 he had been invited by Beecham to
conduct at Covent Garden but his permit to leave Germany was
withheld. He did however appear in London to conduct *Salome*.
After the war he re-emerged and soon established himself with
his interpretations of Beethoven, Brahms, Wagner, Bruckner

and Strauss. His *Parsifal* at Bayreuth in 1951 has become legendary; he continued at Bayreuth although he held the postwar productions in disdain. In 1954 he resumed his directorship at the Munich Opera, but absented himself for an entire year in protest at the delay in rebuilding the National Theatre there. He also made guest appearances to conduct Wagner at Milan and Paris.

Knappertsbusch was a superb conductor whose true genius was revealed in the theatre. His very presence in the pit was sufficient for the atmosphere to become electric with expectation. He was revered by audiences and players alike. Zubin Mehta, who observed him in his student years in Vienna, once remarked that Knappertsbusch put a great amount of tension in music: 'He could play the Brahms *Third Symphony* at half the tempo and you'd still not be bored, because it would make musical sense. He was a great technician and a phenomenal conductor of Wagner operas.' He disliked rehearsing and could never appreciate the need for accuracy when making a record. Culshaw (in *Ring Resounding*) told the story that when Knappertsbusch was recording a Strauss waltz, as usual without rehearsal, at one of the many repeats half the orchestra went on while the other half went back. The resulting chaos lasted only four bars, after which the piece was back on the rails. At the end he called out to Culshaw, 'Can you use that? We don't need to do it again, do we?' Culshaw told him what had happened. He said: '*Scheisse* – do you think anyone else will know?' It is easy to understand that he could not adapt himself to the discipline of the recording studio, where the spontaneity of his interpretations could not flourish. Few of his studio recordings were not wholly successful, but his finest recording was his 1951 Bayreuth performance of *Parsifal*, taped by Decca engineers during rehearsals and the actual performances. On Rosenthal's authority the performance was generally considered the finest of this century, and this great recording is a superb testimony; it captures the magical performance, and has remained one of the best recordings of Wagner opera ever made. Two later *Parsifals*, issued by Philips from Knappertsbusch's 1962 and 1963 Bayreuth performances, have much better sound but did not quite equal the earlier one. Because of his incompatibility with the recording process, he was passed over in favour of Solti for the Decca *Tristan und Isolde* of 1961. Before World War II he had made a number of 78s with the Berlin orchestras for Polydor, HMV and other labels, including Beethoven's Symphonies Nos 3 and 7, and after the war he recorded mostly for Decca, the first important enterprise being the complete *Die Meistersinger* with the Vienna Philharmonic Orchestra *et al.*, which was originally issued act by act, with the Act II among the first LPs issued by Decca. Among his other LPs were Bruckner's Symphonies Nos 3, 4, 5 and 7 (with the Vienna Philharmonic Orchestra for Decca) and No. 8 (with the Munich Philharmonic Orchestra for Westminster), but these also failed to reproduce the magic of the live performance in the recording studio.

KONDRASHIN, Kyril (1914–81). Born in Moscow where both his parents were string players in Koussevitzky's orchestra, and later in the Bolshoi Theatre orchestra, Kondrashin learned the piano as a boy, and when he was still a teenager conducted at the Moscow Children's Theatre in 1931. He studied at the Moscow Conservatory under Khaikin (1931–6), and was an assistant conductor at the Nemirovich–Danchenko Musical Theatre (1934–7), where the first opera he conducted was *Madama Butterfly*. He became conductor of the Maly Theatre in Leningrad (1938–42), and permanent conductor of the Bolshoi Theatre in Moscow (1943–56); he last conducted opera in Chicago in 1958, and then turned his attention to symphonic music. He was conductor of the USSR State Symphony Orchestra (1956–60), then musical director and principal conductor of the Moscow Philharmonic Orchestra (1960–76) and professor at the Moscow Conservatory (1977–8). He toured Europe and the USA, and was guest conductor of the Amsterdam Concertgebouw Orchestra (1975–8); it was his guest appearances with the American pianist Van Cliburn after the latter had won the Tchaikovsky Prize in 1958 that made him an international celebrity. He was awarded two Stalin Prizes (1948 and 1949) and the State Prize of the Russian Soviet Federative Socialist Republic (1969), and was named People's Artist of the USSR (1972). Nonetheless, he felt himself inhibited by the restrictions placed upon artists in the Soviet Union, this impression being confirmed by his visits to the West. He became more interested in performing music by composers such as Britten, Bruckner, Mahler and Rachmaninov, who were not in favour in the USSR, but as this expansion of the musical repertoire was officially disapproved he voluntarily limited his appearances with the Moscow Philharmonic Orchestra. Finally, in 1978 during a tour in the West he sought political asylum in Amsterdam, where he then lived.

Kondrashin saw himself in the same tradition as the great conductors of the past, who strove to produce their own unique sound and style with their orchestras. He wrote several books on conducting, which have yet to be translated into English. His records include the Shostakovich symphonies, which are brilliantly performed, with immense panache and commitment; his other records of Russian music have been equally interesting, but other discs he made in the Soviet Union of symphonies of Beethoven, Brahms and Mahler give a fascinating impression of how the masterpieces of Western musical literature are heard by Russian audiences, although they differ markedly in character from, say, the performances of Svetlanov. Some tempi, the balance and texture of the orchestral sound, the phrasing of many passages, and an acute dynamic control, amounting almost to a mannerism, were the most distinctive characteristics of his interpretations. Philips have issued some discs of him conducting the Amsterdam Concertgebouw Orchestra which are excellent examples of his style; Sibelius's Symphony No. 5, one of the performances, is a startlingly brisk reading. After his defection Kondrashin had fears that Western musicians might find him too authoritarian. Russian musicians see in musical performance the only outlet to express their personalities, which suffers under the official suppression of Soviet society, and so he believed that this made them difficult to lead. But he found in the West that musicians preferred the guidance of a strong personality, and that they responded to him more attentively than did his compatriots in the USSR.

KOŠLER, Zdeněk (b. 1928). Born in Prague where his father was a violist in the National Theatre Orchestra, Košler was a member of the Kühn Children's Choir. He studied piano, composition and conducting, started his career as a coach with the Czech Choir (1945–8), and then studied conducting at the Prague Academy of Music (1948–51), Ančerl being one of his teachers. At the same time he was a répétiteur at the Prague National Theatre (1948–51), and became a conductor there (1951–8). In 1956 he won first prize at the young conductors' competition at Besançon; he was artistic director of the Olomouc Opera (1958–62), chief conductor at the Ostrava Opera (1962–4), again won first prize and the gold medal at the Dmitri Mitropoulos International Conductors' Competition in New York (1963), was assistant conductor to Bernstein with the New York Philharmonic Orchestra (1963–4), was first conductor of the Prague Symphony Orchestra (1964–6), chief conductor at the Berlin Komische Oper (1967–8), permanent conductor of the Czech Philharmonic Orchestra, chief conductor of the Slovak National Theatre at Bratislava (1971–6), and chief conductor at the Prague National Theatre (from 1980). Since 1968 he has visited Japan every year to conduct Japanese orchestras and to teach at the Geijutsu Daigaku University in Tokyo. Although he is little known in the West, he is recognised as one of the most outstanding of the younger Czech conductors. Košler has recorded extensively for Supraphon and Opus, the record company based in Bratislava; most of his discs have been of Czech composers such as Smetana, Martinů, Novak, Foerster, Janáček and Dvořák, whose nine symphonies and symphonic poems he recorded with the Slovak Philharmonic Orchestra.

KOUSSEVITZKY, Serge (1874–1951). Koussevitzky's birthplace was at Tver near Moscow, and almost from childhood he was convinced that he should be a conductor. He won a scholarship to the conservatory of the Moscow Philharmonic Society, but only on condition that he should study the double bass, as there was a vacancy for that instrument in the institute's orchestra. It took him five months to complete the course for the instrument, instead of the prescribed five years. While playing in the orchestra of the Imperial Theatre he also won fame in Russia and abroad as a solo performer on the double bass; he attracted the attention of Nikisch and played one of the Saint-Saëns cello concertos on the double bass at a concert at Leipzig. Later, some records were issued of his double-bass performances, and he also wrote several pieces for the instrument, including a concerto which he composed with Glière's assistance. At the same time as he was giving double-bass recitals in London and Paris, he was studying conducting at the Hochschule für Musik in Berlin, and there observed Nikisch conducting. He himself first conducted in Berlin (1907) and London (1908), and in the years following 1910 he toured Russia with his own orchestra, hiring a boat specially to take him down the Volga River. The story is that when he married the heiress of a Russian tea millionaire, Natalie Oushkoff, he asked for an 85-man symphony orchestra as a wedding present, and it was with this orchestra that he made these legendary tours. With his wife he also founded a music-publishing house in Moscow, Editions Russes de Musique, and actively promoted the new music of Stravinsky, Scriabin and Prokofiev.

The Russian Revolution was a watershed in his life. He lost his wealth and property, but was offered the directorship of the State Symphony Orchestra and of the Grand Opera in Moscow. The new régime, however, had no appeal for him, and in 1920 he and his wife left the country. At first he toured with his double bass, and conducted some concerts in London. In 1921 he settled in Paris, assembled a Russian orchestra and established the Concerts Koussevitzky, which became famous for their programmes of new music. His great opportunity came in 1924 when he was invited to become conductor of the Boston Symphony Orchestra; he was then aged 50, and he remained with the orchestra for 25 years. He elevated it to such a degree of splendour that it was regarded as the finest in the USA, if not in the world. Until 1939 Paris remained his true home, whither he returned each year after the season in the USA; in fact he only slowly assimilated with the American community, and it was only after the outbreak of World War II, when his annual return to Paris became impossible, that he became an American citizen.

His appointment with the Boston Symphony had a hazardous start, since, although he was intuitively a great interpreter, he had an uncertain technique. The orchestra took almost two years to accustom itself to the vagaries of his beat and to his highly personal way of rehearsing. Eventually the players learned to play together by listening carefully to each other and by following their section leaders, and so they developed an excellent ensemble almost in spite of the conductor. His relations with the orchestra were worsened by a number of dismissals and replacements. He kept his orchestra to himself and himself to the orchestra, except for his annual tours to Europe, rarely made guest appearances with other American orchestras, hardly ever conducted opera, and the only guest conductors he would permit with the Boston Symphony were from Europe. Because the Boston Symphony was a non-union orchestra he could rehearse them exhaustively and he allowed no one to be present at rehearsals. Few soloists were engaged for his concerts; the fact was that he was a poor accompanist. The outcome was that he took over a good orchestra and made it a great one. Stories that he could scarcely read a score were nonsense, and arose from his practice of learning scores with a pianist (Jesus Maria Sanroma) play the music as he wished it phrased, while he made the motions of conducting the work with the score.

Koussevitzky was a commanding figure in his day, and his quarter of a century with the Boston Symphony saw one of the most illustrious partnerships in the history of orchestral music. His records were some of the most prized in the 78 r.p.m. catalogue, and one would give a hundred of the present LPs of his successors to have a digital recording of his *Daphnis et Chloé* or *Till Eulenspiegel*. He was one of the great *romantic* conductors, in both his approach to interpretation and in the music which he naturally performed best. He created a glowing orchestral colour that stressed the music's dramatic and lyrical qualities. Ernest Newman once wrote that it was hardly possible for a conductor to raise some works to a higher pitch of nervous incandescence than Koussevitzky did, but the nervousness never got out of hand. 'It is Koussevitzky's servant, not master. The excitement is always perfectly under control; one great plastic line runs through and through the work.' He trained his orchestra to produce the sonorities and expressive nuances of romantic music with extraordinary effect, but when he turned to music of the classical and baroque periods he was much less equipped to match the style. Rhythms tended to become rigid, and string tone not instinctively flexible; expressiveness could not come, as in romantic music, from the orchestral colour or the intensity of the melodic line but had to emerge from the balance and structure of the movement, as much as from phrasing and nuance. This did not mean that all his performances of Bach, Haydn and Mozart were unsuccessful, but his recordings of the Beethoven symphonies would come under fire today because of their idiosyncrasies and tempi variations, a considerable contrast to his contemporary, Toscanini, and to the great conductors that followed him, such as Karajan, Klemperer and Szell.

Lasting fame for Koussevitzky and the Boston Symphony, at least for the world at large, came from their recorded performances of many works by a handful of composers—Berlioz, Debussy, Ravel, Tchaikovsky, Prokofiev, Sibelius and Strauss —which were of an incredibly high standard. He thought that some of his readings of these composers were as good as they could possibly be, and although this is an overstatement, his *Daphnis et Chloé* Suite No. 2, *Till Eulenspiegel*, Prokofiev's *Classical Symphony*, and *Tapiola* come close to it. His Sibelius recordings were as significant as any in widening the popularity of the composer; the recordings of some of the Strauss tone poems were shattering in their day. Russian music was his speciality; he gave the first performance of the Ravel orchestration of *Pictures at an Exhibition* in 1923, and recorded it in 1931. The prelude to Act I of *Khovanshchina*, played at a very slow tempo, was remarkably beautiful; a contrast was the *Classical Symphony*, which was taken at an extremely fast tempo, and has not been surpassed for its wit and sparkle. The first recording the Boston Symphony made with him, in 1928, was *Petrushka*, and while his concert performances of *Le Sacre du printemps* were much admired, he never recorded the work. Maybe the most famous of his Russian recordings were the last three Tchaikovsky symphonies, the *Romeo and Juliet* fantasie-overture, and *Francesca da Rimini*, which exhibited his exceptional dramatic power and the orchestra's superb playing. Debussy and Ravel were also particularly suited to the orchestra's magnificent tonal qualities; his recording of *La Mer* was celebrated, but many of its interpretative ideas raise eyebrows today, and the opening is slower than in most performances. His best recordings of American music were *El Salón México* and *Appalachian Spring* of Copland, and Roy Harris's Symphony No. 3. Two major works that have scarcely been eclipsed since were Berlioz's *Harold in Italy* (with Primrose) and Liszt's *Mephisto Waltz*; *Harold in Italy* displayed all the virtues of both conductor and orchestra—rock-like firmness and an inevitability about the performance, which was powerful and expressive. Curiously, Koussevitzky was less certain with Wagner, and recorded very little of the composer; on the other hand, his Brahms Symphony No. 3 was an exemplary performance. Some of his performances are now available on historical re-issues, regrettably not yet on compact disc.

KRIPS, Josef (1902–74). Born in Vienna and son of a doctor, Krips sang as a boy in the choir of the Carmelite Church in Vienna, studied at the Vienna Academy of Music, and with Weingartner and Mandyczewski. He was first violinist at the Volksoper (1918–21), and was engaged by Weingartner in 1921 as coach and choirmaster there. That year he made his début as a conductor in *Un ballo in maschera*, substituting at short notice and conducting the opera without a score. He also conducted his first symphony concert at the Redoutensaal in Vienna in 1921. He became chief conductor at Aussig an der Elbe (1924–5), conductor at the Dortmund Municipal Theatre (1925–6) and general music director at Karlsruhe, conducting both opera and concerts (1926–33). There he led a Bruckner festival in 1929 and a Handel festival in 1930, and appeared in other European cities. He left Karlsruhe and was appointed permanent conductor at the Vienna State Opera (1933–8), first conductor at Salzburg in 1935, and was made professor at the Vienna Academy of Music (1935–8). After the annexation of Austria by Germany in 1938 he was dismissed from these positions as his grandparents were Jewish, although Krips himself was a Catholic. He conducted concerts and opera at Belgrade (1938–9), but was forced to leave because of German influence there. During World War II formal musical activities were denied to him, but he managed

to work as a clandestine opera coach while working as a store-
keeper in a food-processing factory.

After World War II the Soviet occupation authorities immediately gave Krips the responsibility of reconstructing musical activities in Vienna, and he proceeded to re-establish the
Staatsoper virtually singlehanded. He conducted *Fidelio* two
weeks after the war in Europe ended, and in May 1945 the
Staatsoper opened at the Volksoper building with *Le nozze di
Figaro*. From 1945 to 1950 he was at the Staatsoper, conducted
the Vienna Symphony Orchestra, was chief conductor of the
Hofmusikkapelle, and took part in the Salzburg Festivals. Between 1947 and 1950 he toured with the Vienna Staatsoper and
the Vienna Philharmonic Orchestra in France, Belgium, England, Switzerland and Italy; their performances of *Le nozze di
Figaro*, *Don Giovanni* and *Così fan tutte* at Covent Garden in
1947 made an indelible impression. In 1950 he was invited to
conduct the Chicago Symphony Orchestra, but when he arrived
in New York, he was refused admittance by the immigration
authorities, presumably because he had conducted in Soviet
Russia in 1947. He was principal conductor of the London
Symphony Orchestra (1950–4), and contributed to making it
the great orchestra it is today. He eventually made his début in
the USA with the Buffalo Philharmonic Orchestra in 1953,
which led to his appointment as conductor of the orchestra
(1954–63). He also conducted the Montreal Symphony Orchestra, toured Australia, Mexico, *et al.*, appeared at the New York
Metropolitan Opera, returned to Covent Garden, led the New
York Philharmonic Orchestra for ten weeks in 1964–5, which
included a cycle of the Bruckner symphonies, conducted
Beethoven cycles in London, Vienna and New York, and was
conductor of the San Francisco Symphony Orchestra (1963–70).
In 1955 he was awarded the medal of the Bruckner Society, and
in 1962 the Ehrenring of the City of Vienna.

Although nurtured on the Viennese classics, Krips had a
broad repertoire. At Karlsruhe he conducted German, French
and Italian operas; he was a celebrated conductor of Haydn,
Mozart, Beethoven, Schubert, Brahms, Bruckner, Mahler,
Johann and Richard Strauss, yet he was also impressive with
Bartók, Hindemith and Stravinsky, and gave local first performances of much new music, including major works by Janáček,
Britten, Blacher and Shostakovich. In his own words, 'I conduct
everything. And everything I try to do as if it were by Mozart.' A
veneration for Mozart was the cornerstone of his musical life,
and he advised students wishing to become opera conductors to

start by studying the Mozart operas: 'Every opera is by Mozart; even Wagner, even Richard Strauss, has to sound clear, transparent and spirited, or we have a bad performance.' He once said that Mozart's Symphony No. 40 was one of the most difficult pieces ever written, and that he spent 25 years studying it before he was prepared to conduct it. 'Mozart is, of all composers, the most difficult to conduct. And I can tell you why: two bars and you are suddenly transported to heaven. It is very hard to keep your bearings when you are there.' Like Mahler, he had a high opinion of *Carmen*; he considered it one of the most sophisticated scores in the literature, and thought it essential to stick meticulously to Bizet's instructions. Although he had conducted it scores of times and heard many other performances, he said that he had never heard a real *Carmen*, because nobody could realise the dynamic shadings and nuances.

Having experienced this preparation himself, Krips believed that an opera conductor should play the piano, should have studied the voice, should have a period as a coach, and should know the languages of the operas he conducts. He warned that young conductors should be patient and not accept assignments for which they are not ready. In the opera house he personally took charge, from the first piano rehearsals to the first night. In conducting the orchestra, he sought to make the instruments sing or breathe, and this lyricism typified all his music-making. While he maintained a firm discipline over the orchestra, he was a genial, cheerful leader, exuding enthusiasm and enjoyment in his task. This was admirably demonstrated when he conducted *Till Eulenspiegel*, when his animation and gestures reflected the fun and mock-tragedy of the story. He cautioned that good conductors take many years to mature: 'Only after 25 years can a conductor teach an orchestra. For the first 25 years a conductor learns from an orchestra.' Krips's seemingly inborn feeling for Mozart and the great Viennese and German symphonic classics was imbued with warmth and lyricism, but a lack of tension sometimes affected the dramatic quality of the music and made it sound facile and lightweight. His *Don Giovanni*, for instance, was perfectly proportioned and phrased, but in the process the dramatic urgency, the demon, was lost.

Krips came to London after World War II and recorded for EMI and Decca on 78s. Apart from overtures and accompaniments to instrumentalists and singers, the major works were Schubert's Symphony No. 6 and Brahms's Symphony No. 4 (with the London Symphony Orchestra). His mono LPs for Decca included symphonies by Haydn, Mozart, Schubert and

Mendelssohn, and an excellent coupling of Schumann's Symphonies Nos 1 and 4 (again with the London Symphony Orchestra), Brahms's Symphony No. 1 and Tchaikovsky's Symphony No. 5 (with the Vienna Philharmonic Orchestra), Mozart's *Requiem* (with the Vienna Hofmusikkapelle *et al.*), Beethoven's Symphony No. 4 and Schubert's Symphony No. 9 (with the Amsterdam Concertgebouw Orchestra), *Elijah*, *Don Giovanni* and the first of his two recordings of *Die Entführung aus dem Serail*, the second being for EMI. His later recordings included the nine Beethoven Symphonies and some overtures (with the London Symphony Orchestra for Everest), some major orchestral works for La Guilde Internationale du Disque, which were also issued on the Concert Hall label, the five Beethoven Piano Concertos, the Schumann Piano Concerto and Brahms's Piano Concerto No. 2 (with Rubinstein and the Symphony of the Air for RCA), and the Mozart Symphonies Nos 21, 31, 33, 35, 36, 38, 39, 40 and 41 (with the Amsterdam Concertgebouw Orchestra for Philips), a series which he left incomplete at the end of his life.

KUBELÍK, **Rafael** (b. 1914). Born in Bychory in Czechoslovakia, Kubelík is the son of the great violin virtuoso Jan Kubelík, who taught him to play the violin so that he could perform the concert repertoire. He attended the Prague Conservatory (1928–33), made his début as a conductor with the Czech Philharmonic Orchestra in 1934, and was sufficiently accomplished as a pianist to accompany his father on tours in Europe and the United States (1934–6). He also conducted when Jan Kubelík performed 30 violin concertos at a cycle of ten concerts. He became acting conductor of the Czech Philharmonic (1936–9), and in 1937 took the orchestra to Belgium and England. He was conductor at the Brno National Theatre (1939–41) and then artistic director of the Czech Philharmonic Orchestra (1942–8). During World War II he consistently refused to co-operate with the Nazi occupation authorities in Prague; when the Communists took control of Czechoslovakia in 1948 he was in Britain conducting *Don Giovanni* with the Glyndebourne Festival Opera at the Edinburgh Festival, and he did not return to his native country. He conducted in Britain, Mexico and South America, and began his association with the Amsterdam Concertgebouw Orchestra.

His first appearance in the USA was with the Chicago Symphony Orchestra in 1949; he made such an impression that he was appointed music director of the orchestra in 1950. In Chicago he was the centre of controversy; one issue was the high proportion of new pieces included in his programmes, another was the black artists he invited to perform with the orchestra. As a final gesture of propitiation following his resignation in 1953 he led a concert performance of *Parsifal*. Sharing the podium with van Beinum he toured the USA with the Concertgebouw Orchestra, and in 1957–8 conducted the New York Philharmonic Orchestra. He was appointed music director of the Royal Opera House at Covent Garden in 1955, but resigned three years later when he was deeply offended by a public attack on Covent Garden by Sir Thomas Beecham. In his years at Covent Garden he had scored notable successes with *Otello*, *Les Troyens*, *Jenůfa* and *Die Meistersinger*; he was criticised for giving more rehearsals for new productions than previously, which tended to limit the repertoire. He was appointed chief conductor of the Bavarian Radio Symphony Orchestra (1961–79), touring Japan (1965) and the USA (1968) with the orchestra. In 1973 he had a short-lived term of six months as music director of the New York Metropolitan Opera; he resigned under pressure because his commitments in Munich made it impossible for him to give the time expected of him to the New York company. He became a Swiss citizen in 1967, and in 1978 appeared as guest conductor for six weeks with the New York Philharmonic Orchestra. His second wife is the Australian soprano, Elsie Morison, who had sung in his London performance of *The Bartered Bride*, and her last performance as a professional singer was with her husband conducting in the recording of Mahler's Symphony No. 4. He devotes much time to composing, and his output includes two operas, *Veronika* and *Cornelia Faroli*, three symphonies, a violin concerto, a cello concerto and three Requiems, the third written on the death of his first wife, the violinist Ludmilla Bertlová. His honours include the Gustav Mahler medal which he was awarded in 1960.

Kubelík is an intense and dynamic conductor, whose performances of a repertoire from Mozart to Berg are thoroughly considered, unmannered, straightforward, and devoid of eccentricity. Although they may not be illuminated with arresting strokes of genius or by the highest inspiration, they are exemplary in their musicianship, warmth and sensitivity. If he has a fault it is that his natural expressiveness occasionally tends to produce a rhythmic slackness and a rubato that may be excessive and can rob the music of some of its strength. As a young man he heard Toscanini, Krauss, Weingartner and Walter, and was profoundly impressed by them. He has no open preference for any particular composer or school of composition. He is sufficiently self-critical to admit that he is scarcely able to reach the high artistic aims he sets for himself: 'There was never in my life an evening when I could have said that it was really as I thought it should be. And I have conducted thousands of performances.' He prefers to perform before an audience, and before making a recording he performs the work in public. In the studio he goes straight through the work, listens to the tape to ensure that it sounds exactly as he heard it on the podium, and then the second take is the final recording. He values recordings because they often reveal more of the music than can possibly be heard in the concert hall; Mahler, for instance, can be better heard on record than at a concert.

HMV recorded Kubelík on 78s with the Czech Philharmonic Orchestra in music of Dvořák, Smetana and Janáček, and he also recorded with the orchestra for Supraphon. A series followed, on 78s and then LPs, with the Philharmonia and Royal Philharmonic Orchestras, the major works being symphonies of Dvořák and Brahms, Bartók's *Concerto for Orchestra* and several concertos of Beethoven and Brahms. He also recorded with the Vienna Philharmonic Orchestra, the chief discs being the four Brahms symphonies, Mahler's Symphony No. 1 and Dvořák's Symphonies Nos 7 and 9 and Cello Concerto (for Decca), and Smetana's *Má Vlast* (for EMI). Decca produced discs with him and the Israel Philharmonic Orchestra too. In 1951 Mercury recorded a series of outstanding LP discs with Kubelík conducting the Chicago Symphony Orchestra, noted for the distinction of the performances as much as for their exceptionally fine technical quality. The most notable in this series were Tchaikovsky's Symphonies Nos 4 and 6, *Pictures at an Exhibition*, Brahms's Symphony No. 1, *Má Vlast*, and pieces by Hindemith, Bartók, Janáček, Schoenberg and Bloch. During his period with the Bavarian Radio Symphony Orchestra, he recorded exclusively for DGG, and the most impressive of these discs were the nine symphonies of Mahler. He did not add the Symphony No. 10 completed by Deryck Cooke, believing that Mahler so often altered his ideas during composition that his final version really cannot be guessed at, and that it is not possible to put oneself in Mahler's mind. Kubelík's series appeared at much the same time as those of Solti, Abravanel, Haitink and Bernstein; the tone is not particularly beautiful, as it is not the lyrical and introspective element in Mahler that attracts him, but the dramatic quality of the composer's idiom, and his readings are expressive, sensitive and musically convincing. Other major enterprises for DGG were Weber's *Oberon*,

Schoenberg's *Gurrelieder*, Dvořák's symphonic poems, Janáček's *Glagolitic Mass*, Orff's *Antigone* and *Oedipus the Tyrant*, and Hartmann's Symphonies Nos 2, 4, 5, 6 and 8 (with the Bavarian Radio Symphony Orchestra), Dvořák's Symphonies Nos 6, 7, 8 and 9 and the four Schumann symphonies (with the Berlin Philharmonic Orchestra), *Má Vlast*, again (with the Boston Symphony Orchestra), *Rigoletto* (with the La Scala Orchestra), and the nine Beethoven symphonies. DGG departed from the usual practice of recording all the Beethoven symphonies with one conductor and orchestra by having Kubelík record each one with a different orchestra. These were the London Symphony (for No. 1), the Concertgebouw Orchestra (No. 2), the Berlin Philharmonic (No. 3), the Israel Philharmonic (No. 4), the Boston Symphony (No. 5), l'Orchestre de Paris (No. 6), the Vienna Philharmonic (No. 7), the Cleveland Orchestra (No. 8) and the Bavarian Radio Symphony Orchestra (No. 9).

L

LEINSDORF, Erich (b. 1912). Born in Vienna, Leinsdorf learnt the piano
as a boy, studied at the University and the Academy of Music in
Vienna, and in 1934 went to Salzburg to assist Walter at the Festival. He worked with Toscanini at the Festivals in 1935–7, also
helped to prepare performances at the Florence May Festivals
in 1935–7, and conducted concerts and opera in Italy, France
and Belgium. In 1937 he migrated to the USA, and on Toscanini's recommendation was engaged to assist Bodanzky at the
New York Metropolitan Opera, where he made his début with
Die Walküre in 1938, also conducting *Elektra* and *Parsifal* in the
same season. In Kolodin's words he 'performed with vitality and
excellent musical taste, demonstrating a control of unrehearsed
ensembles uncommon in so young a man'. After Bodanzky's
death in 1939 he became responsible for the German repertoire,
and remained there until 1943. In that year he was appointed
conductor of the Cleveland Orchestra, and was then the
youngest man to lead a major symphony orchestra in the USA.
He was conscripted into the US army, and was then discharged
after eight months, found that he had lost his position at
Cleveland, conducted at the Metropolitan Opera, with the St
Louis Symphony and the Los Angeles Symphony Orchestras,
and then was re-appointed to the Cleveland Orchestra in 1945.
He was musical director of the Rochester Philharmonic Orchestra (1947–55) where he led a season of contemporary operas
which was an artistic success but a box-office disaster, music
director of the New York City Opera (1956), and musical con-
sultant and conductor of the Metropolitan Opera (1957–62).
Then he succeeded Munch as musical director of the Boston
Symphony Orchestra (1962–9); since then he has conducted in
the USA, Western Europe and elsewhere, especially in Vienna,
and was principal conductor of the Berlin Radio Symphony
Orchestra (1977–80).

A man of short stature and always impeccably dressed, Leinsdorf has the reputation of being a good talker and a great wit.
His professionalism is much admired by his players and he
controls singers with unusual sympathy. He is a strong disci-
plinarian with a passion for thoroughness and precision. As a
musical interpreter his intellectual interest in musical structure
predominates over lyrical line and emotional expression, in

fact his performances are objective and tightly reined to the point where he is regarded by many as too cold and unfeeling. Certainly he eschews dramatic exaggeration and sentimentality, and his readings err on the side of plainness and severity. As Paul Henry Lang put it when describing Leinsdorf's recordings of the Beethoven symphonies, 'he is not adept at those nearly imperceptible tempo and dynamic adjustments that give life to music'. His musical preferences also reflect this outlook, for while his repertoire is based essentially on the great masterpieces of the 19th century, he dislikes the sentiment and easy-going lyricism of composers such as Glazunov and Saint-Saëns; characteristically he prefers late to early Prokofiev, and early to late Stravinsky. Like Boulez, he believes he has a duty to perform the music of the second Viennese school (Schoenberg, Berg and Webern), which is the bridge from the late romantic composers to modern music. However, in his view it is the disappearance of amateur music-making that has caused the lack of interest in music written since Mahler, and consequently 'composers have come to write for their own satisfaction, not to be listened to or performed'. In common with many other conductors, he holds that a recording can never be anything more than a single performance: 'the recording is a performance, one performance of a work. . . . I warn all young musicians not to study with recordings.' He listens to records for pleasure, but certainly not in any reference to the work he may be preparing. His book *The Conductor's Advocate* is primarily of interest to budding conductors, and in it he demonstrates his exhaustive knowledge of composers and styles, recommending, *inter alia*, that if a conductor is to interpret French music adequately, for example, he must be fluent in the French language. There are many *bons mots* in the book, such as his description of *Der Rosenkavalier* as 'souped-up musical comedy'.

Leinsdorf's career reached its zenith when he became conductor of the Boston Symphony Orchestra in 1962. He took it over from Munch, who had inherited a superb musical institution from Koussevitzky. Munch's relaxed and expressive approach modified the style of the orchestra, but with Leinsdorf its precision was certainly restored; yet most have agreed that in the last years of his tenure the orchestra became something less than it was. His somewhat rigid, unsmiling concept of the standard repertoire eventually affected its former brilliance as an interpretative instrument. He is at his best in opera, where his command of large forces and musical structures is a considerable virtue. To be fair, he was put in a difficult position; he became conductor of the Boston Symphony with a major recording contract which made it mandatory for him to record the great Austrian and German classics which have the greatest record sales, but these call for a style more lyrical and sympathetic than he could bring to them. As a recording artist, he has been remarkably active, from some Beethoven symphonies with the Rochester Philharmonic Orchestra to recordings with the London orchestras for the Decca Four-Phase series in the late 1970s. His discography includes the complete symphonies of Mozart (with the London Philharmonic Orchestra), Beethoven, Brahms and Prokofiev (with the Boston Symphony Orchestra), and about 20 complete operas. The orchestras with which he has recorded are virtually a list of all the major ensembles in the USA and Europe, as well as a number of lesser ones, and he has been contracted to many record companies. Probably his most distinguished recordings have been some of the operas, such as *Die Walküre*, *Turandot* and *Ariadne auf Naxos*; the greatest enterprise of all his discs with the Boston Symphony Orchestra was the complete *Lohengrin*, the largest operatic recording made in the USA.

LEPPARD, Raymond (b. 1927). Born in London and brought up in Bath, Leppard was a choral scholar at Trinity College, Cambridge (1948–52) where he was the music director of the Cambridge Philharmonic Society, and came under the influence of Boris Ord. He made his début as a harpsichordist at the Wigmore Hall, London, in 1952, and in that year formed the Leppard Ensemble which eventually merged with the Goldsbrough Orchestra to become the English Chamber Orchestra. He was the keyboard player with the Philharmonia Orchestra (1953–4), musical director of the Royal Court Theatre, London, was engaged as a répétiteur at the Glyndebourne Festival Opera (1954–5), and in 1957 returned to Cambridge to lecture in music, remaining there for ten years. In the meantime his conducting career proceeded, especially with the English Chamber Orchestra, and in the 1960s he was permanent conductor of the Essex Youth Orchestra. In 1962 he prepared the complete *L'Incoronazione di Poppea* of Monteverdi for performance at Glyndebourne; the next year he took five months' sabbatical leave to search libraries in Italy for the scores of the operas of Monteverdi and Cavalli, which led to new productions of their operas in Britain. After he left Cambridge in 1968 he toured with the English Chamber Orchestra, conducted at festivals, made his début in the USA in 1969 with the New York Philharmonic Orchestra, later made his American operatic début at Santa Fé in 1974 with Cavalli's *L'Egisto*, led some Mozart operas at Covent Garden (1972), and also conducted operas at San Francisco, the Scottish Opera, Stockholm and Oslo. In 1970 he premièred Maw's *The Rising of the Moon* at Glyndebourne, and in 1980 was commissioned by the Paris Opera to prepare a performing edition of Rameau's *Dardanus*. He was principal conductor of the BBC Northern Symphony Orchestra from 1973 to 1980, and has composed scores for a number of films. He has now taken up permanent residency in the USA.

Leppard became an authority on the music of the baroque era, particularly of Venetian music of the 17th century. He prepared editions of Monteverdi's operas *L'Incoronazione di Poppea* in 1962, *La favola d'Orfeo* in 1965 and *Il ritorno d'Ulisse in patria* in 1972, and of Cavalli's *L'Ormindo* in 1967 and *La Calisto* in 1969, and these operas were performed at Glyndebourne with much success. *L'Incoronazione di Poppea* was recorded by Pritchard in 1964, with the Glyndebourne production in Leppard's edition; Leppard himself conducted the recordings of *L'Ormindo* and *La Calisto* for Argo in 1969 and 1972 respectively. These operas have come down to us in fragmentary form, existing only in short scores and containing mostly only the voice parts and bass line. Leppard has attempted to make them readily accessible to present-day audiences, but in doing so he has aroused the hostility of musicologists and musical purists who believe that he has misrepresented the composers' intentions. In the first place, the length of the arias, and indeed the scores themselves, have been cut to fit into contemporary performing conventions. This has had the effect of seriously altering the roles of some of the major characters and of drastically simplifying the plots. The second objection is that his scoring is far too opulent and that this is historically false. A third is the transposition of the arias from other works to the operas, but as this was the custom at the time, the objection can scarcely be sustained. The fact is that Leppard has rescued these works from oblivion and has made them acceptable to audiences accustomed mostly to operas of the 18th and 19th centuries. He has responded to these criticisms, saying: 'I was an academic myself once. They're interested in the idea of the 19th-century urtext. But you take a look at this,' (producing a skeletal manuscript displaying an unadorned vocal line and a sparse bass accompaniment), 'and you can see that *that's* no urtext! This music is sensuous, emotional, and passionate. You have to re-create the composer. You can't stand back from this music like a vestal virgin, you have to be wedded to it.' His revival of Rameau also rouses his enthusiasm: 'Rameau is the last unknown man, the last great one.'

Leppard has recorded more than 100 LPs, for a number of labels. In addition to the Cavalli operas his other major contribution to the gramophone catalogues is the orchestral music of Handel (except the organ concertos) which he recorded with the English Chamber Orchestra and the oboist Holliger and which was released by Philips on nine records in 1973. He also directed a number of British singers, the Glyndebourne chorus, the Ambrosian Singers and the English Chamber Orchestra in Monteverdi's madrigals. His other recordings include Purcell's *Dido and Aeneas*, the Bach Suites and *Brandenburg Concertos*, *Messiah*, *Samson*, Mendelssohn's Symphonies Nos 4 and 5, Bax's Symphony No. 5, and Virgil Thomson's *The Mother of Us All*.

LEVINE, James (b. 1943). Born in Cincinatti into a musical family, Levine studied the piano from the age of 3 and at 10 performed Mendelssohn's Piano Concerto No. 2 with the Cincinatti Symphony Orchestra. He studied with Levin, the first violin of the La Salle Quartet, chamber music, orchestral repertoire, style and interpretation, with Rosina Lhevinne and with Serkin at the Marlboro Festival, and was at the Juilliard School where he studied conducting with Morel. In 1964 he joined the Ford Foundation's American Conductors Project; Szell heard him and invited him to become a member of the conducting staff of the Cleveland Orchestra. First an apprentice conductor, he was assistant conductor (1964–70), attended Szell's rehearsals, concerts and recording sessions and analysed operatic and symphonic scores with him. He filled guest engagements with major orchestras in the United States and Europe, and in 1971 made his début at the New York Metropolitan Opera with *Tosca*; the next year he was appointed its principal conductor and in 1976 became musical director. He spends seven months of each year at the Met., and in the remaining five months conducts elsewhere and occasionally gives piano recitals. In 1972 he first conducted the New York Philharmonic Orchestra, was musical director of the Cincinatti May Festival (1974–78), from 1973 has been the musical director of the Ravinia Festival in Chicago where he conducts the Chicago Symphony Orchestra; in 1974 he made his début at Covent Garden with *Der Rosenkavalier*, from 1975 conducted opera and concerts at the Salzburg Festival, first conducted at the Bayreuth Festival in 1982, and has annual guest engagements with the London Symphony and Berlin Philharmonic Orchestras.

At the New York Met. Levine has specialised in Italian opera, and, outgrowing an earlier brashness, is now a subtle and finished opera conductor. He has received wide acclaim in European opera houses as well as in New York for his command of the operas he conducts; he believes strongly in thorough preparation and in an intimate knowledge of the score, insisting that the conductor must know the music by memory if he is to lead the orchestra conceptually (*sic*). He is convinced that the most difficult of all composers, as far as capturing their style, are Mozart and Verdi: 'For a modern conductor with a modern orchestra the hardest styles are Mozart–Haydn–Schubert on the one side, and Verdi–Puccini–Mascagni–Giordano on the other. In both cases it is because the notes are harmonically very simple, because the objective technicalities are few, because the music looks pretty metrical, and yet with all this, everything about the style is utterly intrinsic.' Mahler, for instance, is easier to conduct than Verdi, as Mahler tells the conductor exactly what to do. Others, such as Stravinsky, present certain problems, but once you have conducted the piece effectively, there can be little interest left in it. 'I gave up doing *The Rite of Spring* as a guest conductor because it was solving the same problems all over again. Whereas the simplest Mozart symphony, with a different orchestra, with the same orchestra another time. . . .' Again, with Wagner and Strauss: 'We have the two greatest examples of people who have something missing in their persons which shows in their music.' This something is a moral element: 'There's a wholeness in the approach of Mozart and Verdi to the human soul.' His estimate of Richard Strauss contrasts with his reverence for Verdi: 'Take any one of Strauss's best works and you find that with all that extraordinary invention, with all the fullness everywhere else, at the very centre of all the music it's empty.' Of all operas, he believes that *Falstaff* 'may be the most perfect work of operatic art', and 'you've got to be absolutely rehearsed and disciplined down to the last 32nd note, and the whole thing must unwind as if it was being composed while it was played'. Asked if he can define the question of style so important in performing Mozart and Verdi, he answered: 'It is very difficult for me to put into words what the stylistic issue is. It's elements of a certain kind of projection of the text—not only the *meaning* of the text, but the *sound* of the text. It has to do with a certain balance between pointing in a detail and over-pointing

—but this is so with all music. It has to do with finding a tempo which is faithful to the often classical structure of the musical idea, at the same time as it is faithful to the pace of the words.'

Levine has embarked on recording the cycle of Mahler symphonies, and his interpretative approach finds strong sympathy among the younger generation of listeners. He is enormously attracted to Mahler, the man and the composer: 'As a conductor, the more I perform his symphonies and the more I study them, the more fascinated I become with their potential for self-renewal and capacity to offer fresh discoveries. In essence each symphony is simply part of one gigantic piece, and they are inter-related through the use of direct musical quotes, cross-references or ideas hinted at in one symphony only to be fully developed in the next. The ten symphonies are really one big cosmos, a constantly growing organism unified by Mahler's unique musical personality.' He has defined the conductor's task, in general, as to produce a performance as faithful to the composer's intention as possible but he is not interested in technical efficiency for its own sake: 'You can read the words of composers from Bach to Stravinsky, and what you find them screaming into the night about is not the technical execution but the conception, the balance, the spirit, the purpose, what was supposed to be conveyed.' Although his dedication to music is complete, some critics still perceive in his direction of the big romantic scores a detachment which does not go beyond the precise statement of the composer, somewhat reminiscent of his mentor, Szell. Levine himself wishes to record works about which he feels strongly, or which may have some documentary value, and restricts accompanying to artists with whom he has a long and close working relationship. In recording he insists on complete takes, to maintain momentum. His first recording was Verdi's *Giovanna d'Arco*, for EMI in 1973; since then he has gone on to record *Die Zauberflöte*, *Norma*, *Il barbiere di Siviglia*, *La forza del destino*, *Il vespri siciliani*, *Otello*, *Adriana Lecouvreur*, *Andrea Chénier*, *Cavalleria rusticana*, *La Bohème* and *Tosca*. His recordings in the symphonic repertoire have also been extensive and have included the late Mozart symphonies (with the Vienna Philharmonic Orchestra), the four Schumann symphonies (with the Philadelphia Orchestra), the four Brahms symphonies and *Ein deutsches Requiem* (with the Chicago Symphony Orchestra), the Mahler symphonies mentioned above (variously with the London Symphony, Chicago Symphony and Philadelphia Orchestras) and the Beethoven Piano Concertos (with Brendel and the Chicago Symphony Orchestra), as well as other major symphonies and concertos. Most have been for RCA, and many have been issued on compact disc.

LEWIS, Henry (b. 1932). Born in Los Angeles, Lewis was educated at the University of Southern California, and at the age of 16 was playing the double bass in the Los Angeles Philharmonic Orchestra. After military service (1955–9) when he played in and conducted the Seventh Army Symphony Orchestra in Europe, he returned to California and founded the Los Angeles Chamber Orchestra, and toured Europe with it under the auspices of the US State Department. He conducted the Los Angeles Philharmonic and American Symphony Orchestras, and in 1968 was appointed music director and conductor of the New Jersey Symphony Orchestra, and was the first black to lead a state orchestra in the USA. He remained with the orchestra until 1976, then continued to conduct opera and symphony concerts. In 1972 he was engaged to conduct at the Metropolitan Opera, and has appeared as a guest conductor with major orchestras in the USA and Europe. His recordings show him to be a painstaking and straightforward interpreter, whose natural restraint keeps him from imposing himself too much on the music. They include Beethoven's Symphony No. 6, Tchaikovsky's Symphony No. 6, Strauss's *Also sprach Zarathustra*, *Don Juan* and *Till Eulenspiegel*, Massenet's *La Navarraise*, Meyerbeer's *Le Prophète*, Rossini's *Assiedo di Corinto* and *La donna del lago*, and recitals accompanying his wife, the soprano Marilyn Horne.

LOMBARD, Alain (b. 1940). Born in Paris, Lombard joined Poulet's class at the Paris Conservatoire at the age of 9, and two years later conducted his first concert. He studied conducting with Fricsay and was appointed second conductor (1960), then principal conductor (1962–4), at the Lyon Opera. He assisted Bernstein and Karajan at the Salzburg Summer Festival in 1966; in the same year he was awarded the Gold Medal at the Dmitri Mitropoulos International Conductors Competition in New York, and conducted a performance of *Hérodiade* at the New York Metropolitan Opera, at Régine Crespin's bidding. He was musical director of the Miami Philharmonic Orchestra (1966–74), chief conductor of the Strasbourg Philharmonic Orchestra (1971–83), and artistic director of the Opéra du Rhin (from 1974), which was founded in 1972 and performs in the three Alsatian cities of Strasbourg, Mulhouse and Colmar. He has, in addition, been a guest conductor with many European and

United States orchestras and opera houses, and has established a considerable reputation for style and brilliance. His recordings have mostly been of French music, including the symphonies of Berlioz, and the operas *Roméo et Juliette* by Gounod and Delibes's *Lakmé*, as well as music of Strauss and Prokofiev, and Verdi's *Requiem*.

LÓPEZ-COBOS, Jesús (b. 1940). Born in Toro, Spain, into a musical family where his father was a prominent member of Madrid's Wagner Society, López-Cobos studied at the Universities of Granada and Madrid, where he took his doctorate in philosophy. He learned some music in Granada, joined and occasionally conducted the university choir in Madrid, took lessons in conducting with Ferrara in Venice, came under the influence of Cristobal Halffter, was assistant conductor at the Madrid Opera (1964–6), and studied conducting with Swarowsky in Vienna (1966–9). He won third prize at the Nicolai Malko Conductors Competition in Copenhagen (1968), and first prize at the International Competition for Young Conductors at Besançon (1969), and in that year made his professional début at the Prague Spring Festival. He studied conducting with Maag at the Accademia Chigiana in Siena and with Morel at the Juilliard School in New York, and became Maag's assistant in Venice, where he conducted his first opera, Donizetti's *Le convenienze ed inconvenienze teatrali*. He appeared at the Teatro Colón in Buenos Aires, and after conducting at the Deutsche Oper in Berlin in 1970 he was offered a five-year contract as a resident conductor. Symphony orchestras he has conducted are the Vienna Philharmonic at the Salzburg Festival, the four major London orchestras, and others in FR Germany, the Netherlands, Switzerland, Italy and Scandinavia, as well as the Los Angeles Philharmonic; he toured with the London Symphony and the Royal Philharmonic Orchestras in Spain and with the New Philharmonia Orchestra in the Netherlands, and has conducted in opera houses in San Francisco, Munich, Hamburg, Chicago, Paris and London. He is now musical director of the National Orchestra of Spain and of the Cincinatti Symphony Orchestra.

López-Cobos is anxious to dissociate himself from the convention that Latin conductors must only conduct Italian and French works in the opera house: 'In concert, also when I tour in Spain, I play Bruckner, Mahler, all the German masterworks. This is the repertoire I learned and absorbed during the years I studied in Vienna.' He has impressed in concert appearances in

London with his command of the orchestra, his care with detail, his disinclination to exaggerate and his firm clear beat. His recordings include *Lucia di Lammermoor*, Rossini's *Otello* and Liszt's *Dante Symphony*.

LOUGHRAN, James (b. 1931). Born in Glasgow, where he received his education, Loughran began his career as an assistant to Maag at the Bonn Opera, and later held similar positions in Amsterdam and Milan. He returned to Britain in 1961, and won first prize at the Philharmonia Orchestra's Young Conductors Competition; he was appointed associate conductor to Silvestri with the Bournemouth Symphony Orchestra (1962–5), was principal conductor of the BBC Scottish Symphony Orchestra in Glasgow (1965–71), in 1971 was appointed principal conductor and artistic adviser of the Hallé Orchestra, in succession to Barbirolli, and in 1979 became principal conductor of the Bamberg Symphony Orchestra. He has conducted opera at Covent Garden, Sadler's Wells, the Scottish Opera and with the English Opera Group, made his début in the USA with the New York Philharmonic Orchestra in 1972, has been a guest conductor with all the major British orchestras, as well as orchestras in the USA and Europe where he regularly conducts the Munich Philharmonic Orchestra, and has taken part in the Henry Wood Promenade Concerts and the Edinburgh Festival. His contract with the Hallé Orchestra permits him to conduct elsewhere for half of the year; in 1975 he toured with the orchestra in West Germany and Switzerland. In 1969 the European Broadcasting Union invited him to record for broadcast the nine Beethoven symphonies with the London Symphony Orchestra, and the performances were broadcast by the member countries of the Union in 1970, the Beethoven bicentenary year.

Loughran is the first British conductor to be appointed to a major German orchestra, no doubt because of his reputation as an interpreter of the German classical repertoire. Under his leadership the Hallé Orchestra has regained much of its former high standards and vitality, and he has brought many imaginative ideas into arranging the concert programmes, so as to move away from the traditional pattern of overture, concerto and symphony. In his engagements abroad he feels no necessity to conduct a British work for the first time in any place, believing that British conductors should be judged on their performances of the international rather than the national repertoire. He is modest, direct, and shuns flamboyance; he sees his musicians as collaborators, and rather than impose his will he seeks to create mutual understanding and rapport, which can result in sensitive and committed performances. Although he is interested in performing 20th-century music, he is disappointed that, despite the great talent of composers, so little moves beyond the experimental stage, and that so much is unnecessarily difficult to perform. In 1974 the record company Classics for Pleasure commenced a series of recordings with the Hallé Orchestra under Loughran, because the north of England was one area where their record sales were poor. Whatever the reason, many fine discs have resulted, which have re-established the Hallé Orchestra as a recording orchestra, and Loughran as an artist capable of careful, straightforward and thoroughly musical readings. The discs included the four Brahms symphonies and orchestral works, Elgar's two symphonies, *The Planets*, Schubert's Symphony No. 9, *Symphonie fantastique* and Rachmaninov's Symphony No. 2. For Enigma he also recorded the nine Beethoven symphonies with the Hallé Orchestra.

M

MAAZEL, Lorin (b. 1930). Born in Neuilly, France, of a Slav father and a Dutch mother, Maazel was brought to the USA as a child, and from the age of 5 played the violin in a children's orchestra in Los Angeles, and studied the violin, piano and conducting with Vladimir Bakaleinikoff in Los Angeles and then in Pittsburgh. He followed an extraordinary career as a child prodigy; he made his début as a conductor at the age of 7, with a programme of a Handel overture and Schubert's Symphony No. 8; in 1939 he led the New York Philharmonic Orchestra at the Lewisohn Stadium, and between 1941 and 1945 he conducted most of the professional symphony orchestras in the USA, with a repertoire of about 60 programmes. In 1941 Toscanini invited him to appear with the NBC Symphony Orchestra, and after he had conducted Mozart's Symphony No. 40, Toscanini blessed him. In 1945 he made his début in Pittsburgh as a violinist, and several years later he joined the Pittsburgh Orchestra as a violinist and assistant conductor. In 1946 he attended the University of Pittsburgh to study philosophy, fine arts and music, but the conductor Victor de Sabata convinced him that music was his true vocation. In 1951 Koussevitzky invited him to take part in the Tanglewood Festival, and in 1952 he was awarded a Fulbright scholarship and went to Rome to study baroque music. At the end of 1953 he substituted for Pierre Devaux at a concert, and after a number of engagements, a successful performance of Liszt's *Christus* led to concerts in Vienna and in many other European cities, as well as the USA, Australia *et al*. His major appointments have been artistic director of the Deutsche Oper, West Berlin (1965–71), music director of the Berlin Radio Symphony Orchestra (1965–75), associate principal conductor of the New Philharmonia Orchestra (1970–2), music director of the Cleveland Orchestra, in succession to Szell (1971–82), principal guest conductor of the New Philharmonia Orchestra (1976–80), chief conductor of the Orchestre National de France (1977–82) and music director of the Vienna State Opera (1983–4). He led the Cleveland Orchestra on ten tours, to Australia and New Zealand (1973), Japan (1974), Latin America (twice) and to Europe (twice), and at the end of his term was made conductor emeritus, and since 1980 has led the Vienna Philharmonic Orchestra's New Year's Day concerts.

After his abrupt departure from the Vienna State Opera he worked with the Pittsburgh Symphony, Vienna Philharmonic and Munich Philharmonic Orchestras and the Orchestre National de France, and is now conductor of the Pittsburgh Symphony Orchestra. He has conducted opera at La Scala, the New York Metropolitan and Covent Garden as well as in Vienna and Berlin, and was both the youngest conductor and the first American to conduct at Bayreuth, when he led *Lohengrin* in 1960.

Maazel is now one of the most distinguished conductors on the international scene. His major influences were Reiner, de Sabata and Furtwängler; of Reiner he believes that 'his musicianship and sensitivity were underrated because he was rather a tough old bird, and people weren't very fond of him. But the truth of the matter is that if you listen to his recordings you discover a man of great musicianship.' Toscanini's influence on 20th-century conductors has been, in Maazel's estimate, mainly negative, 'mostly because people have not been able to grasp what his contribution was. They mistook the clarity and precision as ends in themselves. All Toscanini was saying was that a *clear* performance was vital to the success of that performance, as having good intonation and clear passage work are on the violin or piano. But that was not the end, and his performances are incredibly powerful if you are sensitive to music as art. He demanded from the listener almost the same extraordinary sophistication that he brought to the music.' Maazel sees himself as one of the few present conductors of his generation who knew the great musicians who were active when he was a young violinist, and which were, in his opinion, superior to most of the present day. 'I have the advantage over many conductors of my generation of having had direct contact with Reiner, de Sabata and Rodzinski. Through a fluke of circumstance I represent a link between a kind of music-making that has all but vanished today.' Present-day conductors, to him, are not of the same intellectual level of those 50 years ago. 'Today's conductors are not well-cultured, not well-read, and not interested in a variety of sister arts that interested musicians of old. De Sabata, for example, was equally at home as a conductor, piano virtuoso, linguist, and connoisseur of poetry who could recite Corneille and others from memory. Who has that kind of intellect today? Who among today's conductors has ever read Thomas Mann? Nine out of ten of today's conductors probably have never heard of Thomas Mann. That is depressing, and it can be heard in their music-making.'

Since childhood, Maazel has been noted for his excellent aural memory—he always conducts without a score—and his sense of perfect pitch. Conducting presents no difficulties for him; orchestral players everywhere recognise him as having a superb baton technique, and he takes the greatest pains to achieve what he wants. His performances are invariably polished, and he has the ability to rouse the players of the most famous orchestras to high levels, although many may resent his methods and his approach to them. His experience as an orchestral string player has given him, he says, 'almost an unfair advantage, because I do understand on an intimate basis the technical problems more than half the orchestra has to deal with. I can also recognise when what they are doing is fine, whereas a piano-oriented conductor may cavil or be insecure in that area or simply break into poetry in trying to describe the kind of sound he wants in the hope that a section leader will ultimately be able to have the technical vocabulary to carry off to the rest of the players what is wanted.' With baroque and classical music he is neat and precise, if not specially perceptive; his recordings of the Beethoven symphonies with the Cleveland Orchestra are straightforward, and have been characterised (in the *New Penguin Stereo Record and Cassette Guide*) as based on sharp rhythms and generally urgent tempi, but with an overall aggressiveness. His strength lies in the larger romantic scores which require fine orchestral control and care for detail. In his musical personality there is a coolness and calculation that gives his performances a clinical brilliance, but in no real sense an emotional involvement. In his earlier years he would sometimes drive the music hard, as if ignorant of its lyricism or nobility. His performances were invariably arresting, but cumulative tension and the inner meaning of the music were not so evident. More recently, his personality seems to have undergone a transformation, both in relation to orchestral players and in his concept of the music. As one concert-master has put it: 'Players see in him a constant struggle between the genius and the human being.' His performances have become less idiosyncratic exhibitions of orchestral technique and more authentic musical experiences.

Maazel's repertoire extends from Bach to Stravinsky and includes some 40 operas, but his interest in modern music is confined to works which have an immediate impact on the listener. He acknowledges the importance of performing contemporary music, for the sake of both the composers and the public, but says that he has not heard a really striking work for some time. Contemporary scores have been interesting, but no more. Records have helped him to come to terms with much modern music: 'I have bought many records of experimental contemporary music and they have made me very tolerant of sonorities at first rather shocking. One gets used to it little by little and is able to differentiate between composers. I listen especially to music I don't know, much baroque, oriental, Indian, and music from the Japanese Imperial Court, which is incredibly interesting.' Mahler and Bruckner are comparative late-comers in his repertoire; he still has reservations about Mahler's Symphonies Nos 3 and 8, although he is recording all the symphonies with the Vienna Philharmonic Orchestra for CBS. He rejects the idea that Mahler reflects the decay and collapse of the modern world: 'Mahler was very sane and well-balanced, both as man and artist. His sanity, humour, and many other facets are delightfully and richly expressed in his music.' Maazel did much to persuade audiences in Paris and Vienna to accept Sibelius with his fine performances of the Finnish composer's symphonies, whose greatness became apparent to him through Barbirolli's interpretations with the Berlin Philharmonic Orchestra. The Cleveland Orchestra under him retained its place amongst American orchestras, but it was no longer the ensemble which excelled all its peers in its execution of the Viennese classics. When he took over the orchestra after Szell, he worked to transform the customary concert programme of overture–concerto–symphony to something new, which would bring the orchestra and audience closer to the creative musician. He programmed unusual music outside the regular subscription series, and part of the orchestra was allocated for a series of contemporary music. Other media were introduced into concerts: poetry readings related to the music were given at the end of concerts, and once dramatised selections from Beethoven's sketch books were presented. At first audiences, accustomed to the standard repertoire performed to perfection by Szell, drastically declined, but Maazel's approach created a new public. He also introduced performances of Beethoven's Symphony No. 9 and Mahler's Symphony No. 2 in which school children sang with the orchestra.

Maazel's first records were an impressive number made with the Berlin Philharmonic Orchestra for DGG in 1958. In the mid-1960s Philips recorded him with the Berlin Radio Symphony Orchestra in works by Bach, Handel, Mozart, Pergolesi and Dvořák, then later for Decca and EMI he made numerous discs with the Philharmonia (and New Philharmonia), Vienna Philharmonic, London Symphony, London Philharmonic and

Israel Philharmonic Orchestras. The most notable of these recordings were the complete symphonies of Tchaikovsky and Sibelius with the Vienna Philharmonic for Decca. There has also been a handful of operatic recordings, including *Tosca*, *La traviata*, *Fidelio*, *Luisa Miller* and *Turandot*. With the Cleveland Orchestra he has recorded the Beethoven and Brahms symphonies; his recent discs with the Vienna Philharmonic include the first of the Mahler series, and with the Berlin Philharmonic Zemlinsky's *Lyrische Symphonie*, as well as two best-sellers, Andrew Lloyd Webber's *Requiem* for EMI and the performance for Rossi's film of *Carmen* for Erato.

MACKERRAS, Sir Charles (b. 1925). Although a fifth-generation Australian, Mackerras was born in Schenectady, New York, but was educated at the New South Wales Conservatorium of Music in Sydney. He played the oboe in cinema and theatre orchestras, then was principal oboe with the Sydney Symphony Orchestra (1943–6). In 1947 he won a British Council scholarship and studied under Talich at the Prague Academy of Music; this experience made him one of the finest conductors of Czech music, particularly Janáček's operas, outside Czechoslovakia. He was a conductor at the Sadler's Wells Opera (1948–53), principal conductor of the BBC Concert Orchestra (1954–6), freelance conductor with most British orchestras, as well as a frequent conductor for radio and television, first conducted at Covent Garden with Shostakovich's *Katerina Izmaylova* (1963), was first conductor at the Hamburg Staatsoper (1966–70), musical director of the English National Opera (formerly the Sadler's Wells Opera, 1970–7), chief guest conductor of the BBC Symphony Orchestra (1977–9), principal conductor of the Sydney Symphony Orchestra (1980–5), musical director of the Leeds Philharmonic Society (1985), principal guest conductor of the Royal Liverpool Philharmonic Orchestra (1986), and musical director of the Welsh National Opera (1987). He has made many tours to conduct concerts and operas in Scandinavia, FR Germany, Italy, Czechoslovakia, Romania, Hungary, the USA, the USSR, Belgium, Holland, South Africa, Canada and Australia, where he conducted the opening concert at the Sydney Opera House in 1973. He has arranged music from the Gilbert and Sullivan operas in a successful ballet suite, *Pineapple Poll* (1951), and also music from the Verdi operas, in *The Lady and the Fool*, and has edited works by Handel and Janáček. He was awarded the CBE in 1974 and was knighted in 1979.

Mackerras is a widely experienced and versatile conductor, and although he resists the tendency to mark him off as a specialist, he is nonetheless noted for his performances of baroque music, as well as an operatic conductor. He was a pioneer in the authentic performance of baroque music, particularly of Handel and Bach, and his performance of *Le nozze di Figaro* at Sadler's Wells in 1966 was exceptional in the introduction of ornamentation in the arias. His interest in the Janáček operas was fired when he studied *Kát'a Kabanová* with Talich in Prague; he introduced the opera to Britain when he returned from Czechoslovakia in 1951, went on to give first performances in Britain of *The Makropoulos Affair* (1964) and *From the House of the Dead* (1965), led *The Cunning Little Vixen* at Sadler's Wells and a broadcast performance of *The Excursions of Mr Brouček* (1970), a new production of *Kát'a Kabanová* in his own edition (1973), and then *Jenůfa* at Covent Garden (1974). He has also conducted most of Janáček's operas in the composer's home town of Brno, and in 1977 his recording of *Kát'a Kabanová* was issued by Decca, the first of a series of the operas which he has been recording with the Vienna Philharmonic Orchestra *et al.*, and which have been widely acclaimed and awarded. His care in preparing operatic performances is typical; he visited Shostakovich to discuss *Katerina Izmaylova* before conducting the work at Covent Garden, and similarly took great pains with his production of *Billy Budd*. During his years with the English National Opera he emerged as a major conductor of the Wagner operas. He has made many recordings, in addition to the Janáček opera series; on the 200th anniversary of Handel's death in 1959, he recorded for Pye the *Music for the Royal Fireworks*, with its original wind scoring of 24 oboes, 12 bassoons and contra-bassoons, 9 horns, 9 trumpets, side drums and 3 pairs of kettle drums. In 1967 he recorded, with great vitality and perception, a revolutionary performance of *Messiah* (with the English Chamber Orchestra *et al.* for EMI), using Basil Lam's edition, which purported to be the kind of performance Handel himself directed, and which added ornamentations and appoggiaturas, authentic bowing and phrasing, although the performance differed from those more recently of Hogwood, Gardiner, *et al.*, in employing modern instruments. His other recordings of Handel include *Israel in Egypt*, *Saul*, *Judas Maccabaeus* and Mozart's arrangement of *Messiah*.

MAKSYMIUK, Jerzy (b. 1936). Born in Grodno, Poland, Maksymiuk studied at the Warsaw Conservatory; originally a composition student, he took conducting lessons to perform one of his own works, and from then devoted his entire time to conducting. He was a prize winner in the Fitelberg and Malawski composition competitions and the Paderewski piano competition, received the Polish Prime Minister's award for composition in 1973, and in that year conducted his ballet *Metaphrases* at a festival at Essen. He became conductor of the Polish National Radio Symphony Orchestra in Katowice; in 1972 he formed the Polish Chamber Orchestra, under the auspices of the Warsaw National Opera. In 1974 he and the orchestra undertook the first of its foreign tours; when they visited London in 1977 they attracted warm praise, and EMI contracted them to make a series of records over the next three years, which included works by Vivaldi, Rossini, Dvořák and Suk. In Poland, Maksymiuk and the orchestra made other records, including the *Brandenburg Concertos*, the performances of which are remarkable for their express tempi. Maksymiuk was appointed principal conductor of the BBC Scottish Orchestra in Glasgow in 1983.

MARKEVITCH, Igor (1912–83). Born in Kiev into an aristocratic family of landowners, Markevitch left Russia with his parents in 1913 and settled with them in Vevey in Switzerland in 1916. He studied at the Collège de Vevey, and was introduced to music when he heard, as a boy, the Suisse Romande Orchestra under Ansermet. He began to study the piano and composition at Lausanne, and attracted the attention of Cortot, who in 1925 took him to Paris to enter the École Normale; there he studied the piano under Cortot, composition under Nadia Boulanger, and orchestration under Rieti. At the age of 16 he met Diaghilev who was so impressed with his talent that he commissioned him to write a piano concerto, which was played a year later at a concert at Covent Garden, with the conductor Desormière. Diaghilev also commissioned a ballet, *Rébus*, but unfortunately died in 1929 before the commission was completed. In 1930 Markevitch studied conducting with Scherchen, who inspired him to take it up as a profession; his début occurred that year, when he was 18, in a programme of his own compositions with the Amsterdam Concertgebouw Orchestra.

During the 1930s Markevitch composed much music, including concertos, ballets, orchestral and vocal works; as a student of Boulanger, his compositions were considerably influenced by

Stravinsky, and remained tonal. The best known are the ballet *L'Envoi d'Icare* (1933), an oratorio *Le paradis perdu* (1935–6) and a *Psaume* for soprano and orchestra (1934); the latter caused a controversy about its merits when it was performed at the ISCM Festival in Florence. He recorded *L'Envoi d'Icare* and another work, *Le nouvel age*, on 78s with the Belgian National Orchestra for HMV; the ferocity and violent dynamics of this music and its apparent absence of sentiment hinted at its close relationship with *Le Sacre du printemps* and with the *Scythian Suite* of Prokofiev, but his later compositions show an infusion of feeling resulting from his view of the ennobling purpose of music. By the end of the 1930s Markevitch had turned his attention more and more to conducting. In 1940 he went to Italy to gather material for a cantata he was writing about Lorenzo the Magnificent, which was completed and premièred by him in Rome in 1941. The entry of Italy into the war compelled him to remain in Florence, and when the city was liberated in 1944 the Allies appointed him to organise the Florence May Festival. After the war he toured Europe to conduct opera and concerts, and appeared at major music festivals. He also taught conducting at the Salzburg Mozarteum (1947–53), at the Pan-American conducting courses in Mexico (1955–6), and more recently at the Moscow Conservatory (1963) and the Jerusalem Academy (1976). His permanent appointments as conductor were with the Stockholm Concert Society Orchestra (1952–5), the Havana Philharmonic Orchestra (1957–8), the Montreal Symphony Orchestra (1956–60), the Lamoureux Orchestra in Paris (1954–61), the Spanish Radio and Television Orchestra which he founded (1965–7), the USSR State Symphony Orchestra in Moscow (1965), the Monte Carlo Opera (1967–72) and the Santa Cecilia Orchestra, Rome (1973–5). He took part in the 1954–5 season at Covent Garden, London, and made his début in the USA with the Boston Symphony Orchestra in 1955, and in 1968 visited Japan to conduct the Japan Philharmonic Orchestra. He also toured many other countries and conducted a great number of the major symphony orchestras. He also prepared an edition of the Beethoven symphonies, with analyses and annotations.

Consistent with his style as a composer, Markevitch brought considerable tension and incisiveness to his conducting, and naturally felt a special affinity with the music of Stravinsky and Bartók: his concert performances and recording of *Le Sacre du printemps* were celebrated. His performances of the Viennese

classics were equally firm and well considered, although on
occasion the geniality of the music was attenuated. He was
particularly successful with ballet scores and highly coloured
romantic music. He was a distinguished teacher of conducting,
and believed that the special circumstances of today call for a far
more intensive training for conductors than before. This training, he stated, should begin at the age of 12 or 14, and should go
on for about ten years. Conductors today are usually required to
give many more concerts than in the past, with much less time to
prepare each; they must command a vast repertoire encom-
passing many different styles, and there are also the demands of
recording. The education of the conductor, he explained, should
include the training of the body in correct breathing, developing
independence of the arms and reflexes and agility, and the
preparation of the ear so that errors can be recognised infallibly.
The would-be conductor should have a knowledge of all the
classical symphonies, the most important operas and oratorios
and the standard concertos and make a close study of the most
important contemporary pieces, of which he gave as examples
Le Sacre du printemps, Bartók's *Concerto for Orchestra*,
Messiaen's *Turangalîla symphony*, Schoenberg's *Variations for
Orchestra* Op. 31, and Boulez's *Le Marteau sans maître*. He adds
to this a comprehensive musical and cultural education, including the study of the life and work of each composer, and a
command of several languages to facilitate contact with orchestral players of many countries. Above all, the conductor can
only recreate a musical work if he knows how to communicate
with his musicians, how to convince them of his approach and to
move them to do what he wants them to do.

Markevitch was a prolific recording artist and made records of
a vast range of music, from his own arrangement of Bach's *Die
Kunst der Fuge* to Dallapiccola's *Canti di Prigonia*. His performances of *Le Sacre du Printemps* were celebrated and he
recorded the work twice with the Philharmonia Orchestra
for EMI, in 1952 and 1960. His major recording achievement was of Tchaikovsky's six symphonies and *Manfred*
with the London Symphony Orchestra for Philips, superb
performances but unfortunately remaining in the catalogue
only a short time. His other LP recordings included symphonies, overtures, suites, concertos and symphonic poems of
Haydn, Mozart, Beethoven, Schubert, Mendelssohn, Wagner,
Berlioz, Brahms, Rossini, Verdi, Berwald, Debussy, Ravel,
Nielsen, Mussorgsky, Prokofiev, Shostakovich, Stravinsky,

Bartók and many others, as well as choral works by Haydn, Mozart, Cherubini, Gounod, Stravinsky, Kodály, Lili Boulanger and Verdi, whose *Requiem* he recorded with the Moscow Philharmonic Orchestra *et al.* However, the only compact discs so far released have been of his accompaniments with the Lamoureux Concerts Orchestra for Clara Haskil playing Mozart's Piano Concertos Nos 20 and 24, Chopin's Piano Concerto No. 2 and Falla's *Nights in the Gardens of Spain*.

MARRINER, Sir Neville (b. 1924). Marriner was born in London and was first taught the violin by his father when he was a small boy. He received lessons from Frederick Mountney, and then went to the Royal College of Music in London at the age of 13. During World War II he served in the British Army, was wounded in France in 1943, and during his convalescence in a military hospital met Thurston Dart, who was to have a crucial influence on his career. After the war he completed his studies at the RCM, then went to Paris to study the violin with René Benedetti and to attend the Paris Conservatoire. Returning to England he was a member of the teaching staff at Eton College for a year, was a founder-member of some chamber-music groups, and formed a duo with Dart, who played the harpsichord, specialising in 17th- and 18th-century music. From this emerged the Jacobean Ensemble, which made records of the Purcell Trio Sonatas for Argo in 1950. Previously, in 1948, Marriner had been appointed professor at the Royal Academy of Music, and in 1956 he joined the London Symphony Orchestra as principal second violin. He remained with the orchestra until 1969; his association with Dart continued until the latter's death in 1971. He was knighted in 1985.

In 1957 Marriner was asked by the director of music at the church of St Martin-in-the-Fields, Trafalgar Square, London, to provide music after evensong. He agreed to arrange six programmes, and formed a chamber orchestra of four first and four second violins, two violas, two cellos and a double-bass, most of whom were principals from the London orchestras. The ensemble was given the name, somewhat lightheartedly, of the Academy of St Martin-in-the-Fields. L'Oiseau Lyre contracted Marriner and the orchestra to record Couperin's *Les Nations*, and an initial favourable review of this disc assured the orchestra's future. At first Marriner conducted the Academy (as he came to call the orchestra) from the first desk, but in 1959 he went to the USA to study with Monteux, who taught him to conduct from the podium. Marriner and the Academy went on to make many more records for Argo and later for Philips and EMI; it is now unquestionably the most successful—maybe the best—chamber orchestra to have made gramophone records. Its players are drawn from a pool; none is under contract, and they are engaged entirely for their quality. Wind players have been added so that the repertoire can be extended to include Haydn, Mozart, Schubert and Beethoven, and Rossini. The orchestra tours extensively, and in fact gives more concerts overseas than in Britain.

In 1969 Marriner received an invitation to go to California and direct the newly formed Los Angeles Chamber Orchestra. This group is made up chiefly of young players as well as others drawn from professional freelance musicians in Hollywood. Until his departure in 1978, Marriner spent twelve weeks each year in Los Angeles with the orchestra, and in 1975 toured with them in Europe. His success in Los Angeles led to invitations to conduct some of the major US orchestras such as the Boston Symphony. New York Philharmonic, Cleveland, Minnesota, National Symphony, San Francisco Symphony and Detroit Symphony, but he found it less easy to be engaged to conduct orchestras in Britain. He was from 1971, for a time, conductor of the Northern Sinfonia, based at Newcastle-on-Tyne, and in 1975 he was musical adviser to the South Bank Summer Festival in London. He also founded a chamber orchestra in Australia, similar to the Los Angeles ensemble, he was conductor and musical director of the Minnesota Orchestra (1978–85), was artistic director of the Meadow Brook Music Festival at Rochester, Michigan (1977), and principal guest conductor of the Stuttgart Radio Symphony Orchestra (1981), of which he has subsequently become chief conductor. His return to the symphony orchestra arose from his concern about becoming stale with the chamber orchestra's repertoire. He has also conducted opera, and has made successful recordings of *Il barbiere di Siviglia* and *Le nozze di Figaro*.

Until his appointment with the Los Angeles Chamber Orchestra, Marriner's name, as a conductor, was inseparable from the Academy of St Martin-in-the-Fields. Since then he has developed a more independent identity and has become respected as a conductor in his own right. Like other conductors of chamber orchestras, records have contributed enormously to his international fame; each of his records sold sufficient numbers to permit him to select his own repertoire. He is a perfectionist and is meticulous in all matters of scholarship in preparing performances, for which his experience with Dart was invaluable. He will not, however, listen to other conductors' recorded performances before he records himself, for, to him, the outcome could only be a subconscious influence or a conscious reaction. While his musical taste is catholic, he has no time for 'squeaky-wheel' avant-garde music which introduces electronics or improvisations, as it generally gives little pleasure to either players or audience. He believes that 'nobody has really advanced string technique satisfactorily since Bartók'. The sound and style of the Academy is frequently characterised as 'athletic' and 'crisp', which tends to indicate a certain slickness and conceals the superb ensemble, sense of style and absolute technical proficiency of the orchestra. Even so, the Academy has a special sound: completely focused, the utmost clarity and a bright tone, which some may feel not entirely right for all the music it plays. Marriner himself believes the Academy to be the best chamber orchestra at the moment, and that its recorded performances have become definitive, although he has great respect for the Polish Chamber Orchestra. But, he admits, 'people may still buy our records of baroque music because they like the way we play it and there are other equally interesting ways of performing it now,' accepting that the baroque repertoire will be taken over by the ensembles who play on original instruments, of which there is an abundance in England.

Marriner and the Academy recorded for Argo, Philips and EMI an enormous amount of music in a repertoire ranging from Bach to 20th-century composers. Much of the major instrumental music of the baroque period is included—Bach, Handel, Vivaldi, Corelli and Telemann, with choral works such as the *Mass in B Minor* of Bach, and *Messiah*, and in addition a wide range of pieces by Albinoni, Boyce, Manfredini, Gabrieli, Purcell, Avison, Arne, Abicastro and others. From the classical and later periods there are *all* Mozart's symphonies, a number of piano concertos (with Brendel), other concertos, serenades, overtures, choral music and *Le nozze di Figaro*, a group of Haydn's symphonies titled with names (such as 'Military'), *The Creation* and *The Seasons*, Beethoven's Symphonies Nos 1, 2 and 3 and Violin Concerto (with Kremer, who includes a controversial cadenza by Alfred Schnittke), Schubert's nine symphonies, Weber's two symphonies, Rossini's String Sonatas, Mendelssohn's Symphonies Nos 3 and 4, Rossini's operatic overtures and *Il barbiere di Siviglia*, Grieg's *Holberg Suite* and excerpts from *Peer Gynt*, Dvořák's two serenades, Tchaikovsky's

Serenade for Strings, Souvenir de Florence and *Nutcracker* Suite, and Strauss's *Metamorphosen*. British music is naturally well represented, with the string music of Elgar and Vaughan Williams, and works of Delius, Butterworth, Warlock, Britten and Maw, and of relatively modern composers Debussy, Ravel, Ibert, Fauré, Bartók, Stravinsky, Prokofiev, Shostakovich, Ives, Copland, Cowell, Creston, Barber, Rodrigo and Romero. He also recorded with the Los Angeles Chamber, London Symphony, Philharmonia, Minnesota and Amsterdam Concertgebouw Orchestras, the Northern Sinfonia and the Dresden Staatskapelle; with the Minnesota Orchestra the recorded repertoire included pieces by Dvořák, Wagner, Britten and Copland. The names of Marriner and the Academy, and indeed Mozart himself, became familiar to many thousands through the soundtrack of the film *Amadeus*; although the story was an absurd and erroneous depiction of Mozart, its one virtue, apart from its merits as a film *per se*, was the introduction of the composer's music to a vast number of people.

MARTINON, Jean (1910–76). Born in Lyon into a musical family, Martinon studied at the conservatoire there (1924–5) and then at the Paris Conservatoire (1926–9) where he was a pupil of d'Indy and Roussel. He played the violin in the Paris Conservatoire Orchestra, gave solo recitals, composed, took a master's degree in Arts at the Sorbonne (1932), and studied conducting with Munch and Desormière. He first conducted when he was asked to direct one of his own compositions at a concert where he was also appearing as a solo violinist, and soon after had to take over unexpectedly from Munch. In World War II he served in the French Army, was taken prisoner-of-war in 1940 and spent two years in a German prisoner-of-war camp, from which he escaped and was recaptured three times. In captivity he wrote a symphony, a motet *Absolve Domine*, in memory of French musicians who perished in the war, and a setting of Psalm 136 which became known as the *Chant des Captifs*. Munch gave this work its first performance in Paris in 1942, and the audience, then suffering under the Nazi occupation, gave it an unusually warm reception because of its obvious implications.

After his return to civilian life in 1943, Martinon was asked to conduct a concert of the Pasdeloup Orchestra as his own symphony was in the programme. His success led to his appointment as conductor of the Bordeaux Symphony Orchestra (1943–5), after which he became assistant conductor to Munch with the Paris Conservatoire Orchestra (1944–6). He made guest appearances in Britain and South America, and was appointed associate conductor to Boult with the London Philharmonic Orchestra (1949–51), artistic director of the Concerts Lamoureux (1951–8), artistic director of the Israel Philharmonic Orchestra (1958–60), general music director at Düsseldorf (1960–4), artistic director of the Chicago Symphony Orchestra (1963–8), director of the principal orchestra of the French radio and television network, the French National Radio Orchestra (1968 onwards), and music director of the Hague Philharmonic Orchestra (1974 onwards), which is also known as the Residentie Orchestra. He toured widely in many continents, both as a guest conductor and with the Paris Conservatoire, French National Radio and Hague Philharmonic Orchestras. His list of compositions is extensive and includes five symphonies, concertos and chamber music; two of his symphonies and his Violin Concerto No. 2 have been recorded. In 1948 he was awarded the Prix Béla Bartók for his String Quartet No. 1; his other honours included the Grand Prix de la Ville de Paris (1945), Officier de la Légion d'Honneur and Chevalier des Arts et Lettres.

Martinon was an elegant conductor with an exemplary technique. Although he enjoyed conducting the French repertoire, his real preference was for the German classics, which he attributed to his Alsatian ancestry. In Chicago he gave polished and impressive performances of Haydn, Mozart, Beethoven, Schubert, Schumann, Mendelssohn, Brahms, Wagner and Mahler, and a Beethoven Symphony No. 9 which he led towards the end of his second season there attracted high praise. But he found that he was always called to conduct French music, and his identification with French composers caused him to regret at the end of his life that he had never been asked to record Mahler. His Beethoven and Brahms in particular stood apart from the accepted interpretations of the German school of conductors; his characteristically French style emphasised clarity at the expense of expression and power. He also believed that the public never took him seriously as a composer, but he was not the only conductor to suffer this fate. His mild temperament and his disinclination to confront orchestras or their managements were part of the reason for his unhappy experience with the Chicago orchestra. His appointment was made without the prior knowledge or approval of Reiner, his predecessor, who had controlled the players with something akin to terror. The orchestra, too, was not sympathetic to conductors of the French school, such as Defauw, who had been their conductor from

1943 to 1949. Furthermore, the critic of *The Chicago Tribune*, Claudia Cassidy, held a disproportionately powerful position in forming local musical opinion, and she was antagonistic to Martinon, as indeed to many others. An untenable situation developed with the orchestra and its supporters divided into two warring camps. After he left he still retained his high admiration for the orchestra, but he described Chicago as a provincial town he was not sorry to leave.

His wide experience of conducting in many countries brought home to Martinon the differences between national styles in orchestral playing, and the problem of the guest conductor in imposing his interpretation on a relatively strange orchestra. It is, for example, difficult to ask players with solo passages in standard works to play them differently from their practice for many years. Then, inadvertently correcting a strong player instead of a weak one can destroy the conductor's rapport with the entire orchestra. He found that orchestras do not always appreciate that French music and German music call for different attacks, endings, and rates of crescendo and diminuendo.

Decca was the first company to engage Martinon as a conductor, at the time when he was with the London Philharmonic Orchestra, and with them he made many discs, mostly of French music. He also recorded then with the Paris Conservatoire Orchestra and the Vienna Philharmonic Orchestra for Decca, the most significant works being Prokofiev's Symphony No. 5 and Tchaikovsky's Symphony No. 6. His many other recordings were for a variety of companies and orchestras and were almost all of French music, but with the Chicago Symphony Orchestra RCA produced a series with him that approached Reiner's in style and brilliance, the best examples being Nielsen's Symphony No. 4, *Daphnis et Chloé* Suite No. 2, *The Miraculous Mandarin* and *Nobilissima visione*. In the years at the end of his life, Vox released in two of their Vox Boxes Prokofiev's seven symphonies (with the ORTF Orchestra), and EMI cast him again in the role of specialist in French music in two superb sets of Debussy's orchestral music (with the ORTF National Orchestra) and Ravel's orchestral music and works for solo instruments and orchestra (with the Orchestre de Paris). Critics have inevitably found fault with some recordings in the two sets, but they contain some of the finest performances of the pieces recorded; the general level of performance aspires to greatness, and makes the series a major recording achievement and undoubtedly Martinon's finest legacy to us.

MASUR, Kurt (b. 1927). Born in Brieg, in Silesian Germany, Masur studied the piano and cello at the national music school at Breslau (1942–4), then after war service attended the Hochschule für Musik at Leipzig (1946–8), where he studied conducting with Bongartz. He started his career as a répétiteur and occasional conductor at the Halle State Theatre (1948–51), was then conductor at Erfurt (1951–3), first conductor at the Leipzig Opera (1953–5), general music director at Schwerin (1958–60), and music director at the Berlin Komische Oper (1960–4), where he worked with Walter Felsenstein, the founder of the new realist school of musical theatre. In these years in the opera house he learnt 65 different operas. In 1953–4 he had been a guest conductor with the Leipzig and Dresden Radio Orchestras and was second conductor of the Dresden Philharmonic Orchestra (1955–8). He then decided to give all his attention to symphonic music, became the chief conductor of the Dresden Philharmonic Orchestra (1967–72), and in 1970 was appointed chief conductor of the Leipzig Gewandhaus Orchestra. The Leipzig orchestra, along with the Dresden Staatskapelle, is the leading orchestra in East Germany and originated in the 16-player ensemble that played Bach's cantatas with the composer at the St Thomas Church. Masur has been a guest conductor in Eastern and Western Europe, Japan and South America, and was awarded the National Prize of the German Democratic Republic twice, in 1969 and 1970. He has conducted the New Philharmonia Orchestra in London, led the Gewandhaus Orchestra at the Edinburgh Festival and has appeared at the Salzburg and Prague Spring Festivals, is principal guest conductor of the Dallas Symphony Orchestra, Texas, first conducted the Cleveland Orchestra in 1974, and after returning to the orchestra in 1982 has conducted it regularly. He is an honorary conductor of the Yomiuri Nippon Symphony Orchestra in Japan.

Masur's first great musical influence were radio performances he heard just after World War II in Berlin of Walter conducting Mozart's Symphony No. 40, and of open rehearsals of Munch with the Boston Symphony Orchestra. He was then able to hear music that was never performed in Germany in the time of the Nazis. He possesses and frequently listens to recordings of Furtwängler, Walter and Toscanini, comparing their styles, and seeking to discover what makes them unique. But he avoids hearing the records of other conductors performing a piece before he conducts it himself: 'There are a lot of young conductors who are trying to copy great conductors, and they are starting not to be creative themselves. And that's a danger.' He recognises that records can never be permanent or definitive statements: 'You make the recording, and before it comes out to the audience, you are really one step beyond it. You always get one of your recordings, listen to it and think, "Oh, my God! What did I do?"' Recording, to him, has special problems, as the performance on record has to be alive and perfect at the same time. A commanding figure before the orchestra, Masur is vigorous and animated in his gestures, and conducts without a score. His performances of Beethoven, Brahms, Schumann, Bruckner, Liszt, Tchaikovsky and Wagner in particular are impressive; he is generally restrained, disciplined and correct, and while his readings tend to be literal rather than romantic, he lacks nothing in virtuosity or majesty. Nonetheless, his performances of Haydn and Mozart are perhaps too inflexible truly to capture the classical style.

Masur's recording career has been remarkable. He recorded first with the Dresden Philharmonic Orchestra, but after he became the conductor of the Leipzig Gewandhaus Orchestra he embarked on a comprehensive recording programme which has so far covered all the string and orchestral symphonies of Mendelssohn, the nine Beethoven symphonies, *Fidelio* and the *Missa Solemnis*, the complete symphonies of Schumann, Brahms and Bruckner, the orchestral works of Liszt, and the concertos and some orchestral pieces of Bruch, with the violinist Salvatore Accardo, with whom he has also recorded the Beethoven and Brahms Violin Concertos. Recordings of the symphonies of Prokofiev, Shostakovich and Tchaikovsky are planned. His stature was recognised internationally after Philips released the nine symphonies and overtures of Beethoven; in these he demonstrated a freshness and sensitivity, and a conception of the music that caused the set to eclipse for many years those of other conductors in the West much more celebrated and internationally renowned. Before making these records Masur had studied the manuscripts, first copies and early editions of the Beethoven symphonies: 'Especially after the Fourth Symphony he supervised less thoroughly once he'd written it. I found many differences. Double woodwind? I try to avoid it. Too often it pushes Beethoven into the wrong kind of heroism. If you double everything, you lose the warmth, tenderness and the homogeneity.' But, as Masur points out, these recordings of the Beethoven symphonies were made early in his association with the Leipzig Orchestra, and he would be interested in recording them all again, as the orchestra has now a much closer understanding of him and his style, which in itself has progressed from the time when the original records were made. In any event, they have now been issued by Philips on compact disc.

MATA, Eduardo (b. 1942). Born in Mexico City into a musical environment, Mata first learned the guitar, then studied at the National Conservatory of Music under Chávez and Halffter, and at the Berkshire Music Center in the USA under Leinsdorf and Schuller, and became the resident conductor there. He made his first impact in Mexico with performances of major avant-garde works, was musical director of the Mexican Ballet Company (1963–4), of the Guadalajara Symphony Orchestra (1965–6), of the University Philharmonic Orchestra of the National University of Mexico (1966–76), principal guest conductor, musical adviser then principal conductor of the Phoenix Symphony Orchestra (1970–8), artistic director of the Pueblo Ciudad Musical Festival (since 1974), music director of the Dallas Symphony Orchestra (since 1977) and artistic director of the Mexican National Opera (since 1973). He has been a guest conductor in many countries; in Mexico he has led first performances of music by Boulez, Stockhausen et al., toured Mexico with the New Philharmonia Orchestra (1976), led a Mahler cycle with the National Symphony Orchestra (1975), and has been awarded the Golden Lyre of the Mexican Union of Musicians (1973) and the Elias Sourasky Prize (1976). His compositions include symphonic and chamber works, ballets and vocal music, and pieces composed directly for tape. Mata is an impressive conductor, with an excellent technique, and has a personality that appeals to orchestral players. Much as he enjoys conducting the major symphony orchestras, he prefers to work with one orchestra and to try to achieve results over a long period, so that his criteria prevail in every aspect of interpretation. In Dallas he has aimed to produce a more European sound with the orchestra, and to play music by Bruckner, Mahler, and composers of the 20th century that have rarely, if ever, been played there. He has made many records in Mexico of local composers, and some records have also been issued with him conducting the Dallas Symphony, London Symphony and Philharmonia Orchestras. Of these, the complete *Daphnis et Chloé*, with the Dallas Symphony Orchestra, is exceptionally fine.

MATAČIĆ, Lovro von (1899–1985). Born in Sušak, Habsburg Croatia (now Yugoslavia), Matačić was a member of the Vienna Boys Choir, studied at the Vienna Conservatory, and began his conducting career as a répétiteur at the Cologne Opera. He was then conductor at Osijek (1919–20), Novi Sad (1920–22), Ljubljana (1924–6), Belgrade (1926–32), Zagreb (1932–8) and Belgrade again (1938–41). After World War II he was conductor at Skopje, general music director of the Dresden Staatskapelle and conductor at the Berlin Staatsoper (1956–8), conductor at La Scala, Milan and in Vienna (1958), general music director at Frankfurt-am-Main (1961–65), regular guest conductor at the Vienna State Opera, and conductor of the Zagreb Philharmonic Orchestra (from 1965). He appeared with orchestras in Europe and North and South America, and at music festivals in Salzburg, Venice, Florence, Rome, Naples, *et al.* In the years 1955–63 he made a number of recordings for EMI, including the celebrated one of *Die lustige Witwe* (with Elisabeth Schwarzkopf *et al.* and the Philharmonia Orchestra); he also recorded symphonies of Beethoven, Tchaikovsky and Bruckner for Supraphon, some of which are re-issued on compact disc. He is an interesting conductor for modern listeners, as he has a concept of interpretation typical of an earlier generation, where basic tempi are quickened and relaxed according to the lyrical or dramatic nature of the passage, imposing in many places an unusual degree of expression on the music which disturbs those who know it exactly as it is written. His interpretations find little favour among today's music critics, who have been deeply influenced by conductors such as Toscanini, Szell and Klemperer, whose literal readings avoid these tempi variations within movements and exaggerated phrasings. His recordings also include his own composition *Symphonie der Konfrontation* (1979), in which he directed the Japanese Broadcasting Corporation Symphony Orchestra.

MEHTA, **Zubin** (b. 1936). Mehta is a Parsi Indian, born in Bombay, where his father Meli Mehta had founded the Bombay String Quartet and the Bombay Symphony Orchestra, of which he was concertmaster then conductor. Meli Mehta also played under Barbirolli in the Hallé Orchestra, and later went to Los Angeles, where he taught and conducted the American Youth Orchestra. Zubin learned the piano and violin as a boy, and at 16 was conducting his father's orchestra at rehearsals. For two years he studied medicine, but abandoned it and went to Vienna in 1954 to enrol in the Vienna Academy of Music, where he studied conducting with Swarowsky, played the double bass in the Vienna Chamber Orchestra, and had the opportunity of observing Furtwängler and Karajan. In 1955 he won first prize in a conducting competition in Liverpool, which enabled him to work with Pritchard and conduct a number of concerts with the Liverpool Philharmonic Orchestra. In the next year he went to the Accademia Chigiana at Siena to study with Zecchi, and after taking part in another competition for conductors at Tanglewood, Massachusetts, he attracted the attention of Munch.

In the following years Mehta was a guest conductor with many orchestras, particularly in Brussels and Belgrade, and substituted for other conductors. In 1961 he became the youngest conductor to lead the Berlin and Vienna Philharmonic Orchestras, and in that year he substituted for Ormandy at a concert of the Montreal Symphony Orchestra, and for Reiner with the Los Angeles Philharmonic Orchestra. These events led to his engagement as musical director of both orchestras; he remained in Montreal until 1967, and his contract in Los Angeles terminated when he took up the appointment as musical director of the New York Philharmonic Orchestra in 1978, in succession to Boulez. In Los Angeles, when the orchestra originally engaged him for guest appearances, he was asked to conduct further concerts but without the knowledge of Solti, who had just been appointed musical director. This caused Solti to resign abruptly, and Mehta stepped into his shoes. Mehta first conducted the Israel Philharmonic Orchestra in 1962; his association with the orchestra grew, he led them on tour in 1966, and at the outbreak of the Israel–Arab war in 1967 he returned to Israel to conduct special concerts. In 1968 he was appointed music adviser to the orchestra and in 1977 music director. He first conducted at La Scala, Milan, in 1962, and at the New York Metropolitan in 1965, and has appeared there and in other major opera houses regularly. In 1962 he toured the USSR with the Montreal Symphony Orchestra. Mehta's Viennese training has implanted in him a strong preference for the Austrian and German classics, for the late romantics such as Bruckner, Mahler, Strauss and Wagner, and for the second Viennese school; composers such as Sibelius, Prokofiev and Vaughan Williams have much less appeal to him, although he is able to direct a score like Ravel's *La Valse* with ravishing effect. The conductor whom he admires most is Furtwängler, and he learnt from him that the music must *flow*, from the first to the last: 'Line seems to me the most essential thing in any performance—you must conceive the end at the beginning—too many climaxes won't work.' Sound, too, is important for him; in Los Angeles he strove to create the 'Viennese' sound with a round, sumptuous string tone, and when he took charge of the orchestra he persuaded the management to invest $300,000 to buy new instruments to improve the orchestra's sound. A Mehta performance is marked by this warmth of tone, and the style and approach to the score is relaxed and lyrical. There is little of the surface tension of Solti, the kinetic energy of Bernstein or the clinical precision of Boulez. He wins ready favour with both audiences and musicians for his charm and respectful manner, as much as for his authoritative musicianship. His gestures are simple and his beat very clear; he usually conducts without a score. Sometimes his interpretations are criticised for being too flamboyant and theatrical, and his performances of major works superficial, as though he were unable to convey his conception of the music's depth. Despite the glamorous image with which he was promoted in Los Angeles, he is a musician of complete integrity, whose natural instinct is to put the composer before himself.

Mehta professes that he does not like to record too much, and that he must perform works often before he commits them to record. His first disc of any significance was Bruckner's Symphony No. 9 with the Vienna Philharmonic Orchestra for Decca; it was an auspicious and unexpectedly fine performance. Later discs with the Vienna Philharmonic included Franz Schmidt's Symphony No. 4 and an impressive Symphony No. 2 of Mahler. Decca's series with him and the Los Angeles Philharmonic was extensive and highly successful commercially, and relied mainly on late 19th-century and 20th-century music: works by Tchaikovsky, Bruckner, Respighi, Saint-Saëns, Dvořák, Ravel, Mussorgsky, Elgar, Scriabin, Strauss, Schoenberg, Ives, Varèse, *et al*. The series with the Israel Philharmonic, also for Decca, included symphonies by Mozart, Schubert, Dvořák, Tchaikovsky and Mahler, Beethoven's ballet *Die Geschöpfe des Prometheus*, *Harold in Italy* (with Benyamini) and Bartók's *Concerto for Orchestra*, and with the New York Philharmonic, for CBS, *Symphonie fantastique* and symphonies of Beethoven and Brahms. His opera sets, *Turandot*, *Tosca*, *Aida* and *Il trovatore*, suggest that his natural gifts and sense of drama make him equally at home in the theatre as with the late Austrian and German classics.

MENGELBERG, Willem (1871–1951). The great Dutch conductor Mengelberg was born at Utrecht of German parents who had come from Cologne; his father was a church architect. He received his training at the School of Music in Utrecht and at the

Cologne Conservatory, where he studied the piano with Seiss and became an excellent pianist. His first professional appearance as a conductor was with the Gürzenich Orchestra at Cologne, and in 1891 he was appointed musical director at Lucerne. In 1895 he was offered the position of music director of the Concertgebouw Orchestra in Amsterdam, which had been established just seven years earlier by Willem Kes. He first appeared in Amsterdam as a pianist playing Liszt's Piano Concerto No. 1 at Kes's farewell concert, and at his first concert as a conductor Beethoven's Symphony No. 5 was on the programme. He remained with the orchestra for 50 years, although poor health restricted his activities in the last few years. In addition he was director of the Toonkunst Choir in Amsterdam (from 1898), of the Museum Concerts Society at Frankfurt-am-Main (1907–20), and conductor of the Caecilienverein there (from 1908). He toured Russia, Norway and Italy with the Concertgebouw Orchestra (1898), first visited London in 1903 to conduct at a Strauss festival, and became a regular visitor there between 1913 and World War II, and conducted in Paris. He was appointed professor of music at Utrecht University in 1933.

Mengelberg visited the United States in 1905 to conduct the New York Philharmonic Orchestra briefly, and was invited by Bodanzky in 1920 to be a guest conductor of his National Symphony Orchestra, which was merged with the New York Philharmonic in 1922 at Mengelberg's suggestion, and he was permanent conductor of the orchestra until 1930. He then resigned from the New York Philharmonic and left the USA for good; his reaction to Toscanini's rising popularity in New York, where he had also been conducting the New York Philharmonic since 1926, was to exaggerate some of his interpretations: this brought about a deterioration in his musicianship. Also, his repertoire was restricted by painstaking and slow preparation, and when the directors of the orchestra insisted on more frequent changes of programme, the new works were apt to be inadequately performed. Another cause of dissatisfaction was his custom of lecturing the orchestra at length at rehearsals about the composer to be played. Nevertheless his years in the USA had a significant effect on standards of orchestral performance there, and conductors who had held sway previously, such as Stransky and Damrosch, were forced to stand aside, a fate that Mengelberg himself suffered at the hands of Toscanini. Under Mengelberg the Concertgebouw Orchestra became one of the finest virtuoso orchestras in the world, and its greatness today had its origin in those times. In 1897 his performance of Tchaikovsky's Symphony No. 6 was sensationally received; Grieg, who was in the audience, leapt on a chair and addressed the audience, urging them to be proud of their orchestra and its conductor. Strauss dedicated his *Ein Heldenleben* to Mengelberg and the orchestra, as did Mahler his Symphonies Nos 5 and 8; Mengelberg promoted the music of both composers, who on occasion conducted the orchestra. He collaborated closely with Mahler in the performance of his symphonies in Amsterdam, and conducted a festival of his music there in 1920. In 1904 Mahler came to Amsterdam to conduct his Symphony No. 4 with the orchestra, and at the same concert half an hour later Mengelberg conducted the same symphony again; for him it was for the first time. An LP of a live recording made in 1939 of Mengelberg conducting the Concertgebouw Orchestra with the soprano Jo Vincent was once issued by Turnabout (in the USA); as Mengelberg's scores of the Mahler symphonies were very carefully marked, almost bar by bar, when he studied them with Mahler himself, and as Mengelberg was familiar with Mahler's interpretations, this performance might be presumed to be close to the composer's own. Mengelberg's performances of *Ein Heldenleben* were legendary; he recorded the work twice, with the Concertgebouw Orchestra and the New York Philharmonic. The latter, a performance of great power and urgency, was recorded by RCA in 1928 and was re-issued on LP in 1975. In 1899 he established the annual Palm Sunday concert of the *St Matthew Passion*, for which he was much admired; compact discs of his recording of this work are now available. He invited the world's most famous conductors and soloists to appear with his orchestra, led a Beethoven festival each year, and his associate conductors with the orchestra were, in turn, Muck, Monteux and Walter. He championed contemporary composers, especially Ravel, Debussy, Reger, Schoenberg and Stravinsky, and presented festivals of Dutch music in 1902, 1913 and 1935. Except on a few occasions in Lucerne, he did not conduct in the opera house. In his early years he composed a Mass for mixed choir, solo voices and orchestra, some songs, a *Praeludium on the Dutch National Hymn* and *Rembrandt Variations*, and he had a reputation for his knowledge of art. During the Nazi occupation of the Netherlands in World War II he collaborated with the invaders and conducted in Germany; after the war the Netherlands Honours Council forbade him from ever participating in the musical life of the country again, and he died in Switzerland in 1951.

Mengelberg achieved his extraordinarily high standards by preparing his scores meticulously and by drilling his orchestra exhaustively. *Till Eulenspiegel* was rehearsed for a full month before it was presented. He believed his role as a conductor was to discover what the composer intended behind the notes, to express it freely, and to improvise as the mood of the work unfolded. Of course, this can be read another way: he discovered what he intended behind the notes, and improvised according to the mood the work invoked in him as it unfolded. This highly subjective and romantic style of conducting, which would cause an uproar today, was more the rule than the exception at the time, and it took the overwhelming influence of Toscanini to sweep it aside. More recently, conductors such as Szell and Karajan, and among the younger generation Haitink and Abbado, who are literalists rather than romantics, have become the ones most admired. Even Jochum, whose performances have attracted frequent criticism for their romantic approach, would be considered literalist in comparison with Mengelberg. Listening to a Mengelberg performance nowadays, on compact disc, with the hindsight of countless later performances of the same piece, one is astonished at the remarkable skill used to achieve the distortions he imposed on the score. Adjectives such as 'wilful', 'exaggerated', 'egotistical' come to our lips, as they did, after all, to his listeners and critics. But Mengelberg believed that the true meaning of the piece was revealed uniquely to him, and that he was at perfect liberty to present this meaning as he found it. To him a literal reading destroyed feeling and life, and limited excitement; it would, in a word, be dull. Many of his performances were interesting and thrilling; in his time the gramophone record was conceived more as a concert performance, when individuality could be admired, rather than as an exact statement of the score, as it has so often become today. A conductor who interposes himself between the music and the listener with his own private inspiration is today, rightly or wrongly, thought to be betraying a trust. Mengelberg followed Strauss's advice to conductors: 'Do whatever you like, but never be dull.'

Mengelberg was a foremost recording artist, from the early 1920s to World War II. Among his first recordings, for Victor, was Liszt's *Les Préludes*, which was described by the American critic David Hall in 1940 as 'one of the most hair-raising things on record'. He went on to record, for a number of companies, over 40 composers, and 90 pieces were issued commercially. The Netherlands Broadcasting Company has another 40 or so pieces in its archives. Some scores—the *Egmont* overture, Beethoven's Symphony No. 1 and Tchaikovsky's Symphony No. 5—were recorded three times. Most of the discs were with the Concertgebouw Orchestra, and some with the New York Philharmonic Orchestra. Included were all the Beethoven and Brahms symphonies, Schubert's Symphonies Nos 8 and 9, Dvořák's Symphony No. 9, Tchaikovsky's Symphonies Nos 4, 5 and 6 and the *Romeo and Juliet* fantasie-overture, the adagietto from Mahler's Symphony No. 5, Strauss's *Tod und Verklärung* and *Don Juan*; Haydn and Mozart were all but missing. Some of these recordings were transferred to LP and now many, including the Beethoven and Brahms symphonies, have been issued on compact disc. Listeners today will surely recognise these as remarkable performances, even though some will dismiss them as perverse. But they will be of the greatest interest to those anxious to learn about the history of performance of symphonic music and of the great conductors of the past. Mengelberg once ranked with Nikisch and Mahler, and his records give some notion of his unique artistry and of the standards of performance and interpretation of a past era.

MENUHIN, Yehudi (b. 1916). One of the most celebrated violinists of the century, Menuhin was born in New York of Russian parents who then moved to San Francisco, and there, as a child, he studied the violin with Louis Persinger. At the age of 7 he played Lalo's *Symphonie espagnole* with the San Francisco orchestra under Hertz, and shortly afterwards made his début in Paris, Berlin, New York and London. He later studied with Adolf Busch and Georges Enesco; his career as a child prodigy and as a mature artist brought him the greatest distinctions and the highest musical accolades. As a violinist and chamber music player he has great warmth of tone and deep intensity, although in recent years his performances have been variable on occasion. He has recorded almost the entire violin repertoire in both concerto and chamber music forms, and one of the most famous recordings he made as a violinist is the Elgar Violin Concerto, which he made with the composer conducting the London Symphony Orchestra in 1932. From 1958 to 1968 he was the artistic director of the Bath Festival, and founded the Bath Festival Orchestra. He was also director of the Festival of Windsor, and for 20 years has been artistic director of the Yehudi Menuhin Festival at Gstaad in Switzerland. In addition he founded a residential school at Stoke d'Abernon in Surrey, to develop young musical talent, from the age of 6. With the Bath

Festival Orchestra and later with the Menuhin Festival Orchestra, Menuhin has made a superb series of recordings for EMI, in which, in many instances, he played the solo violin part besides conducting the orchestra. The works recorded include Bach's Suites and *Brandenburg Concertos*, Handel's Concerti Grossi Op. 6, symphonies of Haydn and Schubert, and a number of works of Mozart including *Die Entführung aus dem Serail*. He has toured with the orchestra in the USA, Australia and the Far East, and from time to time has conducted major symphony orchestras. As a conductor he displays the same qualities as he does as a violinist: warmth, vitality, a fine sense of rhythm, a splendid ear for balance and style, and great musical insight.

MITROPOULOS, Dmitri (1896–1960). Born in Athens, Mitropoulos was the grandson of a priest and the nephew of an archbishop, and it was intended that he should become a monk. However, this was not to be; he studied the piano at 7, and showed evidence of an extraordinary musical gift in memorising by the age of 14 many of the most popular operas. Attending the Athens Conservatory and University, he studied the piano and composition and in 1920 his opera *Soeur Béatrice*, based on a play of Maeterlinck, was produced. Saint-Saëns was present in the audience and was sufficiently impressed to arrange a scholarship for Mitropoulos to study with Gilson in Brussels and with Busoni in Berlin. Busoni was to convince him to abandon composition altogether, and to become an interpretative artist. From 1921 to 1925 Mitropoulos was at the Berlin Staatsoper under Kleiber, as a répétiteur, and on Kleiber's recommendation he was appointed conductor of the symphony orchestra at the Hellenic Conservatory in Athens. He transferred to the Athens Concert Society Orchestra in 1925 and then in 1927 became conductor of the State Symphony Orchestra in Greece. He was invited to conduct the Berlin Philharmonic Orchestra in 1930, and created a sensation by playing and conducting from the keyboard Prokofiev's Piano Concerto No. 3, when the soloist, Petri, was indisposed. This feat he repeated in Paris in 1932, in London and in the USA.

Mitropoulos conducted in Italy, England, the USSR and in Monte Carlo, and in 1936 Koussevitzky invited him to some guest appearances with the Boston Symphony Orchestra. In 1937 he was appointed musical director of the Minneapolis Symphony Orchestra, succeeding Ormandy, and in 1940 he was awarded the American Mahler Medal of Honour for his work in promoting the composer. After twelve years at Minneapolis, during which time he also conducted the New York Philharmonic Symphony Orchestra (1947–9), he was invited to share the principal conductorship of the New York orchestra with Stokowski in 1949, and became the sole conductor that year when Stokowski resigned. He became a US citizen in 1946 and remained in New York until 1959, in the meantime taking Walter's place as musical director of the New York Metropolitan Opera in 1954. In 1951 he led the New York Philharmonic Orchestra (as it changed its name) at the Edinburgh Festival, in 1955 on a tour of Europe, and shared the podium with Bernstein in a tour of Latin America in 1958. He died in Milan while rehearsing Mahler's Symphony No. 3 with the La Scala Orchestra.

Mitropoulos was an incredibly gifted musician, but he stood outside the traditional German school of interpretation. As his conducting career developed he gave up composition; his most important work, *Concerto Grosso*, was premièred in 1929, but he never recorded his own music. There have been several recordings of him as a pianist: Prokofiev's Piano Concerto No. 3 with the Robin Hood Dell Orchestra with himself conducting, and a coupling of Loeffler's *Rhapsody for Oboe, Violin and Piano* and Hindemith's Oboe Sonata, both with the oboist Gomberg. His exhaustive and infallible memory was the wonder of his fellow musicians; he rehearsed even the most complicated works, such as *Wozzeck*, without a score. He would demonstrate his photographic memory by taking the New York telephone directory, opening it at random, studying it for a few minutes, then reciting names, addresses and numbers in perfect detail. He was a tall, lean, bald man, reserved and shy, and lived completely without ostentation in an almost monastic fashion. He avoided the social activities usually imposed on conductors, although he was generous to students and to struggling composers. As a conductor he was exaggeratively demonstrative in his manner; he directed the orchestra with jerky movements of his hands, rarely used a baton, and his body appeared to vibrate with the music. His great nervous intensity brought to bear on the music more expressive weight than it could sometimes take. Virgil Thomson, who witnessed many of his concerts in New York, described him as 'oversensitive, overweaning, overbrutal, over-intelligent, underconfident and wholly without ease. . . . His personal excitement bordered on hysteria and distorted music with nervous passion.' These qualities scarcely fitted him for the music of Haydn, Mozart, Beethoven and the early 19th century, but his readings of later romantic and modern music were highly expressive, individual and subjective, although short of the grand and dramatic gestures of a Stokowski and Koussevitzky. He performed much modern music, perhaps more than his audiences were prepared to listen to, championed Schoenberg, Webern and Berg; of British composers he admired Vaughan Williams, particularly his Symphony No. 4, and Joseph Holbrook, whose neglect he could not understand.

At the New York Metropolitan Opera, Mitropoulos was a dynamic force; he introduced many new operas, and gave highly dramatic performances of the standard repertoire. His *Wozzeck*, *Boris Godunov*, *Un ballo in maschera* and *Vanessa* of Barber, with the Metropolitan company, were recorded by Columbia and Victor (for the last two), and his *Elektra* with the company was released by the Off-the-Air Record Club. Of these, *Wozzeck* was outstanding. Many critics have commented that his concert performances were extremely variable and his interpretations were much subject to the mood of the moment; sometimes the concert performances would be quite different from the rehearsal. His control of the New York Philharmonic was unsure, as he was fundamentally too mild a man to assert his authority. This situation finally led to his resignation, and according to some he left New York a broken man. As a recording artist he enjoyed a substantial career with Columbia (USA), first with the Minneapolis Symphony Orchestra and then with the New York Philharmonic. He avoided the major Viennese classics, except for Beethoven's Symphony No. 6 and Brahms's *Variations on the St Antony Chorale*, although his recording of Mendelssohn's Symphony No. 3 was admired. The recording that took his name around the world was that of Mahler's Symphony No. 1, made in 1941 with the Minneapolis Symphony; it was the first ever of the work in the USA. The last he made was of the same composer's Symphony No. 8, in his final year, in Salzburg. Except perhaps for *Wozzeck*, few of his records can aspire to the status of 'great recordings of the century'; his style was too personal for his readings of the standard repertoire to gain general acceptance. But he was always an interesting and individual artist who had the power to produce absorbing performances. Some of his recordings have been re-issued by Columbia on the Odyssey label and give an excellent impression of his work: *Symphonie fantastique*, Tchaikovsky's Symphony No. 6, *Fantasia on a Theme of Thomas Tallis*, Schoenberg's *Verklärte Nacht* and (in Britain) Vaughan Williams's Symphony No. 4. A memorial to the conductor is the Dmitri Mitropoulos International Competition for Conductors, which is held annually in New York, for young conductors between the ages of 20 and 33.

MONTEUX, Pierre (1875–1964). Born in Paris, Monteux started to learn the violin when he was 6, entered the Paris Conservatoire at 9, conducted his first concert at 12, and then toured with an orchestra with Cortot as soloist. In 1894 he was playing at concerts as a member of a string quartet, and in 1896 shared with Thibaud the first prize for violin playing at the Conservatoire. He then became a violist with the Colonne and Opéra-Comique orchestras, and was appointed choirmaster, assistant conductor, and then conductor of the Colonne Orchestra. He conducted the orchestra at the Dieppe Casino (1910), organised his own Concerts Berlioz at the Casino de Paris (1911), and came to the notice of Diaghilev who engaged him as principal conductor for his Ballets Russes Company, with which he conducted the premières of *Petrushka* (1911), *Daphnis et Chloé* (1912), *Le Sacre du printemps* (1913), *Jeux* (1913) and *Le Rossignol* (1914). The first night of *Le Sacre du printemps* in Paris caused a sensation with uproar among the audience. In 1913–14 he also conducted at the Paris Opéra, was a guest conductor at Covent Garden and Drury Lane in London, as well as in Berlin, Budapest and Vienna. In 1914 he founded La Société des Concerts Populaires in Paris.

Monteux served with the French army in 1913 and 1914, and saw action at Verdun, Rheims, Soissons and the Argonne. He was then recalled from the army to join the Ballets Russes in the USA, and to make propaganda for the Allied cause there. He conducted the Ballets Russes (1916–17), the Civic Orchestral Society in New York (1917), took over the French repertoire at the New York Metropolitan Opera (1917–19), and then was appointed musical director of the Boston Symphony Orchestra (1919–24). He then faced difficulties in Boston, since the orchestra was on strike, trying unsuccessfully to force its members into a union; as a result 20 players, including the concertmaster, left. Monteux resigned, and was succeeded by Koussevitzky. For ten years he was an associate conductor with Mengelberg with the Amsterdam Concertgebouw Orchestra (1924–34), as well as conducting the Amsterdam Wagner Society. In 1928 he returned to the USA to conduct the Philadelphia Orchestra during a temporary absence of Stokowski; he then became conductor of the Paris Symphony Orchestra (1929–38), was permanent conductor of the San Francisco Symphony Orchestra (1935–52), and organised and conducted the first concerts of the NBC

Symphony Orchestra (1937). During Munch's time with the Boston Symphony Orchestra (1949–62) he was a regular guest conductor with the orchestra, became a US citizen in 1942, re-appeared at the New York Met. in 1954 and 1958, was chief conductor of the London Symphony Orchestra (1961, until his death in 1964), and from 1941 trained many student conductors at his home in Hancock, Maine.

Monteux was one of the most charming of men and at the same time one of the most important conductors of this century. His personality completely lacked pretension, and he disliked any form of exhibition or histrionics. Maybe for this reason he was never fully appreciated by audiences on the East Coast of the USA, although in San Francisco he was venerated. Certainly some New York critics recognised his stature; Virgil Thomson wrote in 1944 that he had transformed the New York Philharmonic-Symphony Orchestra with the exceptional beauty he drew from them. He was a short, thick figure, and his manner before the orchestra was almost without emotion, quite restrained and always even-tempered. He rarely needed to use a score, and his conducting seemed effortless. Toscanini remarked that Monteux had the finest baton technique of any conductor he knew. But his eyes and face, particularly his smile, conveyed everything to his players. At rehearsals he spared no effort, but at the concert he directed with unruffled calm. Every piece he conducted was treated as if he were doing it for the first time, although he admitted that some of the scores of Debussy and Ravel, which he was called on to conduct often, had lost their appeal. He continued to be interested in new music until the end of his life; at 80 he was studying music by Hindemith, Britten and Bliss, and first conducted Elgar's *Enigma Variations*, from memory, and the British musicians who played under him declared the performance closer to the composer's than any other. He refused to touch up a score, or to change a note, without, in cases where possible, consulting the composer.

Monteux was nurtured in the music of Mozart, Beethoven and Brahms, and frequently pointed out that he had to learn the French repertoire, since much of it had not been written when he was a young man. Unlike many French conductors, he gave superb performances of Beethoven and Brahms, with a lighter orchestral texture than most European conductors. His Wagner, Strauss and Tchaikovsky were equally fine. He had little interest in post-impressionist music, despite his keenness to programme new works. He had an extraordinary sense of orchestral colour and nuance, and an ability to see each musical piece as a whole and not as a series of episodes. One critic pointed out that he could create a sense in the listener's mind that he was simultaneously hearing sounds from far away, and others from nearby. He never imposed his own personality on the music, saying: 'I have no interpretation, I play the music.' However, he did realise that it was not possible to teach his students any more than technique, declaring that: 'Music must be second nature. That's something you cannot learn.' He compiled rules for young conductors, some of which were that the conductor must always conduct with a baton, so that the players far from him can see the beat; that one must never conduct for the audience; not to adhere pedantically to the metronome time, but vary the tempo according to the subject or phrase and give each its own character; not to be disrespectful to the players; not to forget individuals' rights as persons; and not to undervalue the members of the orchestra or treat them simply as cogs in the machinery. Orchestral players and soloists all appreciated his humanity, scholarship and understanding, yet his self-effacing personality put him at a disadvantage compared to his charismatic rivals, and brought him many personal disappointments. One tragedy he never mentioned was the slaughter of his relatives by the Nazis in World War II, because of their activities in the Résistance in France, and because they were Jews.

Monteux had a long and distinguished recording career, making his first discs with the Paris Symphony Orchestra in the 1930s. He undertook a major series for RCA with the San Francisco Symphony Orchestra, and these 78 r.p.m. and later LP records were technically significant as they were the first to be recorded on magnetic tape. Included were symphonies by Beethoven, Schumann, Brahms, Franck and Chausson, as well as *Le Sacre du printemps*, *Tod und Verklärung*, *La Valse* and the *Daphnis et Chloé* Suite No. 2. On LP he also recorded with the Vienna Philharmonic, London Symphony, Paris Conservatoire, Boston Symphony, Chicago Symphony, RCA Victor Symphony, Amsterdam Concertgebouw and North West German Radio Symphony Orchestras, variously for RCA, Philips, Decca, Westminster and La Guilde Internationale du Disque, the repertoire including symphonies and orchestral pieces by Haydn, Bach, Beethoven, Brahms, Berlioz, Dvořák, Sibelius, Tchaikovsky, Stravinsky and Wagner, as well as the inevitable Debussy and Ravel. His *Enigma Variations*, with the London Symphony Orchestra for RCA, was remarkably idiomatic, and another exceptional recording was Massenet's *Manon*, in which he led the Rome Opera House Orchestra with Victoria de los Angeles heading the cast. Many of these discs were re-issued on cheap labels and are, by any standard, superb performances. They most certainly are not showpieces for romantic extravagance on the one hand, or for breathtaking but cold-hearted precision on the other: they are examples of his unsurpassed ability to perform a score so that the composer is the one to whom we give all our attention, rather than to the interpreter.

MORRIS, Wyn (b. 1929). After studying at the Royal Academy of Music and at the Salzburg Mozarteum, Morris was an apprentice conductor with the Yorkshire Symphony Orchestra (1950–1), musical director of an army band (1951–3), and founded and conducted the Welsh Symphony Orchestra (1954–7). In 1957 he was winner of the Koussevitzky Memorial Prize of the Boston Symphony Orchestra, and then was with Szell at the Cleveland Orchestra as an observer (1957–60), at the same time conducting the Cleveland Orpheus Choir and the Cleveland Chamber Orchestra (1958–60). Returning to Britain, he became conductor of the Choir of the Royal National Eisteddfod of Wales (1960–2), made his début in London with the Royal Philharmonic Orchestra (1963), was conductor of the Royal Choral Society (1968–70), and has been conductor of the Huddersfield Choral Society (since 1969) and of the Bruckner–Mahler Chorale (since 1970). Morris made his name as a conductor of Mahler, and in 1968 was awarded the Mahler Memorial Medal of the Bruckner and Mahler Society of America. With an orchestra called the Symphonica of London he has recorded Mahler's Symphonies Nos 1, 5 and 8, Cooke's reconstruction of the Symphony No. 10, and *Lieder eines fahrenden Gesellen* (with Hermann); he also recorded *Das klagende Lied* and *Des Knaben Wunderhorn* with the New Philharmonia and London Philharmonic Orchestras, respectively. A powerful and sensitive interpreter of Mahler, Morris obtains dramatic playing from his orchestras, perhaps not always with the polish of most of the other conductors who have recorded this music, but this is compensated for by his original and thoroughly convincing understanding of the music.

MRAVINSKY, Yevgeny (b. 1903). Born in St Petersburg, Mravinsky was active in theatrical productions while still at school, and later was an accompanist at the Leningrad Ballet School. He studied at the Leningrad Conservatory (1924–30) under Scherbachov for composition, and Gauk and Malko for conducting. His début as a conductor was in 1929; he was with the Leningrad Opera and Ballet Theatre (now the Kirov Theatre) from 1932 to 1938. In 1937 he premièred Shostakovich's Symphony No. 5, and since then has been closely associated with Shostakovich, leading the first performances of most of his music, including the Symphonies Nos 5, 6, 8, 9 and 10; the Symphony No. 8 is dedicated to him. In 1938 he won the first prize in the All-Union Conductors' Competition, and in the same year he was appointed chief conductor of the Leningrad Philharmonic Orchestra. With the orchestra he toured the USA in 1946 and 1957, and Western Europe in 1956, 1961, and later. In 1946 he was awarded the Stalin Prize, and in 1961 the Lenin Prize.

A tall man with a somewhat aloof appearance, Mravinsky is one of the foremost Soviet conductors, and the Leningrad Philharmonic is one of the most distinguished Soviet orchestras. His interpretations are quite literal in that he performs the music exactly as it is written, and his technique is such that he can make the orchestra play the music precisely as he wishes to hear it. The orchestral texture is exceptionally clear; his readings are not in the least influenced by convention and frequently have an electrifying effect, although a certain restlessness is occasionally present. His selection of tempi is always interesting, and sometimes unusual, as in the relatively slow first movement of Beethoven's Symphony No. 7, and the very fast finale of Tchaikovsky's Symphony No. 4. But there appears to be in his performances a concern for orchestral virtuosity for its own sake, as if he were only performing the notes without heed to the poetic content of the music, so that some music, such as the Symphony No. 6 of Beethoven, gives an impression of chilliness that belies his own love of the score. In the words of his long-time colleague, Kurt Sanderling: 'He has a heart but it does not show.' Nonetheless, it is surprising that such an important artist has appeared so sparsely in the EMI Melodiya series that has been issued in Britain and the USA, and that many of the records released, and indeed available, in the USSR, have been of live concert performances taped years before.

Although Mravinsky made records on 78s, the discs that drew the attention of Western listeners to his great gifts were the mono LPs of Tchaikovsky's Symphonies Nos 4, 5 and 6 with the Leningrad Philharmonic, which were issued by DGG. Since then others have found their way to the West on various labels, including Haydn's Symphony No. 101, Mozart's Symphonies Nos 33 and 39, Beethoven's Symphonies Nos 4, 5, 6 and 7, Schubert's Symphony No. 8, Brahms' Symphonies Nos 1, 2 and

4, Bruckner's Symphonies Nos 8 and 9, Sibelius's Symphony No. 7, Hindemith's *Die Harmonie der Welt*, Stravinsky's *Agon* and *Apollon Musagète*, Scriabin's *Poème d'extase*, Bartók's *Music for Strings, Celeste and Percussion*, Shostakovich's Symphonies Nos 5, 6, 7, 8, 10, 11, 12 and 15, and Prokofiev's Symphonies Nos 6 and 7.

MUNCH, **Charles** (1891–1968). Munch was born in Strasbourg, then part of Germany, into a musical family; the original spelling of the name was Münch. His father was the founder of the Choeur St Guillaume and a professor at the Strasbourg Conservatory, and Albert Schweitzer was a distant relative. Munch studied the violin at the conservatory whose director was then Pfitzner, and went to Paris to continue his violin studies under Capet. He started on a career as a solo violinist, but at the outbreak of World War I he was enlisted in the German army, was gassed at Péronne and wounded at Verdun. After the war, he became a French citizen with the return of Alsace-Lorraine to France, and came to Berlin to study the violin with Flesch. Returning to France, he was professor of violin at Strasbourg Conservatory and concertmaster of the municipal orchestra there (1919–26), but went to Leipzig where he taught the violin at the conservatory and played in the Gewandhaus Orchestra under Furtwängler and Walter. When he refused to become a German national, he was forced to resign from the orchestra in 1929, and with the advent of the Nazis he left Germany altogether.

Munch made his début as a conductor in 1932, at the age of 41, with the Straram Orchestra in Paris, and after conducting the Paris Conservatoire Orchestra in the next year he was invited to conduct other orchestras in Paris, such as the Lamoureux. A fortunate marriage released him from the necessity of supporting himself as a violinist; he devoted himself entirely to conducting, studying it with Alfred Sendry in Paris (1933–40). In 1935 he was appointed principal conductor of the Paris Philharmonic Orchestra, which had been founded by Cortot; he became a professor at the École Normale de Musique (1936), principal conductor for the International Society for Contemporary Music (1937), and conductor of the Paris Conservatoire Orchestra, in succession to Gaubert (1938–46). He kept the orchestra alive during World War II, but refused to collaborate with the Nazis in any way, declining the directorship of the Paris Opéra because it meant involving himself with them. He assisted the Résistance, protected his players from religious persecution, and at his country house Allied pilots and refugees were harboured on the escape route. At the end of the war he was awarded the Légion d'Honneur. However his championship of the music of contemporaries such as Honegger and Milhaud, and his neglect of more familiar music in his programmes, eventually brought his resignation from the Paris Conservatoire Orchestra; he then toured Europe and South America, made his début in the USA in 1946, and visited the USA with the French National Radio Orchestra in 1948. The impression he made brought his appointment as conductor of the Boston Symphony Orchestra, following Koussevitzky (1948–62), and he led the orchestra on a tour of the Soviet Union (1956); it was the first time an American orchestra had played in that country. After some years as a guest conductor he became the first music director of the Orchestre de Paris, which had been founded in 1967 by André Malraux, the Minister of Culture, to create a French orchestra comparable to the leading ones in Europe. Munch died in the USA when he was on tour with the orchestra in 1968.

Munch was the antithesis of Koussevitzky, from whom he had inherited possibly the finest orchestra existing at the time. Koussevitzky was authoritarian, ruthless with his players, and exhaustively painstaking at rehearsal; his readings had superlative polish. Munch was a gracious, charming but shy man, considerate to his musicians, and always mindful of his own experience as an orchestral violinist. His lack of pretension is exemplified in his remark to his friends that he was a conductor 'only because I am too stupid to do anything else'. On occasion he also expressed criticism of Koussevitzky's severity with the orchestra and his rigorous rehearsal methods. But like Koussevitzky he performed the French repertoire with great distinction, and when he brought the French National Radio Orchestra to the USA the elegance and polish of its style and sound were particularly noted. Munch was never concerned with small details in rehearsal, and his performances had a spontaneity missing from Koussevitzky's readings. The Boston Symphony Orchestra remained a great orchestra, if not the greatest one; its position was taken over by the Cleveland Orchestra, who achieved the same standard of precision under Szell. Observers have written that in successive performances of the same work Munch's tempi were not always the same; spontaneity never left him. Despite his early years in Germany, he was a typically French conductor, naturally concerned with colour, clarity and balance rather than with profundity or sentiment. His performances of Haydn, Mozart, Beethoven, Schubert, Brahms *et al.*

had an impetuosity and a somewhat superficial brilliance and attracted the criticism that he was too fast and loud with the central repertoire. Even so, David Woolridge (in his *Conductor's World*, 1970) suggested a different view, writing that Munch's 'performances of the Third, Sixth and Seventh Symphonies of Beethoven, and the First and Fourth of Brahms, were among the ultimate pinnacles of music-making'. Certainly his recordings of Beethoven's Symphony No. 3, Schubert's Symphony No. 9 and Brahms's Symphonies Nos 1 and 4, with the Boston Symphony Orchestra, were revealing examples of his special sound and spirit. On the other hand, Beethoven's Symphony No. 9, also with the Boston Symphony, reduced these qualities to brusqueness and disregard for nuance equal to gross insensitivity. In his book, *I am a Conductor*, Munch wrote that a critic once reproached Richard Strauss for having conducted a Mozart symphony too quickly. Strauss replied: 'These gentlemen of the press seem to have a direct wire to Olympus.'

Munch's recording career started in Paris before World War II, when he made discs for HMV and Columbia with the Paris Conservatoire Orchestra, *inter alia*, mostly of French music. After the war he came under contract for Decca and most of his records were with the Paris Conservatoire and London Philharmonic Orchestras; again French music predominated, but there were some symphonies by Beethoven, Mendelssohn, Schumann and Tchaikovsky. Among these discs for Decca, the *Daphnis et Chloé* Suite No. 2 was specially successful. In the USA, he first made records for CBS, but when he became conductor of the Boston Symphony Orchestra, RCA embarked on a significant series, with a wide-ranging repertoire, from the *Brandenburg Concertos* to Martinů's Symphony No. 6. The most successful performances were those of French music by Berlioz, Franck, Debussy, Ravel, Chausson, d'Indy, Milhaud, Poulenc, Honegger, Saint-Saëns and Bizet. Among the other works were Beethoven's Symphonies Nos 1, 3, 5, 6, 7 and 9, symphonies and major orchestral works of Schubert, Schumann, Mendelssohn, Brahms, Dvořák, Tchaikovsky, Strauss, Stravinsky, Scriabin and others. After he left Boston he made many records with European orchestras, again almost all of French composers. A number of his discs with the Boston Symphony are still available in the USA, but far fewer in Britain.

MÜNCHINGER, Karl (b. 1915). Born in Stuttgart, Münchinger learned several instruments at an early age, and composed cantatas in the style of Bach, to whose works he was devoted. He studied at the Stuttgart Academy of Music, taking his diploma in composition and choral conducting, was a revolutionary young composer, and also organist and choirmaster at St Martin's Church in Stuttgart. He was a pupil of Abendroth in Leipzig, Krauss in Salzburg and came under the influence of Furtwängler, became first conductor of the Lower Saxony Orchestra in Hanover (1941–3), and after World War II returned to Stuttgart, where he founded the Stuttgart Chamber Orchestra, which was made up of musicians many of whom had been his fellow students. He gave his first concert with the orchestra in September 1945, and in its first ten years, under Münchinger, it became internationally famous, primarily for the music of Bach. Subsequently the orchestra's repertoire extended; he was more frequently engaged as a guest conductor with major symphony orchestras, especially the Vienna Philharmonic and the Paris Conservatoire, and he also founded the Stuttgart Classical Philharmonic Orchestra in 1966. He and the Stuttgart Chamber Orchestra toured five continents, and have played more than 3,000, concerts, appeared at festivals in Edinburgh, Salzburg, Athens and elsewhere, and toured in the USSR, in Eastern Europe and in the People's Republic of China, making their début in the USA in San Francisco in 1953.

While the reputation of the Stuttgart Chamber Orchestra arises from its performances of baroque music, especially that of Bach, the orchestra's repertoire includes Mozart and romantics such as Dvořák, and moderns such as Honegger and Martin. In rehearsal Münchinger insists on great accuracy; he never talks about the music, and is extremely demanding about dynamics. His strongly accented rhythms and uncompromising attack could be said to be characteristically German, and contrast with the styles of other celebrated chamber orchestras such as I Musici, the Academy of St Martin-in-the-Fields and the Jean-François Paillard Orchestra, to name only three. Each of these represents a certain national style in its performance of the baroque masters, in particular. In general, the Stuttgart style is straightforward and crisp, and devoid of sentimentality. However, the performance of Bach and the baroque masters by orchestras with modern instruments has now been overtaken by those with original instruments which attempt to reproduce the performing practices of the time when the music was written. Public taste appears now to be moving towards the original-instrument performances of Harnoncourt, Pinnock, Hogwood, Gardiner *et al.*, and while one recognises the excellence of the

Stuttgart Chamber Orchestra under Münchinger, they sound today as from a past era of interpretative practice.

Münchinger and his orchestra have had an exclusive recording contract with Decca almost since the orchestra's inception. The *Brandenburg Concertos*, which were recorded again later for stereo, were first issued in 1951 and quickly became bestsellers. Similarly, their record of Vivaldi's *The Four Seasons* was one of those that aroused almost universal interest in the composer and was the prelude to his enormous popularity and the flood of records of baroque music that followed. Münchinger's other major recordings with the orchestra have been Bach's suites, *St John Passion*, *St Matthew Passion*, *Mass in B Minor*, *Magnificat*, *Christmas Oratorio* and *Easter Oratorio*, a number of other discs of music by baroque composers, Haydn, Mozart, *et al*. The *St Matthew Passion*, which was released in 1965, remains probably the finest recording made of the work and, with one or two exceptions, the other performances are scarcely less good. He also recorded with the Suisse Romande, the Paris Conservatoire, the Vienna Philharmonic and the Stuttgart Classical Philharmonic Orchestras; of these records the most impressive was *The Creation*, with the Vienna Philharmonic *et al*.

MUTI, **Riccardo** (b. 1941). Born in Naples, the son of a doctor, Muti learned the piano and violin as a boy, studied music and philosophy at Naples University, and the piano at Naples Conservatory. He first conducted with a student orchestra there, then studied conducting and composition with Votto at the Milan Conservatory, and was the first Italian to win the Guido Cantelli competition for conducting, in 1967. The next year he made his professional début, accompanying Richter at the Maggio Musicale Fiorentino, and in 1969 was appointed principal conductor of the Florence orchestra. He has conducted opera in many Italian cities, in Vienna and London, and appeared with the Berlin Philharmonic, Vienna Philharmonic, Chicago Symphony and the Philadelphia Orchestras regularly, as well as taking part in the Salzburg and other major musical festivals in Europe. In 1973 he substituted for Klemperer at a concert with the New Philharmonia Orchestra, and as a result became its principal conductor, in 1977, when the orchestra reverted to its original title, the Philharmonia Orchestra. In 1982 his appointment with the Philharmonia came to an end, and he was then made conductor laureate; in that year he also retired from the Maggio Musicale Fiorentino. His association with the Philadelphia Orchestra started when he impressed Ormandy during the orchestra's visit to Europe in 1970; he was engaged for the 1972 season, became principal guest conductor in 1977, and in 1980 was appointed Ormandy's successor as musical director. In 1986 he also became musical director of the La Scala Opera, Milan, relatively close to his permanent home in Ravenna.

Muti is an intensely exciting and dramatic conductor, much in the Toscanini mould; in fact he regards himself as a successor to Toscanini, whom he considers the greatest, and constantly refers to him when rehearsing the orchestra; but he also professes to admire Furtwängler. His performances impress for their precision, intensity and sheer physical exhilaration, but frequently the spiritual content and meaning of the music evades him. He has a somewhat different attitude from an earlier Philadelphian, Stokowski; about re-arranging scores he says: 'I cannot admire the desire to change every score on your desk. I think you shouldn't touch a note. If you don't like a score, don't play it. It is like going to a museum to see the paintings. "Oh, very beautiful," I say, "but here, let me just touch up this corner and add paint there." It is unthinkable in painting, but common in music.' The extreme polish of his performances is the result, at least partly, of his insistence on perfection of execution; he often takes one section of the orchestra and goes over a particular passage slowly, as the individual players would if they were practising. Despite his interest in opera, he is disinclined to undertake more than three new operatic ventures each year, so that his interpretations can be developed from the outset of each production. For the past three years, in October, he has prepared in Philadelphia a concert performance of an opera, but the prohibitive cost of recording opera in the USA prevents these superb performances being available to a world-wide public. He has spent much time studying the Verdi operas and their performance, and believes that it is important to understand the libretto fully before conducting them: 'Verdi was a great man of the theatre; sometimes the dramatic side is even more important than the music. And the recitatives can be even more fantastic than the arias.' He is enthusiastic about his new appointment at La Scala, as the chorus and orchestra there are now at their best: 'Italian operas need the kind of sound they produce so naturally, a sound with a typical Italian colouration: very direct, very pure, sharp but not edgy—the sort of orchestral sound that Toscanini recreated with the NBC Symphony.' Among modern composers, he is attracted to Penderecki, Berio and Ligeti, the last of whom 'has found a way to make the orchestra a contemporary instrument that's both new and very old.' His influence on the

Philadelphia Orchestra has transformed it far from the sound and style of Ormandy; according to the critic Peter G. Davies, it 'is the most versatile, most finely tuned, and most instrumentally refined orchestra in the land'.

Muti has recorded exclusively for EMI since 1975, first with the Philharmonia Orchestra. The first recordings were Cherubini's *Requiem in D*, and *Aida*, which was the beginning of a series of the Verdi operas, including also *Un ballo in maschera*, *Macbeth*, *Nabucco* and *La traviata*. Other operas he has recorded are *I puritani*, *Don Pasquale*, *Orfeo ed Euridice* and *Pagliacci* (with the Philharmonia Orchestra *et al.*) and *Così fan tutte* (with the Vienna Philharmonic Orchestra *et al.*). His other discs with the Philharmonia Orchestra include the complete symphonies of Mendelssohn, Schumann and Tchaikovsky, *Scheherazade* and Verdi's *Requiem*. With the Philadelphia Orchestra he started a cycle of the Beethoven symphonies with Nos 6 and 7, and the other important discs have been Franck's *Symphony in D Minor*, Liszt's *Faust Symphony*, Mahler's Symphony No. 1, *Scheherazade*, *Petrushka*, excerpts from Prokofiev's *Romeo and Juliet* and Scriabin's Symphony No. 1. His first disc with the Berlin Philharmonic Orchestra, issued in 1986, is Bruckner's Symphony No. 4. A number of these latter recordings have made outstanding compact discs.

N

NEUMANN, Václav (b. 1920). Born in Prague into a musical family, Neumann learned the violin as a boy, and played in chamber music groups at high school. He studied history, Czech philology and musicology, but since universities in Czechoslovakia were closed during World War II he entered the Prague Conservatory and studied the violin and conducting. In 1941 he founded, with Antonín Kohout, the chamber ensemble that was later to become famous as the Smetana Quartet. He was a member of the Quartet for seven years, initially as the first violin and later as the viola player. He then became a member of the Czech Philharmonic Orchestra (1945), and in 1948, when Kubelík, the permanent conductor of the orchestra, fell sick, he deputised for him and launched his career as a conductor. He first conducted at Karlovy Vary (1951) and Brno (1954), was conductor of the Prague Symphony Orchestra (1956–63), the Prague Philharmonic Orchestra (1963–4), and was chief conductor of the Berlin Komische Oper (1957–60), where he came to international attention for his presentation of Janáček's *The Cunning Little Vixen* in Felsenstein's production. He was appointed conductor of the Leipzig Gewandhaus Orchestra and general music director of the Leipzig Opera (1964–7); in 1968 he returned to Czechoslovakia as chief conductor of the Czech Philharmonic Orchestra, and up until 1977 he had performed more than 250 compositions and had given almost 500 concerts at home and abroad. He also was music director of the Württemberg State Theatre in Stuttgart, in succession to Leitner (1970–1), he toured Europe with the Leipzig Gewandhaus Orchestra in 1964, and later visited the United States with the Czech Philharmonic. In 1966 he received the National Prize of DR Germany, and was named honoured artist in 1967.

Neumann has emerged as one of the major Czech conductors, and as conductor of the Czech Philharmonic Orchestra is in direct succession to Talich, Kubelík and Ančerl. In addition to being a distinguished interpreter of the music of his native country, his musical sympathies extend to composers such as Gershwin and Elgar. His recordings in Czechoslovakia have been released in the West on a number of labels; he first came to notice as a recording artist with the Prague Symphony Orchestra in Dvořák's Symphonies Nos 1, 2 and 4, which were the first recordings of these works to be generally available. He subsequently re-recorded all the Dvořák symphonies with the Czech Philharmonic Orchestra. He has made a formidable list of recordings for Supraphon, the most notable being the symphonies of Mahler and Martinů, and the operas *The Cunning Little Vixen* and *The Excursions of Mr Brouček* of Janáček, and Smetana's *The Secret*.

NIKISCH, Arthur (1855–1922). Born in Lébényi Szant-Miklós in Hungary, of a Moravian father and a Hungarian mother, Nikisch showed remarkable musical talent in childhood, and at the age of 11 entered the Vienna Conservatory to study the violin and piano. In later life he was to say that all conductors should learn the violin, not only for its own sake, but because of the command it gives to the wrist. As a violinist he played in the Vienna Court Orchestra (1872–4) under Brahms, Wagner, Verdi, Bruckner, Rubinstein and Liszt, and his memory was such that he could recall every detail of their performances for the rest of his life. His career as a conductor started in 1878 in Leipzig, where he was second conductor at the opera; during his lifetime his appointments included conductor of the Boston Symphony Orchestra (1889–93), musical director of the Budapest Opera (1893–5), principal conductor of the Leipzig Opera (1879–89 and 1905–6), conductor of the Philharmonic concerts in Hamburg (1897–1922), and conductor of the Leipzig Gewandhaus and the Berlin Philharmonic Orchestras simultaneously (1895–1922). He toured often in Europe and Russia, frequently visited Britain where he led several cycles of *The Ring* at Covent Garden (1913–14), conducted at the Leeds Festival and with the London Symphony Orchestra, which he took on a tour of the USA (1912). He often appeared in London as piano accompanist to the great lieder singer Elena Gerhardt.

The leading conductor of his day, Nikisch was a unique and incomparable artist. Boult, who studied with him in Leipzig for two years, regarded him as a perfect technical model; Klemperer had the highest opinion of him, saying that he was 'really a virtuoso', and conducted the Schumann symphonies wonderfully; 'His parade pieces were the *Tannhäuser* overture and, above all, Tchaikovsky's *Symphonie Pathétique*, which he did phenomenally—great beauty of sound, controlled and yet very passionate.' His extraordinary power was a combination of a feeling for colour, melodic phrasing, dynamic graduations, rhythmic freedom, rubato, and a constant variation between tension and relaxation, all of which was entirely instinctive.

Even so, many critics disapproved of his supposedly erratic tempi, exaggerated rubatos and dynamics, and some remarked that he never played one piece the same way twice. He had a mesmeric control over every player in the orchestra; he was called *der Magier*, and magical power was attributed to him. Listeners and indeed orchestral players were hypnotised by the movement of his beautiful hands, and by the visible three inches of his sleeve cuffs. He always conducted from memory, and commanded complete obedience effortlessly. His baton technique was so exceptional that it indicated every nuance, his left hand was used sparingly and it never doubled his right. When rehearsing he never stopped, but his left hand and eyes would indicate to the players the need for correction. It is said that he commenced the *Oberon* overture by just raising his eyebrows, and often gave directions with a nod. Boult remembered a remarkable performance of a Brahms symphony in which Nikisch's hand never rose above his face. No matter what orchestra he conducted, his wonderful warm tone was always evident; Boult said 'we could hear Nikisch at work if we listened blindfolded to the first bar of *Tristan*.' At the same time, when he conducted a strange orchestra, he never imposed his will on every detail, but adapted the orchestra's normal reading as close as possible to his own conception. Tchaikovsky saw Nikisch when he was a young man, and wrote: 'Herr Nikisch is elegantly calm, sparing of superfluous movements, yet at the same time wonderfully strong and self-possessed. He does not seem to conduct, but rather to exercise some mysterious spell; he hardly makes a sign and never tries to call attention to himself, yet we feel that the great orchestra, like an instrument in the hands of a wonderful master, is completely under the control of its chief.' Nikisch displayed his intuitive understanding of his players even when talking to them, and he believed that the personality of the different instrumentalists varied according to the instruments they played, so that he would speak quietly and delicately to an oboist or violinist, but would be much more forcible when addressing, say, a trombone player. There are, however, two sides of the coin; Olin Downes wrote that Nikisch was a poor drillmaster and that the technical standard of the Boston Symphony Orchestra was materially lowered during his régime.

Nikisch apparently wrote nothing about conducting, but said that he himself was not conscious of any technical objectives. 'If any one of my colleagues were to ask me after a concert how I had produced this or that effect, I should be unable to tell him. People ask me how I convey my feeling to musicians. I just do so, without knowing how. When I conduct a work, it is the thrilling power of the music that sweeps me on; I certainly do not follow any hard and fast rules of interpretation. I don't sit down and think out in advance how I am going to have every note of the composition played. And so it comes about that the details of my interpretations vary almost with every performance, in harmony with the powers of feeling that are aroused in me most strongly. But I must emphasise, only the details. To experience a Beethoven symphony in one way today and in an entirely different manner tomorrow would be as absurd as it would be illogical.' He did not hesitate to acknowledge the supreme importance of the interpreter: 'It is only through the personality of the conductor that all our modern instrumental music comes to life'; but he also recognised that each interpreter or conductor must, of necessity, give his own individual stamp to the same piece of music. To Henry Wood he once said: 'Music is a dead thing without interpretation. We all feel things differently. A metronome can keep a four-square indication, if they like it that way, but never forget that you should make every performance a great improvisation—even though you direct the same work every day of the year.'

DGG recorded Nikisch conducting the Berlin Philharmonic Orchestra in Beethoven's Symphony No. 5 in 1913, and this was the first recording of a complete symphony. Later in 1920, with the same orchestra, Liszt's *Hungarian Rhapsody No. 1* and the overture *Le Carnaval romain* were issued. In 1914, HMV recorded him with the London Symphony Orchestra performing the overtures *Egmont*, *Le nozze di Figaro*, *Der Freischütz* and *Oberon*, and the *Hungarian Rhapsody No. 1*. G & T and HMV also issued a number of records in which he accompanied Elena Gerdhardt in lieder by Schubert, Schumann, Brahms, Wolf *et al*. Whether the performance of Beethoven's Symphony No. 5 as recorded is truly representative of Nikisch is open to doubt, for Toscanini remarked that he had heard Nikisch conduct the symphony and that the record was not the same. As the records were made in 1913, the technical problems of the primitive recording process as much as Nikisch's variability would be to blame.

O

ORMANDY, Eugene (1899–1985). Born Jenö Blau in Budapest, the son of a dentist who was determined that his son should be a violinist, Ormandy started to learn on an eighth-size instrument when he was 4, and is said to have been able to differentiate between works of music at the age of one and a half. At 6 he entered the Budapest Royal Academy of Music, studied with Hubay, Weiner and Kodály, graduated with a master's degree at 14, and won an artist's diploma for violin at 16. He also took a degree in philosophy at Budapest University, toured Hungary and Germany as soloist and concertmaster with the Blüthner Orchestra, and in 1920 toured Austria and France as a soloist. In the following year he went to the USA—on the ship *Normandie*, hence his name—on the promise of concerts as a violinist, but when this came to nothing he joined the orchestra at the Capitol Theatre in New York, and within a week was its concertmaster. In 1924 he was asked to conduct when the conductor became ill, and this led to his appointment as conductor of the orchestra, where he remained until 1927. He then was engaged by the impresario Arthur Judson to conduct the Columbia Radio Orchestra and some summer concerts with the New York Philharmonic and the Philadelphia Orchestras. He attended the rehearsals of Mengelberg, Furtwängler and Toscanini, who were then conducting the New York Philharmonic Orchestra, and soon came to regard Toscanini as his examplar. In 1927 he became a US citizen.

In 1931 Ormandy substituted for Toscanini at a concert with the Philadelphia Orchestra, and very soon after took Henri Verbrugghen's place as conductor of the Minneapolis Symphony Orchestra. He remained in Minneapolis for five years; when Stokowski sought to reduce his commitment with the Philadelphia Orchestra, Ormandy was appointed co-conductor in 1936, and two years later became the orchestra's music director. He remained for 48 years with the Philadelphia Orchestra, second only to Mengelberg for the length of tenure with the one orchestra. Before World War II he conducted some concerts in Europe—in Budapest and Vienna—and in 1949 he toured Britain with the Philadelphia Orchestra. In 1944 he toured Australia, conducting the Australian Broadcasting Commission's orchestras. He toured the USA regularly with the

Philadelphia Orchestra and occasionally accepted engagements as guest conductor with other orchestras; he conducted at the New York Metropolitan Opera, once, in 1950 and in 1973 took the Philadelphia Orchestra on tour to China. In 1936 the Bruckner Society of America awarded him its medal.

A genial, well-mannered and almost unassuming man, with scarcely a trace of malice towards his fellow conductors and musicians, Ormandy could be termed a self-made conductor. He was virtually the first great conductor to be trained, as a conductor, in the USA. His most important influence in his formative years was Toscanini; later Klemperer also influenced him. He had an infallible ear and a prodigious memory, was extraordinarily quick in assimilating new scores, and conducted all music except concertos and contemporary works from memory, but believed that conducting with or without a score made no difference. He had the remarkable ability of absolute timing: he could tell at any hour of the day the time to the minute, and could judge exactly the length of time it took to perform the work he was conducting. For a time a physical impairment prevented him from using a baton, but when he resumed the baton he insisted that greater precision could be obtained by using the hands alone. Technically he was the equal of any contemporary conductor; his stance on the podium was firm, and he did not feel the need to conduct every note. Mistakes by players did not upset him. An accident in childhood caused a limp, and the injury brought him great difficulties until the end of his life. He did not shrink from altering a score if he thought the change would improve it; he even arranged the choruses from Handel's *Messiah* for orchestra. At Minneapolis he had a reputation for severity, but at Philadelphia his relations with his players relaxed considerably.

Ormandy's experience in Minneapolis gave him a special insight into making records effectively. A flaw in the musicians' contract gave them no extra income for recording, and as RCA was interested in building up its classical catalogue, it recorded the orchestra under Ormandy, in two separate sessions of two weeks for 42 hours each week, in 100 separate works. In addition, these records gave him a national reputation as a brilliant recording artist, the major works recorded including Mahler's Symphony No. 2, Bruckner's Symphony No. 7, Rachmaninov's Symphony No. 2, Sibelius's Symphony No. 1 and Schoenberg's *Verklärte Nacht*; these records made the works familiar to thousands. He readily acceded to the extensive recording programme RCA had for the Philadelphia Orchestra, and then later for Columbia, which was vital for the orchestra's financial welfare. Concert programmes and recording schedules were closely integrated so that a minimum of rehearsals were needed for recording. In contrast to Stokowski, Ormandy cultivated good relations with the orchestra's management, although the intensity of the orchestra's activities strained harmony with the players. He chose programmes with obvious box-office appeal, and reduced the number of new or novel scores performed; in fact, he was criticised for having an outlook primarily economic and utilitarian rather than motivated by artistic values. Even so, Ormandy preferred a conservative approach to programming; his own natural affinity was for Brahms, Dvořák, Sibelius (except the Symphonies Nos 3 and 6 which he claimed he did not understand), Mahler, Smetana, Kodály, Bartók, and the Russian nationalists from Glinka to Shostakovich and Prokofiev, not excluding Rachmaninov. Although he made many fine recordings of music by the later 20th-century composers, including Hindemith, Walton and Penderecki, he had no predilection for their music, believing little music written today can compare with the best work of Stravinsky, Berg or Schoenberg. The style appropriate for Haydn, Mozart and the early Schubert symphonies evaded him, and Schumann and Mendelssohn were not always comfortable to him; recordings of some composers such as Rimsky-Korsakov and Richard Strauss, of whom one would imagine he would have given inspired performances, were often disappointingly routine.

Ormandy's very virtues, as well as those of the Philadelphia Orchestra, have often caused him to be underrated as a conductor. The vast number of records he made with the orchestra are frequently dismissed as highly-polished, glossy performances of little depth or insight, a charge once levelled at Koussevitzky and sometimes more lately at Karajan. The observation has been made, however, that the Ormandy of the recording studio was a contrast to the Ormandy of the concert hall, where passion and spontaneity were certainly not missing. He himself said: 'Every time I walk on the platform I consider that my life depends on that performance. Of course, that doesn't mean that I'm always at my best, or what comes across is everything I should like, but I am always trying.' Stokowski had created an inimitable sound and style with the Philadelphia Orchestra, which Ormandy largely maintained, if somewhat modified. He soon abandoned Stokowski's innovation of individual bowing with the strings but could retain their sumptuous, seamless legato. Indeed, in all its departments the orchestra kept its superb quality. Ormandy claimed that this special sound was his, and not the orchestra's: 'It's me. My conducting is what it is because I was a violinist. Toscanini was always playing the cello, Koussevitzky the double-bass, Stokowski the organ. The conductors who were pianists always have a sharper, more percussive beat, and it can be heard in their orchestras.' It did not take Ormandy long to recreate that same sound when conducting other orchestras, and when Klemperer came to conduct the Philadelphia Orchestra in his latter years, it sounded like the Philharmonia. Probably, the sound we hear is a fusion of Ormandy and the orchestra, as may be the case with Karajan and the Berlin Philharmonic.

Ormandy's first recording with the Philadelphia Orchestra, in 1936, was Tchaikovsky's Symphony No. 6; his last, released in 1986, was a coupling of Strauss's *Tod und Verklärung* and *Metamorphosen*. He started with RCA, then transferred in 1943 to Columbia/CBS, and finally returned to RCA in 1969. The repertoire of his enormous catalogue of recordings is generally concentrated on the later romantic composers, although the Beethoven and Brahms symphonies and concertos are represented. There is an abridged *Messiah*, which was a bestseller, and arrangements of Bach and, at the other end of the spectrum, Penderecki's *Utrenja* and Webern's *In Sommerwind*. Some find the last RCA recordings an unsatisfactory representation of the orchestra, but record collectors have the satisfaction of knowing the sound and the interpretations of one of the greatest orchestras ever, under a very great conductor.

OZAWA, **Seiji** (b. 1935). Born of Japanese parents in Hoten, Manchuria, when it was occupied by the Japanese, Ozawa was introduced to Western music by his Christian mother; his father was a Buddhist. He studied the piano from the age of 7, and before his mid-teens he was familiar with all of Bach's keyboard music. The family moved to Tokyo, and in 1951 he entered the Toho School of Music, studying composition and conducting under Saito (1951–8). Because of an injury to two of his fingers, he was obliged to abandon a career as a pianist; he heard the Boston Symphony Orchestra which was touring Japan with Charles Munch, and took up conducting. In 1954 he conducted the NHK Symphony and Japan Philharmonic Orchestras, but scarcity of opportunity in Japan, apart from writing film music, caused him to go to Europe, having persuaded a Japanese motor company to give him a motor scooter to drive around Europe as a form of promotion. In Paris he studied with Bigot, entered and won the

International Competition for Young Conductors at Besançon in 1959, and then Munch, who was one of the judges, invited him to study at Tanglewood, Massachusetts. There, after a year, he was awarded the Koussevitzky Memorial Scholarship, and made his début as a conductor at Carnegie Hall in New York in 1961. That year he won another scholarship to study in Berlin with Karajan; in Berlin Bernstein met him when he was touring with the New York Philharmonic Orchestra, and took him as assistant conductor on a tour of Japan with the orchestra. Again, in Japan, he found little sympathy for his interpretative approach, and returned to the USA as one of Bernstein's assistants (1961–2). His first professional concert appearance in North America was with the San Francisco Symphony Orchestra in 1962. He was musical director of the Chicago Symphony Orchestra's summer concerts at Ravinia Park (1964–9), and conducted the Lewisohn Stadium Orchestra in New York (1963–4) and the Toho String Orchestra during its tour to New York (1964). He was then appointed musical director of the Toronto Symphony Orchestra (1965–9) which he led on tours to the USA, Britain and France, and at the same time was musical director of the Nissei Theatre at Tokyo. He was musical director of the San Francisco Symphony Orchestra (1970–6) and retained his connection with it in 1976–7 as musical adviser and guest conductor, and has been musical adviser and, since 1968, the principal conductor of the New Japan Philharmonic Orchestra which is a young orchestra of musicians less than 40 years of age. He first conducted the Boston Symphony Orchestra in Boston in 1968, having previously appeared with it for four summers at Tanglewood; in 1970 he became an artistic director of the orchestra and then in 1973 he was appointed its musical director. He toured Europe in that year with the San Francisco Symphony Orchestra; his tours with the Boston Symphony Orchestra have been to Europe in 1976, and, to celebrate the orchestra's centenary, a tour of fourteen cities in the USA, and another to Japan, France, West Germany, Austria and England in 1981. He had made his London début with the London Symphony Orchestra in 1964 in Honegger's *Jeanne d'Arc au bûcher*, appeared at the Salzburg Festival in *Così fan tutte* in 1969, and at Covent Garden in *Eugene Onegin* in 1974. He regularly conducts the Berlin Philharmonic Orchestra, the Orchestre de Paris, the French National Radio Orchestra, the Vienna Philharmonic Orchestra, the Philharmonia Orchestra and the New Japan Philharmonic Orchestra, and in addition to Salzburg and Covent Garden he conducts opera at La Scala and Paris, where he conducted the world première of Messiaen's *Saint François d'Assise*.

Ozawa is one of the foremost of the younger generation of conductors, and possesses an indefinable charismatic quality, maybe learned from his mentors Karajan and Bernstein. In his reluctance to discuss himself, he has a reputation for aloofness and arrogance, not to say inscrutability, with journalists and the public, although he has an extremely good relationship with the players of the Boston Symphony. One has said: 'He is not too lenient nor too over-restrictive. That's why the orchestra is in such good shape, such a wonderful orchestra—it's a reflection of the conductor.' He was criticised in his early years with the orchestra for playing too much French and Russian music, where his real preferences probably lie, but nonetheless his musical tastes are eclectic. Coming from Japan he has had no particular tradition to influence him, and so approaches each work unencumbered. His great influences were naturally his teachers: Saito, who had studied in Germany, taught him the German repertoire, and with Munch he studied the French. Karajan, he says, showed him that 'inside all music there is a great line, a natural line running right through'; in addition, Karajan taught him the importance of *souplesse* (suppleness): 'If you are physically stiff or tense, then your ears are not really open. Before your ears are open, you must relax and this makes for better beating.' His choice of dress eschews the conventional Western manner. He is, nonetheless, an exact, energetic and authoritarian musician, with an exemplary baton technique and a most sensitive ear for tone and balance. The concertmaster of the Berlin Philharmonic Orchestra, Thomas Brandis, described him as 'exciting and so economic in his mind and in what he says and does, which is always perfectly clear'. On the podium his movements are extrovert and graceful. His memory is such that he conducts massive works such as *Gurrelieder* and Mahler's Symphony No. 8 without a score. His performances are praised for their transparent texture, well conceived tempi and superlative playing, and under him the Boston Symphony Orchestra has been restored to the magnificence of its days with Koussevitzky and Munch. Some critics in Boston find his interpretations uninteresting and occasionally superficial, despite their polish; perhaps for this reason he is at his best in the music of the impressionists and the 20th century.

Virtually all the major recording companies except Decca have recorded Ozawa, conducting a variety of orchestras. Among his first discs were the *Turangalîla symphony* of

Messiaen (with the Toronto Symphony Orchestra for RCA) and *Jeanne d'Arc au bûcher* (with the London Symphony Orchestra *et al.* for CBS). With the Boston Symphony Orchestra his most successful recordings have been Berlioz's *Roméo et Juliette*, Schoenberg's *Gurrelieder*, the Berg and Stravinsky violin concertos (with Perlman), *Also Sprach Zarathustra* and *Ein Heldenleben*, *Le Sacre du printemps*, *The Planets*, Mahler's Symphony No. 8 and the five Beethoven piano concertos (with Rudolf Serkin). He also recorded five works by Sessions, Panufnik, Lieberson, Harbison and Wilson, for the centennial of the Boston Symphony.

P

PAITA, Carlos (b. 1932). Born in Buenos Aires, Paita first studied law, but abandoned it for a musical career, although continuing to study philosophy at the University of Buenos Aires. He was a pupil of Neuchoff for piano, Fischer for composition and Rodzinski for conducting, and came into contact with Furtwängler when the latter visited Argentina and later in Europe. Paita's first appearances as a conductor were in Buenos Aires with the National Radio Chamber Orchestra, and in 1964 he led a performance of the Verdi *Requiem* at the Teatro Colón, as a tribute to President Kennedy. In that year he was invited by the United States government to make a study tour of the United States, and when he returned to Buenos Aires in 1965 he conducted a gala performance of Mahler's Symphony No. 2, which was the work's première in South America. During a visit to Europe he was engaged to conduct the Belgian Radio Orchestra; soon after the Decca Record Company took him under contract, but he made only one record for them, a distinguished one of Wagner preludes and other pieces. In 1966 he led the Stuttgart Radio Symphony Orchestra, and in 1979 made his début in the USA with the Houston Symphony Orchestra. With the record company Lodia he has made a series of recordings, some of which have been released on compact disc; many of these are distinguished, and all are highly committed and romantically inspired readings. Included are Beethoven's Symphonies Nos 3 and 5, *Symphonie fantastique*, Brahms's Symphony No. 1, Tchaikovsky's Symphony No. 6, Mahler's Symphony No. 1, Verdi's *Requiem* and Bruckner's Symphony No. 8. The orchestras employed are a variety from Britain and the Netherlands.

PINNOCK, Trevor (b. 1946). Born in Canterbury where he was a chorister at Canterbury Cathedral, Pinnock studied the organ and harpsichord at the Royal College of Music in London, and achieved a reputation as a harpsichordist. He was a member of the Galliard Harpsichord Trio (1966–72) with a flautist and a cellist, playing modern instruments, 'but', he says, 'the more we learned about historical style, the less willing we were to accept the compromises necessary to make the music effective on modern instruments'. In 1973 he formed The English Concert, a group of players performing on baroque instruments, with which his name is now connected. He has toured as a recitalist in Europe, the USA and Australia; in 1983 alone he made three tours of the USA, two as soloist and the third with The English Concert, in addition to concerts in European countries and in Japan, and in 1985 his tours of the USA numbered five. He directed his first opera in 1983 in London, Rameau's *Acante et Céphise*, the next year he made his début as a conductor in the USA in Chicago, in 1985 he first conducted in Canada at Ottawa and Toronto, and in 1986 he conducted both the Boston Symphony and Chicago Symphony Orchestras.

In the USA Pinnock had to overcome a widespread prejudice against the performance of baroque music on instruments of the time, something that had been overcome a decade or so earlier in Britain and Europe. In January 1983 he remarked to Allan Kozinn of *The New York Times*: 'Your program is rather behind and still in the stage of pioneer players and small consorts, with very little in the way of original instrument orchestras. In fact, the impression I've had is that early music is still thought of, here, as something a little homegrown, with elements of amateurism about it. It is not yet accepted as mainstream, serious musicmaking.' He added: 'One sees now that a good baroque orchestra is in no way inferior to a good modern orchestra—which is something that could not be said in 1973. In our case, we knew that we could produce good results with modern instruments, yet each of us wanted to explore the music from a direction that only the old instruments offered. We had to start from scatch, just as I see American ensembles doing now, and we had to watch it develop very gradually. It was jolly tough work. But it has been well worth it.'

Pinnock's recordings were first as a harpsichordist, and were of music by Bach, Handel, Rameau and Scarlatti, for DGG, Vanguard and CRD. The records he has made with The English Concert, mostly for DGG and many on compact disc, are much acclaimed, and take their place alongside those of Harnoncourt, Hogwood, Gardiner, *et al*. Included are Bach's orchestral suites, *Brandenburg Concertos* and harpsichord concertos, Handel's Concerti Grossi Opp. 3 and 6, *Water Music et al.*, and Vivaldi's Op. 8, which includes *The Four Seasons*.

PRÊTRE, **Georges** (b. 1924). Born in Douai, France, Prêtre was educated at the conservatoire there and at the Paris Conservatoire (1939 –44), was a trumpet player, and studied conducting with Cluytens and at the Straram Foundation. As a teenager he had become familiar with the operatic repertoire by sitting through countless performances in the orchestral pit at the Paris Opéra and the Opéra-Comique. His first ambition was to become a composer; he wrote a symphony and several operettas, but found conducting too strong an attraction. He made his début at the Marseille Opera House with *Samson et Dalila* in 1946; he remained at Marseille (1946–7), then was conductor in Lille (1948), Casablanca (1949–50) and Toulouse (1951–4), then became music director at the Opéra-Comique, Paris (1955–9) and conductor at the Paris Opéra (1970–1). His début in the USA was at the Chicago Lyric Opera (1959); he conducted at Covent Garden (1961), the New York Metropolitan (1964–5) and La Scala (1965–6), conducted the major French orchestras, was a permanent conductor at the Vienna State Opera, has been a guest conductor with many major symphony orchestras in Europe and the USA, and has performed at festivals such as Salzburg (1966). In 1962 he was invited by Beecham to conduct his Royal Philharmonic Orchestra, and after Beecham's death was for a time the associate conductor of the orchestra (1962), and toured the USA with them (1963). He is now conductor of the Vienna Symphony Orchestra. He gave the première of Poulenc's *La Voix humaine* in 1959, and has led the first performances of others of the composer's works. He has also been associated with the soprano Callas, in concert, in opera, and on record.

In his native France, Prêtre has always performed a wide repertoire, from Mozart to Wagner and Strauss, and modern French composers such as Poulenc, and is equally committed to operatic and symphonic music. His style is distinctive; in concert performances, especially in French music, he applies more rubato than usual, but on record his performances of Berlioz, in particular, are not notably perceptive. Like many Italian and French conductors, who regularly perform Italian and German operas in their home countries, abroad he is expected primarily to conduct music of his native country; his performances of the rest of the repertoire are regarded as unidiomatic. Perhaps this is another way of saying that French and Italian conductors have traditions of performing the general repertoire different from others, but it may be a simple and inexplicable idiosyncrasy of audiences everywhere. Prêtre has recorded extensively for EMI and RCA, mainly music of French composers such as Poulenc, Saint-Saëns, Franck, Berlioz, Debussy *et al*. Among his many recordings of opera are *Lucia di Lammermoor*, *La traviata*, *Tosca*, *Iphigénie en Tauride*, and *Louise*.

PREVIN, André (b. 1929). Born in Berlin as Ludwig Andreas Priwin, Previn grew up in an intensely musical background under the influence of his father, Jacob Priwin, who was a successful lawyer and judge. He was taken to his first symphony concert —Furtwängler and the Berlin Philharmonic Orchestra—when he was 5, and the next year he was enrolled in the Hochschule für Musik. By the time he was 8 he was a fluent pianist and was playing piano duets with his father, but then he was expelled from the Hochschule because he was Jewish. The family fled to Paris, where Previn was for a year at the Paris Conservatoire, studying under Dupré, and then in 1939 they moved to the USA, to take up residence in Los Angeles, a relative there being the head of the music department at Universal Studios. As a boy, Previn soon became well-known as a pianist, and when still at school he was a professional composer of film music for the MGM Studios. There he had the opportunity to conduct his own music with the studio orchestra, to conduct the players after-hours in some of the symphonic repertoire, and to conduct the California Youth Symphony Orchestra. At this time he took lessons in composition from Castelnuovo-Tedesco, Achron and Toch. He became a US citizen in 1943.

Previn's reputation as a jazz pianist soon spread, and in 1945 he made a couple of records for RCA, which sold over 200,000 copies. As the pianist in a jazz trio he recorded discs for Contemporary, and one of these, an arrangement of *My Fair Lady*, sold over 500,000 copies. Altogether, in his Hollywood years he made over 100 records as a jazz pianist or film com-poser. His first film score, for a Lassie film, was in 1949, and in the 1950s he arranged scores and wrote original music for films. When he was on the staff of MGM he won an Oscar for his arrangement of *Gigi* (1958), and then was awarded three more Oscars for *Porgy and Bess* (1959), *Irma la Douce* (1963) and *My Fair Lady* (1964). At this time his interest was turning more towards serious music; earlier, during a two-year period in the army when he became concertmaster of the Sixth Army Band, he started conducting lessons with Monteux in San Francisco, and continued them for a year after his army discharge. He established a name in Los Angeles as a classical pianist, gave concerts with the Pacific Arts Trio, made records for CBS of the music of Barber, Hindemith, Martin *et al.*, and appeared with major orchestras as a soloist. By 1954 he had determined to cast off his Hollywood activities altogether and to become a conduc-tor, but, because he refused to conduct light-music programmes with the major orchestras, for some time he took engagements with provincial and semi-professional orchestras so that he could perform the classical repertoire.

Records were a critical influence in propelling Previn to the forefront as a conductor. He made his first and only record as a conductor for CBS in 1962, Britten's *Sinfonia da Requiem* and Copland's *The Red Pony* with the St Louis Symphony Orchestra, and two years later recorded accompaniments in London for RCA. In 1965 RCA brought him back to London to record Shostakovich's Symphony No. 5 and Tchaikovsky's Symphony No. 2 with the London Symphony Orchestra; the success of these records led to others with the London Symphony, and to a close collaboration with the orchestra in concert engagements. In the meantime, he was appointed music director of the Houston Symphony Orchestra (1967–9), and in 1969 he became principal conductor of the London Symphony Orchestra in succession to Kertész. In 1976 he was engaged as principal conductor of the Pittsburgh Symphony Orchestra, with whom he toured Europe in 1978 and 1982; his years with the London Symphony finished in 1979 when he was succeeded by Abbado, and in his time with the orchestra he toured with them in the USSR, Japan, South Korea and Hong Kong. After his contract with the Pittsburgh Symphony expired in 1982 he became music director of the Los Angeles Philharmonic and the Royal Philharmonic Orchestras (1985), dividing his time equally between the two. But in 1986 he resigned as music director of the Royal Philharmonic because of his dissatisfaction with the prevailing system under which musicians were hired. Ashkenazy took his place as music director, and he assumed the position of principal conductor. Previn's compositions, apart from his film scores and light music, include concert overtures, a symphony for strings, concertos for piano, cello and guitar, vocal and piano music, and the score for the stage show *Every Good Boy Deserves Favour*, which he wrote in collaboration with the playwright Tom Stoppard. His experience as a composer leads him to comment: 'To a young composer who wants to get played the advice is write something for brass: you will be performed around the clock.'

Previn's period in Hollywood gave him excellent experience in rehearsing and controlling symphony orchestras, even if he were performing music of ephemeral value. Much as he would like to lose his association with film and jazz, he has not entirely been able to do so; his sharp-witted glib volubility, the familiar cosiness of his manner, and his undeniable liking for public exposure on television have scarcely assisted. His years with the London Symphony brought him and the orchestra immense success in concert, on record and as television personalities, and this has been repeated to a lesser extent with the Royal Philharmonic. Nonetheless he cannot be mistaken for anything but a most serious and highly accomplished musician with a superb touch for, in his own words, 'colourful music, with a strong nationalistic flavour'. He professes the greatest devotion to Mozart, but his genius as a conductor is with the music of composers such as Tchaikovsky, Rachmaninov, Shostakovich and Prokofiev. Since his early years he has been attracted to British music, particularly Vaughan Williams, Walton and Britten, and he has been one of their most enthusiastic and effective proponents; in fact he has been said to have done more for 20th-century British music than any other present-day conductor. His compliant personality makes his relationship with the orchestra a relaxed, give-and-take one, the opposite of the usual stereotype. His perfect pitch was evident from childhood; he quickly assimilates scores but does not claim a photographic memory. He retains his facility with the piano, and has recorded and appeared as a soloist and a chamber player. Like many other American conductors, he has an extrovert predilection for tonal weight, and less concern for the finesse of style and touch necessary for Haydn and Mozart, but then the German and Austrian classics are not the natural focus of his musical culture. In fact, Previn finds himself unsympathetic to Bruckner and Wagner, although not to Mahler; contemporary music is also of limited interest, and he dislikes performing music for which he has no feeling. It is facile to dismiss him for the weaknesses in his repertoire rather than to recognise him for his strengths; he has undoubtedly been overexposed as a musician, and anyone who believes a great conductor is judged on how he performs the greatest music must still suspend judgement on Previn.

Ignoring his records as a jazz pianist, solo and ensemble pianist, and taking into account only the records which he has made as an orchestral conductor, Previn has a number of distinguished recordings to his credit. In the series for RCA and EMI with the London Symphony Orchestra there was, *inter alia* Vaughan Williams' nine symphonies, Walton's Symphony No. 1 and *Belshazzar's Feast*, Shostakovich's Symphonies Nos 5, 8, 10 and 13, Rachmaninov's three symphonies and *The Rock*, Britten's *Spring Symphony*, Gershwin's orchestral music, a collection of Berlioz overtures, *The Planets*, the *Turangalîla symphony*, *Carmina Burana*, *Daphnis et Chloé*, *La Mer*, *Images* and *Nocturnes*, *Enigma Variations*, *Scheherazade*, *Nutcracker*, *The Sleeping Beauty*, *Swan Lake* and *Manfred* symphony, and

Prokofiev's *Romeo and Juliet*. His other discs, for various recording companies, have included Mahler's Symphony No. 4, Goldmark's *Rustic Wedding* symphony, Sibelius's Symphony No. 2, Tchaikovsky's Symphony No. 4 and Rochberg's Violin Concerto (with Stern and the Pittsburgh Symphony Orchestra), *Scheherazade*, *Don Juan*, *Till Eulenspiegel* and *Tod und Verklärung* (with the Vienna Philharmonic Orchestra), Shostakovich's Symphonies Nos 4 and 5 (with the Chicago Symphony Orchestra), *Eine Alpensymphonie* (with the Philadelphia Orchestra), and Berlioz's *Requiem* and Rachmaninov's *The Bells* (with the London Philharmonic Orchestra). He also recorded some Haydn symphonies (with both the London Symphony and Pittsburgh Symphony Orchestras), two Mozart concertos in which he was soloist in one and in company with Lupu in the other, and Beethoven's Symphony No. 5 (with the London Symphony Orchestra).

PRITCHARD, Sir John (b. 1921). The son of a professional violinist, Pritchard was born in London, took lessons from his father on the violin, studied the piano with Petri, and went to Italy in his teens to learn about opera. In the army in World War II he was stationed at Derby, where he began conducting with the Derby String Orchestra (1943–51). On Roy Henderson's recommendation he was accepted on the staff of the Glyndebourne Festival Opera in 1947, became chorusmaster in 1949, and made his début as a conductor there when he took over from a sick Busch in the middle of a performance in 1951. He assisted Busch and was largely influenced by him at Glyndebourne; in 1963 he became principal conductor, and in 1969 musical director and artistic counsellor, until his resignation in 1977. He has also been conductor of the Jacques Orchestra (1950–2), music director and conductor of the Royal Liverpool Philharmonic Orchestra (1957–63), principal conductor of the London Philharmonic Orchestra (1962–6), co-director of the Marseille Opera (1966–8), musical director of the Huddersfield Choral Society (from 1973), chief conductor of the Cologne Opera (from 1978), principal guest conductor (1979) and then principal conductor of the BBC Symphony Orchestra, the chief conductor (1982), and joint music director with Sylvain Camberling of the Théâtre Royal de la Monnaie in Brussels (from 1981). He led the London Philharmonic on tours to the Far East in 1962, 1969 and 1973, and to the USA in 1971; on the 1973 tour he conducted the orchestra in Hong Kong and China, and in 1972 took the English Chamber Orchestra on a tour to South America. He first appeared at the Edinburgh Festival in 1951, at the Vienna State Opera in 1951, in the USA with the Pittsburgh Symphony Orchestra in 1963, with the San Francisco Opera in 1970 and at the New York Metropolitan Opera in 1971, has conducted at most of the major opera houses throughout the world, and was appointed musical director of the San Francisco Opera in 1986. At Covent Garden he conducted the premières of Britten's *Gloriana* and Tippett's *The Midsummer Marriage* and *King Priam*. He was knighted in 1983.

In his career Pritchard has avoided any form of specialisation; he is equally at home in the opera house and with the symphony orchestra, and his repertoire ranges from Monteverdi to Henze. When he premièred the Leppard arrangement of *L'Incoronazione di Poppea* at Glyndebourne in 1962 he was a leader in the great awakening of interest in Monteverdi, and he also led the British première of Henze's *Elegy for Young Lovers* at Glyndebourne. Musicians regard him as one of the most reliable conductors with modern scores, and in Liverpool he introduced the Musica Viva series, in which concerts of modern works were preceded by explanatory talks, and were followed by discussion, an educational method later practised to great effect by others. In many ways he is the complete conductor, but his urbanity, indifference to self-promotion, quiet professionalism, and the utter lack of drama or sensationalism in his background have kept him from the highest rewards in British musical life. At the same time, his recorded performances give many examples of his fine musicianship; they are invariably well-executed, but frequently lack strong personal commitment. His recordings have been numerous, ranging over the symphonic repertoire, and of operas he has recorded *Lucia di Lammermoor* and *La traviata*, and the Glyndebourne productions of *Idomeneo*, *L'Incoronazione di Poppea* and Busoni's *Arlecchino*.

R

RATTLE, Simon (b. 1955). Born in Liverpool, the youngest child of musical parents, Rattle demonstrated remarkable talent for music as a child, and at the age of 15 was a percussion player in the Royal Liverpool Philharmonic Orchestra and in the National Youth Orchestra under Boulez. His first experience as a conductor was with the Merseyside Youth Orchestra; in 1971 he began a study of conducting and the piano at the Royal Academy of Music in London and there in 1973 led performances of Mahler's Symphonies Nos 2 and 6, and *L'Enfant et les sortilèges*. In 1974, the youngest to enter, he won first prize in the Bournemouth John Player International Conductors' Competition, and then became assistant conductor with the Bournemouth Symphony Orchestra and the Bournemouth Sinfonietta (1974–6). He conducted the English Chamber Orchestra at Barcelona (1975), appeared with some British provincial orchestras, and led the New Philharmonia Orchestra at the Royal Festival Hall, London (1976). He first conducted at the Glyndebourne Festival Opera in 1977 and returned there in subsequent years; he was appointed assistant conductor of the BBC Scottish Symphony Orchestra (1977) and of the Royal Liverpool Philharmonic Orchestra (1977), principal conductor and artistic adviser of the City of Birmingham Symphony Orchestra (1980) and principal conductor of the London Choral Society (1980). He first appeared in the USA in 1977 when he toured with the London Symphony Orchestra, and in the next year he returned to conduct the Los Angeles Philharmonic and Chicago Symphony Orchestras; in 1981 he was appointed principal guest conductor of the Los Angeles Philharmonic Orchestra, and in 1983 principal guest conductor of the London Choral Society. He is also principal guest conductor of the Rotterdam Philharmonic Orchestra, music director of the South Bank Summer Music Festival in London, and appears with the London Sinfonietta and the Nash Ensemble.

A modest and self-deprecating man, Rattle is nonetheless a lively conversationalist. He has rare gifts for a conductor of his age; his rhythmic sense and capacity to control large forces, evident in Mahler's Symphony No. 2 and in the opera house, have marked him off as an exceptional talent destined for the top flight of British conductors. He recognises Furtwängler as the greatest influence on all conductors, and places Giulini as the only conductor who carries on his school today. Haitink, Boult, Boulez have also been formative influences, and he says that John Carewe, the principal conductor of the BBC Welsh Symphony Orchestra, taught him most of what he knows about conducting. He finds an affinity with many composers, such as Haydn, Berlioz, Dvořák, Mahler, Berg, Ravel and Maxwell Davies, and he has a name as an interpreter of contemporary music, including much 20th-century music in his programmes —works by Messiaen, Milhaud, *et al.*—which have been greeted enthusiastically by his audiences. Mozart he finds, at this stage of his experience as a conductor, too difficult to interpret, and he has said that he finds himself less and less capable of conducting the Beethoven symphonies as he grows older, as the musical problems he faces in these works appear harder. The Brahms symphonies 'remain excruciatingly difficult', not technically, but musically; 'One has to rediscover the culture that they encapsulate again. With three or four exceptions the performances of Brahms—and Beethoven—that one hears today are generally unacceptable, shocking!' The Brahms of Giulini and Boult he deeply admires: 'One wouldn't wish for any note to sound different from the way it does in Boult's recording of the first—yet people abroad just don't know about this man!' On the other hand, Mahler comes naturally to him, as, he believes, it is part of his generation's tradition. After some early scepticism he recorded the version of Mahler's Symphony No. 10 completed by Deryck Cooke: 'It was a very, very difficult work to prepare, but I have always loved Mahler, and if you love Mahler, you have to explore the tenth, because it's of enormous importance. It gives a clue to what all the other 20th-century composers were to do: one movement sounds like Berg—the first, which is like *Lulu*—and another just like Hindemith.' Rattle believes that orchestras should have a good mixture of international players, and of men and women: 'I don't think I want to listen to an all-male orchestra any more. They are sadly lacking. In a string section, you often need the brute force of a man as well as some of the delicacy, detail and quicker response of women. Women usually seem to be the more fulfilled members of orchestras, the ones with fewer grouses and less prone to disillusionment.'

Rattle dislikes recording, because of the difficulty he finds in keeping in balance the two personalities in every conductor —the man who rehearses and the man who performs: 'One should only record with the memory, the aftermath, of a performance fresh inside one. Otherwise it gets very depressing.' He has nevertheless made many successful recordings for EMI with the City of Birmingham Symphony, Bournemouth Symphony, London Symphony, Philharmonia, Los Angeles Symphony and National Youth Orchestras, the London Sinfonietta and the Nash Ensemble, and the outstanding discs have been Britten's *War Requiem*, Mahler's Symphony No. 10 and *Das klagende Lied*, Janáček's *Glagolitic Mass* and Rachmaninov's Symphony No. 2. Also, off the beaten track there have been Weill's *The Seven Deadly Sins* (with his wife, Elise Ross, the soloist), and Britten's *Young Apollo*, *Canadian Carnival*, *Scottish Ballad* and *Four French Songs*.

REINER, Fritz (1888–1963). Born in Budapest, the son of a merchant, Reiner began to learn the piano at the age of 6 under the influence of his mother who was an amateur musician, and then showed evidence of an exceptional memory. At 10 he entered the Budapest Academy of Music, where one of his teachers was Bartók: at 12 he conducted a high school orchestra, at 13 played a Mozart piano concerto in public, and from 15 to 19 he played the kettle-drum in the Academy orchestra. Reiner's father wished him to become a lawyer, and for a time he studied law at Budapest University. Previously the composer Weiner had convinced him that he should be a conductor, and at 20 he became a choral coach at the Budapest Comic Opera, and conducted a performance of *Carmen* when the conductor fell sick. He was then conductor at Ljubljana Opera (1910–14), where he performed *Parsifal* when, for the first time, the opera could be performed away from Bayreuth. He became Royal Court conductor at Dresden (1914–22); on his arrival there he was asked to conduct the four operas of Wagner's *Ring* without rehearsal. There also he came to know Strauss, and directed an early performance of *Die Frau ohne Schatten*. At Dresden he also conducted the Saxon State Orchestra, and was a guest conductor in Berlin, Hamburg and Vienna, but he left in 1922 because he was refused permission to conduct in Rome and Barcelona, where he had also been a guest conductor for a year. When he was invited to succeed Ysaye with the Cincinatti Symphony Orchestra, he migrated to the USA to become the orchestra's conductor (1922–31), and was granted US citizenship in 1928. He was head of the opera and orchestral departments at the Curtis Institute at Philadelphia (1931–41), took part in the opera venture with the Philadelphia Orchestra and the Philadelphia Grand Opera (1934–5), conducted at the Hollywood Bowl, was music director of the Pittsburgh Symphony Orchestra (1938–48), conductor at the New York Metropolitan Opera (1949–53), and finally conductor of the Chicago Symphony Orchestra (1953–62), which he took over at a low ebb of the orchestra's fortunes. He was a frequent visitor to Europe, Mexico and South America, conducted the La Scala Orchestra in Milan (1926–30), led operas of Wagner and Gluck at Covent Garden (1936–7), conducted at the San Francisco Opera (1936–8), and was invited to conduct *Die Meistersinger* at the re-opening of the Vienna State Opera (1955). He toured very little with the Chicago Symphony Orchestra, and rejected the opportunity to visit Europe with the orchestra in 1959 because of the excessive demands made by the travelling schedule.

Reiner was one of the most significant conductors of his time, and together with the Chicago Symphony Orchestra he ranked with Toscanini, Stokowski, Mengelberg, Beecham and Furtwängler with their respective orchestras. His formative influences were Muck, Mahler, Strauss and more particularly Nikisch, whose methods he studied at Leipzig, and who was a model for his own style and technique. Reiner combined extraordinary precision of execution with flexibility in phrasing and expression; his performances, especially in his last years with the Chicago Symphony Orchestra, were incredibly brilliant, with unique qualities of rubato and dynamic shading. He reached these superlative standards through an almost inhuman demand for perfection, and the most meticulous preparation and rehearsal. In both opera and orchestral concerts no detail escaped his scrutiny, and he left nothing to chance. His ear was remarkably acute; at rehearsals his most frequent call to the orchestra was: 'It is *not* clean. It must be clean.' His precision was not for the sole purpose of performing the music exactly as written, but to reveal its inherent dramatic and musical qualities. Stravinsky called the Chicago Symphony Orchestra under Reiner 'the most precise and flexible in the world'. Reiner's musical scholarship was profound, and his repertoire comprehensive. He performed baroque music with exemplary style and once said that his favourite composer was Mozart; he performed Haydn with more freedom than most. His programmes were built around the Viennese classics, but he was also celebrated for his interpretations of Mendelssohn, Berlioz, Brahms, Strauss, Stravinsky, Bartók and Hindemith. His players noted that the tension rose when he conducted Strauss and Wagner. He took great pleasure in performing lighter music, such as Strauss waltzes, and gave them the same scrupulous attention as the most serious symphonies; his discs of Strauss waltzes with the Chicago Symphony show a rare degree of finesse. Although he occasionally programmed American composers, he was scarcely a committed advocate for them. He liked Schoenberg, but his interest in Stravinsky did not go later than *Agon*. With soloists he was an excellent collaborator.

Among musicians Reiner's baton technique was a legend. He could beat any rhythm, but his baton, usually a large one, moved in very small patterns, apparently to make the players keep their eyes on him. He regarded his eyes as the important contact with each player, who were caught in an almost hypnotic effect, in the manner of Nikisch. To the audience he appeared motionless and therefore uninteresting, but he said himself that 'the best conducting technique is that which achieves the maximum musical result with the minimum of physical effort'. Paradoxically, Bernstein was one of his students at the Curtis Institute. At rehearsals he spoke little and in a familiar piece he was precise in his demands; sometimes he would impassively run through the score with his eyes on the music, as if he were making up his mind how it should sound. At concerts he was even more restrained and gave few cues, but always permitted the principal players to phrase in their own way. He had an acid wit, and was known to be amiable but unapproachable in everyday life; however, before the orchestra at rehearsals he was quite irascible: 'any day he failed to lose his temper was a day when he was too sick to conduct,' one player remarked. Musicians respected his knowledge and musical authority, but he was certainly not liked by them. Some even thought that he was trying to fool the orchestra. Later, in 1972, Solti remarked that the Chicago Symphony had lost 'that kind of Reiner fear that the musical director was a natural enemy'. In Chicago he was an enigma, divorcing himself completely from all social activities, which estranged him from the orchestra's management and the civic authorities.

Although he was not interested in recording techniques as such, Reiner always carefully planned and rehearsed his recorded performances, which usually took place after concerts where the works were programmed. He is said to have made records in Europe in 1920, but in the USA his first recordings were made in 1938. He recorded a wide repertoire with the Pittsburgh Symphony Orchestra between 1941 and 1948, and later with some other orchestras, but his most illustrious recordings were made with the Chicago Symphony Orchestra for RCA. These included symphonies by Haydn (No. 88), Mozart

(Nos 36, 39, 40 and 41), Beethoven (Nos 1, 3, 5, 6, 7 and 9), Schubert (Nos 5 and 8), Brahms (No. 3), Dvořák (No. 9), Tchaikovsky (No. 6) and Mahler (No. 4), a number of concertos, major and minor orchestral works such as *Scheherazade*, *Das Lied von der Erde*, *Alexander Nevsky*, Bartók's *Concerto for Orchestra*, *Pini di Roma* and *Fontane di Roma*, and most of the Strauss tone poems, and there were some other notable recordings with other orchestras, for example the Bach orchestral suites, Haydn's Symphonies Nos 95 and 101, and Brahms's Symphony No. 4. Some operas conducted by him have appeared on private and pirate labels. Fortunately, some of these recordings with the Chicago Symphony have now been issued on compact disc, which gives the new generation of listeners the opportunity to hear and wonder at the glory of that great orchestra under one of the greatest conductors, at a golden time in both of their lives.

RICHTER, Karl (1926–81). Born at Plauen, Saxony, the son of an Evangelical clergyman, Richter grew up in an environment closely associated with church tradition and the music of Bach. As a boy he was a member of the Dresden Kreuzchor, and after World War II studied at Leipzig with Mauersberger, Straube, Ramin and Kobler. He was choirmaster at Christ Church, Leipzig (1946), organist at St Thomas's Church there (1949), then he moved to Munich in 1951 to become cantor (i.e. organist, choirmaster, conductor and improviser) at the St Mark's Church. He formed the Heinrich Schütz Circle, to perform the music of that composer, but changed the name to the Munich Bach Choir. The choir consisted of 70 to 120 voices, was an amateur body and gave usually two concerts each month. He also established the Munich Bach Orchestra, and was a professor at the Munich Academy of Music. Richter was one of Germany's most distinguished harpsichordists, organists, choral and orchestral conductors, and had a special reputation for his performances of baroque music, particularly Bach. His style in this music is distinctive; it is literal with marked rhythmic accents, and has great power and vitality. He gave scrupulous attention to the preparation of his performances, to finding the balance between technique, intellect and expression, and the result was performances of the highest technical standard and musicianship. He made over 100 records for DGG, including Bach's *Mass in B Minor*, *St Matthew Passion*, *St John Passion*, *Christmas Oratorio*, *Magnificat*, a number of cantatas and concertos, the orchestral suites and *Brandenburg Concertos*,

Handel's *Concerti grossi* Op. 3 and Op. 6, *Messiah*, *Samson* and *Giulio Cesare*, Gluck's *Orfeo ed Euridice*, Mozart's *Requiem* and Beethoven's *Mass in C Major*, all with the Munich Bach Choir and Orchestra.

ROSTROPOVICH, Mstislav (b. 1927). Born in Baku, Rostropovich took lessons on the cello from his father, Leopold Rostropovich (1892–1942); both his father and grandfather were cellists. He was also taught the piano by his mother, herself an accomplished pianist. In 1935 the family moved to Moscow, where he attended the music school at the Conservatory (1939–41), and first appeared in public as a cellist when he was 13, playing a cello concerto by Saint-Saëns. During World War II he first lived in the Urals, then entered the Moscow Conservatory proper to continue his studies in the cello and composition. His professor of composition was Shostakovich with whom he became a close friend and collaborator. Prokofiev, too, he greatly admired, and when the music of Shostakovich and Prokofiev was banned for two years, he left the conservatory and lived with Prokofiev until the latter's death in 1953. He won prizes in 1944–5 for his performances, graduated in 1946 with the highest honours, soon won great acclaim as a soloist in the USSR, then, after his first appearance in the West in Florence in 1951, in many countries abroad. He is recognised as one of the finest artists of the day, and composers, including Britten, as well as Shostakovich and Prokofiev, have written music especially for him. Up until 1977 58 major works had been dedicated to him, and most were composed at his request. Of all his many recordings as a cellist, he regards the one of the concertos of Dutilleux and Lutosławski as the most significant. In 1953 he became a teacher at the Moscow Conservatory; he was elected professor in 1959, and in 1961 was appointed professor at the Leningrad Conservatory. He married the soprano Galina Vishnevskaya in 1955, and from time to time accompanies her in solo recitals.

Rostropovich has said that his interest in being a conductor was aroused when as a boy he toured with his father who conducted orchestras at spas in the USSR. His initial appearance as a conductor was in 1961, but his first major engagement was to lead *Eugene Onegin* at the Bolshoi Theatre in 1968. He is essentially self-taught as a conductor, but admits to having learned much by observing the many great conductors with whom he has performed as a soloist: 'I played the same repertoire with all of them: very exciting! And at every rehearsal I watched how they obtained their results; noted their weak points, their strong points; saw how each of them coped with this or that problem . . . and I learnt. Maybe I, alone among all of my colleagues, had the benefit of such a first-class school for conductors!' He believes his cello-playing has benefited from his experience as a conductor, and as a string player he has a special advantage as a conductor: 'I know precisely what I can get from a string section. I think string players trust me, too. If I ask them to change the way they bow, they'll agree to it, because they know I am a player myself.' He has a great respect for orchestral players, and has said that, when he reads a review with little mention of the conductor but praise of the orchestral playing, he considers a compliment has been paid to the conductor.

Rostropovich's commitment to conducting is deep. His performances have been criticised for their pronounced and sometimes unorthodox expression, but he has reacted sharply: 'If you take the vastly different interpretation of, say, Toscanini, Furtwängler, Walter, Klemperer, in the past, they were not criticised for each going their own very different way. A strong musical personality is bound to express himself by how he feels the music. Besides, you can't always rely on the metronome, and it isn't very thoughtful, in my opinion, to criticise someone for simply not following the marked speeds. I believe that if an artist has a feeling for the music, understands the meaning of *ritardando* and *accelerando*, then he will have faith in what he's doing and it will sound right.' Other musicians have expressed this differently; Yehudi Menuhin said: 'He doesn't have to follow a dry, metronomic beat. As a string player he knows what it is to form a phrase,' and Seiji Ozawa: 'Slava doesn't interpret, he feels. His music is really his character. He is conducting his life.' For Tchaikovsky, Rostropovich ('Slava', in the musical world) says he has a particular affinity; in his performances of this composer he gives the closest attention to every detail, sometimes maybe at the expense of the movement's structure; tempo and expressive exaggerations are frequent, but nonetheless arresting, and his interpretations are in every way original and personal. His performance of the Tchaikovsky symphonies at the Royal Festival Hall in London in 1976 received the most enthusiastic acclamation from audiences and critics alike, and his subsequent recordings of the works are surely among the finest ever made.

In 1974 Rostropovich left the USSR with his wife, with a two-year visa. Although quite apolitical, he had given sanctuary to Solzhenitsyn when the latter was being harassed by the Soviet authorities before his expulsion from Russia, and this led to intolerable interference in his life as an artist. Recording sessions were stopped without warning, his concert and opera engagements abruptly cancelled, and he was finally barred from performing with orchestras in the major cities. Other bureaucratic impediments offended him, such as the necessity to obtain the approval of a government concern before making records overseas; when he recorded the Dvořák Cello Concerto with Karajan in FR Germany without the relevant authorisation, difficulties followed. In 1976 he accepted the appointment for three years as chief conductor of the National Symphony Orchestra in Washington, DC, in 1977 he was appointed artistic director of the Aldeburgh Festival, and in 1981 he organised the first Rostropovich International Cello Competition in Paris. Nonetheless he has no wish to desert his country: 'All my life I wanted to devote myself to making music in my own country. All I do I am doing for my country. I love my country, but I cannot give up my work. I would not be willing to go back if it meant returning to the conditions under which I had to work.' In March 1978 the Praesidium of the Supreme Soviet took away Soviet citizenship from Rostropovich and his wife, debarring them from returning to the Soviet Union because they had engaged in activities 'harming the prestige of the Soviet Union' (*sic*).

Rostropovich has recorded much of the cello repertoire, and has made seven recordings of Dvořák's Cello Concerto. As a conductor, his records have been of *Eugene Onegin*, with the Bolshoi Opera Orchestra *et al.*, recorded in Moscow before he left the USSR, Tchaikovsky's *Queen of Spades* (with l'Orchestre National de France *et al.*) and Shostakovich's *Lady Macbeth of the Mtsensk District* (with the London Philharmonic Orchestra *et al.*), all three operas with his wife Galina Vishnevskaya one of the principals, the seven Tchaikovsky symphonies mentioned above (with the London Philharmonic Orchestra), suites from Prokofiev's *Romeo and Juliet*, Shostakovich's Symphony No. 5 (with the National Symphony Orchestra), and some concerto accompaniments, Tchaikovsky ballet suites, *et al.*

ROZHDESTVENSKY, Gennady (b. 1931). Born in Moscow, the son of Nicolai Anosov, a leading Russian conductor, and N. P. Rozhdestvenskaya, a prominent soprano, Rozhdestvensky was a pupil at the Gnesin School of Music and at the Moscow Conservatory school for children, where he studied under Oborin, and then entered the Conservatory in 1941 where he studied conducting with his father. His talent for conducting became evident in 1951 when he was working at the Bolshoi Theatre and was asked by the conductor Fayer to take over the rehearsal of *The Sleeping Beauty*, which he conducted entirely from memory. After graduating from the Conservatory in 1954 he was engaged to conduct at the Bolshoi Theatre, visited London that year with the Bolshoi Ballet, and in 1955 brilliantly substituted for Samosud in a performance of Shostakovich's Symphony No. 10. He was principal conductor at the Bolshoi Theatre (1965–70), the youngest ever to hold the position; his departure from the Theatre has been attributed by some to the Soviet authorities' disapproval of his efforts to introduce works of foreign modern composers. He led performances of *Le Sacre du printemps* and Britten's *A Midsummer Night's Dream*; from 1960 to 1965 he was chief conductor and director of the Moscow Radio Symphony Orchestra, and in the concert hall he continued to programme music by Poulenc, Hindemith, Orff, Bartók, Ravel and other comparatively modern composers, works which were being heard for the first time in the USSR. He also revived Prokofiev's Symphonies Nos 2, 3 and 4. He has visited countries in Europe, the USA and Japan as a guest conductor, has appeared in Britain many times, especially with the London Symphony Orchestra, in 1970 led memorable performances of *Boris Godunov* at Covent Garden, and in 1971 conducted the Leningrad Philharmonic Orchestra at three Promenade concerts. He was principal conductor of the Stockholm Philharmonic Orchestra (1974–7), a professor at the Moscow Conservatory (from 1976), is musical director of the Moscow Chamber Opera, became chief guest conductor of the BBC Symphony Orchestra (1978), and for a short time was conductor of the Vienna Symphony Orchestra (1981). A versatile conductor with a decidedly dramatic instinct, he has made numerous records for Melodiya, including incisive and vivid performances of Prokofiev's symphonies, *The Prodigal Son*, *The Gambler*, *On Guard for Peace*, *Le Pas d'acier et al.*, Tchaikovsky's symphonies, *Nutcracker*, *Swan Lake* and *The Maid of Orleans*, the Sibelius symphonies, and a number of other works in the international repertoire such as Strauss waltzes, *Don Quixote*, *Symphonie fantastique*, Bruckner's Symphonies Nos 3 and 9 and Dvořák's Symphony No. 9. Other works off the beaten track recorded include Mussorgsky's *The Marriage*, a suite from Janáček's *The Cunning Little Vixen*, a suite from Bach arranged by Mahler, and Schoenberg's arrangement of Brahm's Piano Quartet No. 1.

S

SABATA, Victor de (1892–1967). Born in Trieste, de Sabata studied conducting and composition at the Milan Conservatory, and won the gold medal on graduation in 1911. He first became known as a composer, particularly for his opera *Il Macigno*, which was produced at La Scala, Milan, in 1917. When his career as a conductor started it was in the concert hall, but in 1918 he was appointed conductor at the Monte Carlo Opera, where he remained for twelve years, and there conducted the world première of *L'Enfant et les sortilèges* in 1925. In 1929 he joined La Scala as a conductor, and later was appointed musical and artistic director. He retired from La Scala in 1953. He first visited the USA in 1927, conducted in Vienna in 1936–7, and led *Tristan und Isolde* at Bayreuth in 1939. Coming to London in 1947, he presented a cycle of the Beethoven symphonies with the London Philharmonic Orchestra of which the performance of No. 9 was especially memorable. He revisited London in 1950 with the La Scala Company, conducting remarkable performances of *Otello* and *Falstaff*, and performed at the same time at the Edinburgh Festival.

Normally an abstemious and placid man, de Sabata was transformed on the podium, where he became a tense and tyrannical personality. He was particularly harsh with singers. Nevertheless it was not unusual for him to be mentioned in the same breath as Toscanini, especially as a conductor of Wagner and Italian opera. Under his baton the orchestra's sound was lighter and lither than under his North European counterparts: he was the archetype of an Italian conductor. He could coax the most delicate sounds but his fortissimi were extremely loud. David Bicknell, who was with EMI for over 40 years, has said that 'de Sabata, like Furtwängler, was a great one for the mood of the moment. And, as with all conductors, he got his own sound from the orchestra. It was a great tragedy that he decided to retire so early—I think his poor reception in New York upset him.' In the USA, de Sabata had a name for the brilliance and eccentricity of his performances, with enormous exaggerations of tempi and dynamics to the point where familiar music lost its cohesion. His memory was incredible; when he was in London in 1947 he found mistakes in the London Philharmonic's scores of the most popular pieces. Even to his last years he was a fine pianist and violinist, and every day played *Scarbo* and *Tzigane*, two of the most difficult pieces for these instruments. He is said to have preferred composition to conducting, and wrote two operas and a number of symphonic poems, some of which were performed. Toscanini conducted two of them, *Juventis* and *Gethsemane*, in his early years in the USA; Maazel revived another, *The Night of Plato*, with the Philadelphia Orchestra in 1968. De Sabata himself recorded *Juventis* with the EIAR Symphony Orchestra for Cetra; although it was reputed to be his best work, it was described by the American critic David Hall in 1948 as a 'not strikingly original essay in a Richard Strauss-cum-Puccini romantic manner'.

De Sabata made records for four European companies—Cetra, Polydor, HMV and Decca, and of those issued originally on 78 r.p.m. discs many have been made available on LP transfers. Many of these recordings were superb, and captured de Sabata at his most electrifying. Undoubtedly the greatest was *Tosca*, which was recorded in 1953 and has been issued on compact discs. It still remains at the top of all operatic recordings, and it is de Sabata's unique direction that gives the performance its inspiration, despite the marvellous contributions of Callas, di Stefano and Gobbi. *Jeux* was significant, for at that time this music was rarely heard, and de Sabata had a special affection for it. Sibelius's *En Saga*, Respighi's *Fontane di Roma* and Mozart's *Requiem* were also exceptional. But some of his recordings were disappointingly eccentric: Beethoven's Symphony No. 3 and Verdi's *Requiem* were both marred by excessively slow tempi. To be fair to de Sabata, he had suffered a heart attack before recording the *Requiem*, and apparently was not really equal to the undertaking.

SALONEN, Esa-Pekka (b. 1958). Born in Helsinki, Salonen studied composition with Rautavaara, conducting with Panula, and the horn, at the Sibelius Academy in Helsinki, and between the ages of 15 and 18 played the horn in local orchestras. In 1979 he made his début as a conductor with the Finnish Radio Symphony Orchestra, and studied composition with Donatoni in Siena and Castiglioni in Milan (1979–81). The next years he divided his time between Helsinki and Stockholm, becoming the principal conductor of the Swedish Radio Symphony Orchestra. His appearance on the international musical scene was spectacular, when he substituted at five days' notice for Tilson Thomas in Mahler's Symphony No. 3 with the Philharmonia Orchestra in London in 1984; he subsequently became the principal guest conductor of the orchestra. His début in the USA, with the Los Angeles Philharmonic Orchestra, followed in the same year, and his first appearance in France, with the French National Orchestra, took place in 1985. Before the orchestra Salonen is reserved, and his directions are elegant and precise. Committed to performing modern compositions, he nonetheless seeks to combine the modern and the traditional in his programmes. Critics have deprecated many of his performances, in concert and on record, for their departures from conventional readings and sometimes from the score itself, but Salonen is clearly a vital and original musician, bringing an original and often arresting impulse to his interpretations. He has a long-term recording contract with CBS, and so far has recorded Messiaen's *Turangalîla symphony*, Nielsen's Symphony No. 4 and *Helios* overture, trumpet concertos by Tomasi and Jolivet (with Marsalis), and Lutosławski's Symphony No. 3 and *Les Espaces du sommeil* (with Shirley-Quirk).

SANDERLING, Kurt (b. 1912). Born in Arys in East Prussia, Sanderling received a private education and started his career as a répétiteur at the Berlin Staatsoper, and at the age of 19 was an assistant conductor there. With the advent of the Nazis, he left Germany for Switzerland and the Soviet Union, on the invitation of relatives living there, as he was Jewish. He was first a répétiteur and then assistant conductor with the Moscow Radio Orchestra (1936–41), was appointed chief conductor of the Kharkov Philharmonic Orchestra (1939), but after a guest appearance with the Leningrad Philharmonic Orchestra in 1941 he joined the orchestra as conductor at Novosibirsk in Siberia, where it was evacuated. From then until 1960 he shared their concerts with Mravinsky, the musical director. In 1944 the orchestra returned to Leningrad, and Sanderling taught at the Leningrad Conservatory, with the title of professor. In 1960 he returned to Berlin and was invited to be the general music director of the Berlin Symphony Orchestra in East Berlin, which had been formed to give the city a permanent symphony orchestra in addition to the Berlin Staatskapelle (the orchestra of the Berlin Staatsoper) and the Berlin Radio Symphony Orchestra (of the GDR Radio). He was also principal conductor of the Dresden Staatskapelle (1964–7), retired from the Berlin Symphony in 1977, but still conducts them from time to time. He visited London in 1972 to substitute for the sick Klemperer at a concert with the New Philharmonia Orchestra; he regards this occasion as immensely important, as he admired Klemperer above all other conductors in his days in Berlin when Klemperer was at the Kroll Opera. He now travels in both East and West, has conducted in Australia and Japan where he is an honorary conductor of the Yomiuri Nippon Symphony Orchestra, but in the USA has performed only with the Dallas Symphony Orchestra.

In addition to Klemperer, Furtwängler, Walter, Kleiber and Toscanini impressed him deeply in Berlin. To Furtwängler he attributes the greatest musical experiences of his life: 'He was interested in only what was written between the notes, and precision in playing was not so important.' As for Toscanini, 'maybe he is the greatest conductor when we are thinking about realisation of the music by the orchestra, but I cannot say that he gave me the greatest musical impression. Perhaps it depended on what he conducted. I cannot imagine better performances of Debussy or Wagner than those of Toscanini, but not his Beethoven or Mozart, or even his Brahms. These days we are now a little more dependent on the written text, probably due to Toscanini's influence, but this can be a bad thing if taken too far. Sometimes perfection can be wrong, if it is the only purpose. In a lot of music it is possible to give excellent performances with precision alone, but a perfectly played *adagio* from the Beethoven Ninth can be nothing, yet an imperfectly played *adagio* can be wonderful.' Of today's conductors, he considers Karajan to be one of the best interpreters of romantic music: his Bruckner, he says, is 'incredible, just right and marvellous'. Of all composers he believes Haydn to be the most difficult to perform: 'It is difficult for the orchestra to play, and it is difficult for the conductor to find the right emotions for the music. Most conductors play Haydn like a composer of earlier days, but he has to be played like a modern composer, as he liked to shock the audience. In his music one has to find the element of originality, as in modern music.' Sanderling was the first conductor to perform all three symphonies of Rachmaninov, but prefers not to conduct them too often now; he recorded the Second with the Leningrad Philharmonic, but would not conduct it again, as he feels that performance cannot be repeated. In fact Sanderling's musical personality is admirably demonstrated in that completely idiomatic recording of Rachmaninov's Symphony No. 2, with the four Brahms symphonies, which were once released in the West and in which he conducted the Dresden Staatskapelle with the greatest warmth and depth, and with the six *Paris* symphonies of Haydn, with the Berlin Symphony Orchestra, which illustrate exactly his words about the composer. He has recorded throughout his career, in both the USSR and DR Germany, and in addition recorded the nine Beethoven symphonies with the Philharmonia Orchestra (for EMI). His other recordings include the seven Sibelius symphonies, Tchaikovsky's Symphonies Nos 4, 5 and 6, Mahler's Symphony No. 9 and Deryck Cooke's completed version of Mahler's Symphony No. 10, all with the Berlin Symphony Orchestra.

SARGENT, Sir Malcolm (1895–1967). Born in Ashford, Kent, Sargent was first an organist, studied music at Durham University, where he was awarded his doctorate at the age of 21, and served in the British army for eight months in 1918. He then studied the piano with Moiseiwitsch, achieved a reputation as a pianist and accompanist, and appeared as a conductor in 1921 when he led his own composition *Impressions on a Windy Day* with the Hallé Orchestra in Leicester, later repeating the performance at a Promenade Concert in London at Sir Henry Wood's request. In 1922 he organised the Leicester Symphony Orchestra, in 1924 moved to London where he conducted the D'Oyly Carte Company in Gilbert and Sullivan operas, the Diaghilev Ballets Russes, the British National Opera Company, the Robert Mayer Children's Concerts and the Royal Choral Society's presentation of *Hiawatha* of Coleridge-Taylor, taught at the Royal College of Music and conducted the first performance of Walton's *Belshazzar's Feast*. From 1928 he was the music director of the Courtauld/Sargent Concerts in which the London Symphony and London Philharmonic Orchestras were conducted by himself and internationally famous conductors. He was particularly in demand as a choral conductor and toured Europe and the USA with the Huddersfield Choral Society, performing *Messiah*: Beecham said that Sargent was 'the greatest choirmaster we have produced'. In 1932 Sargent assisted Beecham when the latter formed the London Philharmonic Orchestra and shared the direction of their concerts with him. He toured Australia in 1936, 1938 and 1939, was conductor of the Hallé Orchestra (1939–43), the London Philharmonic Orchestra (1939), the Liverpool Philharmonic Orchestra (1942–8) and the BBC Symphony Orchestra (1950–7), and was intimately connected with the London Promenade Concerts from 1950 until his death in 1967. He toured extensively after World War II, to the USA, Canada, Japan and in Europe, as well as to South Africa, Australia and New Zealand.

Sargent was generally a good conductor, but only occasionally a great one. In English music he was a lesser figure than Wood, Beecham or Boult, and he was the direct antithesis of a later conductor of the BBC Symphony Orchestra, Pierre Boulez. His strength was in choral, romantic and British music; all these came together in *The Dream of Gerontius*, which he conducted with the utmost conviction, as is testified in his 78 r.p.m. set with the Liverpool Philharmonic Orchestra, the Huddersfield Choral Society *et al.*, recorded in 1945 and re-issued on LP in 1975. An untiring advocate of British music, he once advised the Viennese: 'Elgar is fine, forgive me, a finer composer than Bruckner.' Despite his love of the Viennese classics, he could rarely rise above the routine in interpreting them. He resolutely refused to accede to the present-day practice of performing the oratorios of Handel and the *Mass in B Minor* and Passions of Bach with small choirs and 17th-century instrumentation, maintaining that Handel and Bach intended that their music should be performed by large forces. He had no sympathy with contemporary atonal music, which led the BBC to allocate more and more of the Prom concerts to other conductors competent in this repertoire. He always conducted with the score in front of him, was a rapid assimilator of new scores, and claimed he could conduct immediately a thousand pieces. With the public he enjoyed a vast popularity, set off by the carnation in his buttonhole, and a flair for showmanship unusual among British conductors. To the world he was the very model of the modern Englishman; to many Englishmen he was just 'Flash Harry'. Edward Heath (in his book *Music: A Joy for Life*) summed up Sargent well: 'In the last 20 years of his life he was probably the British conductor and musician best known to the public, particularly to the promenaders, who adored him. In the world of professional music he was rather more controversial and there were always those ready to sneer. Perhaps as a result of his own restless nervous energy, he did conduct too many concerts a year; perhaps his repertoire of major works was somewhat limited; perhaps he did lack sympathy with the avant-garde products of contemporary music festivals; and perhaps he was snobbish in his approach to the non-musical world. For all that, he did a great deal to encourage British music and British musicians.'

Sargent made records from 1924 almost until his death 43 years later. In 1928–30 he recorded five of the Gilbert and Sullivan operas, and in 1940 two more; later he re-recorded them for LP. On 78s he was also a distinguished accompanist, and his recordings of the Beethoven Piano Concertos with Artur Schnabel and the London Symphony and London Philharmonic

Orchestras have now been re-issued on compact disc. Among his many other recordings, the most distinguished were *The Dream of Gerontius* (mentioned above), *Israel in Egypt*, *Elijah* and *Messiah*, which he recorded twice, in 1954 and 1959. Despite the reservations of critics the latter recording was something of a bestseller.

Sargent was the butt of Beecham's wit more than once. Sir Thomas was asked, after he had appointed Sargent as his assistant with the London Philharmonic Orchestra, why he had such a high opinion of him. He answered: 'If you ever appoint a deputy, appoint one whom you can trust technically; but his calibre must be such that the public will always be glad to see *you* back again.' After a tour of the Middle East, Sargent told Beecham he had been detained and released by the Arabs. 'Released,' exclaimed Beecham. 'Had they heard you play?' But Beecham did not always have the last say. Once he arrived at one of his favourite hotels in the provinces unannounced, and asked for his favourite room, to be told that it was already occupied. He suggested that the occupant might be asked to transfer to another room, but the manager of the hotel said that he thought the man had retired. They both went to the room, knocked at the door, and made their request. 'Certainly not. I'll do nothing of the kind,' was the response. 'But,' said the manager, 'this is Sir Thomas Beecham.' The man said: 'I don't care if it's Sir Malcolm Sargent.'

SAWALLISCH, Wolfgang (b. 1923). Born in Munich, Sawallisch showed early evidence of a talent for music, and was learning the piano at the age of 5. At 11 he attended a performance of *Hänsel und Gretel*, which profoundly affected him, so that he determined to become a musician and conductor. After private studies in Munich, he served in the German armed forces (1942–6) and was taken prisoner in Italy. He resumed his studies at the Munich Conservatory after the war, and joined the Augsburg Opera in 1947 as a répétiteur, then became the first conductor of operetta (1950–1), and remained there until 1953. He was assistant to Markevitch at the conductors' course at Salzburg (1952–3), was appointed general music director at Aachen (1953–8), then at Wiesbaden (1958–60), was music director at the Cologne Opera (1960–3), principal conductor of the Vienna Symphony Orchestra (1960–70), head of the conductors' class at the Cologne Academy of Music, general music director of the Hamburg Philharmonic Orchestra (1960–73), general music director of the Bavarian State Opera (since 1971), chief conductor of the Suisse Romande Orchestra (1960–80), honorary conductor of the NHK Symphony Orchestra, Tokyo, and permanent conductor at La Scala, Milan. He first conducted at the Bayreuth Festivals in 1957 with *Tristan und Isolde*, and has also conducted at festivals at Edinburgh, Vienna and Montreux, *inter alia*. His first visit to London was in 1957 as the accompanist to Schwarzkopf in a Wolf lieder recital; he returned to conduct the Philharmonia Orchestra the next year. In 1964 he toured the USA with the Vienna Symphony Orchestra. He is an accomplished pianist, and in addition to accompanying in lieder recitals he has been both soloist and conductor in performances of concertos by Mozart and Beethoven.

Sawallisch is one of the most distinguished German conductors today. But as a personality and as a conductor he is conservative and restrained; his musical preferences are for the great classical and romantic composers which he performs with the highest regard for the printed score. He is unsympathetic to the second Viennese school, believing dodecaphonic music to be an aberration, but performs with enthusiasm the music of Bartók, Hindemith, Honegger, Britten, Orff and Stravinsky (up to, but not including, *Agon*). His disdain for the spectacular, for public acclaim and for the imposition of his personality *per se* on audiences separates him from many of his contemporaries; his correctness as a conductor results in performances that are admirable in many ways, but not for their colour or expressiveness. He has not the musical temperament to be cast as the successor to Walter or Furtwängler; a certain straightforwardness in phrasing and feeling robs his interpretations of composers such as Wagner and Strauss of the final touch of inspiration. He is unattracted to the great international opera houses, has refused approaches from Berlin and New York, preferring to remain with the permanent ensembles of provincial opera houses rather than accepting the conditions imposed by the *ad hoc* ensembles of operatic stars. He conducts from memory, believing that a conductor should be 'so conversant with the music he is interpreting that he has the melody, structure and metre in his head. In this way there can be much deeper and closer contact with the orchestra. It is as though a barrier had been removed. The conductor stands right in the centre of the music, and there is no distraction from having to turn the pages of the score.'

Sawallisch's first major recordings were with EMI and were Orff's *Carmina Burana*, *Die Kluge* and *Der Mond*. He later went on to record the Strauss operas *Capriccio* and *Intermezzo*, the five Mendelssohn symphonies (with the Philharmonia Orchestra *et al.*) and the four Schumann symphonies (with the Dresden Staatskapelle). For Philips were his Bayreuth performances of *Der fliegende Holländer* and *Tannhäuser*, the four symphonies of Brahms (with the Vienna Symphony Orchestra), the complete symphonies and Masses Nos 5 and 6 of Schubert (with the Dresden Staatskapelle *et al.*) and *Elijah* (with the Leipzig Gewandhaus Orchestra *et al.*), and for Supraphon Mozart's Symphonies Nos 38, 39, 40 and 41 (with the Czech Philharmonic Orchestra), to name perhaps the most important of his recordings. These discs, particularly of the Schubert, Schumann and Brahms symphonies, were highly praised for their faithful interpretations and for the complete absence of personal idiosyncracies, and it was evident that Sawallisch could elicit the finest playing from the great orchestras he conducted. Unfortunately by now most of his records have been deleted from the catalogues in the USA and Britain.

SCHMIDT-ISSERSTEDT, Hans (1900–73). Born in Berlin, Schmidt-Isserstedt learned the violin as a boy, studied at the Hochschule für Musik there and at the Universities of Berlin, Heidelberg and Münster, and received his doctorate for a thesis about Italian influences on Mozart's early operas. After hearing Nikisch he decided to become a conductor; his first appointment was as a répétiteur at the Wuppertal Opera (1923–8), where he also played the violin in the orchestra. He was principal conductor at Rostock (1928–31), Darmstadt (1931–3), first conductor at the Hamburg State Opera (1935–42) and general music director at the Deutsche Oper in Berlin (1942–5). Having had no connection with the Nazi Party, he was asked by the British occupation authorities in 1945 to form the Nordwest Deutsche Rundfunk Orchester (i.e. the Hamburg Radio Orchestra), which he conducted for 26 years (1945–71), and then was appointed its honorary conductor. His début in the USA was with the Philadelphia Orchestra in 1961; he had visited Britain with the NWDRO in 1951, and toured the USA with the orchestra in 1969. He also conducted throughout Europe, the USA, visited the USSR and Australia as a guest conductor, was conductor of the Stockholm Philharmonic Orchestra (1955–64), appeared on occasion at the Hamburg Opera, conducted at Glyndebourne (1958), led *Tristan und Isolde* and *Der fliegende Holländer* (1972) at Covent Garden, conducted the Hamburg Opera in Hindemith's *Mathis der Maler* during its visit to New York (1967), and led *Die Entführung aus dem Serail* at the

Bavarian Opera in Munich (1970). In Sweden he was honoured with the Cross of the Commander of the Order of Vasa (1964), and was made a member of the Royal Academy of Music in London (1970). Early in his career he composed orchestral, vocal and chamber music, and a comic opera *Hassan gewinnt*, but later abandoned composition, declaring that 'all the best things have been written already'.

After World War II, Schmidt-Isserstedt's career gravitated from the opera house to the concert hall, where he achieved distinction as one of the finest exponents of the German school of conducting. Under his leadership the Nordwest Deutsche Rundfunk Orchester developed into one of the finest in FR Germany, although he regretted that, for whatever reason, its records could not attract large sales. His taste in music, like his manner as a conductor, was conservative; he enjoyed a distinguished reputation as an interpreter of Mozart, Beethoven, Brahms, Dvořák, Mahler and Bruckner in particular, but he disliked most contemporary music except for Britten, Tippett, Blomdahl and Henze, whom he performed enthusiastically. In the Viennese classics he was above all concerned with keeping the music's architecture in the foreground, and presented performances that were at the one time imaginative, cool-headed and unmannered. In Beethoven he said: 'There must be an ideal balance of head and heart. Paradoxically, this is something that cannot be learned and yet it can be achieved only when a conductor has the music really in his bones.' His recordings of the nine Beethoven symphonies with the Vienna Philharmonic Orchestra (for Decca), which were made in the last seven years of his life, illustrate his strengths and weaknesses as a conductor; they have attracted critical comments ranging from 'straightforward, unmannered' and 'thoughtful, poetic' to 'unimaginative' and 'beautifully polished but without power'. Probably the last remark best epitomises the series, and Schmidt-Isserstedt's approach in general.

Commencing in 1932, Telefunken issued a number of records in which Schmidt-Isserstedt conducted the Berlin Philharmonic Orchestra. After World War II he recorded for many companies with his Nordwest Deutsche Rundfunk Orchester, and of these discs Dvořák's Symphony No. 7 (for Decca) became something of a classic, and Schmidt-Isserstedt himself regarded it as his best with the orchestra. In addition to the Beethoven symphonies, he recorded the Beethoven Piano Concertos with Wilhelm Backhaus and the Vienna Philharmonic Orchestra, and a number of other works with other orchestras for other companies. The only operas he recorded were Mozart's *La finta giardiniera* and *Idomeneo*.

SCHURICHT, Carl (1880–1967). Born in Danzig, of a German father who was an organ builder and a Polish mother who was a fine musician, Schuricht was educated at the Hochschule für Musik in Berlin under Rudorff and Humperdinck, and studied composition with Reger at Leipzig. He first conducted at Zwickau, Dortmund, Kreuznach, Goslar and Weimar, was conductor of the Rühl Choral Union at Frankfurt-am-Main (1909–11), and was conductor and general music director at Wiesbaden (1912–44). In 1944 he found disfavour with the Nazis and fled to Switzerland, which was his home until his death. He first visited the USA in 1927, and toured there with the Vienna Philharmonic Orchestra in 1956, sharing the podium with Cluytens. In 1933–4 he was conductor of the Berlin Philharmonic Choir, and from 1935 was a frequent guest conductor for the Berlin Radio. Before World War II he was a regular visitor to Holland, where he won great acclaim as a conductor; in 1938 Queen Wilhelmina awarded him the Order of Orange-Nassau. After the war he had no permanent post, but took part in many festivals in Europe, and was a guest conductor with the major orchestras. He composed some orchestral and piano music and songs.

Schuricht was a most distinguished conductor of the German school; his performances were noted for their warmth, sonority, close attention to detail and absence of mannerisms. He was not preoccupied with literalness, and with his interpretations one was always conscious that the music was passing through the mind of a musician fully aware of its beauty and meaning. He became recognised for his readings of the classical and romantic repertoire, but it had not always been so. As he once said: 'When I was young, I concentrated on the moderns—Stravinsky, Bartók, Hindemith and others. I still like them. But more and more I'm in demand as an interpreter of classical and romantic music. In France I am considered a Schumann specialist. In Denmark they call me a Brahms specialist. In Holland I am considered a Bruckner specialist. I am essentially an exponent of the old tradition. I have nothing against what music is now, but I feel that it is important to pass a sense of tradition from age to youth.' He was one of the few Continental conductors who championed Delius. Invariably cast as a symphonic conductor, Schuricht recorded extensively in the 1920s and 1930s; after 1945 he made records for Decca, EMI and La Guilde Internationale du Disque, and among these discs were many distinguished performances, especially the early Beethoven Symphony No. 5 with the Paris Conservatoire Orchestra (for Decca), the coupling of Mozart's Symphony No. 35 and Schubert's Symphony No. 8, and Bruckner's Symphonies Nos 3, 8 and 9, with the Vienna Philharmonic Orchestra (for EMI). He also recorded for EMI the nine Beethoven symphonies with the Paris Conservatoire Orchestra, but these performances were not hailed in Britain as being especially distinctive, mostly due to the sound of the French horns, which is disturbing to British ears.

SCHWARZ, Gerard (b. 1947). Born in Weehawken, New Jersey, the son of two Viennese-born medical doctors, Schwarz studied the piano and trumpet as a boy, attended the Juilliard School, and was a trumpet player in the New York Philharmonic Orchestra (1972–5). He made his début as a conductor at the Aspen Music Festival, Colorado (1974), became music director of the SOHO Ensemble (1975), the Waterloo Music Festival in New Jersey (1976), the Y Chamber Symphony in New York (1976), and the Los Angeles Chamber Orchestra (1980–1), was music adviser for the Mostly Mozart Music Festivals in New York (1982–3), and principal conductor and then musical director of the Seattle Symphony Orchestra (1984). He has also been a guest conductor with orchestras in the USA, Canada, Britain, France, Italy, Portugal, Spain, Finland, DR Germany and Hong Kong. He has made a number of recordings, first with the Los Angeles Chamber Orchestra, and also with other orchestras with which he has been connected, including music by Wagner, Prokofiev and Stravinsky with the Seattle Symphony Orchestra.

SEMKOW, Jerzy (b. 1928). Born at Radomsko, Poland, Semkow studied at the Kraków Conservatory and at the Leningrad Conservatory under Mravinsky, and later with Serafin, Kleiber and Walter. He was assistant conductor to Mravinsky with the Leningrad Philharmonic Orchestra and conductor of the Leningrad Opera Studio (1954–6), conductor at the Bolshoi Theatre, Moscow (1956–8), artistic director and principal conductor of the Warsaw National Opera (1959–61), permanent conductor of the Danish Royal Opera and conductor of the Royal Danish Symphony Orchestra (1966–75). He first conducted in the USA in Boston in 1968, conducted the London Philharmonic Orchestra on its Far Eastern tour in 1969, was musical director and principal conductor of the St Louis Symphony Orchestra (1976–9), has been director of the Teatro Fenice, Venice, and in 1979 was appointed artistic director of the Orchestra Sinfonica de Roma della Radio-televisione Italiana. He has conducted the major orchestras in the USA and in London, Berlin, Vienna *et al.*, and at the operas at Covent Garden, La Scala and Rome. He recorded, *inter alia*, the original version of *Boris Godunov* (with the Polish Radio Symphony Orchestra *et al.*) and *Prince Igor* (with the Sofia National Opera *et al.*) for EMI.

SEREBRIER, José (b. 1938). Born in Montevideo of Russian and Polish parents, Serebrier studied the violin as a boy, and at the age of 11 made his début as a conductor with the National Youth Orchestra of Uruguay, with which he gave numerous concerts in South America for four years. After attending the Montevideo School of Music, he came to the USA in 1955 to study with Martinů at the Curtis Institute in Philadelphia. He was an apprentice conductor with Dorati in Minneapolis, graduated from the University of Minnesota, and his Symphony No. 1 (1957), *Elegy for Strings* (1962) and *Poema elegiaco* were given their first performances in New York. He studied conducting with Monteux and Szell, and was associate conductor to Stokowski with the American Symphony Orchestra, assisting Stokowski in 1965 at the première of Ives's Symphony No. 4. He has taught at Syracuse and Michigan Universities and at the Dalcroze School of Music in New York, was invited by Szell to be composer-in-residence with the Cleveland Orchestra (1968–70), was musical director and conductor of the Cleveland Philharmonic Orchestra (1968–71) and of the Worcester Music Festival, Massachusetts, and is principal conductor of the Mexican Opera. In 1970 he made his London début with the London Symphony Orchestra; Elgar, Delius, Vaughan Williams and Britten are included in his repertoire. He recorded Ives's Symphony No. 4 with the London Symphony Orchestra; his other recordings include Poulenc's *La voix humaine*, with the Adelaide Symphony Orchestra (Australia) *et al*.

SHAW, Robert (b. 1916). Born at Red Bluff, California, the son of a minister, Shaw studied at Pomona College, where he conducted the college Glee Club. In 1938 he went to New York to conduct Fred Waring's Glee Club (1938–45); in 1941 he formed the Collegiate Chorale in New York, which was superseded in 1944 by the Robert Shaw Chorale, an entirely professional body. He was head of the choral departments at the Berkshire Music Center (1942–5) and the Juilliard School (1946–50); in 1944 he had also been director of the RCA Victor Chorale. He toured extensively with the Robert Shaw Chorale in the USA and abroad; in 1952–3 he gave 175 performances of the Mozart *Requiem*, and in 1959–60 36 performances of Bach's *Mass in B Minor*. With the Chorale he toured Europe and the Middle East for the State Department (1956), toured the USSR (1962) and Latin America (1964). Previously, he had turned his attention to orchestral conducting, was conductor of the San Diego Symphony Orchestra (1953–7), associate conductor with Szell of the Cleveland Orchestra and conductor of the Cleveland Orchestra Chorus (1956–67), and in 1966 became co-conductor of the Atlanta Symphony Orchestra, becoming the orchestra's musical director in the following year. As a choral conductor Shaw has done more than any other American to raise standards of choral singing in the USA; Toscanini considered him the finest choral director with whom he had ever collaborated and the Robert Shaw Chorale, prepared by Shaw, appeared in many of Toscanini's recordings with the NBC Symphony Orchestra, including Beethoven's Symphony No. 9 and *Missa Solemnis*, and Verdi's *Requiem*. Shaw has made numerous records as conductor with the Robert Shaw Chorale, including Bach's *Mass in B Minor* and *St John Passion*, *Messiah*, Beethoven's *Missa Solemnis* and Brahms's *Ein deutsches Requiem*; recently there has been issued on compact disc his new recordings of *Messiah*, Beethoven's Symphony No. 9, *Ein deutsches Requiem*, and other pieces, in which he conducts the Atlanta Symphony Orchestra and Chorus.

SIMON, Geoffrey (b. 1946). Simon was born in Adelaide, studied at Melbourne University, the Juilliard School and Indiana University, and first conducted with the Bloomington Symphony Orchestra (1969). He studied further with Swarowsky, Ferraro, Markevitch and Kempe, was a prize winner at the John Player International Conductors' Award (1974), was music director of the Australian Sinfonia, which is an orchestra of expatriate Australian musicians in London (1975–9), and was assistant professor of music at the University of Wisconsin-Madison, and later professor at North Texas State University. He became music director of the Albany Symphony Orchestra in New York (1987), and has been a guest conductor with orchestras and opera companies in Europe, the USA and Israel. He records for Chandos, the first disc being Bloch's *Sacred Service*; his subsequent records have included the original versions of Tchaikovsky's Symphony No. 2 and *Romeo and Juliet* fantasie-overture, Szell's arrangement for orchestra of Smetana's

String Quartet No. 1, and lesser known orchestral works of Respighi.

SINOPOLI, Giuseppe (b. 1946). Born in Venice and raised in Sicily in a quite unmusical family, Sinopoli began his musical studies in secret at the age of 12, as his father disapproved of his ambition to become a musician, telling him that he was too intelligent to be one, and that he should qualify as a doctor. Accordingly he studied medicine at the University of Padua, but at the same time took lessons at the Conservatorio Benedetto Marcello in Venice. As soon as he graduated as a doctor in 1971 he went to Vienna and studied conducting with Swarowsky there; he then taught in Venice (1972), Siena (1973), Darmstadt (1976) and at the Paris Conservatoire (1977). In 1975 he formed the Bruno Maderna Ensemble, in 1979 he presented programmes of contemporary music with the Berlin Philharmonic Orchestra, in 1981 his first opera *Lou Salomé* was performed in Munich, and in 1983 he made his début in the USA with the New York Philharmonic Orchestra and conducted *Manon Lescaut* at Covent Garden, London. His first appearance in London had been with the London Sinfonietta when he directed music by Berio and himself; as a composer he uses electronic sounds and computers. In 1981 he was named Artist of the Year by the Deutsche Phono-Akademie; in 1984 he was appointed principal conductor of the Philharmonia Orchestra, in succession to Muti, and he is also conductor of the Orchestra dell'Accademia Nazionale di Santa Cecilia in Rome.

Sinopoli is one of the three Italian conductors (Muti and Abbado are the others) who have come to take a leading part in musical life in London, taking the place of the Hungarians Solti, Kertész and Dorati who did the same 20 years ago. Like his Italian colleagues he also has a reverence for Verdi, and is said to have devoted four years to the study of Verdi alone, making a remarkable impression at the outset of his career with his performances of *Macbeth*. Mahler and Schumann are also among his preferences, and he has revealed his approach to interpretation in the programme note he wrote for his recording of Schumann's Symphony No. 2, which brings an interesting insight to the composer's mental disposition while writing the work. Schumann's psychological and pathological condition, he points out, had an overwhelming importance on the structure and meaning of the music. 'It is time we gave up judging 19th-century music as simply an affair of themes and forms and measuring comparative greatness and success in these terms. In this sense Schumann would not have passed the test. The paranoic and obsessive aspect of his music must be understood not simply as illustrating his medical condition, but as one of the fundamental elements of his composition.' Sinopoli adds that, along with Berlioz, Schumann was perhaps the first instance in the history of music where the sound image prompted by the composer's changing psychological state corresponds with the musical material employed by him. Schumann himself had written after the composition of the symphony: 'I began to feel more myself again when I wrote the last movement,' and Sinopoli believes that his recovery from the state of mind he was experiencing when he wrote the first three movements meant 'the extinction of the terrible fire of invention and demonic fever' that led to the writing of the earlier movements. Be that as it may, Sinopoli's recording of the symphony, and of the *Manfred* overture accompanying it, is original and impressive. His first recording, for DGG, was a disc of music by Bruno Moderna, and his subsequent recordings include symphonies by Mendelssohn and Schubert, Mahler's Symphony No. 5 and the operas *Manon Lescaut* and *Macbeth*.

SKROWACZEWSKI, **Stanislaw** (b. 1923). Born in Lwow (then in Poland, now in the USSR), where his father was a brain surgeon, Skrowaczewski composed his first orchestral piece at the age of 5, and the Lwow Philharmonic Orchestra performed an overture written by him when he was 8. At 11 he made his début as a pianist, later studied at the Lwow University and the Kraków Academy of Music, went to Paris in 1947, studied conducting with Kletzki, and came into contact with Nadia Boulanger. Between 1947 and 1957 he received many prizes for his compositions. He was conductor of the Polish National Radio Orchestra (1949–54) and the Kraków Philharmonic Orchestra (1955–6); after winning first prize at an international competition for conductors in Rome in 1956 he became conductor of the Warsaw National Philharmonic Orchestra (1957–9). He made his début in the USA with the Cleveland Orchestra in 1958, and became conductor of the Minneapolis Symphony Orchestra (1968–79), after which he was made conductor emeritus. The orchestra was renamed the Minnesota Orchestra in 1968. He has been a guest conductor with major orchestras in the USA and Europe, toured Europe with the Amsterdam Concertgebouw Orchestra, Latin America with the Philadelphia Orchestra and Australia with the Cleveland Orchestra, gave the first performances in the USA of Penderecki's *St Luke Passion* (1967) and

The Devils of Loudun (1969), and was appointed principal conductor and musical conductor of the Hallé Orchestra in 1982. He is a versatile musician, is especially good with large-scale works, and is an advocate of contemporary music; because of his somewhat severe intellectuality and an apparent lack of spontaneity in his performances he has been likened to Szell, with whom he has an affinity in temperament and style. He made many records for Mercury with the Minnesota Orchestra, but undoubtedly his most distinguished recording was the complete orchestral works of Ravel, with the same orchestra for Vox, and it is a considerable example of both the orchestra's and the conductor's musicianship.

SLATKIN, Leonard (b. 1948). Slatkin was born in Los Angeles where his father was the conductor and violinist Felix Slatkin, and his mother was Eleanor Aller the cellist; both were members of the famous Hollywood String Quartet. Leonard began playing the violin at the age of 3, and became involved in the intense musical activities of the Slatkin household. He first studied with his father, then with Castelnuovo-Tedesco, and at 17 was playing the viola in the California Youth Symphony. He studied for brief periods at the University of Indiana and the Los Angeles City College, but on the death of his father decided to become a conductor, and made his début at a music camp at Aspen, Colorado. He studied conducting with Susskind and with Morel at the Juilliard School in New York City (1964–8), and his début there occurred with the Youth Symphony Orchestra of New York. On Susskind's invitation he became assistant conductor of the St Louis Symphony Orchestra in 1968, then advanced to associate principal conductor in 1974, but when Susskind resigned from the position of principal conductor, Slatkin declined the appointment and was named principal guest conductor (1976). In the following year, 1977, he was also appointed music director of the New Orleans Philharmonic-Symphony Orchestra; he was a guest conductor with the Dallas Symphony, Chicago Symphony and Minnesota Orchestras, and made his début with the New York Philharmonic Orchestra in 1974, when he substituted for Muti. Then he was guest conductor with the Philadelphia Orchestra, became principal guest conductor of the Minnesota Orchestra (1974–80), made his London début with the Royal Philharmonic Orchestra (1974), and went on to conduct the other major London orchestras, the Amsterdam Concertgebouw and the Berlin Philharmonic Orchestras, and orchestras in Mexico and the USSR.

In 1979 Slatkin became the first American-born music director of the St Louis Symphony Orchestra, which is the second
oldest in the USA, after the New York Philharmonic. Critics
there have noted the progress of the orchestra under Slatkin,
some declaring that it is approaching the standard of the big five,
in New York, Chicago, Cleveland, Boston and Philadelphia.
With the St Louis Orchestra Slatkin has formed the practice of
introducing unfamiliar and contemporary works with a short
talk, illustrating them by himself on the piano; he feels a
responsibility to perform as often as possible music by American
composers, and to develop young musicians as orchestral players. He apparently prefers Russian to German repertoire, and
has a particular affinity with Rachmaninov. The classical composers, especially Mozart, have not such an immediate appeal
for him. He believes he should champion the composers who, in
his opinion, have not received the respect they deserve:
Vaughan Williams, Sibelius, Nielsen, the later Richard Strauss,
and Rachmaninov, who, he says, have one thing in common:
'their recognition of their inability to enter the 20th century.'
He has expressed a nostalgia for the era when the audience
expected much less of a conductor: 'It has really become quite
difficult, what we have to do. It's not just that more pieces have
been written as the 20th century progressed, but now we're
expected to go back before Haydn too. All of a sudden in the last
few years we have had to make conscious decisions about what
to do with *Messiah*! I can't get up there and do it in the so-called
authentic manner. It requires a totally different training. Then
there's the problem of the new music which has become so . . .
so . . . *varietous*. We don't have time to assimilate it all.' He
compares that predicament with Toscanini's situation, who
'never did a Mahler symphony'.

In his years with Susskind at the St Louis Symphony Orchestra, Slatkin recorded a three-disc set for Vox of the orchestral
music of Gershwin. He has also recorded much contemporary
music, and more recently there has been a fine series of compact
discs of him with the St Louis Symphony for Telarc and
Nonesuch, including Mahler's Symphony No. 2, Prokofiev's
Symphony No. 5, and some orchestral works of Debussy.

SOLTI, Sir Georg (b. 1912). Born in Budapest, Solti started piano lessons
at the age of 6, and was giving recitals in Budapest and in the
Hungarian provinces at 12. He studied at the Franz Liszt
Academy under Székely, Kodály, Bartók, Weiner and
Dohnányi, and decided to become a conductor when he heard

Kleiber conduct a Beethoven symphony. At 18 he was a répétiteur at the Budapest Opera; he assisted Walter at the Salzburg Festival in 1935 and Toscanini during the following two years, working with Toscanini in preparing *Die Zauberflöte* and Verdi's *Requiem*; in *Die Zauberflöte* he played the glockenspiel. His experience with Toscanini was decisive, and gave him a great devotion for conducting opera. In March 1938 he made his début as a conductor in Budapest with *Le nozze di Figaro*, but as a Jew his career in Hungary was blocked; he was invited by Toscanini to assist him at Lucerne where Toscanini, Walter and Adolf Busch were organising a festival. He left for Switzerland in August 1939, two weeks before the border was closed. To support himself in Switzerland he returned to the piano, gave lessons and accompanied, and in 1942 won first prize in the Concours International de Piano in Geneva. His only opportunity to conduct during the war was for a few concerts with the Swiss Radio Orchestra in 1944.

At the conclusion of the war, Solti went to Munich on the invitation of the American Military Government to conduct *Fidelio* at the Bavarian State Opera; since conductors implicated with the Nazis were forbidden to appear in public he was invited to become musical director in place of Krauss. In 1952 he moved to the Frankfurt City Opera, and in 1956 conducted *Die Zauberflöte* at the Salzburg Festival, which brought him to international attention. When he was in Munich and Frankfurt, he conducted the local orchestras, and was a guest conductor in London, Vienna, Berlin, Paris, Rome, Florence, Buenos Aires and in other cities. In 1952 he appeared at the Edinburgh Festival, and the next year made his US début at the San Francisco Opera, led the Chicago Symphony Orchestra (1954) and the New York Philharmonic Orchestra (1957), conducted at the New York Metropolitan Opera, and led *Der Rosenkavalier* at Covent Garden, London (1959). The Los Angeles Philharmonic Orchestra engaged him as conductor in 1961, but he resigned before his first concert with them, because the orchestra's management had engaged a conductor (Zubin Mehta) without consulting him. He was musical director at Covent Garden (1961–71), accepting the appointment on Walter's advice; in 1972 he was knighted and became a British citizen. The knighthood was conferred as an expression of gratitude from British musicians for his work in raising Covent Garden to the undisputed status of one of the world's leading opera houses. He was appointed conductor of the Chicago Symphony Orchestra in 1971, was also musical director of l'Orchestre de Paris (1971–5), took the orchestra on a tour of China (1974), was musical adviser to the Paris Opéra, was principal guest conductor of the London Philharmonic Orchestra, and became the orchestra's principal conductor and artistic director in 1979; he remained with the orchestra until 1983, when he was given the title of conductor emeritus. His home is in London, and he visits Chicago for two series of concerts each year.

Despite his late start in Munich after the war, Solti is one of the great operatic and symphonic conductors on the scene today; it would be an exaggeration to claim, as some do, that he is the greatest. Without belittling his great talent, one can say that he is an excellent example of how gramophone records can accelerate a conductor's career. According to his own account, the great musical influence on him has been Toscanini, whose style his most resembles, but Furtwängler, Kleiber and Walter also played their part in his development. From Toscanini he learnt, above all, that one cannot take music seriously enough and learn enough: 'The essential and desperate seriousness of making music. It is no joke and is not easy, and that old man never stopped looking at the score.' But from Furtwängler he learned to moderate Toscanini's rigidities. His musical sympathies are wide, and he has often criticised the tendency in British musical life to categorise musicians as specialists: 'Everyone says you have to be a specialist, and if you conduct Wagner you cannot conduct Mozart—this is nonsense: all my life I have fought against this. Obviously some works will suit you better than others, but I have always made a point of playing those works that are *not* natural to me. I want to do the things that stretch me musically, and fight the tendency to become complacent and do one kind of music—that is the death of a musician.' He named Beethoven and Schubert among his favourite composers, in addition to Bartók, Stravinsky, Schoenberg, Berg and Hindemith. To the listening public, he is best known as a great conductor of late romantic music; in his first year with the Chicago Symphony Orchestra he conducted a sensational series of concerts in New York, leading in successive concerts Mahler's Symphony No. 5, Bruckner's Symphony No. 8, Mahler's Symphony No. 7 and *Das Rheingold*. He has little interest in music after Schoenberg, and believes that too many of the early works of the great composers are relatively unknown and are not performed. In the opera house, he is acclaimed for his Wagner, Strauss and Verdi, and in the concert hall especially for his Mahler. In fact, he feels in complete sympathy with the music of

Mahler, and says that he can approach him classically and not as a super-romantic.

Solti is revered by his musicians, but he can be imperious, impatient and sometimes autocratic; he drives them to the utmost, which has on occasion led to eruptions. He admits this, but believes that he has changed over the years: 'In my orchestra I hate slackness, idle talk and lost time. I always hated this and still hate it. But I can achieve much more when I am quiet and not shouting.' As a musical director, he believes that he must have complete authority. Rehearsals are tense and exacting, but at performances he is relatively relaxed. He does not stop the orchestra for mistakes, but points out subtle points of interpretation to section leaders and individual players later. His advice to aspiring young conductors is that technique is the least important thing: 'Above all, you need the gift to lead people. You can learn all about music, but this gift to lead, one cannot learn. The next step follows, the really big hurdle. The conductor learns the piece and has a clear picture of it, and then comes the difficult step, to realise the picture.' His own beat is at first hard to follow, and his movements are angular and jerky, sometimes almost grotesque. Nonetheless, he is acknowledged to be one of the most dynamic conductors alive. Players note that he does not beat rhythms, but the bar lines and accented notes. Although his tempi can be unusually fast, he demands absolute precision, and in the opera house he is vitally concerned with every aspect of the production. The score is always before him at rehearsals and concerts, although he knows it by heart; this, he believes, dispels any nervousness on the part of the soloists.

Tension is the most obvious thing about a Solti performance, with a Toscanini-like concentration, with fast tempi and exact rhythms. It is with composers who can take this treatment that he excels: Bartók, Kodály, Mahler, Tchaikovsky, Wagner and Verdi. The music of Haydn and Mozart and the early romantics such as Schubert, Schumann and Mendelssohn is kept on a very tight rein, and is often driven too hard to reveal its lyrical qualities, and in this respect he comes close to Toscanini. In the concert hall he sometimes conducts Mozart with more tension than the music can stand, but even so, three of his finest recordings are *Die Zauberflöte*, *Così fan tutte* and *Le nozze di Figaro*. His Beethoven is another story; it tends to be cautious and correct, even laboured, and in the last analysis sounds too uncommitted to be convincing. He was at first greatly influenced by Toscanini's Beethoven, with one tempo going through the

movement from beginning to end, but later acquaintance with
Furtwängler broadened his view: 'Now obviously somewhere in
the middle is the truth of Beethoven symphonies for me. Between the two men, somewhere, a truth is lying, and that is what
I try to find. One must not be too flexible but not too rigid, not
afraid to decide about phrasing, but not break up the movement
into little pieces.' His Bruckner is inclined to suffer the same
way, when the long paragraphs and the profound sense of
mystery can sometimes elude him. His many Wagner records
have called forth both high praise and carping criticism; he is at
the opposite pole to Knappertsbusch, Kempe, Karajan and
Goodall, and sacrifices breadth and depth to headlong excitement. He is not at all lyrical in the German mould, but is a
dramatic and intense conductor who has his own unique sound
and style. Whether the Chicago Symphony Orchestra has completely retained its magnificence since 1971, based on the refinement, precision and tonal qualities developed by Reiner, is
another matter about which there is not always general agree-
ment, but it must be true that the orchestra now plays exactly as
Solti wants it to play.

Since he was placed under contract by Decca in 1947, Solti has
made an enormous contribution to the record catalogues, and
has recorded with a number of orchestras, the chief ones being
the Chicago Symphony, Vienna Philharmonic, London Symphony and London Philharmonic Orchestras. His discs with the
Chicago Symphony have included the Beethoven symphonies
and piano concertos (with Ashkenazy), *Symphonie fantastique*
and *La Damnation de Faust*, Brahms's four symphonies, two
overtures, *Variations on the St Antony Chorale* and *Ein deutsches Requiem*, Bruckner's Symphonies Nos 4, 5, 6, 7 and 9,
Haydn's Symphonies Nos 94, 100, 102 and 103 and *The Creation*, Mahler's Symphonies Nos 2, 3, 4, 5, 6, 7 and 8 and *Das
Lied von der Erde*, *Le Sacre du printemps*, *Also sprach
Zarathustra, Till Eulenspiegel* and *Don Juan*, and Verdi's
Requiem and *Pezzi sacri*. With the Vienna Philharmonic he
recorded *inter alia* Beethoven's Symphonies Nos 3, 5 and 7,
Schubert's Symphony No. 9, Schumann's Symphonies Nos 3 and
4, *Ein Heldenleben* and Verdi's *Requiem*, with the London
Symphony Bartók's *Concerto for Orchestra* and Mahler's Sym-
phonies Nos 1, 2, 3 and 9, and with the London Philharmonic
Elgar's two symphonies, *Falstaff, In the South*, *Cockaigne* and
Violin Concerto (with Chung), *The Planets*, and *Belshazzar's
Feast*. Important as these discs are, the list of operas he has
recorded is even more impressive: *Orfeo ed Eurydice*, *Die*

Zauberflöte, Così fan tutte, Le nozze di Figaro, Fidelio, Eugen Onegin, Un ballo in maschera, Don Carlos, Otello, Rigoletto, Falstaff, Carmen, La Bohème, Die Meistersinger, Parsifal, Tannhäuser, Der fliegende Holländer, Tristan und Isolde, Rheingold, Die Walküre, Siegfried, Götterdämmerung, Salome, Elektra, Der Rosenkavalier, Arabella and *Moses und Aron*. Some of these, including the four operas of *The Ring*, have been re-issued on compact disc.

STEIN, **Horst** (b. 1928). Born in Wuppertal, Stein studied at the Musik Gymnasium in Frankfurt-am-Main and at the Hochschule für Musik in Cologne, and received his first appointment at the age of 19 as a répétiteur at the Wuppertal Town Theatre (1947–51). He was conductor at the Hamburg State Opera (1951–55), and at the State Opera in East Berlin (1955–61), then returned to Hamburg as assistant general music director (1961–3). He became general music director at Mannheim (1963–70), first conductor at the Vienna State Opera (1972–6), and general music director at the Hamburg State Opera (1972–6), at the same time being a professor at the Hochschule für Musik there. He has been a guest conductor in opera houses throughout Europe, North and South America, first conducted in the USA at the San Francisco Opera in 1965, has frequently conducted the Berlin Philharmonic and Vienna Philharmonic Orchestras, in 1968 led acclaimed performances of *The Ring* at the Vienna Festival, since 1969 has regularly conducted at the Bayreuth Festivals, where he has led *The Ring*, has conducted the NHK Symphony Orchestra in Japan of which he is now conductor laureate, led the first performance of Schoenberg's *Gurrelieder* in South America in Buenos Aires in 1964, has conducted at many festivals in Europe, and has toured West Germany and Austria with the Vienna Symphony Orchestra. He was artistic director of the Suisse Romande Orchestra (1980–5), and from 1986 has been principal conductor of the Bamberg Symphony Orchestra.

In appearance Stein could have walked out of a Gerard Hoffnung cartoon, but as his curriculum vitae demonstrates he is an accomplished and immensely experienced conductor in the very best tradition of the German *Kapellmeister*, giving thoroughly musical performances through the breadth of the repertoire. He has made numerous records for Decca, DGG, EMI/Electrola, Ariola, *et al.*, the most prominent being the five Beethoven piano concertos and Bruckner's Symphonies Nos 2 and 6 (with the Vienna Philharmonic Orchestra, and with Gulda in the concertos, for Decca), and Kienzl's *Der Evangelimann* (with the Bavarian Radio Symphony Orchestra *et al.* for DGG).

STEINBERG, William (1899–1978). Born in Cologne as Hans Wilhelm Steinberg, Steinberg studied at the Cologne Conservatory under Abendroth, and as a boy learned the violin and piano. At the age of 19 he won the Wullner Prize for conducting in Cologne, and became assistant to Klemperer at the Cologne Opera in 1920. Soon he was appointed a conductor there, and was subsequently first conductor at the German Opera, Prague (1925–9), where he became director in 1927, music director at the Frankfurt-am-Main Opera and conductor of the Frankfurt Museum Concerts, also conducting at the Berlin Staatsoper. In Frankfurt he led the second production of *Wozzeck*, and the world premières of Weill's *Aufsteg und Fall der Stadt Mahagonny* and Schoenberg's *Von Heute auf Morgen*.

With the advent of the Nazis, Steinberg was dismissed from all his posts in 1933. He then founded a Jewish Cultural League which gave concerts for the Jewish communities in Frankfurt and Berlin, but he left Germany for Palestine in 1936, taking with him many musicians; there he was co-founder with Huberman of the Palestine Symphony Orchestra (now the Israel Philharmonic Orchestra), and trained it for its first concert in December 1936, which was conducted by Toscanini, who accepted Huberman's invitation without hesitation. Steinberg conducted the orchestra in the first years of its existence, and in 1938 went to the USA on Toscanini's invitation to assist in founding and training the new NBC Symphony Orchestra. He was assistant conductor to Toscanini with the orchestra, and appeared as a guest conductor with many other American orchestras, eventually becoming a naturalised US citizen in 1944 and changing his first name to William. He conducted at the San Francisco Opera (1944–8), was musical director of the Pittsburgh Symphony Orchestra (1952–76), of the London Philharmonic Orchestra (1958–60) and of the Boston Symphony Orchestra (1968–72). He conducted at the New York Metropolitan Opera (1964–5), toured Europe and the Middle East with the Pittsburgh Symphony Orchestra in 1964, conducted the Israel Philharmonic Orchestra on its tour of the USA in 1967, and was principal guest conductor of the New York Philharmonic Orchestra in 1964. A performance of Beethoven's Symphony No. 9 with the New York Philharmonic Orchestra in 1965 drew an audience of 75,000. In the last years of his life Steinberg suffered a grave illness which forced him to curtail his activities; he was obliged to retire from his position with the Pittsburgh Symphony Orchestra in 1976, and then was appointed conductor emeritus. Under his leadership the orchestra had become one of the finest half dozen in the USA.

Steinberg's formative influences were Toscanini and Klemperer, from whom he learnt, above all, a single-minded devotion to his profession and faithfulness to the score. 'Toscanini and Klemperer were the great masters. They served two purposes, the orchestra and the music, and absolutely nothing more. For one wrong tempo at a rehearsal, Klemperer would not speak to me for weeks.' He deprecated personal interpretations at the expense of the composer's intentions. He said that the conductor can only demonstrate the meaning of a piece by allowing the work to speak for itself; to achieve this he must have all the implied spiritual traits and virtues of character, illuminated by intuition and inspiration and sufficient modesty to avoid the attentions of a crowd seeking entertainment or provocation. His fine musicianship ensured that his intentions were generally convincing and eloquent, although sometimes unexciting; his interpretations were honest and literal. He gave his players freedom in their phrasing, in contrast to many of his peers. Steinberg was at his best in Beethoven, Brahms, Wagner, Bruckner and Mahler, but not quite so exemplary in French music. He believed that conductors had an obligation to perform at least some contemporary music for the benefit of their audiences; programmes should inform as well as entertain. He pointed out the advantage of the long experience in opera houses enjoyed by European conductors: 'At the opera house one starts at the bottom. This is the principal mistake of conductors in America, who start at the top.' He judged American orchestras better than most others: 'The top 20 orchestras in North America are superior to those in Europe, with the exception of the Berlin Philharmonic.'

Most of Steinberg's recordings were on LP with the Pittsburgh Symphony Orchestra, for Capitol and Command, and included many distinguished performances: the nine Beethoven and the four Brahms symphonies, and others by Haydn, Mozart, Schubert, Mendelssohn, Tchaikovsky, Bruckner, Rachmaninov *et al.*, as well as a number of other works from the orchestral repertoire. He recorded some contemporary pieces, such as symphonies by Harris, Toch, Schuman and Honegger, some for the label Pittsburgh's Festival of Contemporary Music. In his last years he recorded with the Boston Symphony for DGG, and of these he himself was most pleased with Schubert's Symphony No. 9 and Bruckner's Symphony No. 6.

STOKOWSKI, Leopold (1882–1977). Stokowski was born in London, the son of a Polish cabinetmaker and a mother of Irish descent. His grandfather had brought the family from Lublin, where farmers were being dispossessed of their lands by the Tsarist secret police. As a boy he learned the piano and violin, and it was the violin that remained his favourite instrument throughout his life. In London he studied at the Royal College of Music, graduated from Queen's College, Oxford, with a B.Mus., and also studied at the Paris Conservatoire and at Munich. He became a Fellow of the Royal College of Organists, and his first musical appointment was organist at St James's Church in Piccadilly, London, in 1902. His true name became a controversial point later in his life, but his birth certificate bears the indisputable name Leopold Antoni Stokowski. In 1905 he crossed the Atlantic to become organist at St Bartholomew's Church in New York, where his performances of the music of Bach brought him some local celebrity. The summers he spent in Europe studying conducting; he made his début as a conductor in Paris in 1908, and appeared in London under the sponsorship of Henry Wood, of whom he had been a pupil. In 1909 he was offered the post of conductor of a new orchestra in Cincinatti, Ohio; he established his first reputation there, but after three years he resigned peremptorily before the expiration of his contract to become conductor of the Philadelphia Orchestra.

Stokowski remained with the Philadelphia Orchestra until 1936, that is for 24 years, and in that time he and the orchestra became a legend throughout the USA and the world, on account of the orchestra's superb qualities, Stokowski's spectacular personality, and the exceptional series of gramophone records they made. He became a US citizen in 1925, although by then he had assumed a European accent, which he appeared to drop at will. In 1931 he was appointed musical director of the orchestra, but with the onset of the Depression the board controlling the orchestra asked him to restrict his activities, such as performing new works for large orchestras which required more rehearsals than the usual repertoire, and which had little appeal to audiences. The inevitable clash with the board led to his resignation in 1934, but he nonetheless agreed to remain, provided he had final authority in artistic matters. The new arrangement was not to last, since Stokowski's interest had turned to other fields, and the 1935–6 season was his last as principal conductor. Eugene

Ormandy, who was with the Minneapolis Orchestra, joined him as co-principal conductor, and in 1938 he was appointed musical director; Stokowski then ended his contract, but continued to conduct some concerts each year until the season of 1940–1; after a performance of the *St Matthew Passion* he walked off the stage without acknowledging the applause, and did not return to conduct the orchestra again for 19 years.

Other conductors were frequently in awe at the magnificence of the Philadelphia Orchestra in Stokowski's years with it. The orchestra retained this quality for years after Stokowski's departure, and under Ormandy and Muti it has remained one of the finest orchestras in the USA, if not the world. In 1941 Toscanini undertook a series of recording sessions with the Philadelphia Orchestra; Charles O'Connell, then the music director of RCA records, wrote that 'the conductor was amazed and delighted with the orchestra. Its quickness, agility, musicianship, glorious tone and unique sonority were a revelation to him. At the first rehearsal he went completely through the programme without once interrupting the orchestra. At the end he bowed, smiled, told the men that there was nothing he could suggest to improve the performance and walked off the stage in high good humour.'

After terminating his activities in Philadelphia, Stokowski devoted his attention to film-making, technological advances in sound reproduction, and other areas of interest, but his ventures elsewhere had no lasting effect, and in the end it is still his achievement as a conductor *per se* that has won him lasting fame. He appeared in several films, and then in 1939 he collaborated with Walt Disney in making the film *Fantasia*. The original idea was for Stokowski and the Philadelphia Orchestra to provide the sound track for a Mickey Mouse cartoon on the legend of the sorcerer's apprentice, to Dukas' music; the project blossomed and developed to include cartoons to other music played by the orchestra. Mickey Mouse as the sorcerer's apprentice was a happy inspiration, and the abstract patterns to Bach's *Toccata and Fugue in D Minor* were novel and striking. But there was also a representation of the evolution of life on the planet Earth to the music of *Le Sacre du printemps*, as well as a gentle satire on Greek mythology to Beethoven's Symphony No. 6, which was cut to 22 minutes. Stravinsky objected to this treatment of his score, but was powerless to prevent it. Beethoven's opinion could not be sought, but the cartoons of romping centaurs whose feminine charms were coyly concealed with brassières of flowers, as required by the Hays Office, the Hollywood censorship authority, have haunted the memory of many ever since.

Fantasia has recently been revived, but with Stokowski and the Philadelphia Orchestra's contribution replaced by another orchestra and conductor.

In 1940 Stokowski founded the All-American Youth Orchestra; he searched the USA for the best orchestral talent between 15 and 25 years of age, and in a short time this ensemble reached a standard of performance approaching the Philadelphia Orchestra itself. The All-American Youth Orchestra continued until 1942, and toured the USA and South America with Stokowski; it was briefly revived with a new group of players six years later. Stokowski appeared with the NBC Symphony Orchestra for a season, but his predilection for modern music, as well as Toscanini's dislike for his conducting methods, caused NBC to terminate the contract. In fact, Schoenberg's Piano Concerto received its première under Stokowski at an NBC radio concert. In 1944, on the invitation of the mayor of New York, he formed the New York City Symphony Orchestra, to present low-priced concerts at the New York City Center. The next year he was made musical director at the Hollywood Bowl in Los Angeles, from 1946 to 1949 he was a guest conductor with the New York Philharmonic-Symphony Orchestra, and became co-conductor with Mitropoulos in 1949–50. On Beecham's invitation he visited Britain for the first time in 40 years in 1951, and also appeared at the Salzburg Festival. Between 1951 and 1961 he was a guest conductor at the New York City Opera, and in 1961 he made his one appearance at the New York Metropolitan Opera with *Turandot*. From 1955 to 1961 he was musical director of the Houston Symphony Orchestra, and in 1962 he founded the American Symphony Orchestra, made up of comparatively young players, which he conducted without fee, and with which he gave an annual series of concerts in New York. With them he gave the world première of Ives's Symphony No. 4 in 1965; he was then 83, and he subsequently recorded the work. Into his nineties he was still active, conducting and recording in London. He was married four times; his first wife was the pianist Olga Samaroff, and the last Gloria Vanderbilt. He returned to England for the last years of his life; he said that he spent his days studying the scores of the great masters: 'Except when I am sleeping, I am thinking of the next time I must conduct great music.' Despite the immense fortune he made from music, he once said: 'I've never done a real day's work in my life. I simply make music, and people have always been foolish enough to pay me for it. I never told them that I would have done it all for nothing.'

Stokowski's eminence as one of the truly great conductors of the 20th century was the product of a number of factors. First, there was the unique sound of his orchestras, best exemplified by the Philadelphia Orchestra when he was its director. Then there was the imaginative quality of his musical interpretations; he was no literalist, and to him music became great when the conductor revealed its beauty and power through the agency of his mind. Those who knew him best believe that he had a profound comprehension of the essential meaning of music; he himself said that the conductor must have a complete understanding of the music's emotional content. He went to great trouble to understand the instruments of the orchestra by learning to play them, and when he was in Philadelphia he went to Paris every summer to study a new instrument. The other factors were the records he made, first with the Philadelphia Orchestra, and later with the many others with which he was associated; his constant exploration of new music; and finally, his own charismatic personality.

The remarkable, inimitable character of Stokowski's sound is its firm, thick, lustrous *legato* quality, often with a hint of *portamento*. Many commentators have said that this feeling for *legato* originated in Stokowski's early experience as an organist; others have pointed out that when he directed the orchestra he varied and mixed sound textures as an organist changes his stops. He was a supreme master of orchestral texture, and one is tempted to believe that for him every piece of music was simply a vehicle for this interplay of textures. His sound was majestic, sensuous and seamless; Neville Cardus once said that Stokowski 'embalmed music'. The basis of this sound was his much-discussed innovation of free bowing with the strings, as he insisted that every string player should bow independently of the rest; he also introduced individual breathing for wind and brass, and he was as much concerned with the tonal quality of the instruments his musicians played, as with their technical capacities. He had been known to ask an oboist to change his reed because it was too bright for the grey he wanted. Also, he was careful to place the orchestra according to the demands of the score, and placed 12 double basses in a line across the back of the orchestra.

Stokowski was an unabashed showman, and in him there was a certain narcissistic quality. When he appeared in the opera house he was concerned that the lighting should play on his hands and on his white hair. Despite his birth and education in England, he affected an indeterminate, curious, foreign accent, but he acted this role so much in his life that he slipped into the person of the one he was acting. He astonished a member of the London Symphony Orchestra who was travelling with him in a taxi across Westminster Bridge in London, in his last years, by pointing to Big Ben and asking him what it was, in his best foreign accent. A delightful example of his flair for showmanship was at an opening concert of a summer series with the Philadelphia Orchestra; after the final number on the programme, Stokowski moved down to the audience, the manager pleaded for an encore, suddenly he sprang to the podium, motioned to the orchestra, and directed a superbly poised performance of the *Blue Danube* waltz. The enchanted audience did not know that there was indeed nothing spontaneous in the act; the orchestra had carefully rehearsed the piece a couple of weeks before, but was puzzled because it was not programmed. When he came to Philadelphia, Stokowski battled with the aberrations of the Friday-afternoon audience, late-coming and early-leaving; he once directed a concert which opened with a piece by Lekeu in which the music permitted the orchestra to take their seats one by one, and concluded with Haydn's *Farewell* Symphony, where the orchestra leaves one by one, leaving finally only the conductor.

During his lifetime Stokowski is said to have conducted 7,000 concerts live, to ten million people. His repertoire covered most orchestral music from Bach to the present day. Haydn and Mozart received fine performances, but unlike some of his contemporaries he did not seek a great revival of their music. His art was best displayed in the romantic music of the 19th century, and the great scores of the French and Russian masters, all of which gave him full scope for his devotion to orchestral sound. When he arrived in Philadelphia, in 1912, he immediately announced that he would include contemporary composers such as Debussy, Elgar, Sibelius and Strauss in his programmes, and every year he visited Europe and brought back new scores to perform. He gave an extraordinary number of first performances; the number has been estimated at 2,000. Musicians have derided his arrangements of Bach's music for the modern symphony orchestra, but there is a case to be made in their favour, at least as much as for Beecham's arrangements of Handel. Stokowski had a great devotion to Bach, and believed that only the symphony orchestra could truly reveal the music's majesty. If it is possible to forget temporarily all historical and stylistic reservations, then the gravity, dignity, vigour, serenity and expressiveness of the music represented in his arrangements are impressive indeed. He wished to introduce Bach to his audiences at a time when this music was unfamiliar, although it has been said that the arrangements were intended primarily as orchestral exercises. His favourite piece was the *Toccata and Fugue in D Minor*, which he recorded five times. With all music, he had little respect for the literal reading of the score; he once said: 'That's a piece of paper with some marking on it. We have to infuse life into it.'

Stokowski thought it unimportant whether a conductor conducted from a score or from memory. He said that the ideal was to conduct with a score and yet know the music from memory, but in practice he rarely used a score. As a result of an injury to his arm, he discarded the baton early in his career, perhaps also to exploit the dramatic effect of the expressive gestures of his hands. His directions were simple and direct, avoiding impulsive actions. His relations with his players were pleasant but impersonal. At rehearsal he was methodical and cold, and preferred sarcasm when moved to reprove a player. Although he left his players little opportunity for spontaneous expression, he did not prepare his performances as meticulously as, say, Toscanini did. When he was preparing the Philadelphia Orchestra for its two weekly concerts—on Friday afternoon and Saturday evening —he was allowed four rehearsals; at the first he would go straight through the music in the order of the programme, giving attention to special passages, the next rehearsal would be taken up with intensive work on the programmed pieces, in the third he played through any new music in which he might be interested at the time, and the final rehearsal was again a straight run through of the programme. He never tired the orchestra at rehearsal, leaving the final element of expression to the concert itself. In fact, he is said to have preferred rehearsals to concerts.

Stokowski's first records were made with the Philadelphia Orchestra for RCA Victor in 1917; the Schubert *Unfinished* was the first complete symphony he recorded, in 1924. His series with the Philadelphia Orchestra was the greatest of its time, rivalled only by Beecham's with the London Philharmonic, which commenced in 1932. Stokowski's last records with the Philadelphia Orchestra were made in 1940, except when he returned briefly to record again with them in 1960. His early recordings were relatively straightforward readings, exhibiting the orchestra's sumptuous tone, and were probably the finest performances he recorded during his life. The tendency to mannerisms and distortions of the music came in later years, with the Philadelphia Orchestra and after. The music encompassed by the Philadelphia series was considerable even in comparison with today's standards. The sound, too, was exceptional for the records of that time, and O'Connell wrote that the main reason for their excellence was the acoustic properties of the Academy of Music in Philadelphia. Even so, Stokowski was always intensely interested in orchestral tone and its reproduction. Afterwards, he recorded with many orchestras and with many companies. In 1961 he recorded for Capitol with the London Symphony Orchestra and the Orchestre National de la Radio-diffusion Française; then in the last decade or so in his life he made a remarkable series for Decca with some London and European orchestras, including excerpts from *Messiah*, Beethoven's Symphonies Nos 5, 7 and 9, Schubert's Symphony No. 8, *Symphonie fantastique*, Brahms's Symphonies Nos 1 and 4, Tchaikovsky's Symphony No. 5 and *Romeo and Juliet* fantasie-overture, *Scheherazade*, *Pictures at an Exhibition*, *Enigma Variations*, orchestral excerpts from the Wagner operas, and some of his Bach arrangements. Reissues from his earlier recordings have been made by dell'Arte, including Bach arrangements and *Le Sacre du printemps* and *L'Oiseau de feu* (with the Philadelphia Orchestra), excerpts from *Boris Godunov*, Sibelius's Symphony No. 2, Bartók's *Concerto for Orchestra*, Schumann's Symphony No. 2, the overtures *Le Carnaval romain*, *Leonore No. 3*, *Rosamunde*, *William Tell* and *Don Giovanni*, and his famous coupling of Tchaikovsky's *Francesca da Rimini* and *Hamlet*. Compact discs of Stokowski are the overtures mentioned above (for PRT), Debussy's *Ibéria* and *Nocturnes*, and Ravel's *Alborada del gracioso* and *Rapsodie espagnole* (for EMI), Shostakovich's Symphony No. 11 (for Angel, in the USA), and a collection of short pieces with the title *Stokowski Spectacular* (for PRT).

STRAUSS, Richard (1864–1949). Strauss, the composer of the great and familiar tone poems, operas and songs, was one of the leading symphonic and operatic conductors of his day. His career as a conductor began in 1883 when he was assistant conductor at Meiningen with von Bülow, whom he succeeded there in 1885. He went on to fill many of the most important musical positions in Germany and Austria: conductor of the Munich Court Opera (1886–9), first conductor of the Weimar Court Orchestra (1889), successor to von Bülow as conductor of the Berlin Philharmonic Orchestra (1894–5), conductor of the Berlin Opera (1898–1918), co-director with Schalk of the Vienna Opera (1919–24), and conductor of the Leipzig Gewandhaus

Orchestra (1933). He led *Tannhäuser* at Bayreuth at the age of 30, and was a frequent conductor at Salzburg and at other major European opera houses. When the Nazis came to power in Germany in 1933, Strauss did not hesitate to take Walter's place with the Leipzig Gewandhaus Orchestra when the latter was expelled from Germany. He also accepted the chairmanship of the Reichsmusikkammer, the organisation set up by the Nazis to control music; like some other prominent German musicians, he was largely indifferent to the fate of his Jewish colleagues. However, in 1935 he came into conflict with the Nazis for his collaboration with Stefan Zweig, a Jew, in preparing the libretto for *Die schweigsame Frau*, and from then on his relations with the Nazis were uneasy. In 1939 he was actually placed under house arrest for voicing opposition to the invasion of Poland, and Nazi displeasure was also provoked when his son married a Jewess. After World War II he faced a special court in Munich investigating collaborators with the Nazis, and was exonerated, but nevertheless his music to this day is proscribed in Israel, along with that of Wagner and Lehár. When he was asked why he did not leave Germany during the Nazi era, he said that in Germany there were 56 opera houses, and in America two: 'That would have reduced my income.'

In 1935, Strauss received a State questionnaire to determine whether he was an Aryan, which requested the names of two witnesses to his professional ability. He answered 'Mozart and Richard Wagner'. He was especially celebrated for his performances of the Mozart and Wagner operas: in Mozart, many thought him a conductor of genius, and Klemperer considered that in conducting Mozart his own creative nature was evident, as he himself was apparent in the music. In the Mozart operas, Strauss would accompany the recitatives himself on the harpsichord, and introduce little decorations. Klemperer also remarked that Strauss once told him, to his astonishment, that he could not conduct a Beethoven symphony unless he had some sort of literal meaning in his mind. Strauss's father had been a leading horn player at the Munich Opera, and had detested Wagner, but Strauss was held by his contemporaries to be an exceptional conductor of the Wagner operas; Rosé, the leader of the Vienna Philharmonic Orchestra before World War II, said that Strauss's *Tristan und Isolde* was one of the most unforgettable experiences in music, with an intensity equalled only by Furtwängler. The economy of his conducting style, which required extreme concentration in the musicians, led many in the audience to misunderstand the quiet appearance he assumed when conducting a work like *Tristan*; but the musicians who were watching his eyes, the expression on his face, and the small movements of his baton, knew differently. He once wrote: 'You should not perspire when conducting; only the audience should get warm,' and in Klemperer's words: '*He* did not throw himself around like a madman, but the orchestra played as though *it* were possessed.'

Opinions vary about Strauss as a conductor of his own music. Some say that it was wonderful, others, such as Szell and Beecham, thought he could be dull, and Strauss himself once remarked that it bored him to perform his own music. In the recordings he made of his own works, he is intense, lyrical, casual and cold, frequently in the same work, and occasionally there are patches of poor orchestral ensemble. Fritz Busch explained this phenomenon this way: 'The lack of genuinely warm feeling which Strauss's music often shows was recognised by the composer himself. He knew exactly the places where his music became sentimental and trashy. Nothing annoyed him more than when conductors wallowed in his lyrical outpourings, and thus unpleasantly brought his sins before his eyes. He himself, the older he grew, passed over more indifferently and unemphatically such passages when conducting, as if he were ashamed at having composed them. His inconsistency showed itself in his continuing to write such things. The puzzle of Strauss, who in spite of his marvellous talents, is not really penetrated and possessed of them like other great artists but in fact simply wears them like a suit of clothes which can be taken off at will—this puzzle neither I nor anyone else has yet succeeded in solving.' Boult wrote of a performance of Mozart's Symphony No. 40 by Strauss in 1910: Strauss lavished the greatest attention on the symphony in rehearsal, working on it for five hours. It was, in the end, 'a wonderful performance, and obviously the result of much thought and preparation and precision in rehearsal'. Boult was struck by the slow tempi for the first and last movements, but because his accentuation was so widely spaced, the music appeared to flow along quickly. But Boult added: 'A thoughtful friend of mine has linked Strauss's precise rehearsal craftsmanship with his love of card games; his care in planning his resources in rehearsal was in parallel with his playing a hand of his favourite skat.' Strauss recorded much of his own orchestral music, variously with the Berlin Philharmonic, Berlin State Opera, Bavarian State, London Symphony and Vienna Philharmonic Orchestras, for Polydor, Siemens, Columbia and HMV, and many of these performances have been reissued on LP. Included in the works recorded were *Don Juan*, *Till Eulenspiegel*, *Tod und Verklärung*, *Also sprach Zarathustra*, *Ein Heldenleben*, *Don Quixote*, *Die Alpensymphonie*, *Symphonia domestica*, the Dance from *Salome*, the *Le Bourgeois gentilhomme* suite, waltzes from *Der Rosenkavalier* and the *Schlagobers* waltz. His other recordings were the Mozart Symphonies Nos 39 and 40 and overture to *Die Zauberflöte* and the Beethoven Symphonies Nos 5 and 7 (with the Berlin State Opera Orchestra), the overtures to *Euryanthe*, *Iphigénie en Aulide*, *Der Barbier von Bagdad* and *Der fliegende Holländer*, and the prelude to Act I of *Tristan und Isolde* (with the Berlin Philharmonic Orchestra).

SUITNER, Otmar (b. 1922). Born at Innsbruck, the son of a Tyrolean father and an Italian mother, Suitner studied the piano at the Salzburg Mozarteum (1941–3), and was a pupil of Krauss for conducting. He was first a concert pianist, then made his début as a conductor at the Innsbruck Theatre (1942–5), was a conductor at Remscheid (1952–7), general music director at the Palatinate Symphony Orchestra at Ludwigshafen (1957–60), at the Dresden State Opera and conductor of the Dresden Staatskapelle (1960–4), general music director of the Berlin Staatsoper (in East Berlin) and conductor of the Berlin Staatskapelle (1964–71 and again from 1974). He has been a guest conductor throughout Europe, in the USSR, North and South America and in Japan, where he is an honorary conductor of the NHK Symphony Orchestra. He conducts regularly at the San Francisco Opera, has appeared at many international festivals, led *Der fliegende Holländer* in 1965 and *The Ring* in 1966 and 1967 at the Bayreuth Festivals, was director of the conductors' course at the Salzburg International Summer School (1975–6), and now teaches conducting at the Academy of Music in Vienna. In 1973 he was awarded the Gregorian Order by Pope Paul VI. Suitner is one of the leading conductors performing in East Germany, and his performances of the Mozart, Wagner and Strauss operas are particularly authoritative. He led the first performance of *Parsifal* permitted at the Berlin Staatsoper, as well as a concert performance of Pfitzner's *Palestrina*. He has made numerous records for the East German label, Eterna, including the later Mozart symphonies and the operas *Die Zauberflöte*, *Così fan tutte*, *Die Entführung aus dem Serail*, *Le nozze di Figaro*, *Hänsel und Gretel*, *Il barbiere di Siviglia*, *Salome* and Dessau's *Einstein* (with either the Berlin Staatskapelle or the Dresden Staatskapelle *et al.*). Recently there has been issued on compact disc Suitner's performances of the nine Beethoven symphonies, with the Berlin Staatskapelle; admittedly, this is a very competitive field, and many critics have not welcomed the series with much enthusiasm. Suitner's readings have a straight-forwardness and solidity characteristic of all his interpretations.

SVETLANOV, Evgeny (b. 1928). Born in Moscow where his father and mother were singers at the Bolshoi Theatre, Svetlanov was educated at the Gnessin Music Education Institute and the Moscow Conservatory, studying under Shaporin, Neuhaus and Gauk. While still a student he won a competition for the post of assistant conductor with the Bolshoi Symphony Orchestra; he appeared also as a pianist at the outset of his career, after graduating from the Conservatory in 1951, but in that year he also made his début as a conductor with the Moscow Regional Philharmonic Orchestra. He joined the music department of Moscow Radio, was répétiteur and then conductor with the Bolshoi Theatre (1954–62), and succeeded Melik-Pashaev as chief conductor there (1962–4). In 1965 he took Ivanov's place as conductor of the USSR State Symphony Orchestra. He first conducted outside the USSR at Bucharest in 1953, then in Warsaw in 1955, has toured Italy, the Netherlands and Britain, where he conducted the London Philharmonic Orchestra in 1970, and visited La Scala, Milan, with the Bolshoi Theatre Company. He is married to the soprano Larissa Avdeyeva, and received the award People's Artist of the Russian Republic in 1964. His compositions include a symphony, the tone poem *Festival Poem*, *Daugava*, *Siberian Fantasy*, *Rhapsody for Orchestra*, a cantata *My Native Fields*, a string quartet, some ballet scores based on music by Bartók and Rachmaninov, *Poem* for Violin and Orchestra and a *Piano Concerto in D Minor*; he has recorded the two latter works, with Igor Oistrakh and Petrov, respectively, and the USSR State Symphony Orchestra, as well as the *Festival Poem*.

Svetlanov is one of the leading Soviet conductors, and is a committed and highly effective performer of Russian music in particular, having a preference for Rachmaninov, Shostakovich and Prokofiev, and among non-Russians for Mahler, whom he conducts with conviction; in fact, he is reported to have said that he considers 'Mahler the greatest genius of all peoples and all times'. He also choses to conduct Bach, Mozart, Brahms, Debussy, Ravel, Stravinsky, Bartók, Honegger and Elgar, but of his Beethoven a Russian critic wrote that while he conducts him well, 'he accepts Beethoven more with his mind than with his heart'. Svetlanov recognises the influence of Golovanov, Mravinsky and Stokowski on his development, and is also interested in Bernstein, Karajan and Maazel. On the podium he is restrained in gesture and has a firm disciplinary control of the orchestra. Despite his earlier experience at the Bolshoi Theatre, he prefers to conduct symphonic music: 'Opera is a very complex medium in which the conductor only too rarely is a true interpreter of the music. Too often he is merely a glorified répétiteur or an accompanist. You are so dependent on other people and factors—the producer, designer, artists. If anyone happens to be feeling ill or off-colour, your own performance is bound to suffer. On the concert platform, I hardly need say, the conductor is *really* in charge.'

Along with Rozhdestvensky, Svetlanov is the most recorded Soviet conductor, and his records have included a range of Russian composers, from Glinka to Shostakovich. He has recorded the complete symphonies of Tchaikovsky and Scriabin, but there are very few contemporary Russians represented in his discography. More interestingly, he has made records of music by Beethoven (the Symphony No. 3), Debussy, Ravel, Saint-Saëns (the Symphony No. 3), Bruckner (the Symphony No. 8), Brahms (the Symphonies Nos 1 and 2), Wagner and Elgar (the Symphony No. 2 and *The Dream of Gerontius*). All his performances have the utmost conviction; he shows himself to be an uninhibited interpreter of Russian music, gilding the lily. Some recordings are very fine, such as *Scheherazade* and the *Manfred* symphony, giving the works a power and atmosphere not often heard in interpretations by Western orchestras and conductors. Sometimes this approach borders on brashness, as in the Borodin Symphony No. 2, *Hamlet* and *Romeo and Juliet*, and some critics have taken exception to Svetlanov's addition of percussion parts to the scores of some of Scriabin's pieces, uncharacteristic of the composer's orchestral style. Svetlanov has also recorded as a pianist; the recording of *Festival Poem* was received rather acidly by Western critics, William Mann, writing in *The Times*, said that it is 'a blameless pastiche of your favourite Russian nationalistic music, with a big tune irresistible to those who love Tchaikovsky or Rachmaninov—definitely Tsarist by affiliation.'

SZELL, **Georg** (1897–1970). Born in Budapest where his father was a businessman and lawyer, Szell spent most of his childhood in Vienna. He showed a prodigious talent for music at an early age, and made his début as a pianist at the age of 10 with the Vienna

Symphony Orchestra. A year later he played at the Royal Albert Hall in London, with Landon Ronald in a programme that included a Mendelssohn concerto and an overture that he himself had composed. He studied at the Vienna Academy of Music under Förster and Mandyczewski, and in Leipzig under Reger, at 15 appeared with the Berlin Philharmonic Orchestra as pianist and composer, and at 17 substituted for the regular conductor of the Vienna Symphony Orchestra. Richard Strauss accepted him as an assistant at the Berlin Staatsoper and encouraged him to make conducting his career; with Strauss's sponsorship he succeeded Klemperer as first conductor at the Strasbourg Municipal Theatre (1917–24), and at the same time was principal conductor at the Darmstadt Court Theatre (1921–4) and at Düsseldorf (1922–4). He returned to Berlin and became chief conductor of the Berlin Staatsoper and of the orchestra of the Berlin Broadcasting Company (1924–9) and professor at the Hochschule für Musik in Berlin (1927). Moving to Prague, he was appointed musical director of the German Opera House there (1927–37), conducted the Czech Philharmonic Orchestra, and was also a professor at the German Music Academy. In Prague he impressed the pianist Schnabel, who arranged for him to conduct at the Courtauld/Sargent concerts in London (1933); he conducted the major British orchestras and then became conductor of the Scottish Orchestra (1937–9) as well as the Residentie Orchestra at The Hague. His first appearance in the USA was in St Louis (1930–1); on his return from his second visit to Australia in 1939 he found himself in New York at the outbreak of World War II, and thereafter made his career in America. At first he conducted the Los Angeles Philharmonic Orchestra in some concerts at the Hollywood Bowl; in 1941 he made his début in New York with the NBC Symphony Orchestra, became principal conductor at the New York Metropolitan Opera (1942–6), conducted the New York Philharmonic-Symphony Orchestra (first in 1944), taught composition at the Mannes School, and became a US citizen (1946). Finally, he was appointed conductor of the Cleveland Orchestra (1946), where he remained until his death, and also for a year was joint-conductor of the Amsterdam Concertgebouw Orchestra (1958–9).

Szell was, by common consent, one of the greatest conductors of the 20th century, and some would claim that his only superior was Toscanini. In his early years he was much influenced by Strauss, after whom he modelled his technique; Toscanini and Nikisch he also revered. However, he doubted whether the

present day would tolerate Nikisch's spontaneous and impro-
visational approach, despite the wonderful sound and freedom
of the orchestra. From Toscanini he learned his strict artistic
earnestness, his close adherence to the score, a distaste for
showmanship of any sort, and the unvarying, single-minded
insistence on the highest standards of performance. There was
absolutely nothing routine about any Szell performance; rehearsals were serious and meticulous, and he always brought
with him the complete rehearsal scores of the works to be
performed, densely marked with his own bowings and phrasings. He said that every week his orchestra gave seven concerts,
two of which were in public. He made no attempt to ingratiate
himself with his players or even to be pleasant to them, and he
had a reputation as a ruthless autocrat who inspired respect but
scarcely affection. Tall and broad-shouldered, he commanded
with a chilly severity and was never inhibited in his criticisms of
persons or institutions that did not meet his own exacting
standards. The San Francisco Symphony Orchestra was the
victim on one occasion after an unsatisfactory guest-engagement
and after his abrupt departure from the New York Met. in 1954,
someone said to Rudolf Bing, the manager, that 'George Szell is
his own worst enemy,' to which Bing answered, 'Not while I am
alive.' In fairness, Bing made it up with Szell later. Szell's
memory was phenomenal; when recording he would play each
movement through, and then would correct missed notes or
faulty balances.

Szell's name is inevitably connected with the Cleveland
Orchestra, which he brought to a pinnacle of excellence,
perhaps not equalled, certainly not bettered, by any other
orchestra in the USA or Europe. It was essentially a classical
orchestra, with a superb style and tone for the music of Haydn,
Mozart and Beethoven. Although he succeeded in blending
American virtuosity and tonal purity with a European sense of
tradition, the Cleveland Orchestra was ultimately a purely
American product. A certain clinical inflexibility and the avoid-
ance of even the slightest degree of sentiment resulted in performances that were breathtaking for their clarity and clean
execution, but spontaneity, warmth and expressiveness were
usually discounted; one of his players said: 'He even rehearsed
the inspiration.' He believed that the music should speak for
itself, and all it required was an accurate performance, which
very often was of the very highest imaginable degree of technical
proficiency, with a superb sweep and power frequently reminiscent of Toscanini. Tempi were not always brisk, but elegant

phrasing and shortened note values gave his Haydn, Mozart and Beethoven an incomparable crispness and clarity, perhaps not always justified by the score. Paul Meyers, who produced many of Szell's records, said: 'He always paid the listeners the greatest possible compliment by assuming that they shared an equal knowledge of the work and therefore had the good sense to allow the music to speak for itself without overemphasis or unnecessary histrionics.' He insisted that his players perform as in chamber music, listening to each other, so that their ensemble was exceptional. When the Cleveland Orchestra toured Europe with Szell in 1957, a Polish critic summed up his reaction writing that the orchestra played 'like one magnificent soloist'. Szell has had a significant influence on a number of young conductors, but there is always the danger that the lesson learnt from him is that precision is enough.

Szell's repertoire was limited to the music to which he was attracted: 'If I cannot perform something with complete conviction, I cannot make it sound convincing to the listener.' The composers he performed regularly were Haydn, Mozart, Beethoven, Schubert, Schumann, Brahms, Dvořák, Tchaikovsky, Strauss, Mahler and Bruckner; his programmes also included some Sibelius, Bartók, Prokofiev and Walton. American composers received his attention, for which he received the Laurel Leaf Award of the American Composers Alliance, but he performed comparatively little French or Russian music. He was not particularly at home with Schoenberg, Berg or Webern, although he 'found' the Berg Violin Concerto as late as 1968. His scepticism about programming contemporary compositions was real: 'I do not believe in the mass grave of an all-contemporary concert.' In later years he confined his repertoire to what he felt was the most important in the symphonic literature and discarded many works that he had enjoyed and conducted in early times but which no longer held great interest for him.

Before World War II Szell made records in Berlin, Vienna, Prague and London. Included were the legendary performances of Dvořák's Cello Concerto (with Casals and the Czech Philharmonic Orchestra for HMV), Brahms's Piano Concerto No. 1 (with Schnabel and the London Philharmonic Orchestra for HMV), and Beethoven's Violin Concerto and Lalo's *Symphonie espagnole* (with Hubermann and the Vienna Philharmonic Orchestra for Columbia). In the USA he first recorded on 78 r.p.m. discs with the New York Philharmonic-Symphony Orchestra, and these performances of Beethoven's Symphony No. 6 and overtures and other pieces by Mendelssohn, Weber,

Wagner and Smetana were reissued on LP transfers by Odyssey. With the Cleveland Orchestra he recorded a series of discs which rank with the finest ever contributed to the gramophone. All were for CBS-Epic. They spread over the mono and stereo eras, and some works were later re-recorded. The music recorded included symphonies and other works by Haydn, Mozart, Beethoven, Schubert, Schumann, Mendelssohn, Rossini, Brahms, Bruckner, Dvořák, Smetana, Tchaikovsky, Wagner, Johann Strauss, Debussy, Ravel, Richard Strauss, Mahler, Mussorgsky, Prokofiev, Bartók, Janáček, Hindemith, Stravinsky, Walton and some others. He also recorded with the Amsterdam Concertgebouw Orchestra, both for Philips and Decca; two of these discs, early mono LPs, are classics of the gramophone: Brahms's Symphony No. 3 and Dvořák's Symphony No. 8. Several discs he made for EMI were of concert arias by Mozart, Strauss's *Vier letzte Lieder* and other songs, and Mahler's *Das Knaben Wunderhorn* (with Schwarzkopf, Fischer-Dieskau and the London Symphony and Berlin Radio Symphony Orchestras); the Strauss Lieder have been reissued on a compact disc, as have a number of his recordings with the Cleveland Orchestra.

T

TATE, Jeffrey (b. 1943). Born in Farnham, Tate taught himself the piano as a child, was a distinguished boy soprano, studied at Cambridge University and St Thomas Medical School, and qualified as a doctor of medicine. Before his graduation he won a place at the London Opera Centre, and decided to make his career as a conductor. In 1971 he joined the Royal Opera House, Covent Garden, as a répétiteur; he worked with Boulez at Bayreuth, Karajan at Salzburg and Levine at the Metropolitan Opera, New York, made his début as a conductor at Covent Garden with Mozart's *La Clemenza di Tito* (1971), and appeared at opera houses in Göteborg, Paris, Hamburg, Geneva, Nice, Cologne, New York and San Francisco, and at the Salzburg Festival (1985). He first conducted the English Chamber Orchestra in 1983 and in 1985 was appointed principal conductor of the orchestra, and in the same year became principal conductor at Covent Garden. Because of physical disabilities, Tate conducts sitting down, but nonethless his psychological contact with his players is complete, and he is recognised as a brilliant and meticulous musician. His first records were of Mozart symphonies (with the English Chamber Orchestra), and he has gone on, under an exclusive contract with EMI, to record some Mozart concertos and arias and Haydn symphonies, and also with the Dresden Staatskapelle symphonies by Beethoven, Schubert and Bruckner.

TEMIRKANOV, Yuri (b. 1938). Born in the Kabardino-Balkarsk region of the USSR, Temirkanov graduated from the Leningrad Conservatory in viola and conducting, and made his début at the Maly Opera House in Leningrad with *La traviata*, and won first prize at the Second All-Union Conductors' Competition in 1966. He was conductor of the Leningrad Philharmonic Orchestra (1968–76), became principal conductor of the Kirov Opera and Ballet Theatre (1976), conducted orchestras in the United States, Canada, Mexico, Europe and Japan, and in 1979 was appointed principal guest conductor of the Royal Philharmonic Orchestra. His repertoire includes music from Beethoven to contemporary composers, and he has performed Mahler's Symphonies Nos 2 and 3 in Leningrad; his recording of Mahler's Symphony No. 2, with the Kiev Opera Orchestra *et al.* has been released by Melodiya. He has appeared as conductor on a number of compact discs, including *Boris Godunov*, *Scheherazade*, *Le Sacre du printemps* and Tchaikovsky Symphonies Nos 5 and 6, which have won him recognition as an idiomatic and imaginative interpreter of Russian music.

TENNSTEDT, Klaus (b. 1926). Born in Merseberg, Germany, Tennstedt studied the violin and piano as a boy, attended the Leipzig Conservatory, and became leader of the orchestra at the Municipal Theatre at Halle (1948). An injury to a finger cut short his career as a violinist; he coached singers at the theatre, then in 1953 he substituted for a sick conductor and made his début with Wagner-Régeny's opera *Der Günstling*. He was appointed music director of the Dresden Opera (1958–62), and of the Schwerin State Orchestra and Theatre (1962), at the same time conducting the Dresden Philharmonic, the Dresden Staatskapelle, the Leipzig Gewandhaus and the Berlin Radio Symphony Orchestras, and touring Czechoslovakia, the USSR and other countries in Eastern Europe. He left the German Democratic Republic (East Germany) in 1971 and sought asylum in Sweden where he conducted in Göteborg and Stockholm, and in the following year became general music director at the Kiel Opera (1972–6). His first appearances in North America were at Toronto and Boston (1974), where he made an exceptional impression, leading to engagements at the Berkshire Music Festival at Tanglewood (1975), returning there in the following years; his performances of the Beethoven symphonies and concertos at the Festivals were rapturously acclaimed. In the USA he went on to conduct the National Symphony, the New York Philharmonic and other major orchestras, and his début in Britain was with the London Symphony Orchestra in 1976. He first conducted the London Philharmonic Orchestra in the next year, and became its regular guest conductor. After three years as chief conductor of the North German Radio Orchestra in Hamburg (1979–82) he succeeded Solti as principal conductor and music director of the London Philharmonic. In 1983 he also led *Fidelio* at the New York Metropolitan Opera.

Tennstedt's arrival on the international concert scene after his defection from East Germany was greeted with enthusiasm, almost relief, as he is clearly in direct line with the great German conductors who perform the Austro-German romantic repertoire with conviction, individuality and authority, a breed that many fear might become a threatened species. He has been compared with Solti, both in appearance and deportment: a tall man, he towers over the orchestra. He regards the London Philharmonic as 'a fantastic romantic orchestra', and one of the orchestra has described him as having the best qualities of both of its previous two music directors, Haitink and Solti: Haitink's relaxed phrasing and feeling for line, and Solti's vitality. Tennstedt believes that experience as a player in an orchestra is important for a conductor, as 'you can build a sound when you understand how to get it'. He recognises the balance that must be achieved between emotion and expression on the one hand, and intellect and control on the other. Some critics have observed that the acuteness of this balance is the source of the extraordinary impact of Tennstedt's performances, and this is specially true of his recordings of the Mahler symphonies. He came to Mahler relatively late in life: 'When you decide to conduct Mahler, you should not, I think, be too young. You need a lot of human experience. Mahler, probably more than any other composer, united in his music all the human conditions—all human experience, all human suffering. So, in order to be able to conduct him well, you really need to bring an enormous background of personal experience to bear. All the qualities which make up a man's character can be found in Mahler: joy, sorrow, love, anger, parody.'

Tennstedt's recordings have been with the London Philharmonic and Berlin Philharmonic Orchestras, and paramount among these have been the Mahler symphonies with the London Philharmonic, which are nearing completion. Talking in October, 1984 (in *The Gramophone*) he said that his recording of the Symphony No. 6 was his favourite so far. He will be completing his recordings of the Brahms symphonies, adding *Ein deutsches Requiem*; in interpreting Brahms, he said that the two elements of symphonic weight and lyrical warmth had to be reconciled. But not all of his performances in the concert hall have been free from controversy; an example was the Verdi *Requiem* which he presented with the London Philharmonic Orchestra *et al.* in London; it was described by Hugh Canning as 'feverish', and stylistically way off-mark. But, when Tennstedt is at his best, you feel, in Canning's words, that 'you have participated in a huge struggle with the music, joined in a journey of exploration with a clearly envisioned end'.

THOMAS, **Michael Tilson** (b. 1944). Thomas was born in Hollywood, where his father was a film writer, producer and director; his grandfather was Boris Tomashefsky who had come to the USA from Kiev and had helped to found the Yiddish Theatre in New

York, and his cousin was the actor Paul Muni. Thomas was playing the piano by ear at the age of 5, and later studied the piano and oboe as a boy. At the University of Southern California he first studied science but changed to music, taking theory and conducting with Ingolf Dahl. His career as a conductor started with the Young Musicians' Foundation Orchestra and at the Monday Evening Concerts at the Los Angeles Museum, which were noted for presentations of new music. He assisted Boulez at the Ojai Festival in California, then went to Bayreuth in 1966 to study at Friedland Wagner's classes, but stayed to assist Boulez rehearse *Parsifal*, and to play the glockenspiel at the actual performances. He has said he came to Bayreuth to examine the reasons for his antipathy to Wagner, but remained to admire. In 1968 he was conducting fellow with the Boston Symphony Orchestra at Tanglewood, was awarded the Koussevitzky Prize, and was engaged as assistant conductor with the Boston Symphony Orchestra. In October 1969 he substituted for the ailing Steinberg in the middle of a concert, was immediately acclaimed as a remarkable conducting talent, and went on to conduct 37 more concerts with the orchestra that season. In 1970 he was appointed associate conductor, and then was offered the position of permanent conductor; he refused it, and instead became musical director of the Buffalo Philharmonic Orchestra (1971–9). He has appeared as a guest conductor in London, Tokyo, Tel-Aviv and in other musical centres, as well as conducting major orchestras in the USA, and in 1981 was made principal guest conductor of the Los Angeles Philharmonic Orchestra, with Simon Rattle.

Boulez was Thomas's major teacher of conducting, and his baton technique is clear and easy to follow, his movements on the podium economical and graceful, and his manner with the orchestra warm and appreciative. He has an exceptional memory, assimilates scores quickly, plans rehearsals carefully, and while he is meticulous in preparing performances, he prefers to leave the final touches to the inspiration of the moment at the concert itself. Reflecting the cultural background of his childhood and youth in Los Angeles, his musical interests are extraordinarily wide, and embrace literally every form of music, without any apparent discrimination. He does not believe that one kind of music is intrinsically superior to any other; away from the symphony orchestra he listens to Japanese, Balinese, Indian and other ethnic music, is a connoisseur of rock music and is a warm admirer of James Brown, the soul singer. His own favourite composers are Stravinsky, Tchaikovsky, Mahler,

Ravel and Debussy, as well as Renaissance and early baroque music. 'I am perplexed to the point of vexation by snobbery concerning Tchaikovsky,' he has said. 'The enormous generosity of spirit and the incredible inventiveness is so wonderful. And in even the slightest piece just little touches of such perfection.' While he frequently performs some of the Mahler symphonies, he has so far refused to record any of them: 'We've all heard enough performances of Mahler which are a great orchestra playing music. It's very lush sounds, it's very beautiful, it's very together, it's all very lovely. I think now we have a right to expect something more than that. That is what I'm hoping to give the public. I can do it some of the time; I can't do it all of the time, and I want to wait until I can do it all the time.' At Buffalo he gave his audiences the widest musical perspectives, on the principle that they should hear the music of the past eight centuries, not one and a half centuries. His criticism of fellow conductors who only know and perform music from Haydn to the early 20th century almost borders on scorn; he believes that it is scarcely possible to perform even this music without understanding what came before it, back as far as the Middle Ages.

When DGG signed up the Boston Symphony Orchestra in 1970, Steinberg and Thomas were included in the contract, and with the orchestra he recorded a brilliant Debussy disc, *Le Sacre du printemps* coupled with Stravinsky's cantata *The King of the Stars*, and works by the Americans Ives, Piston, Ruggles and Schuman. He has embarked on a series of the Beethoven symphonies with the English Chamber Orchestra, for CBS, and so far has recorded the Symphonies Nos 4, 5, 6 and 7: 'The most important thing is to have different kinds of versions of these pieces, whether it's large orchestra, small orchestra, old instruments, new instruments, whatever—to keep shaking it up,' otherwise 'we will turn classical music into a kind of version of Kabuki theatre, which will become even fewer pieces in even more stylised ways.' But he has strong reservations about the performance of classical music on original instruments: 'Although I have heard some performances that are interesting, I must say that in terms of real illumination of the spiritual message of the pieces, I don't think yet anybody has approached an understanding of that on original instruments. I'm not sure that the return to original instruments, as interesting as that is, actually is as direct a line as some of the more traditional approaches to cultivated Mozart and Haydn playing may have been that was always the province of people like Szell and people of this kind. . . . The real frontier of that music, which will obviously be aesthetic, is the question of the missing sub-text. In Mozart's mind there was a kind of subtext operating at all times, that really every piece that he wrote in a way is an operatic scene, has a vocal model. . . . What's so affecting in the music is these little turns of phrase which create such strong feelings of hopefulness or resignation or slightly pathetic and sentimental overtones. Each artist has to work these things out for himself. Knowing the operas and the songs, knowing the arias and the actual words that Mozart did set to certain kinds of note patterns, is of course an immense clue. A lot of the rest of it comes out of just knowing a great deal of music and living a great deal of life.'

Thomas has also made the closest study of the music of Gershwin, and originally recorded the *Rhapsody in Blue*, with Gershwin's 1925 piano roll furnishing the solo part. With the Los Angeles Philharmonic he has recorded, both as soloist and conductor, the music for piano and orchestra and the overtures of Gershwin. His other recordings include a two-disc collection of music by Ruggles (with the Buffalo Philharmonic Orchestra), and Ives's Symphonies Nos 1 and 3 and *Orchestral Set No. 2* (with the Amsterdam Concertgebouw Orchestra), all for CBS.

TOSCANINI, **Arturo** (1867–1957). Born in Parma, Italy, Toscanini was the son of a tailor, Claudio Toscanini, who was a fervent follower of Garibaldi. Neither of his parents were musicians, but the household nevertheless resounded with the popular operatic arias and choruses of the day. At the age of 9 he entered the Parma Conservatory, graduated at 19 as a cellist (1885), and the next year joined an Italian opera company which was to tour South America. When the company was in Rio de Janeiro, it suddenly found itself in an impossible situation. A Brazilian conductor had been engaged for the tour, but his incompetence had so incensed the Italian singers that he was forced to resign; to save face he claimed that ill-health was the cause of his resignation. As the theatre was full and the orchestra had taken its place in the pit, it was announced in desperation that a substitute conductor would lead the performance. There was an uproar in the audience, and the substitute fled from the theatre. Some of the singers, striving to retrieve the situation, thought of the 20-year old musician, the leader of the cellists, who had also coached several singers and the chorus, apparently without looking at the score. A woman in the chorus begged him, Toscanini, to attempt to conduct the performance; the young man strode to the conductor's podium, took the baton and, without a glance at the score, conducted *Aida* from beginning to end. He continued as conductor of the company for the rest of the tour, and led 26 performances of the eleven operas in the company's repertoire, all from memory.

Toscanini was one of the greatest, if not the greatest, musicians of the 20th century, and probably in the history of musical performance. His career spanned 68 years; most of his fellow conductors, the musicians who played for him, the soloists and singers he accompanied, and the public who heard him, never doubted his precedence over all others. In the words of Sir Adrian Boult, he 'controlled a higher candlepower of concentration than any other human being except perhaps a few great orators'. Puccini, for whose *La Bohème*, *La fanciulla del West* and *Turandot* Toscanini led the premières, said of him that 'he conducts a work not just as the written score directs, but as the composer imagined in his head, even though he failed to write it down on paper'. Toscanini himself could not recognise anything exceptional in his powers: it was real, not false modesty that caused him to remark: 'I am no genius. I have created nothing. I play the music of other men. I am just a musician.' There have been and there are many other great conductors, but Toscanini's impact on the art of conducting and orchestral performance was overwhelming.

After the opera company returned to Italy, Toscanini conducted at many opera houses there (1887–95), was a cellist in the La Scala Orchestra at the première of Verdi's *Otello* (1887) and led the first performance of *Pagliacci* (1892). He became the conductor of the Turin Regio Opera House (1896), led the first Italian performance of *Götterdämmerung* and the première of *La Bohème* (1896), as well as leading *Tristan und Isolde* and *Die Walküre*. His first orchestral concerts were in Turin in 1898; the programme of the first was Brahms's *Tragic Overture*, the Entry of the Gods into Valhalla from *Das Rheingold*, the *Nutcracker* suite, and Schubert's Symphony No. 9. These concerts were remarkably successful, and after one Saint-Saëns congratulated Toscanini, saying that it was the first time the Schubert symphony had been played with the correct tempi throughout. Toscanini was then appointed principal conductor at La Scala, Milan (1899–1908); here he opened his first season with *Die Meistersinger*, gave the first performances in Italy of *Siegfried*, *Eugene Onegin*, *Salome*, *Pelléas et Mélisande* and *Louise*, and also performed many operas unknown today, such as Leoncavallo's *Zaza*, Mascagni's *Le maschere*, Isodore de Lara's *Messaline*, Galleti's *Anton*, Franchetti's *Germania* and *Asrael*,

Ponchielli's *I Lituani* and Sinareglia's *Oceana*. In these years he also conducted in Bologna, Turin, Rome and in South America; in 1902, at the age of 35, he led his first performance of the complete Beethoven Symphony No. 9, and during 1905–6 conducted the orchestra at the Accademia di Santa Cecilia and the Turin Municipal Orchestra, with which he toured northern Italy.

Toscanini first appeared at the New York Metropolitan Opera in 1908; in the same year he became the principal conductor and remained there until 1915. At his first encounter with the Met. orchestra he attempted to rehearse *Aida*, but the players were suspicious of the music and the man. He asked them to put the Verdi away, and rehearsed the entire *Götterdämmerung* without once consulting the score. After this the orchestra's cooperation in performing Verdi was unreserved. He gave the première of *La fanciulla del West* (1910) and made his début as a symphonic conductor in the USA with Beethoven's Symphony No. 9. In 1915 he returned to Italy and until the end of World War I gave performances for soldiers and war sufferers, without fee. Recalled to La Scala in 1919, he reformed the orchestra and took it on a triumphant tour of Italy and the USA, conducting 32 concerts in as many days in Italy, 68 in 77 days in the USA, and then 36 in 58 days in Italy. When in the USA he and the orchestra made records for the Victor Talking Machine Company at Camden, New Jersey. He remained at La Scala until 1929, in that period leading the première of *Turandot* (1926), but in 1926–7 was a guest conductor with the New York Philharmonic Orchestra, and subsequently became the orchestra's regular conductor until 1928, sharing the season with Willem Mengelberg. In 1928 the New York Philharmonic and the New York Symphony Orchestras were merged to form the New York Philharmonic-Symphony Orchestra, and Toscanini became its principal conductor (1929–36).

After his departure from La Scala in 1929 Toscanini transferred his main activity from the opera house to the concert hall. Except for appearances at Bayreuth (1930–31) and Salzburg (1935–7) and studio performances of operas with the NBC Symphony Orchestra, he did not conduct opera again. Thus it was not until he was 60 years of age that he became the full-time conductor of a major symphony orchestra. He toured Europe with the New York Philharmonic-Symphony (1930), first conducted the Philadelphia Orchestra (1930), the Vienna Philharmonic Orchestra (1933) and the BBC Symphony Orchestra (1935); he conducted in Sweden and Denmark (1933) and led the newly-formed Palestine Symphony Orchestra, predecessor to the present Israel Philharmonic Orchestra and made up of Jewish musicians, refugees from Hitler's Germany, in its inaugural concert in 1936, coming back to conduct the orchestra again the next year. In 1931 he had been assaulted by Fascists in Bologna for refusing to play the *Giovinezza*, a Fascist anthem, before a concert in memory of the composer Martucci, and consequently he left Italy and did not conduct there until after World War II. He was the first non-German conductor to appear at Bayreuth (1931), but refused to return in 1933 because of the treatment of Jewish musicians in Nazi Germany. After triumphant appearances at the Salzburg Festival, he finally refused to conduct there in 1937 because the Jewish conductor Bruno Walter's performances at the festival would not be broadcast in Germany. In 1938–9 he conducted at a festival in Lucerne, where the orchestra, led by the distinguished German violinist Adolph Busch, was composed of musicians who had fled from Germany. Toscanini's opposition to Nazism and Fascism was implacable.

In 1937 David Sarnoff, president of the Radio Corporation of America, which controlled the National Broadcasting Company (NBC), approached Toscanini who was living in semi-retirement in Italy, through Samuel Chotzinoff. He offered to engage him to conduct broadcast concerts in the USA and to create a new symphony orchestra expressly for this purpose. Toscanini accepted, and suggested that Artur Rodzinski, then conductor of the Cleveland Orchestra, be invited to select and train the orchestra. It was made up of 31 players from the already existing NBC house orchestra, and principal players recruited from other American orchestras. Rodzinski rehearsed the orchestra, the French conductor Pierre Monteux led it in its first concert in November 1937, and after five more concerts under Monteux and Rodzinski, Toscanini conducted it for the first time on Christmas Day 1937, in a programme which included Mozart's Symphony No. 40 and Brahms's Symphony No. 1. The broadcast was heard by an audience of 20 million people. He toured with the orchestra in South America (1940) and in a transcontinental tour of the USA (1950), continued to conduct the BBC Symphony Orchestra (1939), the Philadelphia Orchestra (1941–2 to 1944) and on occasion the New York Philharmonic-Symphony Orchestra (1944–5), and travelled to London to conduct the Philharmonia Orchestra in two Brahms concerts at the Royal Festival Hall (1952). Except for the 1941–2 season, when he broke with the NBC because of his dissatisfaction with the orchestra's other commitments with other conductors and other radio programmes, Toscanini remained with them until 1954. The last concert of the 1953–4 season was his last public appearance; he had a lapse of memory during the bacchanale from *Tannhäuser*. He died in his home at Riverdale in New York, and his body was flown to Milan for burial. At the cathedral in Milan the mass was read by Cardinal Montini (later Pope Paul VI); Victor de Sabata led the La Scala company in *Libera me* from Verdi's *Requiem*, and at the entrance to the cemetery a vast chorus sang *Va pensiero* from *Nabucco*, which Toscanini had conducted there 56 years earlier, as a tribute to Verdi.

Toscanini was a small man, slightly bent at the knees, with a high receding forehead, a sharp nose, a short moustache and bushy eyebrows. His head and hands dominated his body, and his small eyes were in absolute control of the orchestra. Every player believed he was being watched all the time. In private life he was a most frugal person and fundamentally a kind and generous man; he was in no way religious. Although he was completely, utterly possessed by music and had an exhaustive knowledge of his profession, he knew much of classical and romantic literature and the visual arts. His concentration when conducting has been compared with that of a mystic in contemplation. He had a single-minded conviction of what the composer intended and an unswerving determination to reproduce his mental image of this intention which he derived from an exhaustive study of the score. He was a perfectionist whose ideals were rarely, if ever, realised, and so conducting was an experience which appeared to bring him suffering rather than joy. He was often dissatisfied with his own performances, and although his tantrums, baton-throwing and smashing, abuse of players and abrupt departures were often directed at failures among his musicians to measure up to his own standards of musicianship, his anger was more towards himself. He was unsparing with both; in the opera house or with the orchestra the atmosphere was invariably tense and occasionally unbearable, as everyone was stretched uncompromisingly to the limit of his ability. Yehudi Menuhin has told the story of the time when he was rehearsing the slow movement of Beethoven's Violin Concerto at Riverdale, with Toscanini playing the piano. The telephone rang; Toscanini stopped playing, strode to the wall, ripped out the telephone with wire and plaster flying, then calmly resumed without a word. Because of his scenes with the orchestra rehearsals were usually in secret. Although he was patient with players' technical mistakes, any lapse in musical taste or any disrespect for the great masters would cause uproar. He disliked applause first because he regarded it as an unmusical sound, but in addition he truly feared that the audience might be applauding him and not the composer.

Toscanini scarcely had an exemplary baton technique; he said himself that it was impossible to teach it, and his own was undoubtedly intuitive. His right arm created circles so that the bars were transformed into long phrases; his left hand was especially expressive, yet sparingly used, and would indicate pianissimos; he would clutch it over his heart in a passage of feeling. But it was mainly with his eyes that he controlled the orchestra, and with them he registered the smallest flaw of intonation. He frequently sang with the orchestra; at Salzburg he was once rehearsing the orchestra, and his own voice soared above the instruments. He stopped the players and demanded: 'Silence, who is singing here?' When no-one owned up, he added: 'Well, whoever it was will now kindly shut up.' Much has been made of his incredible memory, and many conductors have since attempted to emulate his feat of conducting all his concerts and operatic performances from memory. The truth is that he was obliged to memorise his scores from the very beginning because his short-sightedness prevented him from reading a score on the podium. It is estimated that at the end of his career he had in his memory 250 symphonic works, 100 operas and numerous chamber, piano, cello and violin pieces and songs. Some of the stories about his memory are almost beyond belief: in 1942 he saw the score of Tchaikovsky's opera *Yolanta* which he had last come across in 1885, but nonetheless he was able to recall the introduction. The NBC had programmed the Prologue to Boito's *Mefistofele*, which required a backstage band, but the night before the rehearsal the orchestra's librarian found that the parts for the band had been mislaid. That evening Toscanini wrote out the parts from memory. In Vienna once he was challenged to write out the second bassoon part in Act II of *Die Meistersinger*, which he succeeded in doing. His knowledge of scores was absolutely complete, and the exact way the sound should occur from the visual score in his mind was also clear to him. Nonetheless, before every concert he would study the score again, no matter how familiar.

Toscanini would never accept that he was *interpreting* the music. Understanding and producing an impeccable performance of a work was not, to him, interpreting it. He said: 'I have often heard people speaking of the *Eroica* of conductor X, the

Siegfried of conductor Y, and the *Aida* of conductor Z. And I have always wondered what Beethoven, Wagner and Verdi would have said about the interpretations of those gentlemen, as if through them their works assumed a new paternity. I think that confronted by the *Eroica*, *Siegfried*, *Aida*, an interpreter, entering as deeply as possible into the spirit of the composer, should only be willing to render the *Eroica* of Beethoven, the *Siegfried* of Wagner, and the *Aida* of Verdi.' So from the very first he claimed absolute fidelity to the score and the clearest and most accurate performance of it as his only acceptable objective. This has, however, been shown by many writers to be in practice somewhat wide of the mark, as he did alter scores as freely as most other conductors. Additions and amendments were made to the Beethoven symphonies and overtures, especially in the wind and timpani parts. But these were done so discreetly that they largely remained unnoticed. Other pieces he altered were the *Manfred* symphony of Tchaikovsky, *Pictures at an Exhibition*, *Moldau* and Schumann's Symphony No. 3.

Before the time of Toscanini's arrival on the scene, many performances had degenerated through romantic excesses and mannerisms. He brushed aside these slovenly conventions and fought an unrelenting battle against poor performing standards, and against singers, impresarios, publishers and audiences who could not appreciate the finest standards. The other major conductors of the day who were then active in the USA, such as Stokowski, Furtwängler and Mengelberg, infuriated him because of their departures from strictly literal readings of scores in their search for expression. In his orchestra Toscanini sacrificed tonal beauty to clarity, with the lines separated rather than blending. String tone was necessarily transparent, a quality that distinguished the NBC Symphony Orchestra, perhaps to its detriment, compared to say the Vienna Philharmonic or Philadelphia Orchestras. Rhythm had to be exactly right; at La Scala he was criticised for the dryness of his rhythm, but it resulted from his demand for accurate playing. This precision and clarity distinguished him from Mengelberg and Furtwängler, who also conducted the New York Philharmonic-Symphony Orchestra; he showed that it was possible to perform a piece of music of metrical pattern with one tempo throughout. He came to every rehearsal completely prepared; with the orchestra he was painstaking and thorough, and never rehearsed them more once the work was played to his satisfaction. Frequently final rehearsals were more perfect performances than the concerts, as the tension of the concert could cause the players to make mistakes.

Audiences were expected to be punctual, the auditorium had to be in darkness, and encores were not permitted. The critic W. J. Turner once used the analogy that a Toscanini performance was a poem printed clearly and correctly on good paper, compared to a poem printed in smudged ink on blotting paper with the punctuation wrong.

In his early years Toscanini was regarded as a most versatile conductor. A glance at the list of operas he conducted shows him to be an energetic proponent of the young Italian realist school of composers. Until he was 60, the keystones of his musical culture were Verdi and Wagner; he had first performed the German symphonic repertoire, particularly Beethoven and Brahms, as he had heard German conductors perform it, but later the leanness of his orchestral tone and the usually faster tempi he adopted produced, by contrast, an electrifying effect. But his faster tempi were sometimes deceptive, arising from the accuracy and clarity of the playing, as well as the taut rhythm. Like many conductors, as he grew older he became less inclined to perform the music of the day: 'I am the man who did Wagner when Wagner was new; who performed all the moderns from Strauss and Debussy to Malipiero and Sibelius. Now let the other men do what I did when I was young. . . . I want, I crave the time in these, my last years, to come a little nearer to the secrets of Beethoven and a few other great masters.' So while he was with the New York Philharmonic-Symphony Orchestra the standard works of Beethoven, Brahms and Wagner comprised 40 per cent of the programmes. In the USA from 1925 to 1954, the works he most frequently performed in concerts were the prelude to *Die Meistersinger* (54 times), Debussy's *La Mer* (53), Beethoven's Symphony No. 3 (52), the prelude and Liebestod from *Tristan und Isolde* (45), Brahms's *Variations on the St Antony Chorale* (40), Beethoven's Symphony No. 6 (38), Beethoven's Symphony No. 7 (35), the scherzo from *A Midsummer Night's Dream* (35), Brahms's Symphony No. 2 (34) and Debussy's *Iberia* (31). Bach was omitted, except for Respighi's arrangement of the *Passacaglia and Fugue in C Minor*; French music, apart from some Debussy and Ravel, and the Russians, even Tchaikovsky, were largely neglected, and British and American music was virtually absent from his programmes. He was often criticized for performing the Rossini overtures, which he loved; someone said to him about the *William Tell* overture, 'Isn't it cheap music?', to which he replied: 'You try and compose something as good.'

Toscanini first made records with the La Scala Orchestra for

Victor in the USA in 1920–21, and much later with the NBC Symphony Orchestra he made many studio recordings for RCA in his years with them from 1937 to 1954. In between times he also recorded with the New York Philharmonic-Symphony Orchestra, the Philadelphia Orchestra and the BBC Symphony Orchestra. The NBC Symphony recordings covered a considerable repertoire, but they were not entirely satisfactory, technically, due to the fact that many were made in the notorious Studio 8H at Radio City, New York, which pleased Toscanini acoustically but was disastrous for recording. Toscanini himself was bored by recording and apparently too little interested in the tonal quality of his recordings, although the technical perfection of the performances always concerned him. A vast improvement occurred later, when recording was transferred to Carnegie Hall. Despite attempts to improve the tonal qualities of his NBC recordings by techniques such as half-speed mastering and being remastered to digital compact discs, there has only been a marginal improvement. The BBC Symphony and Philadelphia Orchestra recordings were much better, in fact it could be claimed that his records with the BBC Symphony were, taken altogether, the best representation he left on disc. If one were to choose the records which epitomise his greatness as a conductor, the Beethoven and Brahms symphonies would come first, especially the incandescent *Eroica* of 1953; others would include *La Mer*, *Pictures at an Exhibition*, *Harold in Italy*, the Wagner excerpts, the *Tragic Overture* and the *Leonore No. 1* overture (the two latter with the BBC Symphony Orchestra), and the four Verdi operas, *La traviata*, *Un ballo in maschera*, *Otello* and *Falstaff*. For these Verdi operas, let James Levine, the present artistic director of the New York Met., speak: 'The best recorded Verdi from any conductor is, a million miles ahead, Toscanini's, without any question. Now there's some *good* Verdi by other conductors, but only because they are dealing with perceptive singers. Sit with a score sometime, and go get every recording of the last-act *Traviata* prelude, and listen to them all, and look at the score, and then play the Old Man's. I think that you will find it a jaw-dropping experience. I mean, the fiddles, they're crying, they're sobbing, they're singing. It sounds like some sort of cosmic Italian vocal phenomenon manifest in those sixteen NBC Symphony first violins. The way they connect—they use every *legato* in the book, from a sharp shift to a smooth *glissando* slide, in exactly the right way, in exactly the right places, with exactly the right amount of gauge and judgment and color. The accompaniment is perfectly balanced. It neither holds the melody in a straightjacket nor lets it go all over the place. The dramatic hopelessness of the situation is there in the piece and Toscanini gets that across. All of the other performances you'll hear of it are either too dissected, too square, not dramatic enough, not *legato* enough, not with the right *spinto* kind of tone-quality. This is only to clarify how complex the composer's challenge is and how rarely it is ideally met.'

V

VARVISO, Silvio (b. 1924). Born in Zürich where his father was a singing teacher, Varviso studied piano and conducting at the Conservatory there, and was first an accompanist. He was engaged as assistant conductor at the St Gallen City Theatre (1944–50), and made his first public appearance there with *Die Zauberflöte*. He became assistant, then principal conductor at the Basel Opera (1950–62), being appointed its artistic director in 1956, conducted at the Berlin Staatsoper (1958–61), in Paris (from 1958), at the San Francisco Opera (1959), the New York Metropolitan Opera (1962–6), the Glyndebourne Festival Opera (1962), Covent Garden, London (1963) and Vienna, was appointed principal conductor at the Royal Opera, Stockholm (1962–72), in 1969 first conducted at Bayreuth, directing *Der fliegende Holländer*, was general musical director of the Württemberg State Opera at Stuttgart (1972–80), and was appointed musical director at the Paris Opéra (1980).

An immensely experienced and sensitive conductor, especially of opera, Varviso has distinguished himself in the *bel canto* repertoire of Bellini, Donizetti and Rossini. His performance of *Die Meistersinger* at Bayreuth in 1974 was recorded by Philips; of him the authors of the *Penguin Stereo Record Guide* (1977) wrote that he 'proves to be the most persuasive Wagnerian, one who inspires the authentic ebb and flow of tension, who builds up Wagner's scenes concentratedly over the longest span, and who revels in the lyricism and textural beauty of the score'. His other complete opera recordings are *L'Italiana in Algeri*, *Il barbiere di Siviglia*, *Norma* and *Cavalleria rusticana*.

W

DE WAART, Edo (b. 1941). Born in Amsterdam, de Waart's interest in being a conductor was aroused as a boy when he heard Josef Krips conducting *Till Eulenspiegel*. He studied the oboe with Stotijn at the Music Lyceum in Amsterdam, then studied conducting with Spaanderman; in 1961 he became co-principal oboe with the Amsterdam Philharmonic Orchestra, and with the Concertgebouw Orchestra in 1963. The next year he took the conducting course under Ferrara at Netherlands Radio at Hilversum, made his first appearance as a conductor with the Netherlands Radio Philharmonic Orchestra, and won a prize at the Dmitri Mitropoulos Competition for Conductors in New York, which entitled him to a year as assistant conductor with the New York Philharmonic Orchestra (1965–6). He has said that he did not regard this as a useful experience, as in the whole year he conducted only three and a half hours of music, the rest of the time being spent sitting and watching. In 1966 he was appointed artistic director and conductor of the Netherlands Wind Ensemble; his recordings with the Ensemble, particularly of the wind music of Mozart, were exceptional. He was appointed assistant conductor to Haitink with the Concertgebouw Orchestra, in charge of 35 concerts, toured the USA with the Orchestra (1967), and in the following year became co-conductor with Fournet of the Rotterdam Philharmonic Orchestra, becoming the orchestra's artistic director in 1973. He first conducted in Britain in 1969, conducted at the Netherlands Opera in 1970, and the Santa Fé Festival in the USA in 1971, toured Japan with the Netherlands Wind Ensemble in 1972, and appeared as a guest conductor in many cities in Europe and the USA. In 1974 he was appointed permanent guest conductor of the San Francisco Symphony Orchestra, and became its musical director in 1976. He is now musical director of the Minnesota Orchestra, where he has succeeded Marriner.

De Waart's repertoire includes both the standard works and contemporary scores, although he professes a preference for Mozart, Brahms, Stravinsky and Mahler, and for modern composers Messiaen, Berio, Ligeti and Kagel. He echoes Boulez when he says that audiences cannot be expected to understand the music of our time without having first become familiar with Schoenberg, Berg, Webern and (he adds) Ives. He has also suggested that the symphony orchestra should consist of 150 players, who can interchange between separate groups playing pre-classical music, the classical and romantic repertoire, and modern works. Discussing his love of Mozart, he compares him to Charlie Chaplin, who also has the unique capacity to arouse both tears and laughter. De Waart is aware of the impossible task before the conductor: unless he is a tyrant or a quite incredible person, he cannot really communicate to the orchestra what he wants in just three rehearsals. Secure technique and an accurate preparation of the score may ensure an adequate and safe reading, but the conductor has no chance to fashion the material into a personal statement.

He has made a number of recordings, in addition to the series with the Netherlands Wind Ensemble mentioned above; his one opera on disc has been *Der Rosenkavalier*, with the Rotterdam Philharmonic Orchestra *et al*, and on compact disc there is now available Respighi's *Pini di Roma*, *Fontane di Roma* and *Gli uccelli*, the incidental music for *Peer Gynt*, Saint-Saëns's Symphony No. 3, Rachmaninov's Piano Concertos Nos 1 to 4 (with Kocsis), and Ravel's *Shéhérazade*, Debussy's *La damoiselle élue* and songs by Duparc (with Ameling); among his LP discs are Mahler's Symphony No. 4 and excerpts from Prokofiev's *Romeo and Juliet*.

WALTER, **Bruno** (1876–1962). Walter was born in Berlin in what he described as a 'modest Jewish family'; his father was a book-keeper and the family name was Schlesinger, a common German surname, which he later, at the outset of his career, changed to Walter, inspired by the artistic ideals of Walter von Stolzing of *Die Meistersinger*. When it was discovered that he had extraordinary musical talent, his mother taught him the piano as a young child, and at the age of 9 he entered the Stern Conservatory in Berlin. At 13 he made his first public appearance as a pianist with the Berlin Philharmonic Orchestra, playing Moscheles's *Piano Concerto in E Flat*. He remained a fine pianist throughout his life, apparently with the ability to retain his technique without constant practice. Also at 13 he heard Hans von Bülow conduct and decided to become a conductor himself. His first engagement as such was at the Cologne Opera, at the age of 17, with *Der Waffenschmied*, where he had been engaged as an assistant conductor. He moved to Hamburg again as assistant conductor in 1894, and there first met Mahler, who had a profound influence on the young man, with his artistic ideals, literary culture and powerful music. From Hamburg

Walter had successive appointments, as his career moved rapidly upwards, at Breslau (1896), Pressburg (1897), Temesvár in Hungary, Riga (1898) and then at the Berlin Staatsoper (1900), where he succeeded Schalk and came into contact with Muck and Strauss. In Berlin he conducted his first symphony concert which included the *Symphonie fantastique* of Berlioz, and at the Kroll Opera House one of the first operas he conducted was *The Mikado* of Gilbert and Sullivan. At the same time he also conducted his first *Ring*.

In 1901 Mahler invited Walter to Vienna to become his assistant, and director of the Vienna Court Opera; he remained in Vienna until 1913, working with Schalk, but his close connection with Mahler attracted criticism from the press, who saw it as their way of attacking Mahler indirectly. He was undoubtedly Mahler's closest associate and collaborator. To him Mahler played his Symphony No. 3 on the piano, and Walter prepared the soloists for the first performance of the Symphony No. 8 in 1910. After Mahler's death, he gave the first performance of *Das Lied von der Erde* in Munich in 1911 and of the Symphony No. 9 in Vienna in 1912. Mahler entrusted him with the authority to modify the orchestration of his symphonies to suit the acoustics of the halls in which they were to be performed. In Vienna Walter was also a frequent performer in chambermusic ensembles, giving recitals with artists such as Casals and Arnold Rosé; indeed Casals thought Walter would have become a very great pianist if he had not chosen to conduct instead. Walter became seriously ill, and only recovered after a course of treatment with Sigmund Freud. In 1909 he first visited London to conduct for the Royal Philharmonic Society, and in the next year led *Tristan und Isolde* in the Beecham season at Covent Garden.

In 1913 Walter left Vienna to become Mottl's successor at the Bavarian Court Opera at Munich, where he stayed for ten years. In Munich he reached full maturity as a conductor, achieving international recognition for his performances of the Mozart and Wagner operas; his Verdi was highly regarded too. The Mozart operas under Walter at Munich were celebrated for their unique perfection, the result of his own meticulous preparation. His reason for leaving Munich is not clear; he himself wrote in his autobiography that he had finished his work there, but others say that it was anti-semitism and envy that drove him away. In 1923 he made his home in Vienna again, having previously become an Austrian citizen in 1911. He had made his American début with Damrosch's New York Symphony Orchestra, but these concerts in New York were not entirely successful, apparently because he could not overcome the orchestra's antagonism to Germans. He returned later to the USA for concert tours in 1924 (New York and Minneapolis), 1925, 1927 (Cleveland and Los Angeles) and 1932–5 (New York). His concert at the Augusteo, Rome, in 1923 was the scene of a disturbance when he performed Schoenberg's *Verklärte Nacht*, and it caused his absence from musical life there, although he conducted at La Scala in 1926. Threats against him caused him to leave Vienna. He was appointed general music director at the Berlin Staatsoper in 1925 and in these years conducted in many European centres, as well as Moscow where he led Mahler's Symphony No. 4 (1923) and Leningrad (1926). He conducted in Paris (1927) and at the Salzburg Festivals (1925–38), where his Mozart performances reached new pinnacles of glory, and where Toscanini was one of his collaborators. Toscanini was one of the few other great conductors for whom he declared admiration; others were Furtwängler and Beecham. At Covent Garden he was in charge of the German repertoire in 1924–31, and his appearances were distinguished by superb performances of *The Ring*, *Der Rosenkavalier* and the great Mozart operas. The historic cast of Lotte Lehmann, Elizabeth Schumann and Richard Mayr in *Der Rosenkavalier* under Walter first came together in London in 1924, and these artists recorded extensive scenes from the opera in Vienna in 1933, but as Walter was not available, Heger substituted as conductor for the recording. The records have often been re-issued on LP transfers and are an imperishable reminder of the operatic standards of the time. Walter also conducted the London Symphony Orchestra in 1924 in Elgar's Symphony No. 2. His cycle of Mozart operas at Covent Garden in 1927 was later repeated in Paris with equal acclaim, he conducted at the Sargent-Courtauld concerts, and during his visit to Leningrad in 1926 he met the young Shostakovich and took his Symphony No. 1 to present it in Berlin.

In 1925 Charlottenburg was incorporated into Greater Berlin and the German Opera House there was re-opened as the Municipal Opera, with Tietjen as intendant (administrator) and Walter as conductor. He was in Berlin until 1929, and in that time the Municipal Opera flourished as one of the finest opera houses in the world. Furtwängler was then with the Berlin Philharmonic Orchestra, Klemperer with the Kroll Opera and Kleiber with the State Opera. But in 1929 disagreements with the municipal authorities about programmes and production caused Walter's resignation, and after a tour to the USA to conduct at the Hollywood Bowl, he succeeded Furtwängler as the conductor of the Leipzig Gewandhaus Orchestra. The advent of the Nazis to power brought his expulsion from Germany, when his concerts in Leipzig were banned on the grounds that they threatened 'public order and security', and his place at Leipzig was taken over first by Richard Strauss and then by Abendroth. He went to London and to Vienna, was guest conductor with the Vienna State Opera, and in 1935 was appointed its artistic adviser and permanent conductor, and also conducted the Vienna Philharmonic Orchestra. Again with the *Anschluss* he had to flee from the Nazis when they occupied Austria, took up residence in France at the invitation of the French government, became a French citizen only to have his citizenship abrogated in 1940. He conducted the Amsterdam Concertgebouw Orchestra and shared an international festival in Switzerland with Toscanini, who invited him to conduct the NBC Symphony Orchestra in New York in 1939.

Walter finally migrated to the USA, where he conducted the Los Angeles Philharmonic Orchestra when Klemperer was ill (1939) and led the NBC Symphony, New York Philharmonic-Symphony and Minneapolis Symphony Orchestras (1939–41), first conducted at the New York Metropolitan Opera in 1941 with *Fidelio* and then *Don Giovanni* and *The Bartered Bride* in memorable performances, and continued to appear with the New York Philharmonic-Symphony Orchestra as its conductor and musical adviser (1947–9). He returned to Vienna after World War II to lead *Fidelio* at the State Opera, and was re-united temporarily with the Vienna Philharmonic Orchestra at the first Edinburgh Festival in 1947 in *Das Lied von der Erde* with the great British contralto, Kathleen Ferrier. This performance was later recorded (also with Patzak, the tenor) and Walter considered it, with Ferrier's *Kindertotenlieder*, the recording in which he took special pride. It is now magnificently transferred to compact disc. In 1950 he also came to Salzburg to conduct the Vienna Philharmonic in Mahler's Symphony No. 4, with Seefried the soloist, which has been issued on compact disc by Varèse Sarabande,* and ten years later he returned to Vienna to lead the Vienna Philharmonic in the same symphony on the 100th anniversary of Mahler's birth. He had received the Gold Medal of the Royal Philharmonic Society in 1957, but in that year suffered a heart attack and had to restrict his conducting, living in Los Angeles where he died in 1962. He published an autobiography, *Theme and Variations*, in 1947, its sequel *Of*

---

* Issued in the USA. (VCD 47228)

Music and Music Making appeared in 1957, and a monograph *Gustav Mahler* in 1958. Early in his career he composed two symphonies and some chamber music, but then abandoned composition altogether.

It is ironic that one of the greatest German musicians of the 20th century was expelled from his own country; anti-semitism made his life uncomfortable no matter where he went in Germany and Austria even before the Nazi era. Some of his fellow German–Jewish conductors have criticised him for his allegedly equivocal attitude to these provocations, accusing him of seeking to ingratiate himself with the authorities. Be that as it may, he followed a distinguished career and enhanced many of the greatest opera houses and orchestras in Europe and the USA, where his performances of Mozart, Beethoven, Schubert, Schumann, Brahms, Mahler, Bruckner, Wagner and Strauss in particular were acclaimed. His performances were idio-syncratic—warm, lyrical, and romantic in the best sense. Precision was not a preoccupation, and this may have prevented him from giving Beethoven especially its ultimate dramatic stature. Technique took second place to expression; he himself said: 'By concentrating on precision one arrives at technique; but by concentrating on technique one does not arrive at precision.' He was always conscious of the spiritual dimension of the great central European masters and ever sought to express it. His humility in the face of these classics may have been exaggerated when he said that he did not conduct Mozart's Symphony No. 40 until he was 50 because he 'felt the responsibility of such a task'. His interpretations were markedly different from Toscanini's, lacking the latter's fire and intensity, and they did not have the improvisatory character of Furtwängler's, but enveloped the listener with their lyrical beauty. Yet his tempi were not exaggerated, as is evident in, say, his recordings of Beethoven's Symphony No. 7.

Walter had a reputation for gentleness and courtly persuasiveness, and his person radiated with the love of music. At rehearsals his temper was under firm control, he had a ready wit, but although tension between him and his players was low, concentration was uppermost. With his players he was very articulate and talked a lot, regarding them as sympathetic collaborators. He scorned the dictatorial methods of many other conductors, but his own personality failed to impress many players, particularly in the USA, where Toscanini's old orchestra, the New York Philharmonic-Symphony, called for a much stronger hand. Gaisberg, who recorded the Vienna Philharmonic for

HMV in the 1930s, wrote that they were a 'cynical lot, snobbish and blasé', who could only be tamed by Toscanini, but nonetheless out of respect for Walter gave him their best. To some musicians this image of Walter as the quiet imperturbable man is misleading, and they would claim that he was in reality as demanding and ruthless as any other. Certainly he was extremely meticulous in achieving the results he sought. In 1955, Walter recorded Mozart's Symphony No. 36 with the Columbia Symphony Orchestra, at this time a group of freelance musicians who had played with the NBC Symphony Orchestra and similar ensembles. As he had not performed the work before with these musicians, he carefully rehearsed it from his own marked parts. But unbeknown to him, the entire rehearsal was recorded, and when he was told about it, he exclaimed: 'I have been ambushed, and I am not sure that I approve of this look into the workshop.' He was persuaded, however, to agree to the commercial release of the rehearsals, which became the best-selling set, *The Birth of a Performance*. As Peter Munves, who was present at the rehearsals, has said: 'It was a document of a truly great artist at work, teaching a by now lost central European tradition to gifted instrumentalists.'

There has always been criticism of Walter's interpretations of symphonic music, as opposed to his magnificence in the opera house; for instance, Virgil Thomson wrote in 1942 that he was undependable technically and that 'sloppiness of beat and general indifference to ship-shapeness of execution' were evident even in the best of his concerts in New York at the time. Burghauser of the Vienna Philharmonic in the 1930s said that the rhapsodic nature of Mahler's music, with which Walter had had life-long familiarity, was transferred to the music of other composers, and that his weakness in rhythm brought him to include the Bruckner symphonies in his repertoire, because the public accepted a rhapsodic style as appropriate to Bruckner, although professional musicians were aware that it dissolved the music's rhythmic anatomy. But Burghauser concurred that Walter's operatic performances in the decades between the wars were incomparable, as opera did not call for a rigid rhythmic framework and that his flexibility as an accompanist suited the singers. In fact, a predominant characteristic of Walter's style was that the music had to breathe naturally as if it were being sung, which impaired a strict rhythmic pattern. Walter's decision to perform Bruckner had nothing to do with Burghauser's explanation. Walter related that originally he felt a stranger to the composer's extremes of expression, but after a long illness and the opportunity for re-assessment he came to understand Bruckner's 'solemnity and religious greatness'. With Mahler, Walter naturally emphasised the lyrical and softer side of the music, which made him such a moving interpreter of the Symphony No. 4 and *Das Lied von der Erde*; his recording of the Symphony No. 4 with the New York Philharmonic Orchestra and Desi Halban is an object-lesson in string-playing and was one of the significant recordings which brought the composer to a wider public. His earlier recording of the Symphony No. 9 with the Vienna Philharmonic Orchestra had a special poignancy as it was made in 1938 three months before the *Anschluss* at an actual concert in the Musikverein at which Chancellor Schuschnigg and most of the Austrian cabinet were present. Schuschnigg was later held prisoner by the Nazis, and Walter, Rosé, and many other members of the Vienna Philharmonic were soon to leave Vienna. The performance, re-issued on an LP dubbing by Turnabout, is, despite its faults, arresting in its commitment and intensity. Cardus once asked Klemperer about Walter as a conductor of Mahler. 'Quite good, but not altogether satisfactory,' was the answer. 'Why?' Cardus asked; to which Klemperer grunted, 'Too Jewish'.

Although a man of deep musical and literary culture, Walter had little concern for historical correctness and performed classical music with large orchestras, corrupt texts and an ignorance of the performance conventions of the times. But he was not alone in this regard among the great conductors of his generation, and even of the present day. He disregarded repeats in Haydn, Mozart, Beethoven and others, his acute sense of structure impelling him to move on with the musical argument. In rehearsal he did not always correct poor ensemble, believing that he could manage it at the performance. Orchestras of less than first rank were not belaboured to produce standards impossible to them. He conducted from the score until his eyesight grew weaker later in his life, and when he memorised the music he found that without the score he was in much closer contact with the players. His actual baton technique was, according to Boult, not so expressive as that of Nikisch, but 'he was so immersed in the music he was doing that he managed somehow to convey it just as telepathically I think as by putting it into the stick'. He was one of the first to conduct from the piano when he performed a Mozart concerto, although he could not always resolve the ensuing problems of ensemble. The restricted repertoire of his later years concealed the fact that earlier he performed a wide range of music, and was noted for his interpretations of Verdi and Tchaikovsky. All his life he was however antipathetic to twelve-tone music.

Walter's first gramophone recordings were made in Berlin in 1900, and his last records were prepared just prior to his death in Los Angeles, 62 years later. This remarkable career stretched from the days of the most primitive recordings to the era of stereophonic sound. In the early days he recorded with the Berlin Philharmonic, the Berlin Staatsoper, the BBC Symphony, the London Symphony, the Royal Philharmonic and the British Symphony Orchestras. His Master's Voice chose to record him with the Vienna Philharmonic when he was in Vienna in the 1930s, and when he left Vienna another series followed with the Paris Conservatoire Orchestra. After his arrival in the USA he recorded with the New York Philharmonic-Symphony, which became the New York Philharmonic, the Philadelphia Orchestra and the Columbia Symphony Orchestra. The latter was assembled from Californian musicians from the Hollywood film studios and the Los Angeles Philharmonic, to record his final valedictory series after he had retired from active concert life to Beverly Hills in Los Angeles. Happily, virtually all of these discs have been re-issued by CBS on compact disc: Haydn's Symphonies Nos 88 and 100, Mozart's Symphonies Nos 35, 36, 38, 39, 40 and 41, the Violin Concertos K. 216 and K. 218 (with Francescatti), *Eine kleine Nachtmusik*, *Masonic Funeral Music* and three overtures, Beethoven's nine symphonies, *Coriolan* and *Leonore No. 3* overtures, Brahms's four symphonies, two overtures, *Variations on the St Antony Chorale*, *Schicksalslied* and *Alto Rhapsody* (with Miller and the Occidental College Choir), Bruckner's Symphonies Nos 4, 7 and 9, Dvořák's Symphonies Nos 8 and 9, Mahler's *Lieder eines fahrenden Gesellen* (with Miller), and the overtures to *Tannhäuser* and *Der fliegende Holländer*, the prelude to *Die Meistersinger*, the prelude to Act I and Good Friday Music from *Parsifal* and the *Siegfried Idyll*. Performances re-issued on compact disc by CBS with the New York Philharmonic Orchestra are Schubert's Symphonies Nos 5 and 8, and Mahler's Symphony No. 2 (with Cundari, Forrester and the Westminster Choir), and *Das Lied von der Erde* (with Miller and Haefliger). Among his 78 r.p.m. discs, later transferred to LP, pride of place must be taken by the Act I of *Die Walküre*, which, with the soloists Lotte Lehmann, Lauritz Melchior and Emanuel List, must be one of the very finest recordings ever made of a Wagner opera, or part thereof.

WAND, **Günter** (b. 1912). Born in Elberfeld, Wand studied philosophy and musicology at the University of Cologne, at the Cologne Academy of Music, where his teacher for conducting was von Hoesslin, and at the Munich Academy of Music. He was first conductor of Detmold, then became conductor at the Cologne Opera (1939–44), but after the destruction of the opera house by Allied bombing, he moved to Salzburg where he was conductor at the Mozarteum (1944–6). He returned to Cologne at the end of the war, and was appointed general music director at the Cologne Opera (1945–8); in 1947 he became chief conductor of the symphony orchestra at the Gürzenich concert hall, one of the oldest orchestras in Germany, its concerts beginning in 1857. He remained with the orchestra until 1974; from 1948 he was also professor of conducting at the Cologne Conservatory. He has also been a guest conductor in Europe, Japan and the USSR, which he visited in 1959, and first conducted in Britain, with the London Symphony Orchestra, in 1951. Previously the Gürzenich Symphony Orchestra had been under the rather conservative direction of Abendroth, and Wand transformed the orchestra's repertoire by including modern and contemporary music, including at least one modern work in each programme. Bartók, Hindemith, Stravinsky and other 20th-century composers, who had not been performed in Germany during the war, appeared frequently. After leaving Cologne he lived in Berne, was a guest conductor with the Berne Symphony Orchestra and also conducted the Berne Choral Society, and since 1982 he has been chief conductor of the North German Radio Symphony Orchestra in Hamburg. He is also principal guest conductor of the BBC Symphony Orchestra. His compositions include several ballet scores, songs with orchestra, a cantata and a concertino.

Wand is a distinguished conductor with a wide range of sympathies, who is not sufficiently well known outside his native Germany, although his more recent records are bringing him a belated recognition. He recorded with the Gürzenich Symphony Orchestra symphonies by Haydn, Mozart, Beethoven, Schubert, Schumann and Brahms, *The Creation* and Beethoven's *Missa solemnis*, as well as music by Bartók, Schoenberg and Webern, for Nonesuch, Counterpoint and Vanguard; Deutsche Harmonia Mundi have issued Schubert's Symphonies Nos 3 and 6, and the four Brahms symphonies (with the North German Radio Symphony Orchestra), and the nine Bruckner symphonies (also with the NGRSO), but only Brahms's Symphonies Nos 1, 2 and 3 have so far appeared on compact disc.

WEINGARTNER, Felix (1863–1942). Weingartner was born at Zara (modern Zadar, Yugoslavia), of a German mother and an Austrian father, and after his father's death when he was a child, the family moved to Graz, where he studied the piano and composition with Remy. He started composing as a boy, and on Brahms's recommendation received a stipend from the state and went to study philosophy at Leipzig University in 1881. He soon transferred to the Conservatory there, and became known to Liszt, who convinced him he should be a conductor. Liszt produced Weingartner's first opera *Sakuntula* at Weimar in 1884, and in that year Weingartner began his career as a conductor at Königsberg. From there, he proceeded to the pinnacles of his profession in Europe, although the restless and irascible side of his nature always kept him on the move. He was in Danzig (1885–7), then became von Bülow's assistant in Hamburg (1887–9); Mannheim followed (1889–91), then the Royal Opera and Royal Orchestra in Berlin (1891–8), the Kaim Orchestra in Munich (1898–1903), the Vienna Opera, where he succeeded Mahler (1908–11), Hamburg (1912–14), Darmstadt (1914–19), the Vienna Volksoper (1919–24) and the Vienna Philharmonic Orchestra (1919–27), then director of the Conservatory and the Symphony Orchestra at Basel (1927–33), and finally the Vienna State Opera again (1935–6). He toured Europe, visited London for the first time in 1898 and the USA in 1905, conducting the Boston Opera Company (1912–3), and received the Gold Medal of the Royal Philharmonic Society in London (1939).

A prolific composer, Weingartner shared with some other great conductors a profound disappointment that his compositions were never more than an ephemeral success. But he had assimilated so much of other composers' music that his own was too eclectic to have any strong individuality. His output included eight operas, six symphonies, two concertos, chamber music and songs. The operas included a trilogy from Aeschylus, but many considered him temperamentally unsuited to operatic composition. His third symphony was entitled *Le Sermon d'amour* and its finale consisted of variations on a theme from *Die Fledermaus*. Together with Charles Malherbe he edited the complete works of Berlioz, and in fact was one of the first great conductors to pioneer the modern revival of Berlioz. He also edited *Oberon*, *Der fliegende Holländer* and Méhul's *Joseph*. He made a number of orchestral arrangements including Weber's *Invitation to the Dance*, which he recorded himself four times, two ballads of Loewe and songs by Beethoven, Haydn and

Schubert, Beethoven's *Hammerklavier* Piano Sonata (Op. 106), which he recorded with the Royal Philharmonic Orchestra, and Schubert's *Symphony in E Major*. Schubert had sketched this symphony and it was completed in a pianoforte arrangement by the English composer John Francis Barnett in 1882, and Weingartner reconstructed the score in 1934; it has been recorded several times, the last by the Berlin Radio Symphony Orchestra (in East Berlin) conducted by Rögner.

When Weingartner was in Hamburg in 1887–9, there occurred his momentous clash with von Bülow, which led to Weingartner publishing his *On Conducting* in 1895. He objected to von Bülow's romantic exaggerations and excessive rubato, and himself led a performance of *Carmen* that was scrupulous in its observation of all the composer's directions, a great contrast to von Bülow's own performance of the opera. In his book, Weingartner made an explicit attack on von Bülow's freedom of interpretation, and, at one point, after discussing his tempo variations and instrumental amendments in his performances of the Beethoven symphonies, wrote: 'The impression given by performances of this kind was that not the work but the conductor was the chief thing, and that he wanted to divert the attention of the audience from the music to himself.' Along with Muck, Weingartner was one of the first great conductors to insist on strict adherence to the composer's markings, and on consistent and moderate tempi; later Toscanini was to add his overwhelming influence in insisting that the score itself was the sole authority for a performance. Weingartner's own interpretations were always models of sobriety and elegance, and avoided any romantic exaggeration or distortion. His influence as an interpreter, particularly of Beethoven, was crucial, and the vast majority of European conductors since his day have accepted his principles as sacred writ, as do, one might add, today's record critics.

Weingartner was a remote, cold personality, the opposite of the popular stereotype of the egocentric, demonstrative conductor. His baton technique was simple, the wrist doing most of the work, and his manner before the orchestra was restrained, erect and unostentatious; nonetheless his psychological command of the players was complete. Cardus wrote of him in 1939: 'Weingartner does not use the familiar gestures of the modern "dictator" conductors; he retains the old-fashioned belief that an instrumentalist understands how to play his notes correctly and does not need illumination in the form of arts that scarcely belong to that of a conductor—the arts of Terpsichore and of declamation. His gestures are quiet: he is always dignified. He is seldom disturbed from a calm physical balance; his laundry bill probably disappoints those who attend to the weekly linen of most other conductors. He belongs to the cultured epoch of music, the epoch of good manners and taste—and sound scholarship. It is difficult to describe how he obtains his effects; probably the work is done, as every conductor's work should be done, at rehearsal. Weingartner respects the composer's own notes and instructions; he never allows a phrase to carry more expression than consistent with the general flow of the rhythm; in other words, he does not take a phrase out of its context. Yet he is seldom a rigid conductor.' Burghauser, bassoonist of the Vienna Philharmonic Orchestra and the orchestra's chairman from 1933 to 1938, said that Weingartner employed only the subtlest modifications of tempo, and achieved the utmost clarity of rhythm. His performance of works such as Schubert's Symphony No. 8 and *Tristan und Isolde* had an almost unparalleled intensity of expression and dramatic power, although Walter wrote (in his autobiography, *Theme and Variations*) that Weingartner had not a dramatic nature, and for that reason was found wanting as an operatic conductor and director, despite his fiery temperament on the platform. Weingartner never hesitated to cut Wagner, and defended his cuts on artistic grounds. In his first period at the Vienna State Opera (1908–10) he introduced new operas, and had a predilection for comic operas, but in his second period (1935–6) he was apparently too old and resigned to be an effective director.

Weingartner made his first records in 1910, which were some songs of his own, with the American soprano Lucille Marcel, who became the third of his five wives. All of his records were for Columbia. Artistically, his outlook did not go beyond Brahms and Wagner, as his records reflected, and these composers were performed in a typically straightforward and carefully balanced style, perhaps too coolly for many accustomed to the virtuoso readings of Mengelberg, Stokowski, *et al*. His place in the history of musical performance is in his interpretation of Beethoven. His book *On the Performance of Beethoven's Symphonies* had a profound influence and has served as a text book for countless conductors since; in the book he recommended that in many places the symphonies should be rescored, but later in his life he altered his opinion and acknowledged that Beethoven had known better. He recorded all the Beethoven symphonies, some more than once, the most famous being the series he made with the Vienna Philharmonic in the mid-1930s—Symphonies

Nos 1, 3, 7, 8 and 9. Of these, the *Eroica* and *Choral* would have to be included in any short list of the greatest recordings ever made. In Japan alone, the *Choral* sold over 100,000 copies. His Beethoven was firm, with an exact balance between precision and expression; to compare, say, his Beethoven Symphony No. 1 with the Vienna Philharmonic, with the other great recorded performance of the 1930s, Toscanini's with the BBC Symphony Orchestra, is to compare two peaks of excellence—Viennese elegance and style with Italian fire and drama. And yet, Weingartner made these recordings in Vienna under odd circumstances. According to Fred Gaisberg of the Gramophone Company, who supervised them, Weingartner treated his orchestra 'with frigid detachment and they responded with grudging correctness'. All the nine Beethoven symphonies have been re-issued in Japan on LP, and the *Eroica* was included in a three-disc set of LP transfers issued by EMI in 1976, along with Brahms's Symphony No. 2 and other works.

WELLER, Walter (b. 1939). Born in Vienna where his father was a violinist in the Vienna Philharmonic Orchestra, Weller studied at the Vienna Academy of Music, and in 1956 joined the violins of the Vienna Philharmonic. In 1958 he founded the Weller String Quartet, with which he toured internationally and made a number of successful records for Decca. In 1961 he became concertmaster of the orchestra (at the age of 21), and retained that position until 1969. His début as a conductor occurred in 1966, then he conducted at the Vienna Volksoper and Vienna State Opera, was music director at Duisburg (1971–2) and of the Vienna Niederösterreichisches Tonkünstler Orchestra (1975–8), was principal conductor and music adviser on the Royal Liverpool Philharmonic Orchestra (1977), and became principal conductor of the Royal Philharmonic Orchestra (1980). He has been a guest conductor in Europe, Israel, Japan and the USA. Among his recordings are fine accounts of the seven Prokofiev symphonies (with the London Philharmonic Orchestra), the three Rachmaninov symphonies (with the London Philharmonic and the Suisse Romande Orchestras), and Smetana's *Má Vlast* (with the Israel Philharmonic Orchestra).

WILLCOCKS, Sir David (b. 1919). Born in Newquay, Cornwall, Willcocks was a chorister at Westminster Abbey (1929–33), was an organ scholar at King's College, Cambridge (1939–40 and 1945–7), and during World War II served in the British Infantry and was awarded the Military Cross (1944). He was a Fellow of

King's College, Cambridge (1947–51) and conductor of the Cambridge Philharmonic Society (1947), organist at Salisbury Cathedral and conductor of the Salisbury Musical Society (1947–50), organist at Worcester Cathedral (1950), conductor of the Worcester Festival Choral Society and the City of Birmingham Choir (1950–7), conductor of the Bradford Festival Choral Society (1956–74), Fellow and director of music at King's College, Cambridge, organist of Cambridge University and conductor of the Cambridge University Musical Society (1957–74), musical director of the Bach Choir (since 1960), president of the Royal College of Organists (1966–8), and director of the Royal College of Music (since 1974). He has conducted in most European countries, the USA, Canada, Africa, Japan and Australia, conducted Britten's *War Requiem* at La Scala, Milan (1963) and in Japan (1965), and visited Leipzig with the Bach Choir in the year of its centenary (1976). He has composed church and organ music, has been the general editor of *Oxford Church Music, Carols for Choirs* and *Anthems for Men's Voices*, and was awarded the KBE in 1977. He has made over 70 recordings with the King's College Chapel Choir and with the Bach Choir, including *Messiah, St John Passion, The Creation* and the Mass No. 9 (*The Nelson*) of Haydn, *The Dream of Gerontius* and other works of Taverner, Vivaldi, Pergolesi, Palestrina, Fauré, Howells, Britten and Vaughan Williams, *et al*. The Haydn Mass No. 9 was first issued in 1962, and was the first recording that brought the glories of Haydn's late masses before the record-buying public.

WOOD, Sir Henry (1869–1944). Wood was born in London; his father was a prominent singer and his mother gave him his first musical training. At 13 he gave organ recitals, and was appointed organist at the church of Aldermanbury. After studies at the Royal Academy of Music under Prout and Garcia, his first appearance as a conductor was in 1888 when he led a performance of a cantata by McFarren at Clapton; in 1889 he received his first appointment as a conductor with the Arthur Rousbey Opera Company; in 1890 he assisted at rehearsals of Sullivan's opera *Ivanhoe* with the d'Oyly Carte Company, and then conducted with several touring opera companies. At this time he also taught singing. In 1895 the impresario Robert Newman engaged Wood to conduct a series of promenade concerts at the newly-built Queen's Hall in Langham Place, London; Wood led this famous series of concerts for 50 consecutive seasons, until a year before his death. In addition, he conducted numerous other concerts throughout the year with the Queen's Hall Orchestra, and was active in the provinces at many music festivals and with local orchestras. His tours abroad took him as far as the Hollywood Bowl; in 1921 he shared with Nikisch and Pierné the conductorship of the Zürich Music Festival. His commitment to the London Prom concerts brought him to decline overseas engagements and appointments, including the conductorship of the Boston Symphony Orchestra. In 1911 he was knighted, and in 1938 celebrated his fiftieth jubilee as a conductor; for this occasion Vaughan Williams wrote his *Serenade to Music*. Wood's first wife was the soprano and Russian princess Ourousoff, whom he accompanied at many recitals; she died in 1909.

From 1923 Wood taught conducting at the Royal Academy of Music, and many generations of musicians came under his influence. Through the Prom concerts and his many other musical activities he was the first great positive influence in orchestral performance and popular musical appreciation in England; in Boult's words, 'Sir Henry was the greatest popular conductor (in the finest sense of the adjective) that the world has ever seen.' Starting with programmes of unsophisticated appeal, he gradually introduced the music of Beethoven, Wagner, Brahms and Tchaikovsky, so that his audience came more and more to appreciate the standard repertoire. He performed, often for the first time in England, a prodigious amount of new music: the Russian nationalists, Strauss and Schoenberg became familiar to concertgoers, and in the years 1895 to 1919 he presented over 200 works by British composers. Contemporary composers including Strauss, Debussy, Elgar, Delius, Sibelius, Rachmaninov, Bloch, Reger and Scriabin were prominent in his programmes, and many were invited to conduct their own works. Composers were anxious for him to give first performances of their music because his readings were invariably faithful and absolutely clear and accurate. While his orchestra could play virtually any standard repertory work without rehearsal, he took great trouble over new pieces; before Strauss came to conduct *Ein Heldenleben*, Wood had 17 rehearsals to prepare the work. He prepared all his scores very meticulously before rehearsals, and his rehearsals were organised so as not to waste a minute. His baton technique was compared to that of Nikisch in its perfection; he used a very long baton to save arm movement, and to be clearly visible to orchestra and choir. At rehearsals he very often played straight through the work, shouting comments rather than stopping. He was able to have adequate rehearsal time for his normal Queen's Hall concerts, established sectional rehearsals, took immense trouble to have every player accurately tuned, and insisted on unanimity in bowing. He adopted the Continental low pitch (A:435), and introduced women into the orchestra. An extreme case of his care in rehearsal was the preparation of Bach's *Mass in B Minor* in Liverpool for which he had 50 rehearsals. For a performance of the *St Matthew Passion* at Sheffield he personally copied breath and expression marks into 400 vocal scores. In fact he was sometimes criticised for being too careful and laborious; Ernest Newman wrote: 'Whatever else might be said against him, it could never be said that he was anything but thorough. In the preparation of some great work, especially, there were no limits to the trouble he was prepared to take.'

An early battle was fought over the prevailing system of deputies in the Queen's Hall Orchestra, which Wood refused to tolerate. Players would send substitutes to attend rehearsals, themselves coming only to the concert performance itself. As a result those players who would not accept his insistence that they attend both rehearsals and concerts left the Queen's Hall Orchestra and in 1904 formed the London Symphony Orchestra. The Queen's Hall Orchestra under Wood performed in the Proms season continuously for ten weeks with six concerts a week; their repertoire became enormous, and their skill at sight-reading the wonder of visiting conductors. Wood acknowledged that the orchestral playing at the Prom concerts was not the most polished, but countered that this was not his aim. Even so, he achieved a considerable improvement in the standard of orchestral playing in London. He earned the warmest respect from his fellow musicians; Goossens wrote of him that he had 'never encountered a sincerer artist or a more resourceful, experienced and versatile conductor'. He was the first to make orchestral conducting a full-time occupation for a British-born musician. An amusing sidelight of his career was his arrangement of Bach's *Toccata and Fugue in D Minor*, which he published under the pseudonym of Paul Klenovsky; he did not reveal his identity as the arranger until years later.

Wood was one of the first major conductors to make gramophone records, and in 1915 he recorded a number of works for Columbia. Many were in abbreviated versions; for instance, the *Coriolan* overture was abridged to one side of a 12-inch disc, *Till Eulenspiegel* to two sides, and the Elgar Violin Concerto to four sides. This practice continued until 1923, when a Beethoven Symphony No. 3 conducted by Wood was issued on three discs, but criticism was so severe about this and other abbreviated works that the record companies discontinued issuing condensed versions of standard works. He went on to record a wide repertoire with the Queen's Hall, New Queen's Hall and other orchestras, including symphonies by Haydn, Beethoven, Schubert, Tchaikovsky and Franck. Except possibly for the works of Vaughan Williams which he recorded, none of Wood's recordings established itself as an imperishable classic of the gramophone. His critics may have been right when they described him as a master of the grand gesture but less impressive in the meticulous expression of nuances and mood, essential for successful records. But Wood did more than anyone to pave the way for the later excellence of London as an international music centre.

Z

ZINMAN, David (b. 1936). Born in New York, Zinman studied the violin at Oberlin Conservatory, where he was also a choral director, and then graduated from the University of Minnesota. He studied conducting at the Berkshire Music Center and later with Monteux, who took him to Europe in 1961 as his assistant with the London Symphony Orchestra. In 1963 he appeared with the Netherlands Chamber Orchestra at the Holland Festival, substituting for Paul Sacher, and his reception was such that he was at once appointed music director of the orchestra, remaining with them until 1977. He appeared with the orchestra at many European festivals, and toured Australia and the Far East in 1974. His début as a conductor in the USA occurred in 1967 with the Philadelphia Orchestra, and after conducting many other major orchestras there he was appointed music director of the Rochester Philharmonic Orchestra in 1974. In Europe he was a guest conductor with the Amsterdam Concertgebouw Orchestra, the London Symphony Orchestra, the BBC Symphony Orchestra, the Royal Philharmonic Orchestra, the Suisse Romande Orchestra and the Israel Philharmonic Orchestra, and in 1985 he conducted the Berlin Philharmonic Orchestra for the first time. He was appointed principal guest conductor of the Rotterdam Philharmonic Orchestra (1977–9) then was appointed chief conductor (1979–82); he became principal guest conductor of the Baltimore Symphony Orchestra in 1983, and succeeded to musical director in 1984. From 1977 he has also been a professor at the Eastman School at Rochester University. Of his numerous discs—over 40—the most remarkable with the Netherlands Chamber Orchestra were the sets of sinfonias by J. C. Bach, which were models of precision, vitality and style. He received a Grand Prix du Disque for his record of music inspired by Maeterlinck's play *Pelléas et Mélisande*, by Schoenberg, Sibelius and Fauré, with the Rotterdam Philharmonic, and his one compact disc so far is with that orchestra, a coupling of suites from Rimsky-Korsakov's *Le Coq d'Or* and *Tsar Sultan*.

APPENDIX

Compact Disc Recordings

This appendix lists compact discs of works specifically mentioned in the text and which, at the time of going to press, are generally obtainable through retail outlets in Great Britain. Under each conductor, recordings are listed alphabetically by composer. When a work appears as part of a concert recording no note is given of other pieces on the disc if they are not mentioned in the text. Readers are referred to the *Gramophone Compact Disc Catalogue*, published by General Gramophone Publications Ltd, with the aid of which this appendix has been compiled.

ABBREVIATIONS: *Orchestras, choirs, etc.*

AAM	Academy of Ancient Music
ASMF	Academy of St Martin in the Fields
BPO	Berlin Philharmonic Orchestra
CBSO	City of Birmingham Symphony Orchestra
ch.	choir
chor.	chorus
CO	chamber orchestra
COE	Chamber Orchestra of Europe
ECO	English Chamber Orchestra
FNO	French National Orchestra
FNRO	French National Radio Orchestra
LAPO	Los Angeles Philharmonic Orchestra
LSO	London Symphony Orchestra
NYPO	New York Philharmonic Orchestra
Op.	Opera/Opus
Philadelphia	Philadelphia Orchestra
Philh.	Philharmonia Orchestra
PO	Philharmonic Orchestra
ROHO	Royal Opera House Orchestra Covent Garden
RPO	Royal Philharmonic Orchestra
RSO	Radio Symphony Orchestra
SNO	Scottish National Orchestra
SO	Symphony Orchestra
SRO	Suisse Romande Orchestra
St. Op.	State Opera
VCM	Concentus Musicus Wien
VPO	Vienna Philharmonic Orchestra

ABBREVIATIONS: *Recording labels*

ARAB	Arabesque
ARCH	Archiv Produktion/PolyGram Classics
ARGO	Argo/Decca
ASV	Academy Sound & Vision
CAPR	Capriccio
CBS	CBS
CHAN	Chandos
CHNT	Le Chant du Monde
CRD	CRD
DECC	Decca
DELO	Delos

DENO	Denon
DGG	Deutsche Grammophon/PolyGram Classics
DHM	Deutsche Harmonia Mundi
ERAT	Erato
EURO	Eurodisc
HUNG	Hungaroton
JVC	JVC-Melodiya
LODI	Lodia
L'OI	L'Oiseau-Lyre/Decca
ORFE	Orfeo
PHIL	Philips/PolyGram Classics
PRO	Pro Arte
PRT	PRT
RCA	RCA
RODO	Rodolphe
SUPR	Supraphon
TELA	Telarc
TELD	Teldec
TRAX	Trax Classique
UNIC	Unicorn-Kanchana
VOX	Vox Prima

Abbado, Claudio

BEETHOVEN: Symphony No. 3. VPO. (DGG) 419 597-2GH
Symphony No. 9. VPO. (DGG) 419 598-2GH

MAHLER: Symphony No. 1. Chicago SO. (DGG) 400 033-2GH
Symphony No. 3. VPO. (DGG) 410 715-2GH2
Symphony No. 4. VPO. (DGG) 413 454-2GH
Symphony No. 7. Chicago SO. (DGG) 413 773-2GH2

MOZART: Symphonies Nos 40 and 41. LSO. (DGG) 415 841-2GGA

ROSSINI: Il barbiere di Siviglia. Ambrosian Op. Chor., LSO. (DGG) 415 695-2GH2
La cenerentola. Scottish Op. Chor., LSO. (DGG) 415 698-2GH3
Il viaggio a Reims. Prague Phil. Chor., COE. (DGG) 415 498-2GH3

VERDI: Aida. La Scala Chor., La Scala Orch. (DGG) 410 092-2GH3
Macbeth. La Scala Chor., La Scala Orch. (DGG) 415 688-2GH3
Simon Boccanegra. La Scala Chor., La Scala Orch. (DGG) 415 692-2GH2

Abravanel, Maurice de

TCHAIKOVSKY: Manfred Symphony, Utah SO. (VOX) MWCD7123

Almeida, Antonio de

Portrait of Frederica von Stade. Philh. (CBS) MK39315

Ansermet, Ernest

BORODIN: Prince Igor *and*

RIMSKY-KORSAKOV: Scheherezade. SRO. (DECC) 414 124-2DH

DEBUSSY: Orchestral Works. SRO. (DECC) 414 040-2DH

MUSSORGSKY: Orchestral Works. SRO. (DECC) 414 139-2DH2

RAVEL: Orchestral Works. SRO. (DECC) 414 046-2DH

SAINT-SAËNS: Symphony No. 3. SRO. (DECC) 414 034-2

STRAVINSKY: L'Oiseau de feu. New Philh. (DECC) 414 141-2DH

Ashkenazy, Vladimir

BEETHOVEN: Symphony No. 5. Philh. (DECC) 400 060-2DH

Symphony No. 6. Philh. (DECC) 410 003-2DH

RACHMANINOV: Symphony in D minor and Symphony No. 3. Concertgebouw. (DECC) 410 231-2DH

Symphony No. 1. Concertgebouw. (DECC) 411 657-2DH

Symphony No. 2. Concertgebouw. (DECC) 400 081-2DH

SIBELIUS: Symphony No. 1. Philh. (DECC) 414 534-2DH

Symphony No. 2. Philh. (DECC) 410 206-2DH

Symphonies Nos 3 and 6. Philh. (DECC) 414 267-2DH

Symphony No. 4. Philh. (DECC) 400 056-2DH

Symphony No. 5. Philh. (DECC) 410 016-2DH

Symphony No. 7. Philh. (DECC) 411 935-2DH

TCHAIKOVSKY: Symphony No. 6. Philh. (DECC) 411 615-2DH

Beecham, Sir Thomas

Beecham conducts Delius. RPO/T. (EMI) CDS7 47509-8

PUCCINI: La Bohème. RCA Victor SO. (EMI) CDS7 47235-8

Berglund, Paavo

SHOSTAKOVICH: Symphony No. 7. Bournemouth SO. (EMI) CDC7 47651-2

SIBELIUS: Orchestral works. Philh/P. (EMI) CDC7 47484-2

Symphonies Nos 4 and 7. Helsinki PO. (EMI) CDC7 47443-2

Bernstein, Leonard

BEETHOVEN: Symphony No. 3. VPO. (DGG) 413 778-2GH

Symphony No. 6. VPO. (DGG) 413 779-2GH

BRAHMS: Symphony No. 1. VPO. (DGG) 410 081-2GH

Symphony No. 2. VPO. (DGG) 410 082-2GH

Symphony No. 3. VPO. (DGG) 410 083-2GH

Symphony No. 4. VPO. (DGG) 410 084-2GH

FRANCK: Symphony in D minor. FNO. (DGG) 400 070-2GH

MAHLER: Symphony No. 1. NYPO. (CBS) MK42194

Symphony No. 2. LSO. (CBS) M2K.42195
Symphony No. 3. NYPO. (CBS) M2K.42196
Symphony No. 4. NYPO. (CBS) MK42197
Symphony No. 5. NYPO. (CBS) MK42198
Symphonies Nos 6 and 8. NYPO. (CBS) M3K.42199
Symphonies Nos 7, 9 and 10. NYPO. (CBS) M3K.42200
Symphony No. 7. NYPO. (DGG) 419 211-2GH2
Symphony No. 9. NYPO. (DGG) 419 208-2GH2
SHOSTAKOVICH: Symphony No. 5. NYPO. (CBS) MK35854
STRAVINSKY: Le Sacre du Printemps. Israel PO. (DGG) 410 508-2GH
WAGNER: Tristan und Isolde. Bavarian Rad. Chor., Bavarian RSO. (EMI) CDS7 47322-8

Blomstedt, Herbert

BEETHOVEN: Symphony No. 9. Dresden Staatskapelle. (CAPR) 10060
BRUCKNER: Symphony No. 4. Dresden Staatskapelle. (DENO) C37-7126
Symphony No. 7. Dresden Staatskapelle. (DENO) C37-7286
MOZART: Symphonies Nos 38 and 39. Dresden Staatskapelle. (DENO) C37-7146
Symphonies Nos 40 and 41. Dresden Staatskapelle. (DENO) C37-7022

Böhm, Karl

BEETHOVEN: Symphony No. 6. VPO. (DGG) 413 721-2GX2
BRUCKNER: Symphony No. 4. VPO. (DECC) 411 581-2DH

Boulez, Pierre

BERG: Lulu. Paris Op. Orch. (DGG) 415 489-2GH3

Boult, Sir Adrian

BACH and HANDEL Arias: Ferrier, LPO. (DECC) 414 616-2DH
BRAHMS: Symphony No. 1. LPO. (PRT) PVCD8388
Symphony No. 2. LPO. (PRT) PVCD8389
Symphony No. 3. LPO. (PRT) PVCD8390
ELGAR: Symphony No. 1. LPO. (EMI) CDC7 47204-2
VAUGHAN WILLIAMS: A Sea Symphony. LPO. (EMI) CDC7 47212-2
Sinfonia antartica. LPO. (EMI) CDC7 47216-2
Symphonies Nos 4 and 6. New Philh. (EMI) CDC7 47215-2
Symphony No. 5. LPO. (EMI) CDC7 47214-2
Symphonies Nos 8 and 9. LPO. (EMI) CDC7 47217-2

Britten, Benjamin

BRITTEN: Les Illuminations. ECO. (DECC) 417 153-2DH
Nocturne. LSO. (DECC) 417 153-2DH
Peter Grimes. ROH Chor., ROHO. (DECC) 414 577-2DH3

Britten, Benjamin – *cont.*
> Serenade for tenor, horn and strings. LSO. (DECC) 417 153-2DH

Chailly, Riccardo
> BRUCKNER: Symphony No. 3. Berlin RSO. (DECC) 417 093-2DH
>
> Symphony No. 7. Berlin RSO. (DECC) 414 290-2DH
>
> GIORDANO: Andrea Chenier. Welsh Nat. Op., National PO. (DECC) 410 117-2DH2
>
> ORFF: Carmina Burana. Berlin Rad. Sym. Chor., Berlin RSO. (DECC) 411 702-2DH
>
> PROKOFIEV: Alexander Nevsky. Cleveland Orch. Chor., Cleveland Orch. (DECC) 410 164-2DH
>
> STRAVINSKY: The Rake's Progress. London Sinfonietta Chor., London Sinfonietta. (DECC) 411 644-2DH2
>
> TCHAIKOVSKY: Symphony No. 5. VPO. (DECC) 410 232-2DH

Conlon, James
> DVOŘÁK: Symphony No. 9. LPO. (ERAT) ECD88036
>
> JANÁČEK: Idyll and Lachian Dances. Rotterdam PO. (ERAT) ECD88095
>
> LISZT: Dante Symphony. Rotterdam PO. (ERAT) ECD88162

Corboz, Michel
> BACH: St Matthew Passion. Lausanne Vocal Ens., Lausanne CO. (ERAT) ECD880663
>
> St John Passion. Lausanne Vocal Ens., Lausanne CO. (ERAT) ECD88208
>
> MONTEVERDI: Vespro della Beata Vergine. Lausanne Vocal Ens., Baroque Instrumental Ens. (ERAT) ECD88024

Davis, Andrew
> Kiri Te Kanawa sings Richard Strauss. LSO. (CBS) MK76794

Davis, Sir Colin
> BERLIOZ: Les Troyens. ROH Chor., ROHO. (PHIL) 416 433-2PH4
>
> PUCCINI: Tosca. ROH Chor., ROHO. (PHIL) 412 885-2PH2

Dohnányi, Christoph von
> BEETHOVEN: Symphony No. 9. Cleveland Orch. (TELA) CD80120
>
> DVOŘÁK: Symphony No. 8 and Scherzo Capriccioso. Cleveland Orch. (DECC) 414 422-2DH
>
> SCHUBERT: Symphony No. 9. Cleveland Orch. (TELA) CD80110

Downes, Edward
> MAXWELL DAVIES: Symphony No. 3. BBC PO. (BBC) CD560

Dutoit, Charles

> FALLA: El amor brujo and Three-cornered Hat. Montreal SO. (DECC) 410 008-2DH
>
> RAVEL: Alborada del gracioso and Rapsodie espagnole. Montreal SO. (DECC) 410 010-2DH
>
> Daphnis et Chloé. Montreal SO Chor., Montreal SO. (DECC) 400 055-2DH
>
> RESPIGHI: Feste romane, Pini di Roma and Fontane di Roma. Montreal SO. (DECC) 410 145-2DH
>
> RIMSKY-KORSAKOV: Scheherezade. Montreal SO. (DECC) 410 253-2DH
>
> SAINT-SAËNS: Symphony No. 3. Montreal SO. (DECC) 410 201-2DH
>
> STRAVINSKY: The Rite of Spring. Montreal SO. (DECC) 414 202-2DH

Elder, Mark

> BULLER: The Theatre of Memory and Proenca. BBC SO. (UNIC) DKP9045

Fedoseyev, Vladimir

> RACHMANINOV: Symphonic Dances. Moscow RSO. (JVC) VDC523

Ferencsik, János

> BARTÓK: Duke Bluebeard's Castle. Hungarian St. Op. Chor., Hungarian St. Op. Orch. (HUNG) HCD 12254-2
>
> BEETHOVEN: Symphony No. 3. Hungarian St. Orch. (HUNG) HCD 12566-2

Fischer, Iván

> BRAHMS: Violin Concerto. Belkin, LSO. (DECC) 411 677-2DH
>
> DONIZETTI: Don Pasquale. Hungarian Rad. Chor., Hungarian St. Orch. (HUNG) HCD 12610-2
>
> PAISIELLO: Il barbiere di Siviglia. Hungarian St. Orch. (HUNG) HCD 12525/6-2
>
> SCHUBERT: Symphony No. 9. Budapest Fest. Orch. (HUNG) HCD 12722-2

Fischer, Ádám

> GOLDMARK: The Queen of Sheba. Hungarian St. Orch. (HUNG) HCD 12179/81-2

Frühbeck de Burgos, Rafael

> MENDELSSOHN: Elijah. New Philh. (TRAX) TRXCD104

Furtwängler, Wilhelm

> BEETHOVEN: Symphonies Nos 1 and 4. VPO. (EMI) CDC7 47409-2
>
> Symphony No. 3. VPO. (EMI) CDC7 47410-2
>
> Symphony No. 5. VPO. (EMI) CDC7 47120-2

Furtwängler, Wilhelm – *cont.*
> Symphonies Nos 7 and 8. BPO. (DGG) 415 666-2GH
> Symphony No. 9. Bayreuth Festival Orch. (EMI) CDC7 47081-2
> BRAHMS: Symphony No. 1. BPO. (DGG) 415 662-2GH
> WAGNER: Tristan und Isolde. ROH Chor. Philh. (EMI) CDS7 47322-8

Gardiner, John Eliot
> BACH: Mass in B Minor. Monteverdi Ch., English Baroque Soloists. (ARCH) 415 514-2AH2
> HANDEL: Messiah. Monteverdi Ch., English Baroque Soloists. (PHIL) 411 041-2PH
> MOZART: Symphonies Nos 29 and 33. English Baroque Soloists. (PHIL) 412 736-2PH
> PURCELL: King Arthur. Monteverdi Ch., English Baroque Soloists. (ERAT) ECD880562

Gibson, Sir Alexander
> ELGAR: The Dream of Gerontius. Scottish Nat. Chor., SNO. (CRD) CRD3326/7
> SIBELIUS: Symphonies Nos 1 and 7. SNO. (CHAN) CHAN8344
> Symphony No. 2. SNO. (CHAN) CHAN8303
> Symphonies Nos 3 and 6. SNO. (CHAN) CHAN8389
> Symphonies Nos 4 and 5. SNO. (CHAN) CHAN8388
> STRAVINSKY: Symphony in C, Symphony in E flat and Symphony in 3 movements. SNO. (CHAN) CHAN8345/6

Giulini, Carlo Maria
> BRUCKNER: Symphony No. 8. VPO. (DGG) 415 124-2GH2
> VERDI: Don Carlos. Ambrosian Op. Chor., ROHO. (EMI) CDS7 47701-8
> Falstaff. Los Angeles Master Chorale, LAPO. (DGG) 410 503-2GH2
> Messa da Requiem. Philh. Chor., Philh. (EMI) CDS7 47257-8
> Rigoletto. Vienna St. Op. Chor., VPO. (DGG) 415 288-2GH2

Guest, George
> VIVALDI: Gloria and Gloria in D. St. John's Coll. Ch., Wren Orch. (ARGO) 410 018-27H

Haitink, Bernard
> ELGAR: Symphony No. 2. Philh. (EMI) CDC7 47299-2
> MAHLER: Symphony No. 4. Concertgebouw. (PHIL) 412 119-2PH
> Symphony No. 5. Concertgebouw. (PHIL) 416 469-2PH
> Symphony No. 7. Concertgebouw. (PHIL) 410 398-2PH2

Symphony No. 9. Concertgebouw. (PHIL) 416 466-2PH2

MOZART: Don Giovanni. Glyndebourne Fest. Chor., LPO. (EMI) CDS7 47037

SCHUMANN: Symphony No. 3. Concertgebouw. (PHIL) 411 104-2PH

SHOSTAKOVICH: Symphonies Nos 1 and 9. LPO. (DECC) 414 677-2DH

Symphony No. 5. Concertgebouw. (DECC) 410 017-2DH

Symphonies Nos 7 and 12. Concertgebouw. (DECC) 417 392-2DH2

Symphony Nö. 8. Concertgebouw. (DECC) 411 616-2DH

Symphony No. 11. Concertgebouw. (DECC) 411 939-2DH2

Symphony No. 13. Concertgebouw. (DECC) 417 261-2DH

Symphony No. 14. Concertgebouw. (DECC) 417 514-2DH

Symphony No. 15. LPO. (DECC) 417 581-2DH

Handley, Vernon

DVOŘÁK: Symphony No. 8. LPO. (CHAN) CHAN8323

ELGAR: Violin Concerto. Kennedy, LPO. (EMI) CDC7 47210-2

Harnoncourt, Nikolaus

BACH: Cantatas: many issued on compact disc with TELD

Christmas Oratorio. Chorus Viennensis, VCM. (TELD) 2B8.35033

Mass in B minor. Vienna Chor., VCM. (TELD) ZA8.35019

St Matthew Passion. Concertgebouw Chor., Concertgebouw. (TELD) ZB8.35668

Suites, BWV 1066-9

1,2. VCM. (TELD) ZK8.43051

1,2. VCM. (TELD) 8.43633

1-4. VCM. (TELD) ZK8.43051/2

3,4. VCM. (TELD) 8.43634

HANDEL: Belshazzar. Stockholm Chbr. Ch., VCM. (TELD) ZK8.35326

Jephtha. A. Schönberg Ch., VCM. (TELD) 2B8.35499

MONTEVERDI: La Favola d'Orfeo. VCM. (TELD) ZA8.35020

L'Incoronazione di Poppea (Excs) VCM. (TELD) 8.43635

MOZART: Idomeneo. Zurich Op. Hse. Chor., Zurich Op. Hse. Mozart Orch. (RODO) RPC32467/8

Requiem in D minor. Vienna St. Op. Chor., VCM. (TELD) ZK8.42756

Thamos. Netherlands Chamber Ch., Collegium Vocale, Concertgebouw. (TELD) ZK8.42702

RAMEAU: Castor et Pollux. Stockholm Chbr. Ch., VCM. (TELD) 8.35048

Hogwood, Christopher

> HANDEL: Messiah. Christ Church Cath. Ch., AAM. (L'OI) 411
> 858-20H3
>
> Music for the Royal Fireworks and Water Music. AAM.
> (L'OI) 400 059-20H
>
> MOZART: Requiem in D minor. AAM Chor., AAM. (L'OI) 411
> 712-20H
>
> All the symphonies except Nos 28, 30, 32, 33, 35, 36
> and 37 are available on Decca or L'Oiseau-Lyre with
> AAM

Inbal, Eliahu

> BRUCKNER: Symphony No. 3. Frankfurt RSO. (TELD)
> ZK8.42922
>
> Symphony No. 4. Frankfurt RSO. (TELD) ZK8.42921
> Symphony No. 8. Frankfurt RSO. (TELD) ZK8.48218

Janowski, Marek

> WAGNER: Götterdämmerung. Leipzig Rad. Chor., Dresden St.
> Op. Chor., BPO. (DGG) 415 155-2GH4
>
> Das Rheingold, Dresden Staatskapelle. (EURO) 610 058
> Siegfried. Dresden Staatskapelle. (EURO) 610 070
> Die Walküre. Dresden Staatskapelle. (EURO) 610 064

Jansons, Mariss

> TCHAIKOVSKY: Symphony No. 1. Oslo PO. (CHAN) CHAN8402
> Symphony No. 3. Oslo PO. (CHAN) CHAN8463
> Symphony No. 4. Oslo PO. (CHAN) CHAN8361
> Symphony No. 5. Oslo PO. (CHAN) CHAN8351
> Symphony No. 6. Oslo PO. (CHAN) CHAN846

Järvi, Neeme

> PROKOFIEV: Symphonies Nos 1 and 4. SNO. (CHAN)
> CHAN8400
>
> Symphony No. 2 and Romeo and Juliet Suites. SNO.
> (CHAN) CHAN8368
>
> Symphony Nos 3 and 4. SNO. (CHAN) CHAN8401
> Symphony No. 5. SNO. (CHAN) CHAN8450
> Symphony No. 6. SNO. (CHAN) CHAN8359
> Symphony No. 7. SNO. (CHAN) CHAN8442
>
> SHOSTAKOVICH: Symphonies Nos 1 and 6. SNO. (CHAN)
> CHAN8411

Jochum, Eugen

> WAGNER: Die Meistersinger von Nürnberg. Berlin German Op.
> Chor., Berlin Op. Orch. (DGG) 415 278-2GH4

Joó, Árpád

> LISZT: The Legend of St Elisabeth. Hungarian St. Orch.
> (HUNG) HCD12694/6-2

Karajan, Herbert von
BACH: Brandenburg Concertos. BPO. (DGG) 415 374-2GH2
BEETHOVEN: Symphonies Nos 1-9. BPO. (DGG) 415 066-2GH6
BRAHMS: Ein deutsches Requiem. VPO. (DGG) 410 521-2GH2
BRUCKNER: Symphonies Nos 1 and 5. BPO. (DGG) 415 985-2GH2
Symphony No. 6. BPO. (DGG) 419 194-2GH
Symphony No. 7. BPO. (DGG) 419 195-2GH
Symphony No. 8. BPO. (DGG) 419 196-2GH2
Symphony No. 9. BPO. (DGG) 419 083-2GH
HAYDN: Symphonies Nos 82–87. BPO. (DGG) 419 741-2GH3
Symphonies Nos 94 and 101. BPO. (DGG) 410 869-2GH
Symphonies Nos 96 and 100. BPO. (DGG) 410 975-2GH
Symphonies Nos 103 and 104. BPO. (DGG) 410 517-2GH
MAHLER: Symphony No. 4. BPO. (DGG) 415 323-2GH
Symphony No. 5. BPO. (DGG) 415 096-2GH2
Symphony No. 6. BPO. (DGG) 415 099-2GH2
Symphony No. 9. BPO. (DGG) 410 726-2GH2
TCHAIKOVSKY: Symphony No. 1. BPO. (DGG) 419 176-2GH
Symphony No. 2. BPO. (DGG) 419 177-2GH
Symphony No. 3. BPO. (DGG) 419 178-2GH
Symphony No. 4. VPO. (DGG) 415 348-2GH
Symphony No. 5. VPO. (DGG) 415 094-2GH
Symphony No. 6. VPO. (DGG) 415 095-2GH
WAGNER: Götterdämmerung. Berlin German Op. Chor., BPO. (DGG) 415 155-2GH4
Das Rheingold. BPO. (DGG) 415 141-2GH3
Siegfried. BPO. (DGG) 415 150-2GH4
Die Walküre. BPO. (DGG) 415 145-2GH4

Kegel, Herbert
BEETHOVEN: Symphonies Nos 1 and 2. Dresden PO. (CAPR) CAPR1001
Symphony No. 3. Dresden PO. (CAPR) CAPR1002
Symphonies 4 and 9. Dresden PO. (CAPR) CAPR1006/7
Symphonies Nos 5 and 8. Dresden PO. (CAPR) CAPR1003
Symphony No. 6. Dresden PO. (CAPR) CAPR1004
Symphony No. 7. Dresden PO. (CAPR) CAPR1005

Kertész, István
DVOŘÁK: Symphony No. 4. LSO. (DECC) 417 596-2DH
Symphony No. 6. LSO. (DECC) 417 598-2DH

Kleiber, Carlos
BEETHOVEN: Symphony No. 4. Bavarian State Orch. (ORFE) C100841
Symphony No. 5. VPO. (DGG) 415 861-2GH

Kleiber, Carlos – *cont.*
    Symphony No. 7. VPO. (DGG) 415 862-2GH
    BRAHMS: Symphony No. 4. VPO. (DGG) 400 037-2GH
    SCHUBERT: Symphonies Nos 3 and 8. VPO. (DGG) 415 601-2GH
    STRAUSS: Die Fledermaus. Bavarian St. Op. Chor., Bavarian St. Op. Orch. (DGG) 415 646-2GH2
    VERDI: La Traviata. Bavarian St. Op. Chor., Bavarian St. Op. Orch. (DGG) 415 132-2GH2
    WAGNER: Tristan und Isolde. Leipzig Rad. Chor., Dresden Staatskapelle. (DGG) 413 315-2GH4

Kleiber, Erich
    BEETHOVEN: Symphony No. 3. VPO. (DECC) 414 626-2DH
    Symphonies Nos 5 and 6. Concertgebouw. (DECC) 417 637-2DH

Klemperer, Otto
    BEETHOVEN: Overtures. Philh. (EMI) CDC7 47190-2
    Symphonies Nos. 1 and 7. Philh. (EMI) CDC7 47184-2
    Symphony No. 3. Philh. (EMI) CDC7 47186-2
    Symphonies Nos 2 and 4. Philh. (EMI) CDC7 47185-2
    Symphonies Nos 5 and 8. Philh. (EMI) CDC7 47187-2
    Symphony No. 9 Philh. (EMI) CDC7 47189-2
    BRAHMS: Ein deutsches Requiem. Philh. (EMI) CDC7 47238-2
    MAHLER: Das Lied von der Erde. New Philh. (EMI) CDC7 47231-2
    Klemperer conducts Wagner, Vol. 1. Philh. (EMI) CDC7 47254-2
    Klemperer conducts Wagner, Vol. 2. Philh. (EMI) CDC7 47255-2

Knappertsbusch, Hans
    WAGNER: Parsifal. Bayreuth Festival Chor., Bayreuth Festival Orch. (DECC) 417 143-2DH4

Košler, Zdeněk
    SMETANA: The Bartered Bride. Czech Phil. Chor., Czech PO. (CHAN) 8412

Kubelík, Rafael
    SMETANA: Má Vlast. Bavarian RSO. (ORFE) C115842H

Leppard, Raymond
    BACH: Brandenburg Concertos. ECO. (PHIL) 420 345-2PM
    HANDEL: Music for the Royal Fireworks and Water Music. ECO. (PHIL) 420 354-2PM
    PURCELL: Dido and Aeneas. ECO. (PHIL) 416 299-2PH

Levine, James
    BEETHOVEN: Piano Concertos Nos 1–5. Brendel, Chicago SO. (PHIL) 411 189-2PH3

BRAHMS: Ein deutsches Requiem. Chicago Sym. Chor., Chicago SO. (RCA) RD85003

GIORDANO: Andrea Chénier (Conc). National PO. (RCA) RD83091

MAHLER: Symphony No. 1. LSO. (RCA) RD80894
  Symphony No. 4. Chicago SO. (RCA) RD80895
  Symphony No. 5. Philadelphia. (RCA) RD89570
  Symphony No. 7. Chicago SO. (RCA) RD84581(2)
  Symphony No. 9. Philadelphia. (RCA) RD83461
  Symphony No. 10. Philadelphia. (RCA) RD84553

MASCAGNI: Cavalleria Rusticana. Ambrosian Op. Chor., National PO. (RCA) RD83091

MOZART: Die Zauberflöte (Conc). Vienna St. Op. Chor., VPO. (RCA) RCD 14621

VERDI: Otello. Ambrosian Op. Chor., National PO. (RCA) RD82951-1

Maazel, Lorin

BEETHOVEN: Symphony No. 9. Cleveland Orch. (CBS) MK76999

BIZET: Carmen. French Radio Chor., FNO. (ERAT) 880373

MAHLER: Symphony No. 1. VPO. (CBS) MK42141
  Symphony No. 2. VPO. (CBS) M2K.38667
  Symphony No. 3. VPO. (CBS) M2K.42178
  Symphony No. 4. VPO. (CBS) MK39072
  Symphonies Nos 9 and 10. VPO. (CBS) M2K.39721

VERDI: Luisa Miller. ROHO. (DGG) 415 366-2GH

WEBBER: Requiem. Berlin Philh. (EMI) CDC7 47146-2

ZEMLINSKY: Lyrische Symphonie. BPO. (DGG) 419 261-2GH

Mackerras, Sir Charles

JANÁČEK: Cunning Little Vixen. Vienna St. Op. Chor., VPO. (DECC) 417 129-2DH2
  Jenůfa. Vienna St. Op. Chor., VPO. (DECC) 414 483-2DH2

Markevitch, Igor

CHOPIN: Piano Concerto No. 2.
  and
FALLA: Nights in the Gardens of Spain. C. Haskil, Lamoureux Concerts Orch. (PHIL) 416 443-2PH

MOZART: Piano Concertos Nos 20 and 24. C. Haskil, Lamoureux Concerts Orch. (PHIL) 412 254-2PH

Marriner, Sir Neville

BACH: Mass in B minor. ASMF Chor., ASMF. (PHIL) 416 415-2PH2
  Messiah. ASMF. (EMI) CDC7 47027-2

BEETHOVEN: Symphony No. 3 ASMF. (PHIL) 410 044-2PH

Marriner, Sir Neville – *cont.*
>   Violin Concerto. Kremer, ASMF. (PHIL) 410 549-2PH
>   DVOŘÁK: Serenades Opus 22 and 44. ASMF. (PHIL) 400 020-2PH
>   GRIEG: Peer Gynt. Ambrosian Sngrs., ASMF. (EMI) CDC7 47003-2
>   HAYDN: The Creation. ASMF Chor., ASMF. (PHIL) 416 449-2PH2
>   The Seasons. ASMF Chor., ASMF. (PHIL) 411 428-2PH2
>   MENDELSSOHN: Symphonies Nos 3 and 4. ASMF. (ARGO) 411 931-27H
>   MOZART: Le Nozze di Figaro. Ambrosian Op. Chor., ASMF. (PHIL) 416 370-2PH3
>   Symphonies Nos 22–41. ASMF. (PHIL) 412 954-2PH6
>   ROSSINI: Il barbiere di Siviglia. Ambrosian Op. Chor., ASMF. (PHIL) 411 058-2PH3
>   SCHUBERT: Symphonies Nos 1, 2, 3, 6, 7, 8, and 9. ASMF. (PHIL) 412 176-2PH6
>   Symphonies Nos 4 and 5. ASMF. (PHIL) 410 045-2PH
>   TCHAIKOVSKY: Serenade Opus 48 and Nutcracker Suite. ASMF. (PHIL) 411 471-2PH
>   WEBER: Symphonies Nos 1 and 2. ASMF. (ASV) CDDCA515

Masur, Kurt
>   BEETHOVEN: Fidelio. Leipzig Rad. Chor., Leipzig Gewandhaus. (EURO) 610 093
>   9 Symphonies and 4 Overtures. Leipzig Gewandhaus. (PHIL) 416 274-2PH6

Matačić, Lovro von
>   BEETHOVEN: Symphonies Nos 2 and 7. Japanese Broadcasting Corp. SO. (DENO) CO-1002
>   Symphony No. 3. Czech PO. (SUPR) 28C37-4
>   BRUCKNER: Symphony No. 8. Japanese Broadcasting Corp. SO. (DENO) 33CO-1001
>   LEHÁR: Lustige Witwe. Philh. Chor., Philh. (EMI) CDS7 47178-8
>   MATAČIĆ: Symphonie der Konfrontation. Japanese Broadcasting Corp. SO. (DENO) CO-1004

Mehta, Zubin
>   BEETHOVEN: Symphony No. 9. NYPO. (RCA) RD84734
>   BERLIOZ: Symphonie fantastique. NYPO. (DECC) 400 046-2DH
>   MAHLER: Symphony No. 2. VPO. (DECC) 414 538-2DH2
>   PUCCINI: Tosca. John Alldis Ch., New Philh. (RCA) RD80105
>   Turandot. John Alldis Ch., LPO. (CBS) M2K.39160

Mengelberg, Willem

BACH: St Matthew Passion. Amsterdam Toonkunst Ch., Concertgebouw. (PHIL) 416 206-2PH3

BEETHOVEN: Symphonies 1 and 2. Concertgebouw. (PHIL) 416 200-2PH

Symphony No. 3. Concertgebouw. (PHIL) 416 201-2PH

Symphonies 4 and 5. Concertgebouw. (PHIL) 416 202-2PH

Symphony No. 6. Concertgebouw. (PHIL) 416 203-2PH

Symphonies Nos 7 and 8. Concertgebouw. (PHIL) 416 204-2PH

Symphony No. 9. Concertgebouw. (PHIL) 416 205-2PH

BRAHMS: Symphony No. 1. Concertgebouw. (PHIL) 416 210-2PH

SCHUBERT: Symphonies Nos 8 and 9. Concertgebouw. (PHIL) 416 212-2PH

STRAUSS: Don Juan. Concertgebouw. (PHIL) 416 214-2PH

Mravinsky, Yevgeny

TCHAIKOVSKY: Symphonies Nos 4, 5 and 6. Leningrad PO (DGG) 419 745-2GH2

Munchinger, Karl

BACH: Suites BMV 1066–9. Stuttgart CO. (DECC) 414 505-1DH

Muti, Riccardo

BRUCKNER: Symphony No. 4. BPO. (EMI) CDC7 47352-2

MAHLER: Symphony No. 1. Philadelphia. (EMI) CDC7 47032-2

PROKOFIEV: Romeo and Juliet Suites. Philadelphia. (EMI) CDC7 47004-2

RIMSKY-KORSAKOV: Scheherezade. Philadelphia. (EMI) CDC7 47023-2

SCRIABIN: Symphony No. 1. Philadelphia. (EMI) CDC7 47349-2

TCHAIKOVSKY: Manfred Symphony. Philh. (EMI) CDC7 47412-2

Neumann, Václav

DVOŘÁK: Symphony No. 3. Czech PO. (SUPR) C37-7668

Symphony No. 4. Czech PO. (SUPR) C37-7442

Symphony No. 6. Czech PO. (SUPR) C37-7242

Symphony No. 7. Czech PO. (SUPR) C37-7067

Symphony No. 8. Czech PO. (SUPR) C37-7073

Symphony No. 9. Czech PO. (SUPR) C37-7002

MAHLER: Symphony No. 3. Czech PO. (SUPR) C37-7288/9

Symphony No. 8. Czech PO. (SUPR) C37-7307/8

Symphony No. 9. Czech PO. (SUPR) C37-7340/1

Ormandy, Eugene

TCHAIKOVSKY: Symphony No. 6. Philadelphia. (DELO) D/CD3016

Ozawa, Seiji
BEETHOVEN: Piano Concerto No. 3. Serkin, Boston SO. (TELA) CD80063

Piano Concerto No. 5. Serkin, Boston SO. (TELA) CD80065
BERG: Violin Concerto *and*
STRAVINSKY: Violin Concerto. Perlman, Boston SO. (DGG) 413 725-2GH
HOLST: The Planets. Boston SO. (PHIL) 416 456-2PH
MAHLER: Symphony No. 8. Boston SO. (PHIL) 410 607-2PH2
SCHOENBERG: Gurrelieder. Tanglewood Fest. Chor., Boston SO. (PHIL) 412 511-2PH2
STRAUSS: Also sprach Zarathustra. Boston SO. (PHIL) 400 072-2PH

Ein Heldenleben. Boston SO. (PHIL) 400 073-2PH

Paita, Carlos
BEETHOVEN: Symphony No. 5. PSO. (LODI) LO-CD781
BERLIOZ: Symphonie fantastique. LSO. (LODI) LO-CD777
BRAHMS: Symphony No. 1. National PO. (LODI) LO-CD779
BRUCKNER: Symphony No. 8. PSO. (LODI) LO-CD783/4
TCHAIKOVSKY: Symphony No. 6. National PO. (LODI) LO-CD778
VERDI: Requiem. LP Ch., RPO. (LODI) LO-CD772

Pinnock, Trevor
BACH: Brandenburg Concertos. English Concert. (ARCH) 410 500-2AH; 410 501-2AH

Concertos. English Concert. (ARCH) 413 634-2AH3

Orchestral works. English Concert. (ARCH) 413 629-2AH4
HANDEL: Concerti Grossi, Opus 3. English Concert. (ARCH) 413 727-2AH

Concerti Grossi, Opus 6. English Concert. (ARCH) 410 897-2AH

Water Music. English Concert. (DGG) 419 410-2GH
VIVALDI: 12 Concerti. English Concert. (ARCH) 400 445-2AH

Previn, André
BRITTEN: Spring Symphony. LSO. (EMI) CDC7 47667-2
DEBUSSY: Images. LSO. (EMI) CDC7 47001-2

La Mer and Nocturnes. LSO. (EMI) CDC7 47028-2
HOLST: The Planets. LSO. (EMI) CDC7 47160-2
ORFF: Carmina Burana. LSO. (EMI) CDC7 47411-2
RACHMANINOV: Symphony No. 2. LSO. (EMI) CDC7 47159-2
RAVEL: Daphnis et Chloé. Ambrosian Sngrs. LSO. (EMI) CDC7 47123-2
RIMSKY-KORSAKOV: Scheherazade. VPO. (PHIL) 411 479-2PH

TCHAIKOVSKY: Symphony No. 4. Pittsburgh SO. (PHIL) 400 090-2PH
VAUGHAN WILLIAMS: A Sea Symphony. LSO. (RCA) RD89689
Sinfonia antartica and Symphony No. 8. LSO. (RCA) RD89883
Symphony No. 4 and Pastoral Symphony. LSO. (RCA) RD89827
Symphony No. 5. LSO. (RCA) RD89882
Symphonies Nos 6 and 9. LSO. (RCA) RD89883

Rattle, Simon
BRITTEN: War Requiem. CBSO Chor., CBSO. (EMI) CDS7 47034-8
MAHLER: Das Klagende Lied. CBSO Chor., CBSO. (EMI) CDC7 47089-2
Symphony No. 10. Bournemouth SO. (EMI) CDS7 47301-8
RACHMANINOV: Symphony No. 2. LAPO. (EMI) CDC7 47062-2

Reiner, Fritz
BRAHMS: Piano Concerto No. 1. Rubinstein, Chicago SO. (RCA) RD85668
Piano Concerto No. 2 and Tragic Overture. Gilels, Chicago SO. (RCA) RD85406
Violin Concerto. Heifetz, Chicago SO. (RCA) RD85402
RACHMANINOV: Rhapsody on a theme of Paganini and Piano Concerto No. 2. Rubinstein, Chicago SO. (RCA) RD84934

Richter, Karl
BACH: Cantatas. Munich Bach Ch., Munich Bach Orch. (ARCH) 413 646-2AH3
Christmas Oratorio. Munich Bach Ch., Munich Bach Orch. (ARCH) 413 625-2AH3
St John Passion. Munich Bach Ch., Munich Bach Orch. (ARCH) 413 622-2AH2
St Matthew Passion. Munich Bach Ch., Munich Bach Orch. (ARCH) 413 613-2AH3

Rostropovich, Mstislav
DVOŘÁK: Cello Concerto. BPO. H. Karajan (cond.) (DGG) 413 819-2GH
SHOSTAKOVICH: Symphony No. 5. Washington NSO. (DGG) 410 509-2GH

Sabata, Victor de
PUCCINI: Tosca. La Scala Chor., La Scala Orch. (EMI) CDS7 47175-8

Salonen, Esa-Pekka
LUTOSŁAWSKI: Symphony No. 3 and Espaces du sommeil. BPO. (PHIL) 416 387-2PH

Salonen, Esa-Pekka – *cont*.
>   MESSIAEN: Turangalîla symphony. Philh. (CBS) M2K.42271
>   NIELSEN: Symphony No. 4 and Helios. Swedish RSO. (CBS)
>   MK42093
>   TOMASI: Trumpet Concerto *and*
>   JOLIVET: Trumpet Concerto. Marsalis, Philh. (CBS) MK42096

Sanderling, Kurt
>   TCHAIKOVSKY: Symphony No. 5. Berlin RSO. (DENO) C37-7100
>   Symphony No. 6. Berlin Staatskapelle. (DENO) C37-7062

Sargent, Sir Malcolm
>   BEETHOVEN: Piano Concertos Nos 1 and 2. Schnabel, LSO.
>   (ARAB) Z6549
>
>   Piano Concertos Nos 3 and 4. Schnabel, LPO. (ARAB)
>   Z6550
>
>   Piano Concerto No. 5. Schnabel, LSO. (ARAB) Z6551

Serebrier, José
>   IVES: Symphony No. 4. LPO. (CHAN) CHAN8397
>   POULENC: La Voix humaine. Adelaide SO. (CHAN)
>   CHAN8331

Shaw, Robert
>   BEETHOVEN: Symphony No. 9. Atlanta SO. Chor., Atlanta SO.
>   (PRO) CDD245
>   BRAHMS: Ein deutsches Requiem. Atlanta SO. Chor., Atlanta
>   SO. (TELA) CD80092
>   HANDEL: Messiah. Atlanta Sym. Chamber Chor., Atlanta SO.
>   (TELA) CD80093

Simon, Geoffrey
>   SMETANA: String Quartet No. 1. Smetana Qt. (SUPR) C37S-
>   7339
>   TCHAIKOVSKY: Symphony No. 2 (orig. version). LSO. (CHAN)
>   CHAN8304
>
>   Romeo and Juliet fantasie-overture. LSO. (CHAN)
>   CHAN8310/11

Sinopoli, Giuseppe
>   MAHLER: Symphony No. 5. Philh. (DGG) 415 476-2GH
>   MENDELSSOHN: Symphony No. 4 *and*
>   SCHUBERT: Symphony No. 8. Philh. (DGG) 410 862-2GH
>   PUCCINI: Manon Lescaut. ROH Chor. (DGG) 413 893-2GH2
>   SCHUMANN: Symphony No. 2 and Manfred. VPO. (DGG) 410
>   863-2GH
>   VERDI: Macbeth. Berlin German Op. Chor., Berlin German Op.
>   Orch. (DGG) 415 688-2GH3

Slatkin, Leonard
>   DEBUSSY: Orchestral works. St. Louis SO. (TELA) CD80071

MAHLER: Symphony No. 2. St. Louis SO. (TELA) CD80081-2

PROKOFIEV: Symphony No. 5. St. Louis SO. (RCA) RD85035

Solti, Sir Georg

BEETHOVEN: Fidelio. Chicago Sym. Chor., Chicago SO. (DECC) 410 227-2DH3

Piano Concertos Nos 2 and 5. Ashkenazy, Chicago SO. (DECC) 417 703-2DM

BERLIOZ: La Damnation de Faust. Chicago Sym. Chor., Chicago SO. (DECC) 414 680-2DH2

Symphonie fantastique. Chicago SO. (DECC) 417 705-2DM

BIZET: Carmen. John Alldis Ch., LPO. (DECC) 414 489-2DH3

BRAHMS: Academic Festival Overture. Chicago SO. (DECC) 414 488-2DH

Ein deutsches Requiem. Chicago SO. (DECC) 414 627-2DH2

Tragic Overture. Chicago SO. (DECC) 414 487-2DH

BRUCKNER: Symphony No. 4. Chicago SO. (DECC) 410 550-2DH

Symphony No. 6. Chicago SO. (DECC) 417 389-2DH

Symphony No. 9. Chicago SO. (DECC) 417 295-2DH

MAHLER: Lied von der Erde. Chicago SO. (DECC) 414 066-2DH

Symphony No. 1. Chicago SO. (DECC) 411 731-2DH

Symphony No. 2. Chicago SO. (DECC) 410 202-2DH2

Symphony No. 3. Chicago SO. (DECC) 414 268-2DH2

Symphony No. 4. Chicago SO. (DECC) 410 188-2DH

Symphony No. 5. Chicago SO. (DECC) 414 321-2DH

Symphony No. 6. Chicago SO. (DECC) 414 674-2DH2

Symphony No. 7. Chicago SO. (DECC) 414 675-2DH2

Symphony No. 8. Chicago SO. (DECC) 414 493-2DH2

Symphony No. 9. Chicago SO. (DECC) 410 012-2DH

MOZART: Le Nozze di Figaro. London Op. Chor., LPO. (DECC) 410 150-2DH3

Die Zauberflöte. Vienna St. Op. Chor., VPO. (DECC) 414 568-2DH3

PUCCINI: La Bohème. John Alldis Ch., LPO. (RCA) RD80371

SCHOENBERG: Moses und Aron. Chicago Sym. Chor., Chicago SO. (DECC) 414 264-2DH2

SCHUBERT: Symphony No. 9. VPO. (DECC) 400 082-2DH

STRAUSS: Elektra. VPO. (DECC) 417 345-2DH2

Der Rosenkavalier. Vienna St. Op. Chor., VPO. (DECC) 417 493-2DH3

Salome. VPO. (DECC) 414 414-2DH2

VERDI: Un ballo in maschera. London Op. Chor., National PO. (DECC) 410 210-2DH2

Solti, Sir Georg – *cont.*

      Requiem. Vienna St. Op. Chor., VPO. (DECC) 411 944-2DH2

      WAGNER: Der fliegende Holländer. Chicago Sym. Chor., Chicago SO. (DECC) 414 551-2DH3

      Götterdämmerung. VPO. (DECC) 414 115-2DH4

      Die Meistersinger. Vienna St. Op. Chor., VPO. (DECC) 417 497-2DH4

      Parsifal. Vienna St. Op. Chor., VPO. (DECC) 417 143-2DH4

      Das Rheingold. VPO. (DECC) 414 101-2DH3

      Siegfried. VPO. (DECC) 414 110-2DH4

      Tannhäuser. Vienna St. Op. Chor., VPO. (DECC) 414 581-2DH3

      Die Walküre. VPO. (DECC) 414 105-2DH4

Stokowski, Leopold

      DEBUSSY: Iberia. FNRO. (EMI) CDC7 47423-2

      Nocturnes. BBC Chor., LSO. (EMI) CDC7 47423-2

      RAVEL: Alborada del gracioso. FNRO. (EMI) CDC7 47423-2

      Rapsodie espagnole. LSO. (EMI) CDC7 47423-2

      Stokowski Overtures. National PO. (PRT) CDPCN6

      Stokowski Spectacular. National PO. (PRT) CDPCN4

Suitner, Otmar

      BEETHOVEN: Symphonies Nos 1–9. Berlin Staatskapelle. (DENO) C37-7251/7256

      HUMPERDINCK: Hänsel und Gretel. Dresden Krenzchor, Dresden Staatskapelle. (TELD) ZA8.35074

Svetlanov, Evgeny

      BORODIN: Symphony No. 2. USSR SO. (CHNT) LDC278.782

Szell, Georg

      STRAUSS: Vier letzte Lieder. Berlin RSO. (EMI) CDC7 47276-2

Tate, Jeffrey

      BEETHOVEN: Symphony No. 7. Dresden Staatskapelle. (EMI) CDC7 47815-2

      SCHUBERT: Symphony No. 9. Dresden Staatskapelle. (EMI) CDC7 47478-2

Tennstedt, Klaus

      BRAHMS: Symphony No. 1. LPO. (EMI) CDC7 47029-2

      MAHLER: Symphony No. 1. LPO. (EMI) CDC7 47885-2

      Symphony No. 2. LPO. (EMI) CDS7 47041-8

      Symphony No. 3. LPO. (EMI) CDS7 47405-8

      Symphony No. 4. LPO. (EMI) CDC7 47024-2

      Symphonies Nos 5 and 10. LPO. (EMI) CDS7 47104-8

      Symphony No. 6. LPO. (EMI) CDS7 47050-8

      Symphony No. 7. LPO. (EMI) CDS7 47879-8

Symphony No. 8. LPO. (EMI) CDS7 47625-8

Symphony No. 9. LPO. (EMI) CDS7 47113-8

Thomas, Michael Tilson

GERSHWIN: Piano and Orchestral Works. LAPO. (CBS) MK39699

IVES: Orchestral Set No. 2 and Symphony No. 3. Concertgebouw. (CBS) MK37823

Toscanini, Arturo

BEETHOVEN: Symphonies Nos 1 and 3. NBC SO (RCA) RD87197

Symphonies Nos 2 and 7. NBC SO (RCA) RD87198

De Waart, Edo

GRIEG: Peer Gynt incidental music. San Francisco SO. (PHIL) 412 712

RACHMANINOV: Piano Concertos Nos 1 and 2. Kocsis, San Francisco SO. (PHIL) 412 881-1PH

RAVEL: Shéhérazade *and*

DEBUSSY: La damoiselle élue *and*

DUPARC: Songs. Ameling. San Francisco SO. (PHIL) 410 043-2PH

RESPIGHI: Pini di Roma, Fontane di Roma and Gli uccelli. San Francisco SO. (PHIL) 411 419-2PH

SAINT-SAËNS: Symphony No. 3. SFSO. (PHIL) 412 619-2PH

Walter, Bruno

BEETHOVEN: Symphonies Nos 1 and 2. Columbia SO. (CBS) MK42009

Symphony No. 3 and Coriolan. Columbia SO. (CBS) MK42010

Symphonies Nos 4 and 5. Columbia SO. (CBS) MK42011

Symphony No. 6. Columbia SO. (CBS) MK42012

Symphonies Nos 7 and 8. Columbia SO. (CBS) MK42013

Symphony No. 9. Columbia SO. (CBS) MK42014

BRAHMS: Schicksalslied and Alto Rhapsody. Columbia SO. (CBS) MK42025

Symphony No. 1. Columbia SO. (CBS) MK42020

Symphony No. 2 and Academic Festival Overture. Columbia SO. (CBS) MK42021

Symphony No. 3 and Haydn Variations. Columbia SO. (CBS) MK42022

Symphony No. 4 and Tragic Overture. Columbia SO. (CBS) MK42023

HAYDN: Symphonies Nos 88 and 100. Columbia SO. (CBS) MK42047

MAHLER: Das Lied von der Erde. NYPO. (CBS) MK42034

Symphony No. 2. NYPO. (CBS) M2K.42032

Walter, Bruno – *cont.*

> MOZART: Symphonies Nos 35 and 39. Columbia SO. (CBS) MK42026
>
> Symphonies Nos 36 and 38. Columbia SO. (CBS) MK42027
>
> Symphonies Nos 40 and 41. Columbia SO. (CBS) MK42028
>
> Violin Concertos Nos 3 and 4. (CBS) Francescatti, Columbia SO. MK42030.
>
> SCHUBERT: Symphonies Nos 5 and 8. Columbia SO. (CBS) MK42048
>
> WAGNER: Overtures and Preludes. Columbia SO. (CBS) MK42050.

Wand, Günter

> BRAHMS: Symphony No. 1. NDRSO. (DHM) CDC7 47824-2
>
> Symphony No. 2. NDRSO. (DHM) CDC7 47871-2
>
> Symphony No. 3. NDRSO. (DHM) CDC7 47872-2

Zinman, David

> RIMSKY-KORSAKOV: Le Coq d'Or and Tsar Sultan. Rotterdam PO (PHIL) 411 435-2PH